Your Official America Online®

Internet Guide,

3rd Edition

Your Official America Online®
Internet Guide,
3rd Edition

David Peal

AOLPress

Dulles, VA

Your Official America Online® Internet Guide, 3rd Edition

Published by

AOL Press

An imprint of IDG Books Worldwide, Inc.

An International Data Group Company

919 E. Hillsdale Blvd., Suite 400

Foster City, CA 94404

www.aol.com (America Online Web site)

ISBN: 0-7645-3452-1

Printed in the United States of America

10 9 8 7 6 5 4

1B/QT/QU/QQ/IN

Distributed in the United States by IDG Books Worldwide, Inc. and America Online, Inc.

For general information on IDG Books Worldwide's books in the U.S., please call our Consumer Customer Service department at 800-762-2974. For reseller information, including discounts and premium sales, please call our Reseller Customer Service department at 800-434-3422.

Library of Congress Card Number: 99-66799

 is a trademark of America Online, Inc.

 is a registered trademark or trademark under exclusive license to IDG Books Worldwide, Inc. from International Data Group, Inc. in the United States and/or other countries.

Welcome to AOL Press™

AOL Press books provide timely guides to getting the most out of your online life. AOL Press was formed as part of the AOL family to create a complete series of official references for using America Online as well as the entire Internet — all designed to help you enjoy a fun, easy, and rewarding online experience.

AOL Press is an exciting partnership between two companies at the forefront of the knowledge and communications revolution — America Online and IDG Books Worldwide. AOL is committed to quality, ease of use, and value and IDG Books excels at helping people understand technology.

To meet these high standards, all our books are authored by experts with the full participation of and exhaustive review by AOL's own development, technical, managerial, and marketing staff. Together, AOL and IDG Books have implemented an ambitious publishing program to develop new publications that serve every aspect of your online life.

We hope you enjoy reading this AOL Press title and find it useful. We welcome your feedback at AOL keyword: **Contact Shop Direct** so we can keep providing information the way you want it.

AOL Press

About the Author

David Peal teaches in the Educational Technology Leadership MA program at George Washington University in Washington, DC. As the former editorial manager of AOL's Internet Connection, he developed forums about the Internet and helped create AOL's first comprehensive online source of Internet help. In addition to this book, David has written two other books for AOL: Student's Guide to the Internet (1998) and AOL Guide to Digital Imaging (1999), both of which are available online, through AOL. He wrote Access the Internet! (1994), edited the Lycos Small Business Web Resource Guide (1997), and developed one of the first newsletters devoted to the commercial use of the Internet (1994-95). He has been a judge for the education category in the Global Information Infrastructure (GII) awards.

Credits

America Online

Technical Editor
Gary Lampal

Cover Design
AppNet, Inc.
DKG Design, Inc.

IDG Books Worldwide

Acquisitions Editor
Kathy Yankton

Development Editor
Colleen Dowling

Technical Editor
Kristin Tod

Copy Editors
Marti Paul
Michael Welch

Project Coordinator
Linda Marousek

Graphics and Production Specialists
Dina F Quan
Jude Levinson
Mario Amador
Ramses Ramirez

Quality Control Specialist
Chris Weisbart

Book Designer
Evan Deerfield

Again, and always, for Carol and the kids

Foreword

At AOL, our mission has always gone beyond building a great service. We want to help build a great medium, one that is central to people's lives.

The results of our most recent Cyberstudy, conducted with the respected Roper Starch organization, underscores the extent to which the Internet is becoming a necessity in people's lives. Fully 78% of Internet users say being online has made their lives better, and, amazingly, 63% of kids prefer going online to watching TV. More and more users are going online to communicate with friends and family, shop, get entertainment information, book travel, bank, and track and trade stocks. Surprisingly, more than 60 percent of those 18 to 24 years of age are already downloading music online — and even a fifth of those over 50.

At AOL, we have in fact played an important role in helping the Internet become a consumer medium and a force that is bringing great benefits to society. After all, a huge percentage of consumers first accessed — and continue to access — the Internet through AOL, with its seamless connections and useful links to the best content, commerce, and services. Exploring the Internet with AOL is a rich fascinating experience — I liken it to traveling first class, with the best tour guides and excellent accommodations. Our customized navigational tools and resources make the Internet accessible and easy to use, with all the support and community you've come to expect from AOL.

But even with AOL serving as a valuable gateway to the Internet, the sheer size and scope of cyberspace can make it daunting for users to find the sites, products, and information from which they could benefit.

That's why we've worked with David Peal — a former editorial manager for the Internet Connection channel on AOL — to produce yet another edition of AOL's Guide to the Internet. David — who has also authored Access the Internet! — takes advantage of his experience in helping design our own links to cyberspace to share insider tips that can turn your Internet experience into something truly extraordinary. His entertaining chapters not only reveal how to use AOL's Internet tools, they also show how AOL adds value to the Internet with our special programming and services. Our publisher, IDG Books Worldwide, Inc., has also drawn on its own expertise in computer book publishing to shape David's work into a truly user-friendly guide designed with your needs in mind.

I hope that you enjoy the results of our efforts — and that with the Internet Guide at your side, you will be able to make AOL and the Internet an even more central and satisfying part of your life, too.

Steve Case
Chairman and CEO, America Online, Inc.

Preface

Welcome to the All New Edition of AOL's Official Internet Guide

"It's in the air. It's in the water. It's in the pizza," a pundit announced recently on the *Charlie Rose Show*. He was talking about the Internet, of course. Thanks in large part to America Online, "ubiquitous computing" has become a reality faster than even the pundits ever dreamed.

▶ Newspaper articles and ads are filled with *h-t-t-p* this and *dot-com* that.

▶ Hotels compete to offer wired rooms for business people and travelers, so that room service now includes technical support.

▶ Local governments post school lunch menus on the World Wide Web.

▶ Pocket-sized computers offer "wireless" access to the Internet (no phone jacks, no plugs, no cables), so you can surf the Web while waiting at the checkout counter.

▶ In many places you can even do your grocery shopping online, leaving you more time for the things you'd rather be doing.

It's hard, in other words, to avoid the Internet. If you have a small business, your competition is probably wired. If you have children, your kids may spend more time online than with you. If you're retired, your grandchildren probably spend time online, and you might have the feeling that you could all stay more closely in touch if only you, too, were online. This book shows how you can take part in that world.

What *is* the Internet? Chapter 1 unravels the mysteries of the Net, with its many software tools, countless information resources, and myriad online communities.

Why Do I Need a *Book* on the Internet?

You might be wondering to yourself, "Why do I need a book about the Internet in the first place?" After all, the Internet seems to undergo some big change every week or so; no book could ever keep up with the pace.

This book conveys what's stable about the Internet so you can understand and adapt to the changes as they come barreling toward you. Chances are, the World Wide Web and electronic mail won't go away, for example, yet both are almost certain to work in different ways and acquire a new look in the next few years. Even more: while the Internet undergoes some big change every week or so, AOL always provides a reliable haven. Dozens of " portals" provide a starting place for your Internet travels, but AOL alone provides the latest tools for exploring *and* a restful online home to which you can always return.

Another reason for using this book: To keep up with the Net, you need to be hanging out in the right places — watching certain Web sites, following the appropriate forums on AOL, subscribing to Net-related mailing lists and newsgroups. This book can keep you up-to-date, no matter how fast the Internet changes.

What's New in this Book

With all the changes on the Internet and AOL, this book has been entirely rewritten. Several new chapters cover the following important subjects:

▶ Customizing AOL to suit your preferences (Chapter 3)

▶ Using Netscape Navigator, the hugely popular and free software you can use with AOL (Chapter 6)

▶ Having fun with live (real-time) communication, including Instant Messages, AOL Instant Messenger, and AOL's fantastic new Internet chat software, ICQ (Chapter 11)

▶ Building Web pages and sites using AOL's new tools (Chapter 14-15)

▶ Understanding the fast new Internet connections that will reshape what you'll be able to do on AOL in the near future (Chapter 18)

▶ Tapping the power of Microsoft's Internet Explorer browser

How to Use this Book

This is a reference book. The book's new organization provides more depth and also makes it easier to find what you need. You can read sections, chapters, and parts in any order.

Part I: A First Look Around

If you're new to the Internet, Chapter 1 introduces the Internet in terms of what you actually *do* on the Net. If you're new to AOL (or a seasoned AOL member who wants an overview of the new features in AOL 5.0), make sure to read Chapter 2. You'll appreciate the many new ways of using AOL as *Internet* software. Chapter 3 goes into customizing AOL, a subject not fully dealt with in previous editions of this book. You will find tips for tweaking *individual* Internet tools (like the AOL Web browser) in the appropriate parts of the book.

Part II: Discovering the World Wide Web

Five hefty chapters are devoted to the World Wide Web. After a charter tour of the many useful things you can do on the Web and on AOL.COM in particular (Chapter 4), you'll find an in-depth look at AOL's built-in Web browser (Chapter 5). Then, learn where to get and how to use the world-famous Netscape browser (Chapter 6). With hundreds of millions of Web pages out there, how do you find what you need on the Web? Chapters 7 and 8 take you into the world of searching for information: the tools, resources, and tricks you *must* know in order to find what you are looking for.

Part III: You and Everyone Else: Communicating with the World

This part is devoted to the tools you use to take part in electronic conversations and online communities on AOL and the Internet. First, you'll discover electronic mail, as powerful as it is simple (Chapters 9 and 10). From there, find out how to take part in the world of live electronic conversations and chat on AOL and the Internet (Chapter 11). The mailing list is the Net's best-kept secret, a great way to take part in small communities of shared interest. Lists also can also keep you informed on the Internet itself (Chapter 12). Unlike lists, newsgroups are *public* forums, easier to use and search than mailing lists, and open to anyone (Chapter 13). Chapter 13 introduces other public forums, including Web-based message boards.

Part IV: Spinning your Own Web Pages

These two chapters cover a very hot topic: building Web pages (Chapter 14) and designing multi-page Web sites (Chapter 15). You'll become familiar with AOL's many old and new tools and the many AOL and Web resources for Web builders. You'll also learn about AOL Hometown, the new virtual community where you can publish on the Web and reach anyone on the globe who has Internet access and a browser.

Part V: Extending Your Internet Connection

Chapter 16 shows how to take advantage of older yet still indispensable Internet tools such as FTP and Telnet. Chapter 17 goes a step further, introducing the many wonderful Internet programs that you can use with AOL: what they do, how you use them, where you get them. Finally, Chapter 18 looks into the near future at some of the benefits and uses of *broad-*

band connections. These superfast Internet connections will transform what is possible on-line, and make AOL even more compelling in the years ahead.

Note

Things change so fast on the Internet that you might find an out-of-date detail or two in this book. Paths change, tools get facelifts, AOL adds resources; the Internet grows at a breakneck pace, with companies growing, merging, and perpetually changing, and the average Web site lasting a couple of months, at best. (Don't worry, though, I've tried to choose sites with a good chance of lasting!) Send an e-mail message to me at AOL (screen name: **dpeal**) with your suggestions and corrections, or just to say hi. Don't hesitate to share discoveries for the next edition.

Finding Your Way through this Book

Windows programs like AOL (and Mac programs like AOL for that matter) have much in common. Basic AOL tasks are grouped in a *menu bar* consisting of five *menus* lined up horizontally at the top of the AOL window: File, Edit, Window, Sign On, and Help. In addition, AOL has its own set of menus, grouped together in the AOL toolbar, below the menu bar. The AOL toolbar's menus can be recognized by the downward-pointing arrows. (Chapter 2 has all the details.) Click a menu on either the menu bar or AOL toolbar to see a "drop-down" list of *menu items* that let you do things (like open a file) or visit places (like one of your Favorite Places).

All menu selections are indicated by the ⇨ symbol. For example, Edit ⇨ Dictionary, means to click on AOL's Edit menu, then to click and release the Dictionary *menu item*. (Did you know AOL puts this dictionary at your disposal whenever you're online?) On the AOL toolbar, selecting My AOL ⇨ Preferences brings up a window with a series of buttons that give you a broad range of ways to customize your AOL and Internet experience. In this book, the ⇨ symbol can take you to buttons to click as well as menu items to select. For example, My AOL ⇨ Preferences ⇨ WWW lets you specify exactly how you want your AOL browser to work.

Icons are small pictures in the book's margins. They pull out important points, provide additional information and cross references, and in general make it easier for you to find your way through the book and online.

 **Cross-Reference**

Cross-references lead you to more detailed explanations elsewhere in the book.

 Tip

Tips call your attention to shortcuts and useful resources.

 Note

A noteworthy and helpful item that is well worth taking the time to read.

 Definition

The definition of a new term at the very place it is used in the text.

 Find It Online

AOL keywords and Internet addresses.

 Caution

Cautions advise you of something *not* to do. Don't worry; you won't find many cautions in this book.

Acknowledgments

Each edition of the *AOL Internet Guide* has more to cover, on more subjects, in fewer pages, in less time, with greater chance of being scooped by the constant growth of America Online and the Internet. To accommodate the many changes in AOL and the Internet since the last edition, this book was rewritten from scratch. The project required, in fact, a team effort that only the Internet could sustain. My biggest debt is thus to the Internet itself. Without its resources, communities, and tools, I could not have completed this project. Not in this millennium, at least.

Many people at AOL have provided tremendous support from the first edition through the current one. Special thanks to Paul Di Vito, for his ongoing support; to John Dyn, for both supporting the book and shoe-horning the project into the schedules of many people at AOL; to Don Crowl, for his behind-the-scenes wizardry; to Gary Lampal, for answering my persistent questions about AOL 5.0; to Michael Dourney, for his recommendations regarding AOL's new search tools; to Thomas Kriese, for keeping me informed about AOL's new and wonderfully simple Web-publishing tools.

At IDG Books Worldwide, Kathy Yankton, acquisitions editor for AOL Press, made substantial improvements to this book's conception and organization. Always friendly despite a ferocious schedule, Colleen Dowling, developmental editor, shepherded the manuscript and approximately one million screen captures into various edits, through production, and to you. Thanks to the following people at IDG for refining the words and pictures, and turning them into the book you're holding: Marti Paul, copy editor, Linda Marousek, production coordinator, Chris Pimentel, production supervisor, Renée Dunn, graphics and production whiz, and Kristen Tod, technical editor.

Fellow computer book authors Ed Willett and Lois Patterson withstood my needling well enough to write early drafts of several chapters, and I am grateful for their hard work. They afforded a difference of perspective — not just because they're both Canadian — that simply made for a better book. Thanks to Christian Crumlish, Waterside Productions, for representing the book.

My cohort in the Educational Technology Leadership program at George Washington University provided more ideas about the Internet and personal support than I could begin to acknowledge. Special thanks to the program's director, Dr. Badrul Khan, a gentleman from Bangladesh who clearly sees how the Internet can improve schools, and not just those in the U.S.

At home, it has been sobering to hear my children talk about *AskJeeves* and *Google* in otherwise normal conversation. During a long and unusually hot summer Gabriel and Ella became rightly frustrated with a father who spent too much time at the computer, while their mom, again, picked up the slack. All three leave no doubt about what matters most, which is why the book is dedicated to them.

Contents at a Glance

Contents

Chapter 3: Making AOL Work Your Way: Parental Controls and Other Preferences 50

Part II: Discovering the World Wide Web   77

Chapter 4: Essential Destinations: Using the World Wide Web to Plan, Improve, and Enjoy Your Life 80

Part III: You and Everyone Else: Communicating With the World   **203**

Attaching One or More Files 240

Embellish Those Messages 242

Emphasizing Text 242

Inserting Links, Text, and Images 243

Caffeinated Stationery and Other Mail Extras 246

Greeting Cards 248

Signatures 249

Creating a Signature 249

**Chapter 11: Live Communication: From Instant
Messages to Internet Chats** **254**

Tête-à-Tête with Instant Messages 255

Using AOL's Instant Messages 256

Click Here If You Want Some Privacy 256

Take It to the Internet with AOL Instant Messenger 258

Downloading, Installing, and Running AOL Instant Messenger . . 259

Finding a Buddy 260

Adding Buddies to Your Buddy List 261

AOL Mail Contacts: Chatting with your E-mail Buddies 262

Groups@AOL 262

Sending Messages with AIM 263

Receiving Messages with AIM 264

Creating and Joining AIM Chats 264

Setting Your AIM Preferences 265

Changing and Formatting Your Screen Name 266

You, Your Shadow, and Your AIM Profile 266

Quick, Buddy 267

Global Communications with ICQ 270

Downloading and Installing ICQ 271

ICQ: Some Key Features 271

Finding and Adding People to Your ICQ List 272

Sending Messages 274

Being Found 275

ICQ's Important Portal 276

Part IV: Spinning Your Own Web Page   331

Chapter 14: Contributing to the Web: Making a Page 334

Chapter 15: Contributing to the Web: Making and Managing a Site 354

Part V: Extending Your Internet Connection   383

Chapter 16: FTP, Telnet, and Such 386

Chapter 17: Internet Software and Where to Find It 406

PART

I

A FIRST LOOK AROUND

Chapter 1

What is the Internet?

The Internet has been compared to a vast library with its contents dumped on the floor. This chapter conveys a more realistic sense of the Internet in terms of what people use it for. You'll also read about some of the many ways in which AOL simplifies and contributes to the Internet experience. Along the way, you'll get a bit of history and a sense of what's behind the Net boom.

The obvious problem with comparing the Internet to a library with all the books on the floor is that you don't actually find many *books* on the Internet. Also, the Internet is becoming much more organized every day; it is getting easier and quicker to find what you want on the Net.

The Inter-what?

Unlike your standard lending library, the Internet is a place
where you can easily contribute your own creations. What you
"borrow" (the stuff you use on your own computer) can usually be kept forever — at least for your own use. Also, while libraries contain things in only one or two formats (printed
materials, mostly), the Internet brings you a diverse and growing variety of content:

▶ Breaking news in text, pictures, audio, and video

▶ Scrolling stock-market tickers and interactive personal-
  finance calculators to plan for a house, college, or retirement

▶ Electronic archives of the past, with old photos, diaries,
  popular magazines of the 1800s, maps, old baseball
  cards, original recordings of presidential speeches, authentic folksongs, and all the odds and ends you'd expect in any respectable attic

▶ Interactive games to play with people you have
  never met

Parts of the Internet resemble a *mall* more than a public library, because you can conveniently and safely buy things, or
even set up shop for yourself. Other parts resemble a *club-
house, pub, or classroom,* where you can readily find people
who share your special interests, hobbies, politics, and causes.
Or, search out new perspectives on the Internet.

A Way to Think of the Internet

Some people define the Internet as a network of physical networks, but that doesn't say much except to telecommunications experts, who are mostly interested in the ways in which
computers are wired together into networks. This book, instead, focuses on how you can make use of this global tangle
of computers and cables. Here's a more down-to-earth definition of the Internet:

Cross-Reference

Different tasks require different tools. The rest of the book goes into individual tools in detail. For example, a Web browser is a tool that lets you read the newspaper in just about any city in the world (Chapters 5 and 6). AOL's e-mail programs let you get in touch with friends and colleagues in any country, at little cost, almost instantaneously (Chapters 9 and 10). That's just the start.

▶ It is a set of tools for doing new sorts of things *across* networks: finding information, retrieving information, and communicating with individuals and groups located anywhere. The specific tools are all available on AOL, and I'll cover them throughout the book.

The word *tool* is a technical-sounding male sort of word. In this book, *tool* refers mostly to software that helps you do things you could not do otherwise. Internet tools make amazing things possible. For example, some Internet tools help you find specific, even obscure, information very fast. Other tools enable you to find out the informative and knowledgeable *people* in any area.

▶ It is a sea of information resources — Web sites and other destinations provide solid information and strong opinion, as well as wisdom, humor, and lunacy. Tools let you visit these destinations and put resources to good use. They turn destinations into virtual malls, libraries, clubhouses, museums, and classrooms.

▶ It is a collection of tens of thousands of communities — people from many countries who share interests, enjoy each other's company, or frequent the same destinations.

▶ Yes, it is a vast physical network of diverse computers that gather, store, process, and share information — sort of like a large human brain.

The striking thing is how the Internet contributes to the very normal daily activities of learning, creating, making a living, and hanging out. It's not always a good idea, or true, to think of the Internet as a separate place; instead, it's a very real extension of daily life. The next section looks a little more closely at the ways in which the Internet does all this.

A Global Community? Not Yet

As a community, or group of communities, the Internet is not quite as global as the media would have you believe. The U.S. plus Germany, Japan, the U.K, and Canada comprise approximately two-thirds of the Internet population. Most people in the U.S. get access to the Internet over traditional telephone lines. However, more than half the people in the world have never used a telephone, much less seen or used a computer. On the Internet itself, you can learn about these realities and also join organizations such as the Internet Society (http://www.isoc.org) that are working to overcome them.

Note

AOL provides a complete set of Internet tools, together with access to Internet destinations and communities. AOL itself is not "on" the Internet, since folks on the Internet cannot access all of AOL's destinations and communities. As an AOL member you have full access to both worlds—AOL and the Internet

What's the Difference Between AOL and the Internet?

AOL is a private, easy-to-use network of content and community, most of this network is accessible only to AOL members. It's also a quite unique network *from* which AOL members can access any part of the Internet, using AOL's Internet tools and services. As such, AOL adds layer on layer of value to your Internet experience.

How does AOL improve your Internet experience?

▶ You get full and direct *access* to the Internet at no extra cost.

▶ This access is available, increasingly, *anywhere*. With AOLMail (accessed remotely at www.aol.com), for example, you can now access your AOL electronic mail when you don't have the AOL software (Chapter 9). QuickBuddy, likewise, gives you the advantages of AOL Instant Messenger when you don't have *that* program (Chapter 11). With a PalmPilot handheld computer you can now access your AOL e-mail without even having a computer handy!

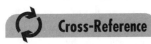

Cross-Reference

Chapter 14 provides a full introduction to AOL's new Web building tools.

Cross-Reference

Chapter 4 introduces many of the essential destinations that can make your life better in many small ways.

Definition

A URL is short for a Uniform Resource Locators. The URL's are the "addresses" used to find a specific Web page.

▶ On AOL you have a complete and well-integrated set of tools for using the Internet, including a World Wide Web browser, an e-mail program, a newsgroup reader, and much more. With AOL 4.0 and 5.0 you get completely new tools for building Web pages and adding them to the huge new community on the Web, AOL Hometown.

▶ AOL contributes to the general Internet community in many ways. Its Web site, AOL.COM, orients millions of people to myriad Internet destinations. AOL's Web Centers, another part of AOL.COM, help you find the very best Internet resources (Web sites, mostly) for your day-to-day purposes (such as finding a movie to see or place to stay at the beach).

▶ AOL develops some of the world's most innovative Internet tools, including the Netscape browser (Chapter 6), ICQ (a full-purpose, mind-blowing communications program), and AOL Instant Messenger (a simple tool for holding electronic conversations with anyone on AOL or the Internet).

▶ On AOL you get information about the Internet, some of it available only to AOL members. Chapter 2 introduces the many sources of Internet-related help on AOL.

The Web and the Net: Not the Same Thing

Many people equate the World Wide Web with the Internet. That assumption is not quite true: the Internet is much bigger. The Internet is a worldwide collection of networks set up to communicate with one another. The World Wide Web is a subset of the Internet. The Web houses millions of Web pages, or documents, that are created with HTML and can be located with URL's.

The Internet contains vast networks of other information that you will never see. What is available to the public is what comprises the World Wide Web. Everything on the Web can be accessed through Web browsers or Internet Service Providers.

Web programs called *browsers* can do the work of many tools — handling electronic mail (see Figure 1-1), providing access to bulletin boards, and enabling file transfers, for example. The Web is *not* the same thing as the Internet, however. Browsers provide uniform access to *other* Internet resources, but it is mostly a Swiss army knife.

AOL's browser is just one Internet tool of many, including your specialized, full-featured AOL tools for reading electronic mail, poking around discussion groups, and downloading files. As a tool in its own right, the browser gives access to multimedia creations (pages) made just for the Web and published by anyone for anyone. On AOL, you can create and make available such pages for free. See Figure 1-2 for AOL Hometown, where you get all the tools you need to create Web pages.

Tip

Despite the huge claims made for the Web, the *Internet* came first and made the Web possible. While the Internet goes back to the late 1960s, the Web wasn't invented until 1989. The Web's dual mission has been (1) to make the scattered and diverse information on the Internet readily available and (2) to make it easy to *contribute* information available to Internet users anywhere. Tim Berners-Lee, the Web's inventor, shares his vision for the Web in his book, *Weaving the Web* (Harper San Francisco, 1999).

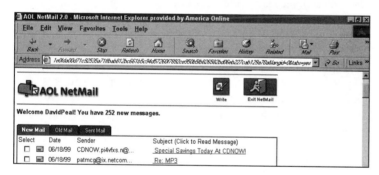

Figure 1-1. Using the Web to access other Internet resources. AOL's AOLMail (see Chapter 9) provides you with what you need to read and write electronic mail.

Cross-Reference

Chapters 2 and 3 provide an overview of the new features (Net-related and otherwise) in AOL 5.0. The features include a new and improved Welcome Screen, You've Got Pictures, and My Calendar.

---

build a homepage now!

"Basically, all you have to do to create this kind of page is type. It's the kind of 'idiot-proof interface' I like." - *Jeff Davis, ZDTV*

IT'S EASY! You can have your own FREE home page in 2 minutes with 1-2-3 Publish. **CLICK HERE** to get your first page now.

Make Your Page About You

Put your picture in your Web profile, or try another template:

- My Collection
- My Favorite TV Shows
- Your Genealogy
- See More Templates ...

Livin' La Vida Loca!
Build a home page shrine to your favorite music star, like the one fergi579 created for her favorite Latin music performer Ricky Martin. For more ideas, browse the full list of templates in our 1-2-3 Publish Gallery.

Advanced Home Page Publisher?
We've got goodies for you in our Advanced Tools area.

Not Using AOL?
Soon 1-2-3 Publish will be available to everyone on the Internet. Be

---

Figure 1-2. Using the Web to create resources. On AOL, you can build your own Web page. Here, AOL's 1-2-3 Publish provides what you need to put together a Web page in a few minutes.

If you've used AOL in the past, you may not notice *all* the new features in its most recent version, AOL 5.0, featured in this book. Some changes lie in improved performance of existing features. Some changes involve greater integration between AOL and its broad range of Internet tools and services. AOL's new AOL Search is a wonderful way to search for anything you need in both AOL the Internet. Learn more about this great new feature in Chapter 7. More than the browser, AOL itself provides comprehensive access to diverse Internet resources.

What Makes the Internet Tick?

By one recent estimate the Web consists of about 800 million pages. Perhaps a hundred million or so pages will be added to this number by the time you read this; perhaps we'll top a billion. Behind the growth is a story of a new medium finding its way into elementary schools, retirement villages, tribal councils, living rooms, boardrooms, beaches, monasteries, and grocery stores.

Binding Forces—Why We All Want to Become Involved

What is powering the Internet's tremendous growth? What's in it for you? Many people want to experience the online world because they are attracted by this new medium's possibilities. At first, they expect to find something new, a sort of virtual world. Instead, they find that the Internet supports and enriches their day-to-day activities in countless ways. Here's what they find.

Information. The Internet is becoming the preeminent way to find out just about anything.

As an information resource, the Internet is the world's preeminent way of learning about many things, such as nutritional trends in Cameroon, how clocks work, the best route to the mountains this summer, ancient civilizations, the number of ant species (9,000), and whatever you happen to want to know.

Do you need to find specific information such as the closest pet store or the weather at the beach? You can find out these things more quickly on the Internet using AOL's Internet tools. Chapter 4 is devoted to finding information of general importance to your life as you make both day-to-day decisions and long-term ones.

Sure, finding specific information on the Web has become daunting. Yet the search sites, after several years of innovation, have vastly improved. As you'll see in Chapters 7 and 8, new services make it ever simpler to find facts, specific types of information (like sound files), and materials on very specific topics.

Tip

There's more to the Web than tracking down information made available by others. With AOL's 1-2-3 Publish, you can create places for others to visit (see Chapter 14). With AOL Calendar, you can create a Web-based calendar for your *own* use only; there you can keep track of personal engagements, work meetings, PTA gatherings, local movie showings, your favorite TV shows, and all the other real-life events you have to juggle (see Chapter 2).

With AOL 5.0 AOL has launched AOL Search, a massive new catalog of hand-selected, annotated, and rated Web sites. Because the sites are hand-picked, you can count on their usefulness, something you *can't* do when you use other search tools. More than that, AOL Search provides a single starting place from which to search an online dictionary and encyclopedia, Internet based yellow and white pages, the message boards available only to AOL members, and other indispensable resources. Chapter 7 has everything you need to know about AOL Search.

Take the example of the recent war over Kosovo. Even before war broke out in Yugoslavia in 1999, the parties to the conflict used the Internet to promote their respective causes. After war broke out, when many journalists were expelled from the country, the Internet became the fastest way to find out about the bombings of Serbia and expulsions from Kosovo. The established media used Web sites to cover the unfolding events around the clock. The BCC's site, in particular, became required reading and viewing, with its up-to-the-minute news reporting, video clips, graphics, interviews, and links to other resources (Figure 1-3). Within a few days of the outbreak of fighting, the NATO Web site offered video clips of Serb targets exploding. NATO's misfires got their share of attention on the Web as well, from every perspective. The Web conveyed the facts of the conflict as well as all opinions about it, with immediacy and fidelity.

Figure 1-3. Using the Web to discover information — on the Web. Long before, during, and long after the war in Yugoslavia, the BBC used its Web site to report on current events in the region, using text, audio, video, and graphics.

Value. The Internet saves time, money, and hassle whenever you have to do product research, compare prices, and get customer service.

The products and services available online go well beyond cyberstores for buying software and hardware. You can shop and do comparison shopping for clothes, toys, jewelry, and anything else that can be sent by mail and many things that can't, including cars and houses (see Chapter 4). The Web brings together storekeepers and shoppers, as well as individuals with something to buy and individuals with something to sell.

When you buy a book from an online bookseller, you're using search tools and resources to get specific information, then actually making a purchase. The book comes to your front door by overnight express or regular postal service. The Web makes it both simpler and faster to buy exactly what you need and to find that unique gift, giving you better choice and freeing you up for other things.

For millions of consumers the Web greatly simplifies the buying and selling of goods and services. The Giga Information Group, a leading business consulting firm, predicts that by the year 2002 between $580 billion and $970 billion in revenues will be generated in the U.S. by electronic commerce — defined broadly as people being influenced by Internet information as well as people buying products online. Big, well-known companies lead the way, with small companies grasping a rare chance to join the giants.

Witness Amazon.com, a company that came from nowhere (no brick-and-mortar stores, at least) to challenge the large book-selling chains. That particular story continues to unfold. As all the large chains now sell on the Web, too, Amazon has started holding auctions and selling toys, just to stay a step ahead. As usual in such situations, the consumer wins: more selection and more convenience at lower prices.

To boot, as a consumer you usually don't have to pay sales tax and you often enjoy discounts shopping on the Web. In the fierce struggle for revenue and market share, companies are busy making services easier to use, beefing up customer service, and extending special offers to frequent customers. On AOL, and especially on the new Shop@AOL center (see Chapter 4), members benefit from the convenience of one-stop shopping and the guaranteed level of service provided by AOL's Certified Merchants and AOL Shop Direct.

 Note

The Internet improves your shopping experience in many ways. You can search for specific items, benefit from the product reviews written by other customers, and do some serious comparison shopping. AOL brings together in one place more than 200 online vendors, many of them Web-based, creating the largest online mall. Start at keyword: Shop@AOL. AOL requires that its vendors offer return policies; it backs up merchants' policies with its own money-back guarantee.

 Find It Online

AOL has partnered with many Web department stores and auction houses to create customized, easy-to-use sites just for AOL members. Auction pioneer E-bay, for example, can be reached directly on AOL at Keyword: **Ebay**. The book superstore, Barnes & Noble, can be reached directly at Keyword: **BN**.

Cross-Reference

A mailing list is an e-mail based community focused on a particular topic. For any field or subject, mailing lists can help you meet the experts, keep up with the new Internet resources, and learn the ropes. Chapter 12 is devoted to mailing lists.

Community. Online communities bring together people who share a hobby, a taste for the same food or type of music, a profession, an ambition, a tradition, a personal or family problem, a belief, or a simple desire to socialize.

Old and new Internet tools make online communities possible: mailing lists, newsgroups, Web boards, and several types of live Internet messaging and chat. Online communities differ from real-world ones in their voluntary character, hence in the high degree of motivation among participants.

"Community," "commerce," and "information" are not mutually exclusive. Online communities generate some of the richest information resources on the Internet, such as the collections of frequently asked questions (FAQs) about hundreds of subjects, collectively maintained by countless people. Community also makes commerce more rewarding on the Web — witness the thousands of people who contribute their often informative book reviews to Amazon.com. All three — community, commerce, and information — get a tremendous boost from the continued trend toward ease of use throughout the Internet.

Simplicity. It's getting easier both to use the Internet and to contribute to it.

Once difficult to access and requiring all kinds of commands to use, the Internet is now used even by young children. The first Internet books set about to make the Internet easier (I wrote one, so I know). Today's books, and this one in particular, take an easy-to-use but sprawling Internet and make it more manageable, more convenient, a greater value, and a more compelling time-saver. In a word, more useful, whatever your needs, and more fun, whenever possible.

The Web is a major driver of Internet growth, and Web browsers get both easier and more powerful every year. The new version of AOL comes packaged with a version of the latest Microsoft browser, Internet Explorer, which displays Web pages faster and more attractively. America Online recently acquired the Netscape browser, whose latest version is freely available to AOL members.

Want to reach a large audience or a small audience of like-minded people? When you contribute a page to the Web, you're contributing to the larger Internet community. Part IV has everything you need to make your mark in this way. The Internet supports your creative contributions as well as your needs to find information and join communities.

Using built-in AOL tools, plus readily available, often free, third-part software, you can build you own home pages and complex Web sites, then publish them (make them available for others) on the Web. AOL provides all that you need at each step: the tools to make pages, the advice and troubleshooting to build them effectively, and a place (AOL Hometown) where you can add your work to bustling Web communities.

The new tools, the new information resources, the spectacular demographic growth, and the great bargains make for an Internet experience that gets better all the time; AOL makes it as easy as possible to enjoy that experience.

Cross-Reference

Chapter 5 is devoted to the AOL browser and Chapter 6 to Netscape. They're all yours, free, on AOL.

Cross-Reference

Chapters 14 and 15 provide all you need to get started building Web pages and sites, and discovering people who share your interests.

How Big Is the Internet?

As I write this, 150 million people in some 240 countries tap into the Internet's resources and communities from schools, homes, and workplaces. By the time you read this, millions of new Internet denizens and perhaps an additional handful of countries will have come on board.

As big as a good-sized country, the Internet possesses all the features of a real nation, with the exception of a standing army, a border, tariffs, and a long history, in human years; in Internet time, the 1970s seems like the 11th century. Though a relatively new country in the scheme of things, the Internet boasts rich traditions owing to its hypergrowth on all fronts. All perspectives are represented on the Internet, and many languages are spoken there, or at least typed; English is the most commonly used language. Conflicts erupt on the Internet, but not shooting wars or even civil wars. Crimes occur on the Internet, but as in any strong community the spirit of neighborhood vigilance runs high. In any Places Rated guide to the Internet, America Online would rank high for its friendly population, safe environment, good services, and excellent schools.

Cross-Reference

If you're interested in the technical details of the Internet, Chapter 18 has a sidebar on voice and data networks ("Making Data Networks Sing"). At the excellent computer-reference, Whatis.com, you'll find a tutorial called "How the Internet Works" (http://www.whatis.com/tour.htm).

A Short, Breathless History of the Internet

It's not fashionable to say this, but the U.S. government can make great things happen. Today's Internet would not exist without strategic long-term support by the U.S. government from the 1960s until the Internet went private in the mid-1990s. Such support made possible the work conducted by the many network heroes who invented TCP/IP (which allows different types of computer to communicate), who cobbled together the first applications for transferring files and sending messages, and who actually used the Internet for fun, games, and socializing a decade or two before these things became a virtual pastime for tens of millions of people.

In many ways the Internet is a '60s kind of thing, designed as a communications network meant to survive disruption in one part of the network (owing to nuclear disaster, runs a somewhat overstated myth of the Internet's origins). A certain anarchy (or suspicion of central control) has been evident from the outset.

In the 1980s the Internet morphed into a set of tools for peaceful academic researchers to exchange messages and data with colleagues across the country. America's ARPANET, then NSFNET, were soon joined to similar "packet-switched" networks in Europe. (ARPANET stands for the Defense Advanced Research Projects Agency network; NSFNET, for the National Science Foundation's research network.) Only in the 1990s, when the government stepped back from managing and financing the Internet, did business and the rest of us discover the joys of networking.

In the last few years America Online has played a key part in Internet history, making the tools, creating the destinations, building the networks, and vastly expanding the communities that hold it all together. In 1995 America Online acquired ANS (Advanced Network & Systems), a company that maintained the Internet's main network (called a *backbone*) in the early 1990s. In early 1996 arrangements with both Microsoft and Netscape gave AOL's members access to superior Internet tools, making AOL in many ways the leader of the commercial Internet in the U.S. Acquiring Netscape in 1998, AOL now owns and develops the Net's most popular Internet software, which it is developing on many fronts.

Want to know more? Pick up a copy of the paperback (you can buy it online!), *Where Wizards Stay Up Late: The Origins of the Internet,* by Katie Hafner and Matthew Lyon (Touchstone Books, 1998). Or, read the online history, *Netizens,* by Rhonda Hauben (`http://www.columbia.edu/~hauben/netbook/`). My favorite place to get an overview of Internet history is the Internet Society's well-maintained "All About the Internet" page (`http://www.isoc.org/internet-history/`).

Some Facts About the Internet

"In late 1998, there were 147 million users of the Internet; just over half (52%) or 76 million logged on in the U.S. The number of users grew by more than 50% in [both] 1997 and 1998. Japan, Germany, the U.K, and Canada also sent contingents of more than five million to the Internet." (*Source: Computer Industry Almanac Inc., an Arlington Heights, Ill.-based reference information publisher; cited in a mailing list.*)

"By 2003, nearly eight million new-car purchases will be influenced by the Internet, and half a million new vehicles will be purchased entirely online, Forrester Research predicts. Last year, more than two million consumers used the Internet to research new car purchases, the Cambridge, Mass.-based firm reported." (*Source: CBS MarketWatch,* `http://cbs.market watch.com/news.`)

"A University of Texas study, financed by Cisco Systems, found that US companies generated US$301 billion in revenue last year from online-related goods and services. The total, derived from interviews with about 3,000 companies participating in the Internet economy, included $102 billion worth of e-commerce, such as sales of books by Amazon.com [and] toys at eToys.com...." (Source: Wired News, June 10, 1999.)

"By the end of this year [1999], a research firm estimates, almost nine million [American] teenagers will be using the Internet." (*Source: 2/19/99* `finance@infobeat.com,` *InfoBeat.*)

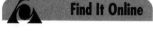
Find It Online

The Internet isn't just about buying stuff. It provides tremendous opportunities for giving, as well. AOL underwrites a Web site (Keyword: **Helping.org**) where you can find out about more than half a million non-profits, safely donate to them over the Internet, and learn about volunteer opportunities in your neighborhood.

"The number of schools using the Internet has grown from 82 percent in 1998 to 89 percent in 1999 — an increase of 8.5 percent. Research and database company Quality Education Data expects every school to have Internet access by the end of the 1999-2000 school year...." (*Source: Finance - Internet Daily, 8/26/99.*)

"Replacing an industry classification that has existed for 60 years, the U.S. Commerce Department has introduced a new system that recognizes this leap into the information age.... The Commerce Department also says that more e-mail than snail mail was sent in 1997, and that U.S. consumers bought more computers than automobiles." (*Source: 3.18.99 FROM EDUPAGE.*)

"A recent poll conducted by Louis Harris and Associates indicates that the average online computer user in the U.S. spends six hours a week surfing the Web. That time does not include *sending and receiving e-mail*, which is the most popular on-line activity. Sixty-three percent of online users say they use e-mail "often"....The next most popular activity (39%) was *conducting research for work or school.* Thirty-one percent of users shop online, with books the most frequently purchased item (software ranked in second place). (*Source: EduPage 3/25.*) Emphasis added.

A Quick Look Back . . . and Ahead

This very short chapter does no more than give a sense of the Internet as a whole. It's so easy to get overwhelmed by the Internet that it's important to keep some perspective on its simple underlying principles.

The Internet:

- ▶ Is available through AOL, and enhanced by AOL's tools and services. AOL contributes to the Internet through its free software (like AOL Instant Messenger) and vast Web resources (like AOL.COM and AOL Hometown).

- ▶ Consists of collections of diverse tools, myriad information resources, virtual communities, and diverse computers and networks.

- ▶ Is not the same as the Web. The Web is a subset of the Internet.

- ▶ Is very big (150 million people) but not yet global.

From here, your path through this book depends entirely on your background and interest. It helps to be familiar with the interface of the new version of AOL, so you might want to skim the next chapter, whatever your background.

CHAPTER

2

I'M ON AOL.
WHERE'S THE INTERNET?

Chapter 2

I'm on AOL.
Where's the Internet?

Ready to go? First thing you probably want to do is *sign on* (or *connect*) to AOL, so you can start exploring. How you sign on depends on whether you're using a modem or some type of network. This chapter briefly goes into all this preliminary stuff (including what to do when you're done — signing off). If you can already sign on and off, jump ahead to the tour of AOL (starting with "An AOL Road Map"). This particular tour has a very specific purpose: to show you where to find the Internet tools, resources, and help on AOL.

A Word about Keywords

Throughout this book you will be seeing *keywords*. An AOL keyword is a word or two that takes you directly to an AOL area or (in some cases) a specific Web site.

1. Enter a keyword into either the AOL Address box shown in Figure 2-1 or the Keyword window, which you get by clicking the little Keyword button to the right of the Address box.

Cross-Reference

Notice the little Search button to the left of the Keyword button? Type a search term like **millennium bug** or **Maui vacation** in the Address box, and click Search to do a combined search of AOL and the Internet using the new AOL Search. See Chapter 7 for more on AOL Search.

2

I'm on AOL. Where's the Internet?

Click keyword, regardless of what's entered in Address box   Click Go for AOL keyword or web address; Search for a search term

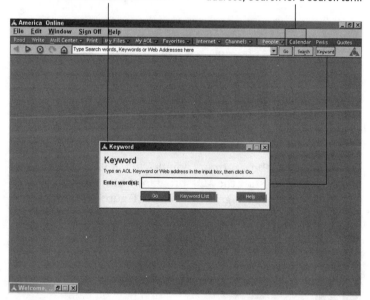

Figure 2-1. The main AOL window, showing the Keyword box. Elsewhere in this book you might see slight differences in the ordering of the tools on the toolbar.

2. In the Address box or Keyword window, type a keyword and click the little Go button. For example, type the Keyword: **Web** and click Go to visit AOL's home page on the Web. Use Keyword: **Keyword** for a list of AOL's keywords.

To use this book effectively you need a PC or laptop outfitted with a modem or network connection, and you should have already installed AOL 5.0. If you are not quite ready to go, Jennifer Watson and Dave Marx's *AOL Tour Guide*, also published by IDG, serves as the perfect prequel.

Signing on to AOL Using a Modem

In some ways AOL works just like any Windows program. Before signing on, you must first install AOL on your hard drive, using either a CD-ROM (like the one in this book) or Keyword: **Upgrade**. To upgrade AOL online, you must be an AOL member using an earlier AOL version. Or, you can use any Internet account and download the software from AOL's Web site (http://www.aol.com), registering and installing as prompted.

Signing on to AOL gives you complete access to AOL and all of AOL's Internet tools and resources, plus all the great AOL content available only to AOL members. Here's how:

1. Start the AOL program. Windows 95/98 conveniently provides you with many *shortcuts* to the program. The AOL shortcut looks like this (Figure 2-2):

Figure 2-2. A shortcut to AOL is available almost anywhere you happen to be. Notice the small arrow on the shortcut, which is how all shortcuts are indicated in Windows 95/98.

2. Single-click the shortcut (double-click if it's in Windows Explorer) to start the AOL program. In the AOL window, you'll see a Sign On window (Figure 2-3), which has boxes for screen name, password, and location.

Figure 2-3. Screen names are automatically remembered and listed here; you have the choice of storing your password on your PC (as in this figure). After storing your password, you won't see the Enter Password field any more; all you do is choose a screen name and press Enter!

3. Since you've already installed and set up the AOL software, some of your personal information is ready for

you to use. If you've upgraded from an earlier version of AOL, all your existing screen names and locations are available in the AOL 5.0 Sign On screen. Choose a screen name from the Select Screen Name box (click the downward-pointing triangle in Figure 2-3).

Upon signing on *for the first time*, you must enter your unique password (the one you chose while first setting up AOL). You will be prompted to have your computer store your password, so you won't have to enter it again. (*Prompted* means you'll see a small window in which the AOL software requests some information.) Click Sign On or press Enter when you've selected a screen name, confirmed the location, and provided a password.

The *location* gives AOL information about how you are connecting:

a. Using a modem to dial an AOL access number in a specific area code

b. Using a network or Internet Service Provider (ISP), regardless of your geographical location

Using a modem, you'll be using one of AOL's access numbers, and the location tells your AOL software which access (telephone) numbers to use and how many times to try each number if it's busy. The upcoming "Signing On to AOL Over a Network" section shows how to set up a location if you'll be accessing AOL over a network or ISP.

4. If everything goes right, you'll now go through the sign-on process. The AOL program dials the AOL access number, establishes a connection, "talks" to the network, passes on your screen name/password information, and, if everything checks out, welcomes you online. If the phone lines are busy, which happens with every Internet service provider from time to time (especially during peak evening hours), you can try again later or have AOL redial automatically, as explained below in the "Locations: Where You are When You're Online" section.

5. Welcome! Pretty quickly, all this sign-on stuff will be second nature. If you're staying put, and your screen name and location won't be changing, all you do to sign on is open AOL and press Enter (which is the same as clicking Sign On)!

Note

Once you've signed on, then signed off, this window--where you enter screen name, password, and location--is called Goodbye from America Online. The name of a window is always provided in its Title Bar--the horizontal strip of text along the window's top edge.

Tip

In Chapter 3 you will read about Parental Controls, which adults can use to restrict kids' access to certain tools and types of online content. If you (the adult, or AOL master account holder) have your PC remember your password, another person in your household will be able to sign on to AOL using your screen name and password. Make sure to weigh the convenience of storing it against the possible risks of somebody else using it.

Signing on with Screen Name *Guest*

Cross-Reference

Read about Favorite Places in Chapter 3, and the Address Book and PFC in Chapters 9 and 10.

Sometimes you don't have your computer available but still need to check your AOL e-mail or stock portfolio, or do something on the Web. If a friend of yours has a computer loaded with AOL (any version), you can sign on using the screen name *Guest*, which is available from the drop-down Screen Name list.

Once connected as Guest, you will be prompted to provide your real screen name and password. As a guest, you will be able to use the Web, visit AOL areas, and send and receive e-mail and Instant Messages, but you won't be able to do anything requiring access to your friend's hard drive: using Favorite Places, accessing the Address Book, or saving messages in the Personal Filing Cabinet (PFC).

Where'd My AOL Go?

Lost your AOL? Figure 2-4 shows you some places to look.

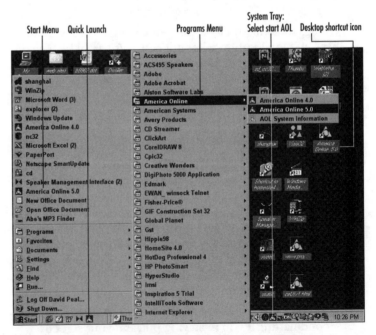

Figure 2-4. Some of the places where you can find and open AOL

▶ On the top half of the Windows 95/98 Start menu, if you chose to place it there during installation (The

Start menu is that little button in the lower left corner of your Windows display.)

▶ On the Windows 95/98 Start Menu: select Programs ➪ America Online > America Online 5.0

▶ In Windows 95 and 98 it might be on Windows's Quick Launch toolbar, which you'll see at the bottom of your screen (sometimes you'll have to drag your mouse arrow to the bottom of the display for the toolbar to pop up)

▶ Also in Windows 98, the AOL shortcut might be in the "system tray" — the clutch of program icons on the far right of the Windows toolbar. This particular AOL short-cut provides information of particular use to users with broadband connections (cable and ADSL, described in Chapter 18).

▶ The shortcut is added automatically to the Windows desktop when you install AOL 5.0.

Signing On to AOL Over a Network

The modem has been the most popular access method since AOL's beginnings in the 1980s.

Since 1996 another access method has grown in popularity: accessing AOL over a network. In the years ahead, you may be using network connections such as DSL (Digital Subscriber Line), so it's a good idea to familiarize yourself with non-modem access. Signing on to AOL over a network means one of several things:

▶ Accessing AOL over your work (or home) LAN, if it has an Internet connection. Ask your systems administrator if you have questions about your work connection.

▶ Accessing AOL over your Internet service provider (ISP).

▶ Accessing AOL over a DSL connection.

▶ Accessing AOL over your cable company, if it provides Internet connectivity services (in this case you'll need additional hardware, as explained in Chapter 18). This doesn't mean you'll use AOL on TV, just that you can use the cable wire to run AOL on your PC. To see AOL

Not enough shortcuts? Make a new one by right-clicking any existing AOL shortcut and clicking Copy. Then, go to the folder or toolbar where you want to place a new shortcut, right click, and se-lect Paste. Presto!

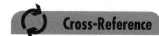

Chapter 18 goes into more detail about DSL and other broadband (superfast) Internet connections through which you can (or soon will be able to) access AOL.

AOL is currently working on a version of the AOL software that will add DSL to the exist-ing choices (modem and ISP/LAN). That choice will be part of the setup process de-scribed in this section.

2

 **Definition**

A LAN, or Local Area Network, links together a company's or other organization's computers, printers, and other resources at a single site. LANs require computer gateways to enable individual users to access the Internet. Most LANs provide much faster access to the Internet than via modem. Home networking is becoming more popular as families start to use many computers, for more purposes, with more competition for access to printers, scanners, and the Internet. See Chapter 18 for more about home networking.

on your TV, you'll need a set-top box or satellite connection, as explained in Chapter 18.

If you have a network connection, you can join AOL on the Bring Your Own Access plan, which gives you full access to AOL's content, but not through AOL's physical network. The plan is lower in price than the standard plan, for modem users. Keyword: **Billing** has everything you need to know about the choices among billing options.

To access AOL over a network, you must first set up an ISP/LAN location, as follows:

1. From the Sign On screen (or Goodbye screen if you've signed off AOL without closing the AOL application), click Setup to bring up the window shown in Figure 2-5.

2. At the America Online Setup window, click the button called "Create a location for use with new access numbers or an ISP." Click Next.

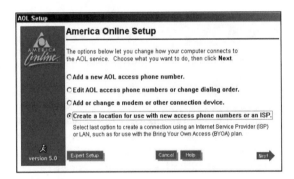

Figure 2-5. Start here to indicate that you'll be using a network or ISP to access AOL. By switching locations in the Sign On screen, you can go back and forth between modem and ISP/network.

3. In the Add Location window (Figure 2-6), click the button called "Add a custom connection." In the Name box, you'll see ISP/LAN Connection, which is the name that will appear in the future in your Locations box in the Sign On screen, unless you choose to name the connection something else (like *Cable* or *Network* or *Mindspring* or *Work*). Click the Next button. Your connection is created and named, and the name appears in the Sign On screen.

4. Now, to sign on, use the Sign On window to select the new ISP/LAN location and click Sign On.

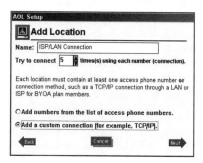

Figure 2-6. Create a custom location so you can use AOL with your ISP, DSL (Digital Subscriber Line), cable modem, or network connection. I've kept the connection's name *ISP/LAN Connection*. You can call it anything you like, such as *Home Network* or *My ISP*.

To run AOL over a network connection:

1. Establish the ISP, network, or cable connection to the Internet.

2. Open the AOL software, select the ISP/LAN location (or whatever you've named it) in the Sign On screen, and click Sign On. The process usually takes place a bit faster than when using a modem, but don't forget to factor in the time required to establish the network connection in the first place.

Using AOL as Internet Software

AOL 5.0 gives you the option of making AOL the *default Internet application* when you use the Web, e-mail, or newsgroups. You can choose this option during installation, and you can change it at any point thereafter.

Here's what this option is likely to mean for you:

Many applications let you embed Internet links in documents. Microsoft Word and the other Microsoft Office applications, for example, let you link directly to Web sites. In addition, the Microsoft Internet Explorer Web browser lets you create shortcuts to Web pages and put those shortcuts on your desktop.

Tip

Here's a fast way to get online when you have a network connection. In the Windows 95/98 "system tray" (along the lower right-hand edge of your Windows display, on the Windows toolbar), right click the AOL icon (shown in Figure 2-4) and select AutoStart Options. Click *Automatically start AOL*. AOL now starts whenever a network connection is detected. AutoStart AOL is new to AOL 5.0.

Note

If you choose AOL as your default program, you'll notice that any Windows desktop *shortcuts* (links to Web sites) have clickable AOL icons. Sometimes, it can be a little tricky to tell which of these icons is an Internet shortcut and which is a shortcut to AOL itself! Check out the icon's name if you're unsure, or right click the icon and select Properties to see whether it's pointing to a Web address, in which case it's *not* an AOL icon.

Note

In automatically attempting to connect, AOL attempts to work with the most recent location you used. If you were using an ISP/LAN connection and are not now connected to a network, you will have to manually connect to the network before you can establish the AOL connection you need to use a link, shortcut, or Internet application.

What happens when you click such a link (in a document) or Web shortcut (on your desktop)? If you're online and AOL is your default Internet application, the AOL software opens automatically whenever you click a link or Internet shortcut.

Or, suppose you're currently *not* online. When you click a link or shortcut, or attempt to use Internet software like AOL Instant Messenger, ICQ, or one of the programs profiled in Chapter 17, you automatically make AOL open and connect, in order to create a connection so you can use the software.

To make AOL your default Internet application:

1. Select My AOL ⇨ Preferences.
2. Click the Associations button. Read the instructions and click OK to make AOL your Internet application. In practice, that means that whenever you try to launch a Web site or open the browser, you'll automatically sign onto AOL first. AOL will be your default Internet application even if your connection to the Internet is through an ISP, LAN, or cable modem; in other words, you'll have to establish a network connection first.

Change your mind? Want the stand-alone Microsoft Internet Explorer browser and Microsoft e-mail program as your default Internet applications? Go to your Windows 95/98 desktop and right-click the Internet Explorer icon. Select Properties. In the Internet Properties window, click the Programs tab. Click the Reset Web Settings button. You'll be asked whether you want to restore your MSIE default settings. Click Yes to confirm that you do. Click OK to close the Internet Properties window. Instead of AOL icons for all your Web links (shortcuts) on your desktop, you'll see lots of little MSIE icons.

Locations: Where You are When You're Online

In a world of virtual everything, "locations" have to do with where you *really* are (in what town or city) when you're on AOL. Let's say you are travelling to San Francisco on business, and you've got a laptop in tow. You'd need to find a local phone number for your laptop's modem to dial up, and you'd need to store those access numbers in a special location for easy retrieval. Here's how to find and use the AOL access codes in the 415 area code.

1. On the Sign On screen (or Goodbye screen, depending on whether you've been online today), click Setup. In the Setup window, select the "add a new AOL access number" button.

2. In the Search for AOL Access Numbers window, type (for example) **415** into the Area Code box (Figure 2-7).

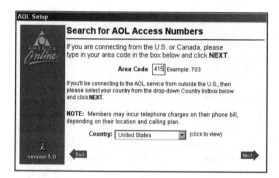

Figure 2-7. Setting up a new location means adding new phone numbers for AOL to use when you're travelling out of the area code where you live. First step: enter an area code.

3. From the long list of phone numbers on the left, select one phone number and click Add; repeat so that you select at least two phone numbers. *AOL requires you to choose at least two.* In choosing phone numbers, bear in mind your modem's speed; you'll want to choose access numbers fast enough to support that speed. Also consider whether any of the numbers carry a toll charge, as many calls do within the country's larger area codes. Sometimes adjacent area codes will be listed along with the area code you chose (search for 415 in San Francisco, and you'll pull up a couple of 510 numbers in the East Bay, for example). When you click the Add button to move access numbers to the right-hand window, you get the chance to edit your choice, specifying whether you want the area code included, for example, or want to add the number 9 (in a business or hotel requiring a 9 to reach an outside number). See Figure 2-8.

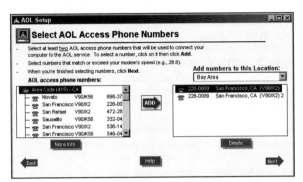

Tip

If you're using a network connection, make sure you've selected the corresponding location. You won't be able to connect.

Figure 2-8. Setting up a new location with two or more access numbers for that location. Create a new location on the spot by selecting Add Location from the drop-down list labeled *Add numbers to this Location.*

4. Before leaving this window, choose a location into which to include the new access numbers. Either place the new number into an existing location, or, for new locations, click Add Location from the drop-down list of locations and create a new location. A location, remember, is usually a group of access numbers you use when you're traveling.

Somewhat confusingly, a *location* is also a way of distinguishing network from non-network connections. A network connection is generic, by the way: you can use the same ISP/LAN location for network connections in any geographical location, whether it's Phoenix or Halifax.

To create a new location at any time, go to the Sign On (Goodbye) window and click Setup. In Setup window, click Expert Setup (Figure 2-9 shows mine). Here you can add new locations and new phone numbers to existing locations.

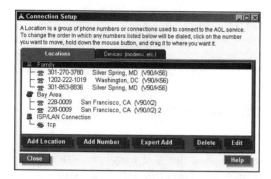

Figure 2-9. *Add Location* lets you add a new location for dial-up access or a new location for your ISP/LAN (or cable or network) connection. *Add Number* lets you add a phone number to a location. Right-click any location to edit, delete, or rename it.

Switching Screen Names without Signing Off

In the new version of AOL 5.0, every master account on AOL now can have up to seven screen names (see the next chapter for more about setting up screen names and their corresponding passwords and Parental Controls). You can switch from screen name to screen name without having to first sign off and then sign on again. During busy times, this can be a godsend.

1. From the Sign Off menu, select Switch Screen Name.
2. From the list of names that comes up, choose one and select Switch.

You'll be told just how long the previous screen name was online (if you're on a billing plan that tallies the minutes in order to bill the hours). If you chose to have the new screen name's password stored on your PC, you'll be whisked to a new Sign On screen, with new mailbox, new Favorite Places (see next chapter), and all the other items tweaked for the screen name to which you wish to switch.

Signing Off AOL
The simplest way to leave AOL is to select Sign Off from the Sign Off menu.

Here are a few wrinkles having to do with:

▶ Whether you're on a network

Signing Off AOL

The simplest way to leave AOL is to select Sign Off from the Sign Off menu.

Here are a few wrinkles having to do with:

▶ Whether you're on a network

▶ Whether you want to close the *AOL program* when you terminate your *AOL connection* (they're two different things)

If you're using a modem (not a network):

> ▶ Choosing Sign Off ⇨ Sign Off disconnects you from AOL. The AOL software, however, remains open, so you can quickly sign on again later (just press Enter to sign on).

> ▶ Closing the AOL program (e.g., by choosing File ⇨ Exit) closes the AOL program and disconnects you. To sign on again, you'll have to reopen the AOL software.

If you're using a network connection (not a modem):

> ▶ Signing off AOL (Sign Off ⇨ Sign Off) keeps the AOL program open but *doesn't terminate the underlying network connection.*

> ▶ Closing the AOL application (pressing Alt-F4, or clicking the Close box, or using File ⇨ Exit) closes your AOL program without disconnecting your network connection. Using both major types of connection, I have learned the hard way how easy it is to run up bills with an ISP because the connection remains open after the AOL application is closed.

Note

Sometimes, after you've chosen to sign off, AOL will take a moment to remove graphics it's temporarily stored on your computer; sometimes, AOL will download small feature enhancements that will be available next time you use AOL.

Caution

As long as that network connection is active, you may be incurring costs from your ISP or hourly charges from the phone company. Why? Even if you close the AOL application, the underlying network connection is still going.

An AOL Road Map

If you're familiar with a Web browser, you'll recognize two aspects of the AOL interface right away: the toolbar and the navigation bar (Figure 2-10).

Figure 2-10. AOL 5.0 looks a lot like AOL 4.0: the toolbar and navigation bar give you simultaneous control of AOL and Internet; the menus at the top of the window give you control of AOL as a Windows application. The following windows come up automatically when you start AOL: the Welcome screen, your Buddy List, and AOL Search. See above comment.

The toolbar simplifies access to AOL content and Internet tools. It also lets you set your preferences and tweak AOL to your liking. Chapter 3 is devoted to the growing number of personal preferences available to you on AOL 5.0.

The navigation bar, shown in Figure 2-10, provides joint control of AOL and the Web. The Forward, Previous, Stop, Refresh, and Home buttons are especially useful in controlling your Web experience, as you'll see in Chapter 5. In the navigation bar's Address box, you can enter either a Web address (or URL) or an AOL keyword. Clicking Go is the same as pressing Enter.

Definition

The Point-to-Point Protocol (PPP) makes your PC part of the Internet while you're browsing the Web, reading e-mail, or doing anything else on the Net.

Note

The AOL 5.0 software works with Microsoft's new Windows 2000 operating system, as well as with Windows 95, Windows 98, and Windows NT.

New Internet (and Other) Features in AOL

AOL 5.0 sports a greatly enhanced and much more useful Welcome screen, described in the next chapter. Otherwise, if you've used AOL 4.0, you'll be right at home with AOL 5.0. Behind the scenes, however, are important technical enhancements that add up to superior access to and experience on AOL and the Net.

▶ You can now create up to seven screen names. Instead of two megabytes of free storage space per screen name (as in earlier versions of AOL), you now get both more screen names and, for each screen name, more storage space on AOL's computers to use when you create Web pages. All the details are in Chapter 14.

▶ AOL includes the latest version of the Microsoft Internet Explorer browser (version 5), popularly known as *MSIE*. This browser displays pages faster, includes improved search features, supports more types of multimedia, and includes other changes discussed in depth in Chapter 5.

▶ AOL has added something called PPP, short for the Internet's Point-to-Point Protocol. You may not notice the difference, but PPP means that AOL will be more efficiently managing your Internet connection. PPP applies to modem-based connections, not connections over an ISP or network.

▶ Closing in on 20 million members, AOL has always had to manage the large numbers of members who sign on to the service during busy hours. Now, when you've been inactive for about 45 minutes, a new alert sound gives you the chance to resume working if you wish. If you're working on another program (word processing, for example), the timer is a useful way of alerting you that AOL is about to automatically sign you off. Also new to this version: if you are writing an e-mail message when AOL does sign you off automatically, the message will remain active for continued writing and editing offline.

▶ Both the Address Book and the Favorite Places folder, discussed in the next chapter, can now be saved as a file for safekeeping and for synchronizing copies of AOL maintained by one person using the same screen name on *different computers*. Your Address Book helps you keep track of complicated Internet e-mail addresses for all your contacts, while Favorite Places help you keep track of all your favorite Internet destinations. As a laptop user, I love this new tool for keeping my desktop and laptop in synch.

▶ AOL can now detect modems that use your computer's COM 5 port, increasing the number of connection options available to you. When installing a modem, AOL can automatically detect and configure it.

▶ When you install the latest version of AOL, you get the option of making AOL your default Internet application (explained earlier in " Using AOL as Internet Software").

▶ AOL 5.0 enables you to add signature files to your e-mail messages. This addition to your messages provides contact information, quotes, jokes, or anything else you want to provide.

▶ Once online, you'll see that AOL has consolidated its search features. In the last version, AOL Find enabled you to look for specific AOL areas of interest; AOL Search did the same (on a much bigger scale) for the Web. Now, using AOL Search, you can conduct a joint search of both AOL and the Internet. Chapter 7 has all the details. A Search button on the AOL navigation bar (Figure 2-11) takes you instantly to the AOL Search Web site, so you search AOL, the Web, or just about anything else on the Internet.

The improved Welcome screen is always available. Closing the Welcome screen minimizes it without making it go away. Figure 2-12 shows the Welcome screen.

2

I'm on AOL. Where's the Internet?

Type Search words, Keywords or Web Addresses here ▾ Go Search Keyword

Figure 2-11. The new AOL navigation bar provides a Search button, giving you instant access to a truly comprehensive AOL/Web search service.

AOL's Red Carpet: The Welcome Screen

AOL's Welcome screen (Figure 2-12) has undergone a facelift in AOL 5.0. Many new features — You've Got Pictures, My Weather, My Calendar, My Places — extend your ability to customize AOL. Chapter 3 is devoted to customizing AOL. Consolidation, expanded features, and improved customization

capabilities make the Welcome screen much more valuable as
the point from which to set out on either AOL or the Internet.

▶ Most notably, the Welcome screen has been consolidated with the old Channels menu; AOL channels are
   now listed alphabetically along the Welcome screen's
   left side.

▶ Underneath the famous You've Got Mail button is a
   new button for AOL's new You've Got Pictures and
   My Calendar features.

▶ The new AOL Search window, which lets you search
   AOL and the Net at the same time, is a click away,
   too, thanks to a button in the Welcome screen's
   upper-right corner.

▶ My Places, a new feature, lets you add up to five of your
   favorite links to AOL areas, creating a custom menu of
   your favorite destinations.

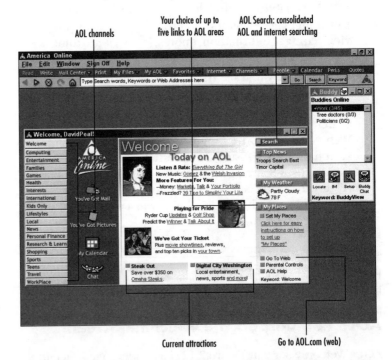

Figure 2-12. The greatly expanded Welcome screen now offers direct access to AOL
channels, new services such as You've Got Pictures and My Calendar, customized links
to AOL areas (My Places), and breaking news stories.

Other new features on the Welcome screen — You've Got Pictures and My Calendar — were just being released as this book went to press.

Familiar features can still be found on the Welcome screen. The Chat button takes you to the People Connection channel. Go to the Web is the same as selecting Go to the Web from the Internet menu; both take you to AOL.COM (AOL's Web site). In the lower-right corner of the Welcome screen, you'll also find a link to Parental Controls.

Down the middle of the Welcome screen are the links to AOL's new areas, live events, and special promotions, as well as breaking news stories of general interest. These links change many times daily.

Channeling Your Energy

AOL orders its online world into 18 or so *channels* of information, communities, and shopping districts, arranged in large, familiar subjects. The Health channel, for example, shown in Figure 2-13, with its message boards, online pharmacy (Planet rX), online magazines, polls, chat, access to doctors, a myriad of connections to hand-selected Web sites, text articles available only on AOL, and a great deal more. While no AOL channel covers the Internet as such, every channel takes you to hand-picked Web sites directly related to the channel's theme. The Computing channel, in particular, shown later in Figure 2-20, provides a massive collection of resources on using specific Internet tools, building Web pages, buying Internet software, learning programming, and much else.

Cross-Reference

Parental Controls are covered in depth in Chapter 3. AOL.COM is the subject of Chapter 4.

2

I'm on AOL. Where's the Internet?

Figure 2-13. AOL's Health channel — for advice, support, and reliable information

Tip

The Internet menu on the AOL toolbar takes you to mostly all of AOL's Internet-related tools and Help resources.

Cross-Reference

In later chapters, especially Chapter 17, you find out about third-party (non-AOL) tools that you can use on AOL.

Where Do They Keep the Tools Around Here?

On AOL you can use any Internet tools you want (as long as they work on your Mac or Windows operating system, of course). You can also easily use different types of tools at the same time, and use AOL's tools with third-party tools. See Figure 2-14 for fast ways to find AOL's Internet tools.

What follows is a list of some of the tools you need to use the Internet. All the following tools are built right into your AOL software (on your computer) or directly available on AOL itself (on its computers).

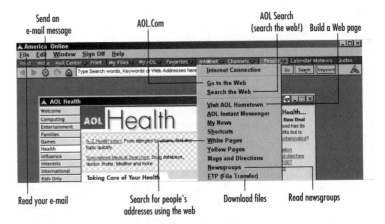

Figure 2-14. The Internet at your fingertips

- ▶ **An e-mail program**, so you can send and receive messages or files to anyone on AOL or the Internet. Just click the Read or Write buttons on the AOL toolbar.

- ▶ **A newsgroup program**, available at keyword: Newsgroups, so you can take part in tens of thousands of public Internet bulletin boards, to which anyone with Internet access can post messages and read others' messages.

- ▶ **A Web browser**, so you can use a billion or so pages of information.

- ▶ **A Web-page creator** (also known as an HTML editor), for making and posting your own pages. In Chapter 14, you'll learn about the *two* free Web-publishing tools AOL makes available.

▶ **An FTP program,** available at keyword: FTP and keyword: MyPlace, for downloading and uploading files —
indispensable in creating a Web site of your own.

AOL Roadside Assistance for Internet Travelers

AOL provides complete outfitting services for your Internet
adventures, round-the-clock troubleshooting, training, help,
places to swap experiences, occasional wisdom, maps, tips,
and all the gear you need. Even if you already know your way
around, Net technology changes so fast and new destinations
emerge so frequently that you should get familiar with AOL's
resources for getting help and staying up-to-date. The following overview helps you navigate AOL's excellent, if somewhat
scattered help resources. As you'll notice right away, Help resources come in all sorts of formats, so you can choose the
one that matches your needs and the way you like to learn.
Some resources help you learn to use certain AOL and
Internet tools; others help you deepen your knowledge or do
some troubleshooting. Use these resources (and this book)
whenever you need help.

Watch a Slideshow to Get an Overview of the Most Important Features

The slideshow, bane of many a childhood, has enjoyed a big
comeback thanks to new multimedia tools and new possibilities of watching them on your own time and at your own
pace. Available at Keyword: **Visual Help**, AOL Slideshows
present simple animations, with voiceovers. For a general
introduction, visit Keyword: **Slideshow**. Slideshows currently
cover topics such as downloading files and managing computer viruses, but many more are planned. Revisit Keyword:
Slideshows to stay up-to-date. Save it as a Favorite Place as
explained in Chapter 3. Figure 2-15 shows a single image
from a longer slideshow with voice and animation.

Tip

If you want to know *about*
the big-i Internet—the companies, personalities, policies, and trends—go to
keyword: **Internet Pros**.
Among other things you can
find out about hot new products and Internet-related jobs
of all sorts.

Figure 2-15. You can enjoy Slideshows on your own and quickly pick up new Internet skills or learn about new AOL features like (in this case) You've Got Pictures.

Teach Yourself Step-by-Step, in Pictures

A newer resource on AOL serves the needs of what teachers like to call "visual learners" (Figure 2-16). Also at Keyword: **Visual Help**, you will find more than two dozen simple, annotated graphics covering basic AOL tasks and a few Internet tasks, such as purging your cache, clearing your history trail, and downloading files from the Web. Bear in mind that a tutorial provides a single set of steps and can't capture every particular context or need.

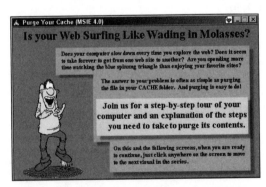

Figure 2-16. At Keyword: *Visual Help*, you get illustrated overviews of basic Internet tasks. Some, like this one, consist of several screens.

Take an Online Class to Learn HTML (and Other Things)

Chat put AOL on the map, and AOL does a good job turning tools people love into tools they can use for something useful.

Keyword: **Basics** provides a growing list of chat-based classes, lead by experts; many of them are AOL-focused, some Net-focused, and some cover both worlds. For each topic, information is available in several forms, so you can learn the way you like. For example, click Basic HTML Workshop in the List of Classes, and you find a web of related information

The main window shows a schedule of chat lessons to be held in the next few weeks. If a chat session is in progress, you can click Enter the Classroom to join the guide and AOL members eager to learn HTML. If you never liked classroom learning, you can read a transcript, a full written introduction to the topic with numerous *links* to AOL and Internet resources on HTML.

Use the AOL Message Boards to Ask Internet Questions

Chat, message boards, e-mail, and now Hometown AOL form the backbone of AOL's vigorous community life. Message boards provide public bulletin boards in which you can explore specific topics. While chat is transient (it lasts as long as the typing takes place), your message-board postings are available over long periods of time.

Message boards in particular give AOL members the chance to ask each other for help when they get stuck with some tricky bit of HTML script or a malfunctioning scanner. Other members can strut their stuff, share similar experiences, and provide links to AOL and Internet resources.

The Computing channel has the most numerous and best Internet-related message boards on AOL. From the channel's main window, click Chat & Messages to see a list of available boards, some of which have more to do with the Net than others. (The Computing channel focuses on PCs and Windows. At the channel's Help Desk you can acquire Windows 95/98 basics such as copying files, creating folders, and formatting disks.) Figure 2-17 shows the message board devoted to Building Home Pages. Remember, if you go there it will look somewhat different, with new topics and a different number of subjects per topic.

Definition

It's worth pausing at the word *links.* On a Web page, a *link* refers to a bit of text (sometimes a picture) you click *once* with your mouse in order to jump to related information. Text links usually appear in a different color and underlined. You'll know you can click on a link when the mouse pointer turns into a pointing hand.

Tip

Here's how to visit a Web address: type the following into the AOL Address box: http://www.aol.com/nethelp /home.html and click the Go button (or press Enter).

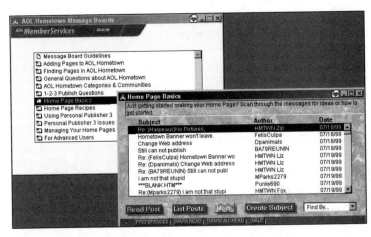

Figure 2-17. An AOL message board, available only on AOL, where you can get your questions answered

NetHelp: Web-based Internet Help

AOL's first comprehensive Internet help resource (NetHelp) went live in late 1996; I was lucky to have been part of that effort. Today, NetHelp is available on the Web at the following address: `http://www.aol.com/nethelp/home.html` (Figure 2-18).

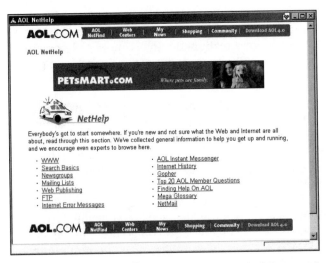

Figure 2-18. The Internet-related information you need, when you need it

On AOL, Keyword: **NetHelp** takes you to a central help kiosk on the AOL service that's even more comprehensive than NetHelp on the Web. Everything appears in the single compact window shown in Figure 2-19. In the left-hand window, you can see either a high-level list of topics or a longer, alphabetically arranged index. *Topics* is the more useful tab for most purposes. Keep double clicking topics and subtopics in the left until the article you need appears in the box on the right.

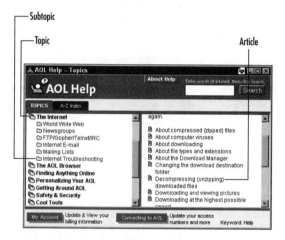

Figure 2-19. Don't flounder, use NetHelp

Keyword: **NetHelp** now forms part of a larger help resource created by AOL's Member Services group (Keyword: **Help**). Start at Keyword: **Help** if you have any questions about installing AOL, connecting to the service, downloading AOL files, and staying safe online. This comprehensive help resource is searchable.

Buying Computer Gear

Many Internet technologies seem to require "fast" everything — hard drives, processors, modems, printers. New devices such as scanners and digital cameras can enrich your experience but also require that you first make some crucial buying decisions. If you want to contribute to the Internet, you may need to buy graphics programs and an HTML editor, then download a slew of utilities. How do you know what to buy?

AOL recently joined with CNET, the creator of computer-related programs for cable television, to create a series of consumer's guides, which you will find in the Computing channel's main window (Figure 2-20). To purchase software or hardware, you'll need to visit one of the many online vendors who sell direct online (like Dell) or who resell others' products (like Beyond.com and Cyberian Outpost) — Keyword: **Dell**, Keyword: **Beyond**, and Keyword: **Cyberian**, respectively. AOL offers this as well at Keyword: **AOL Shop Direct**. For any product you search on CNET, you can find a comparison of the prices for that product offered by leading online vendors.

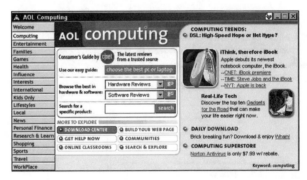

Figure 2-20. Hand-holding for new users, hard data for the experienced: CNET's consumer's guides help with those difficult buying decisions. New software and equipment can help you get more of the Internet.

A Quick Look Back

In this chapter I wanted to present in one place the information you need to use AOL as a base for exploring the Internet:

- ▶ How to sign on to AOL by modem.
- ▶ How to sign on to AOL over a network, LAN, Internet Service provider, or cable.
- ▶ How to create "locations" so you can sign on to AOL by either modem or network. You *must* know about locations if you travel regularly.
- ▶ Along the way you saw how to sign on as a Guest (if you're at someone else's computer) and switch screen names without signing off.

You also got an overview of the new AOL 5.0 *as an Internet application*: how the AOL software has been refined to incorporate Internet features just about everywhere. Changes in the software and on AOL's computers together make for a richer and also simpler experience of the Internet.

The last few pages of the chapter profile AOL's Internet-related help resources, which are available in many forms and many places: offline and online; as text and in pictures; in message boards and chat rooms; and on AOL or on the Web. You can take such support services for granted on AOL, and you won't find them with plain-old Internet service providers (ISPs).

CHAPTER

3

MAKING AOL WORK
YOUR WAY:
PARENTAL CONTROLS
AND OTHER PREFERENCES

Chapter 3

Making AOL Work
Your Way: Parental Controls
and Other Preferences

IN THIS CHAPTER

Keep track of the places you like to visit

Keep track of the people with whom you like to communicate online

Keep track of important information about your personal account

Keep yourself and your family safe in the online world

AOL is a large and feature-packed program, which comes in versions for Windows and the Macintosh. Think of AOL as a tool that makes available and simplifies use of other tools. Other Internet Service providers offer only a bunch of special-purpose tools, such as Web browsers and e-mail readers. AOL takes things a step further by integrating tools and making them easy to use.

This chapter shows you how to make the AOL software work the way you like it. Many of AOL's customization features can be found in the My AOL menu. A few others are available under Favorites in Windows' Control Panels. It pays to explore AOL thoroughly at some point early in your online adventures, just as you'd want to identify the main features of the dashboard on a new car.

Cross-Reference

This chapter looks at ways to customize AOL. Other chapters look at customizing Internet tools and services such as the Web browser (Chapter 4), e-mail (Chapter 9), and newsgroups (Chapter 12). Elsewhere you'll see how to make mailing lists and file-transfer programs work the way you want.

Your Favorite Places

One of the most useful ways of customizing AOL (and the Internet) is to keep your own personal record of where you've been and what you like. Doing so enables you to share with others and to return to those places yourself. AOL gives you several ways to find out about and keep track of your favorite destinations on AOL and the Interet.

You Know What You Like—Do You Know Where to Look?

AOL makes it quite simple to find places of interest to you, and to keep tabs on these places (see the next section, "Favorite Places"). Keyword: **Interest Profiles**, shown in Figure 3-1, should be one of the first stops for new AOL members or longer-time members who are familiar with only one corner of AOL and want to explore further, or who want to stay up-to-date as resources come and go on AOL. By setting up an Interest Profile you'll learn about the new areas on AOL that match your particular interests.

3

Making AOL Work Your Way

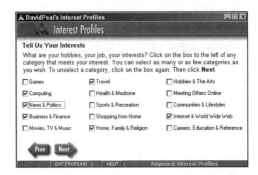

Figure 3-1. Ask AOL to indicate the areas of potential value to you, given the details you provide about topics and subtopics of interest (Keyword: *Interest Profiles*).

If you've never filled in this form before, you'll see a Create button. If you have used the form, the button reads Edit. The process in either case is pretty much the same.

1. Indicate your level of expertise (Beginner, Intermediate, Advanced). Click Next.

2. Put checks in one or more boxes describing your interests and hobbies (Games, Computing, Travel, and so on). This step is shown in Figure 3-1. Click Next.

3. For each interest you checked, you'll see a window with a list of subtopics. Double-click a subtopic (for example, computer programming under Computing) to select it; double-click a selected subtopic to remove it from your list of preferred subtopics.

4. Click Next to walk through all your favored interests. When you see a Done button, click it if you're done. Or, back up to refine your selections.

The only difference between creating and editing your profile is that when you edit one, you encounter the topics and subtopics you selected earlier; just add to them or delete them as you please.

When you're done with the process, AOL sends you an e-mail message, with an automatically generated list of AOL areas of likely interest to you. In the future, whenever AOL adds an area of potential interest to you (based on the information you provided in your Interest Profile), you'll get an e-mail message. As always, browse the how-to articles (Keyword: **Interest Profiles**) for more details about this useful feature.

Favorite Places

Your Favorite Places folder, available from the Favorites menu, lets you keep a list of, and links to, all your favorite destinations. Yes, you can use your Favorite Places as a "hot list" of your favorite Web sites, but you can also add much more:

- ▶ e-mail messages (for example, mailing list Welcome messages and important job-related or personal messages)
- ▶ newsgroups and individual newsgroup messages
- ▶ message boards, even particular postings
- ▶ FTP sites you frequent — or the FTP directories with the best files
- ▶ AOL areas and windows within them (which won't all be directly available by keywords)
- ▶ AOL channels
- ▶ AOL features such as your Buddy List and the AOL Members Directory
- ▶ Individual Web pages obscurely tucked away in those ever-larger sites

Not only can you store different types of sites, but you can also create folders to hold related content. I keep a folder for each of my work and home projects, for example. I also kept folders and subfolders just for this book, so I wouldn't forget to include some of the great resources I've been finding.

You can move folders around within the Favorite Places folder; you can move items around within folders; and both item names and folder names can be changed to suit your needs. Using Favorite Places is a breeze. To add any page, message, site, or AOL area (and so forth) to your personal Favorite Places folder:

1. Click the small heart in the window's upper right-hand corner (Figure 3-2). This heart will not be visible if your window is maximized (made as large as possible — by clicking the square in the window's upper right-hand corner). In this case you can reduce the window size (click the little picture of overlapping squares in the upper-right corner), or press Ctrl+ (hold down the Control key and click the plus key), or select Window ⇨ Add Top Window to Favorite Places.

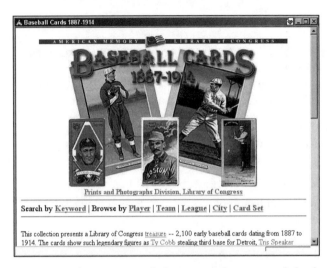

Figure 3-2. Whenever you see the heart in a window's upper right-hand corner, you can add the destination to your Favorite Places folder.

2. A window pops up offering you some choices (Figure 3-3). To save the link in your Favorite Places folder, click Add to Favorites.

Figure 3-3. Store your favorites or share them right away by inserting a live link into an e-mail message or Instant Message.

To view your Favorite Places, select Favorites ➪ Favorite Places. Figure 3-4 shows my folder; yours will differ.

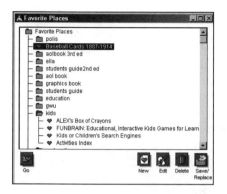

You can even insert a link to individual e-mail messages, message-board postings, and Instant Messages, and share them. If you *really* like to share, you'll see in Chapter 7 that you can create lists of your Favorite Places in Web pages you build with AOL's Personal Publisher.

Figure 3-4. Use the Favorite Places folder to edit, delete, and rename your favorites.

Notice that the Favorites menu itself displays the first 20 or so items in your Favorite Places folder; just select an item to visit the place (Figure 3-5). In this menu list, the actual folders are denoted with little black triangles to the right; move your mouse over the folder's name to see a drop-down list of items in the folder. The drop-down lists also display just 20 items. In both the Favorites menu and drop-down lists, if your entire list does not display, click *More Favorites* (at the bottom of the list). That brings up the standard AOL Favorite Places folder (Figure 3-4).

3

Making AOL Work Your Way

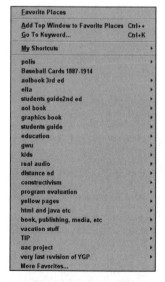

Figure 3-5. A shortcut to your first 20 or so Favorite Places (the File menu); to see all your favorites and to customize them, select Favorites ⇨ Favorite Places.

Favorite Places is not without some endearing quirkiness. When you add an e-mail message to your Favorite Places folder, it is automatically placed at the top of the list. When you add an AOL area or Web page, it goes at the bottom of the list. If you have several subfolders at your list's top, you won't be able to drag an item or folder above those folders in the list; instead, they will fall in a folder! To get around this, add an e-mail message (any old message will do) to your Favorite Places folder. You can now move something above the message (then delete the message if you want).

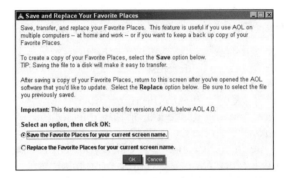

Figure 3-6. One screen name, many machines? AOL 5.0 lets you keep all your Favorite Places folders, even if they're on different computers, up-to-date and synchronized.

Managing Your Favorite Places

In no time the Favorite Places folder can get overgrown with all sorts of links to all sorts of resources on AOL and the Internet. Favorites can be become unrecognizable after a year or two. Here are a few tips for organizing them:

▶ Click the New button, and when the Add New Folder/Favorite Place folder pops up, click the circle by New Folder. Type in a name for the folder and click OK.

▶ Click an item and drag it into a folder. You can also move folders into folders, and you can move folders and items up and down the main list or the list of items in a folder.

▶ Select no-longer-favored places and delete them. Shift-click to select and delete more than one item or folder

(listed one after the other) or Control-click to select and
delete items that aren't next to each other in your list.

▶ If you do have too many favorites, you can keep them
all and retrieve specific items using AOL's search feature, which can also be used in your electronic mailboxes and Personal Filing Cabinets. With the Favorite
Places folder open, click Ctrl-F (Figure 3-7). Type in a
word to search for, and click Find. You can make your
searches case-sensitive by clicking the Match case box
(a case-sensitive search for *TCP/IP* would find *TCP*
but not *tc*).

Adding and Editing Favorite Places

You probably won't want to do this, but you can *add a
Favorite Place from scratch* by clicking New and supplying a
name and a URL: the name is what shows in the folder, the
URL defines the link to the actual destination. This makes
sense only for Web pages, since AOL areas have bizarre nu-
meric URLs meant only for use by computers.

You *will* want to do this: edit a Favorite Place. Just select it and
click Edit (Figure 3-7). I use this feature all the time to provide
names that make sense to me (not all favorites have labels that
make sense); less often, I'll change a URL when the URL itself
changes. Unfortunately, e-mail messages can't be edited — unfortunately, because message names are usually long and not
very useful in identifying their content.

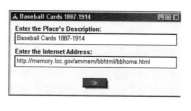

Figure 3-7. Edit your Favorite Places to give them meaningful names and update
their URLs if they change.

My Places

My Places aims to give you your choice of up to five general AOL resources that you want at your fingertips. Remember, the Welcome Screen (where you'll find links to those resources) is always around when you're signed on. To create My Places:

1. Open the Welcome Screen. If it's not visible, go to Keyword: **Welcome**.

2. Along the lower part of the right side of the Welcome Screen, click Set My Places.

3. Click the Choose New Place button. The menu that pops up corresponds to AOL's channel listings. You'll see categories like Entertainment, Sports, and Research.

4. Click a menu item (Baseball in Figure 3-8). Continue making selections for the rest of the My Places categories. Or, stop at any point. You don't have to use them all! Change selections and reorder them until you're happy with your choices, and click Save Changes when you're done.

The Welcome Screen displays your selections right away and whenever you sign on. You can change them at any time.

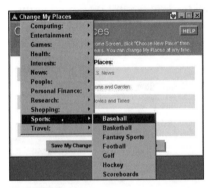

Figure 3-8. My Places puts your favorite AOL sites on the Welcome screen, the most prominent screen on AOL.

My Calendar

My Calendar fills a gap in AOL's customization features and sets another online standard (Figure 3-9). There's probably no way in which AOL better supports your daily activities than with this simple, comprehensive calendar. In one place, you can record your personal schedule, keep track of important birthdays, and make sure you don't miss a movie or baseball game. My Calendar is available from the Welcome Screen, toolbar, and at keyword: Calendar. As with My AOL.COM, no one has access to My Calendar but you.

To add an appointment, meeting, or other personal event, click the date on your calendar, provide a title, time, and any other details, and then click Save to add it to your calendar. My Calendar accommodates repeating events (like those first-Tuesday-of-the-month PTA meetings or your favorite Thursday evening TV show). My Calendar can be viewed in many ways–unlike the old drugstore calendars. The monthly view, shown in Figure 3-10, provides the most convenient overview. The weekly view, indispensable during the work week, shows the week's meetings at a glance, and lets you add to, or edit them. The daily view gives hour-by-hour detail; consider printing it and carrying it around on especially busy days.

Note

New to AOL 5.0, My Calendar gives you online tools to better organize your offline life.

Tip

Use the Calendar and Event Directory tabs to go back and forth between the events in your life (Calendar) and the public events you might *want* in your life (Event Directory). The Tour & Help tab provides clear and comprehensive help; to get familiar with My Calendar's many new features, open the latter tab and take a short, graphical tour!

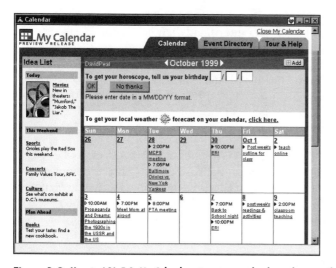

Figure 3-9. New in AOL 5.0, My Calendar gives you a calendar to keep track of meetings, anniversaries, and all the events in your life. You can view the calendar by the day, week, or month; plan ahead; and automatically add movies, sports events, TV shows, and much more.

Movies, sporting, and other events can also be viewed daily, weekly, and monthly. For the monthly view, for example, you can quickly add to your personal calendar a month's worth of movies or cultural events. From any view, you can scroll to the next day, week, or month by clicking the left- and right-pointing triangles flanking the date at the time of the calendar view; you will move to next or previous day, week, or month.

Tip

Think of My AOL as a personalized newspaper, updated almost as often as the news itself. You might consider making My AOL (http://my.aol.com) your home page on the Web — the page to which your AOL browser opens when you click the AOL navigation bar's Home button. Chapter 5 shows how to set your home page.

Little touches like local weather and your horoscope make My Calendar all the more personal.

My AOL

On AOL you can now create a personalized Web newspaper consisting of the articles, sports scores, business stories, and other news items you want to read, in the order you want to read them. The flexible My AOL feature is free to AOL members and nonmembers alike.

The idea is simple. You edit your own online newspaper, putting together your own pages (front page, news, sports, business, entertainment, weather, etc.) from a broad range of wire feeds and other news sources. Here's how it works:

1. Go to Keyword: **My AOL**.

2. The first time you use My AOL, you'll need to register. Click the Register [??] button), and then provide an AOL screen name or AOL Instant Messenger screen name, with the existing password for AOL or AIM. You'll be given the opportunity to save this personal information on your computer. It's a good idea to have this information saved in order to simplify later access. Once registered, you're ready to start reading My AOL and customizing it as you want.

3. My AOL is arranged as a series of Web pages (sort of like newspaper sections) such as Business, Entertainment, and News. Each such page has its own tab, as shown in Figure 3-10. Click a tab to see a different section. The content and layout of every section can be customized to suit your preferences.

   ▶ **Layout.** Like a newspaper, My AOL is arranged in columns (Figure 3-10). Each column has several channels. A channel consists of a small window containing a specific type of information, such as business headlines or weather forecasts. Like any computer window, a channel can be minimized, or made smaller, in order to provide more space for other channels. Or, it can be temporarily closed altogether, after you've read it, for example. Use the small buttons in a channel's upper right-hand corner to edit, minimize, and close that channel. Pass your mouse over the buttons to see descriptions of what will happen when you click.

   To add a new channel to any page, click Add Content. First, use the Select Channel or Tool drop-down list to make your content selection. Then, click one of the buttons designating the column where you want the column to appear. Click Save to return to My AOL. Your changes appear right away.

To remove a channel: In the Add Content or Edit Layout views, select any channel and click the X to its right.

To move a channel from one column to another: click Edit Layout. You can move a channel up or down in a column by selecting it and clicking the up or down button.

▶ **Content.** To edit content, you first switch to a specific section, such as News or Business, by clicking the appropriate tab.

For closer control of channel content, click the Edit button in a channel's upper-right window. Editing the Weather channel, for example, lets you choose any part of the world to display on your opening page, so you can wake up with the day's outlook in Daytona Beach, or the Isle of Man, or McMurdo Station at the South Pole, or all three. Likewise, editing Headlines (in any section) lets you select from among many major news, business, and sports wire sources including AP, Reuters, CNET, and CBS MarketWatch.

Tip

Always available in My AOL is the My AOL Message Center, a set of indispensable communication and personalization tools. Located in the upper right-hand corner of each My AOL section, the Message Center consists of My Calendar (see Chapter 3); Web-based AOL Mail (see Chapter 9); and AOL Instant Messenger and Quick Buddy (see Chapter 11).

Tip

The world's flow of news, weather, business, and other information never ceases. You can have My AOL retrieve up-to-date information as frequently as every five minutes. Click Edit Profile, and choose a refresh frequency from the drop-down list.

3

Making AOL Work Your Way

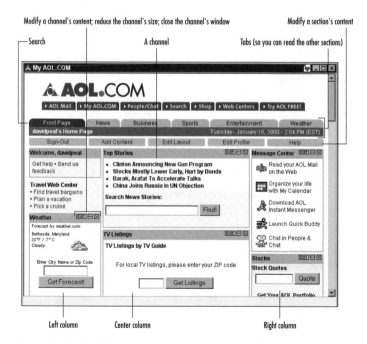

Figure 3-10. My AOL: your personal, always up-to-date Web newspaper.

Tip

To help you keep all your buddies happy, AOL provides a free reminder service (Keyword: **Reminder**) that will send you an automatic e-mail message 14 days before, and again four days before, someone's birthday, anniversary, or other event. The service includes a calendar with the dates of each major holiday in the current year.

Tip

If you want your Buddy List to show up automatically when you sign on to AOL, click the Setup button in Figure 3-12, click Buddy List Preferences, and then put a check in the appropriate box under Online Setup.

Your Friends, Family, and Colleagues

Net newcomers do not always realize that the Internet consists of a wealth of human perspectives, not just a vast source of often valuable information. AOL provides many tools for keeping track of the names and addresses of your online friends and colleagues, the ones you *want* to stay in touch with as well as the ones you *must* stay in touch with.

Buddy Lists

Buddy Lists, new to the previous version of AOL, let you know which of your online friends and colleagues are currently online. If they're online, you can send them an Instant Message (for a one-to-one live conversation) or create a chat room in which to visit (a useful way for a group to discuss a joint project or plan a party). Figure 3-11 shows my list of buddies, grouped into categories such as Politicians and Tree Doctors (in this case).

Buddy lists have become tremendously popular on the Internet, with others more or less "borrowing" AOL's idea. AOL's own Instant Messenger, which you use to talk to people who are on the Internet but are not AOL members, has refined the idea of buddy lists considerably, and you can read all about them in Chapter 12.

Figure 3-11. Your Buddy List lets you know who's online right now and who's not, so you can carry on an electronic conversation with one or more of them.

It's important to take advantage of buddy *groups*, a way of clustering related names. To create a group for buddies, for example:

1. Click Setup in your Buddy List (shown in Figure 3-11).
2. Click Create (Figure 3-12)

Figure 3-12. Set up your Buddy List to work the way you want.

3. In the Create a Buddy List Group window (Figure 3-13), give the group a name. Enter buddies' screen names, one at a time, clicking Add Buddy after each addition. If you don't know someone's screen name, search the Member. Click Save when you're done.

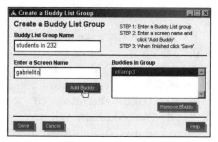

Figure 3-13. Create groups of buddies. Here, I'm adding a new screen name (*gabrielito*) to a group called *students in 232*, which already contains a screen name (*ellamp3*).

To edit a group (to add and remove names), repeat this procedure, but click Edit in Step 2, and in the Edit List window, add buddies on the left and remove buddies on the right as required. Click Save when you're done.

Spend some time familiarizing yourself with your Privacy Preferences, which give you a say about who gets to send you Instant Messages, and to block or allow IMs from specific people. IMs are invaluable, but can be abused. Use Keyword: **Notify AOL** to report such abuses.

Using Buddy Lists takes a little practice. They can be of greatest value in letting you know who's online, so you can pop them an Instant Message. If someone is online, their screen name appears in the appropriate group. A plus sign before a group name indicates a closed folder. A ratio after the group name (such as 0/3) indicates how many buddies are online out of the total number in the group (0 online out of a group of 3 in this case). Double-click an online buddy to bring up the Instant Message window.

Cross-Reference

Chapter 11 shows how to set up Privacy Preferences.

Tip

Info about your buddies is stored on AOL's computers, where the comings and goings of your buddies can be tracked. By contrast, your Favorite Places and Address Book are kept on your hard drive. If you use AOL on several computers (and thus several hard drives), you'll need to synchronize your Favorite Places and Address Book, as explained earlier in this chapter.

Note

AOL 5.0 has a new feature that lets you know whether the sender of an e-mail message, or up to seven of the people who (in addition to you) were recipients of the message, are currently online. A new group appears at the top of your Buddy List called Mail Contacts Online, listing those people who are currently online. If anyone appears on the list and can receive an AOL Instant Message (IM) or an AOL Instant Messenger (AIM) message, click the person's name to send a message. For more on this new feature and on AIM, check out Chapter 11.

Want to create an AOL chat room and invite several buddies? Click BuddyChat, edit the list of names to invite, give the chat room a name, and click Send.

Address Book

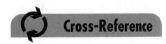

Cross-Reference

Instant Messages (one of AOL's simplest and most useful features) is discussed in more detail in Chapter 10.

Tip

Effective online communication sometimes requires using several tools. New to AOL 5.0 (and not available to people using earlier versions), when you're reading an e-mail message, any senders and recipients of the e-mail message who are currently online appear at the top of your Buddy List window in a new, automatically created Buddy group called Mail Contacts. As a result, it becomes easy to follow up an e-mail message with Instant Messages.

This tremendous feature, new as of the last version of AOL, lets you keep a list of the people to whom you regularly send e-mail, so you never have to remember their e-mail addresses (much less multiple addresses for one person). Chapter 9 provides details on using it, but for now it's enough to say that you can keep notes about each person in the list (making note of phone numbers and alternative addresses). You can also create groups of people you want to contact at the same time. Unlike your Buddy List, your Address Book keeps track of people with either an AOL screen name or an Internet e-mail address.

Like Favorite Places, in AOL 5.0 you can now make a copy of your Address Book to use for the same screen name but on another computer. First, open the Address Book (Mail Center ⇨ Address Book). Then, click the Save/Replace button shown in the lower-right corner of Figure 3-14. Follow the onscreen instructions, then transfer the newly created file to a floppy disk. On the other computer, insert the disk; open the Address Book; click the Save/Replace button; select Replace the Address Book; and click OK. Favorite Places can be synchronized in the same way.

Figure 3-14. The AOL Address Book, for keeping track of the names, e-mail addresses, real addresses, phone numbers, even the pictures of the people with whom you are often in touch.

Member Profile

To add buddies to your Buddy List or Address Book, one useful place to find screen names for people you know online is the AOL People Directory, which you can search by name, location, hobbies, birthdate, language, country, and similar information. Most often, of course, you'll know a screen name from experience or from having received an IM or e-mail message from the person in question.

To make your personal information available to (and searchable by) anyone in the AOL community, go to the setup screen at My AOL ⇨ My Member Profile. Fill in any or all of the boxes, with quotes, the type of computer you have, your city, and so on, and click Update. This information can be retrieved by anyone on AOL, so avoid personal or compromising information. Children and minors should never provide a last name or any contact information.

Note that non-AOL members on the Internet do not have access to this information. With AOL Instant Messenger (AIM) and AOL's ICQ program, however, you can create a personal profile that can be made available to anyone on AOL or the Net who uses this software. Chapter 10 has the details.

Note

In AOL 5.0 you can now keep as many as seven screen names, up from five in previous versions. Each screen name can be as long as 16 characters, as opposed to 10 characters in the older versions, increasing the chances of new members getting the names they want.

Your Personal Account

The most personal information on AOL is your screen name (it's how others recognize and communicate with you), your password (known only to yourself), and your billing information (known only to you and AOL).

Screen Names and Passwords

Screen names are keys that let others know you're online, send you e-mail, or pop you an Instant Message. A screen name is your e-mail address on AOL; non-AOL people sending you an e-mail take your screen name and add **aol.com** (more details follow in Chapter 9).

Here are some guidelines to bear in mind in selecting a screen name.

▶ Every account can have up to seven screen names, including the screen name used upon establishing the account and providing billing information.

▶ You need a screen name when you sign on to AOL; your AOL software remembers your names, so all you have to do is choose from a list of them on the Welcome Screen.

Note

To use Parental Controls (see "Online Safety for You and Your Family"), a parent must first set up a screen name for a child, because controls apply to screen names, not to individuals.

▶ Screen names can be from 3 all the way up to 16 characters (letters, numbers, and/or spaces). The first character in a screen name must be a letter, and will be capitalized automatically. Letters you capitalize *after* the first character appear as capitals in the screen name. Using words likely (or calculated) to offend others can lead to account termination.

To create a screen name, go to Keyword: **Names** and click Create a screen name. (Here's where you go to delete screen names, too.) Any screen name you want to use must be unique on AOL. If the name you prefer is not unique, AOL will offer you a name that may include a string of numbers tacked on to the end of the name you wanted. Keep trying for a name of your own, if you want.

Screen names are stored on the PC where they were created. If you use *several* PCs and add or delete screen names from *one* of the PCs, these PCs can get out of synch. To make all your PCs reflect the most current set of screen names for your account, do the following at each PC: sign on; at Keyword: **Names**, select Update Screen Names; click the button that updates screen names.

Every screen name has its own password. Changing passwords adds security to your account by preventing others' access to it. To change a password, sign on to AOL using the screen name whose password you want to change, and go to Keyword: **Password**. Follow the instructions, remembering to make your passwords difficult to figure out: *don't use familiar names or dates, use at least six characters, and try alternating numbers and letters.*

Online Safety for You and Your Family

With more than 150 million people on the Net, you will encounter some people who want your password, your address, your money, and who knows what else. Sometimes they operate by sending unsolicited e-mail messages to thousands of people. Sometimes they'll drop you an unwanted Instant

Message. Sometimes they'll create obnoxious Web sites and advertise them using links embedded in unsolicited e-mail. Sometimes they'll send files attached to e-mail messages that can harm your system if you download and run the files. And some people use e-mail or Instant Messages to try to separate you from your password while pretending to be AOL employees.

With a little practice, it's easy to recognize fraud and deception online. As a company, AOL provides tools to keep predators at bay, and it pursues the worst offenders in court. It also provides a great deal of advice for keeping you and your family safe.

If anyone *ever* bothers you or your children online, or asks for your password, or is otherwise unpleasant (and if it seems unpleasant to you, that's all that matters), just go to Keyword: **Notify AOL**. There you'll find options for reporting obscene screen names, unwanted password solicitations, and other violations of AOL's guidelines or Terms of Service (Keyword: **TOS**). Everyone who uses AOL (including students whose screen names are registered under someone else's account) must follow these guidelines; ignorance of them is never an excuse for abusing them. They're not only reasonable but are also comparable to the guidelines required when you use any Internet service provider (or even any Web sites with interactive features such as chat rooms and message boards).

Caution

The only person in the world who knows your password is you, plus anyone you share it with. No one from AOL will ever ask you for your password. Use Keyword: **Notify AOL** to report anyone asking for your password.

Online Safety Tips

▶ Never give out information that provides your address, phone number, or other personal information.

▶ Never provide your password to anyone, especially someone claiming to work for AOL. These unbelievably lame requests should be reported at once to keyword: **Notify AOL** (for adults) or **Tell AOL** (for kids).

▶ Never download a file attached to a message sent by someone you don't know; if you do, inadvertently, don't open it.

3

Making AOL Work Your Way

▶ Report unwanted sexual comments and advances using keyword: **Notify AOL** or **Tell AOL**

▶ Kids need to learn to tell your parents when things happen online that make you uncomfortable.

Parental Controls

To provide a first level of defense, AOL has created Parental Controls (Keyword: **Parental**) for restricting access to certain AOL and Internet features. Other ways of getting there:

▶ On the Welcome Screen, click Parental Controls.

▶ From the My AOL menu, select Parental Controls.

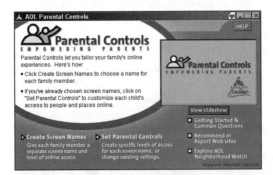

Figure 3-15. Parental Controls provide a full set of services for parents, teachers, and guardians: the ability to create screen names, assign them to age groupings that govern the level of access via e-mail, the Web, and other tools, and customize the level of access for a specific screen name and tool

If you are a parent, and your kids use AOL and the Internet:

▶ Learn about Parental Controls.

▶ Teach your kids the elements of online safety (see "Online Safety Tips") and direct their attention to the kind of resources they can safely enjoy when they're doing homework and projects. Provide them addresses of fun sites when they're done with homework. Keyword: **Netfind for Kids** provides many places to start.

▶ Find a nonintrusive way to keep track of what your kids are doing online: follow their history trail (see Chapter 4); check out the mail they're sending and receiving; do things in common (like genealogy and homework projects).

Keyword: **Neighborhood Watch** pulls together all of AOL's major safety areas, including Parental Controls. You may want to store Neighborhood Watch in your Favorite Places folder for ready access from the Favorites menu (to find out how to use Favorite Places, see the "Favorite Places" section earlier in this chapter).

To start, click Set Parental Controls in the main window (Figure 3-16) to bring up the window shown in Figure 3-17. Every master account (this is the person who pays the bills) can have up to six additional associated screen names, for a total of seven on an account. The many screen names can be used for different people (spouse and kids) and different purposes (work and home). Each screen name has its own password, its own Favorite Places, its own Web-storage space (see Chapter 14), and its own electronic mailbox.

AOL 5.0 makes it easier to set up controls for a specific screen name. Remember, that to set up controls for a child you must first create a screen name for that child; conveniently, you can create screen names directly from the main Parental Controls window, shown in Figure 3-17. Create a password for the new screen name, and keep a record of it in a safe place (with the many other passwords you'll be collecting as you start to use Web services and buy things online).

You can choose from two ways to set up Parental Controls for a child's screen name, and these ways can be used alone or in combination.

1. Assign a screen name to one of AOL's four age categories. Each category defines a *set* of controls for eight different Internet and AOL tools and services, including e-mail, newsgroups, and the Web. If you are content with the level of access set for each of these features, you don't have to set any of the custom controls in Step 2. See "AOL's Age Categories."

Definition

A *control* (in the context of Parental Controls) is a restriction in the degree of access to an Internet or AOL software tool. Tools have many capabilities; controls limit the capabilities that can be used by a specific screen name. For example, AOL offers e-mail controls that can prevent a child from receiving e-mail from someone who is not on AOL or from specific people or specific domains; another e-mail control can prevent a children from receiving *any* messages with attachments. To apply the controls, a child must have his or her own screen name.

Note

For AOL 5.0, Parental Controls have been redesigned to simplify access. From a single window (shown in Figure 3-16), you can select a screen name, assign the screen name to a general category (such as Kids Only or Adult), and then refine the level of access for each of the major Internet tools.

3

Making AOL Work Your Way

Tip

If you are unsure of the level of controls to use for a certain child, consider using one of the age categories, which define a *set* of controls that apply to *several* AOL and Internet features (Step 1). If you have strong preference about specific tools — e.g., the dangers of a child's receiving e-mail or Instant Messages from strangers-- you can make the controls for those tools that much more stringent (Step 2).

2. For a screen name, set particular custom controls for each tool or service. You would use custom controls for a feature like e-mail in order to broaden or tighten the controls created by putting a child in an age category. Or, you could create your own set of controls one at a time instead of using the age categories. See " Using Custom Controls."

An example: an especially mature and trustworthy kid under 12 can be given full access to the Web, instead of being restricted to the sites deemed appropriate to much younger children. At the same time you might assign this child to the Kids Only (under 12) or Young Teen category (for kids aged 13-15) and accept the newsgroup, chat, IM, and other controls automatically set for that age category.

AOL's Age Categories

To assign a screen name to an age, click Set Parental Controls Now at the Parental Controls window (Figure 3-16). At the Set Parental Controls window (Figure 3-17), you assign screen names to age categories as follows:

1. Select a screen name from the drop-down list at the top of the window. All screen names for an account are listed here.
2. Click one of the four buttons at the bottom of the window: General Access, Mature Teen, Young Teen, and Kids Only.

Internet Safety Sites

▶ GetNetWise (http://www.getnetwise.com/)

▶ Safe Surfing (http://www.safesurfin.com/)

▶ Site Seeing on the Internet (http://www.ftc.gov/bcp/conline/pubs/on-line/sitesee/)

▶ Family PC's Kids' Safety & Parental Safety
Clearinghouse (`http://www.zdnet.com/`
`familypc/content/kidsafety/index.html`)

▶ Safe Kids (`http://www.safekids.com/`); includes a
review of Internet filtering software (`http://www.`
`safekids.com/filters.htm`)

▶ Parental Control of the Internet (`http://www.`
`worldvillage.com/wv/school/html/`
`control.htm`)

▶ Safeteens.com (`http://www.safeteens.com/`)

▶ National Center for Missing and Exploited Children
(`http://www.missingkids.com/`)

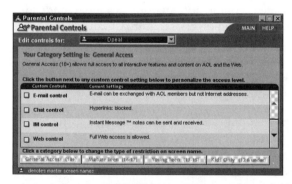

Figure 3-16. Use this window (a click away from the main Parental Controls window, Figure 3-17) to choose a screen name, assign a screen name to an age category, and tighten or loosen controls for a tool.

Note

In the drop-down list at the top of Figure 3-18, note the icon representing a person to the right of the displayed screen name. This person can set Parental Controls for the account.

Here are the four age categories and associated controls:

▶ *Kids Only* access restricts young children to the Kids Only channel (available from the Channels menu). A Kids Only account cannot send or receive Instant Messages (IMs), cannot enter member-created chat rooms, cannot use premium services (games paid for on an hourly basis), and can only send and receive text-only electronic mail (that is, kids cannot send or receive either file attachments or embedded pictures, e-mail features described in Chapter 9).

▶ Parents of teenagers might want to select *Young Teen* (aged 13-15) or *Mature Teen* (aged 16-17). Young Teens may visit some chat rooms, but not member-created rooms or private rooms. Mature teens can download files and use IMs. Both teen categories are restricted to Web sites appropriate for their respective groups. Both groups are also blocked from downloading files from newsgroups and from reading adult newsgroups. Nor can they use AOL's premium gaming services. The choice between "young" and "mature" is a judgment call that depends more on level of maturity than age, and also depends on your concerns and readiness to work with your child learn to use the Net.

▶ The *18+* provides unrestricted access to all features on AOL and the Internet.

Setting up a new account (and providing billing information) automatically puts the account owner in the 18+, or General Access category, which entitles that person to unlimited access to AOL and Internet features. Master account-holders can then assign Parental Control privileges to other screen names in the same account. Two parents would have equal control-setting privileges in this way.

Using Custom Controls

Custom controls let you define more precise settings for the individual tools and services covered by Parental Controls. To set custom controls, start at the Parental Controls window (Figure 3-16):

1. Select a screen name from the drop-down list at the top of the window.

2. In the Custom Controls column, click the small square button to the right of a tool name, such as E-mail. You can set controls for one tool, for several, or for all. Once set they can be changed at any time. A scroll bar on the window's right-hand side lets you see the entire list of controls you can set.

E-mail Custom Controls

Mail controls (shown in Figure 3-17) let you choose from *one* of six options listed on the left. Click any button to select the option.

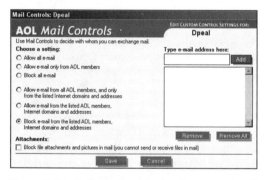

Caution

Changing from one of the last three options to another does not automatically remove the list of addresses/domains you set up for the original option. When making such a change, make sure to click Remove All, then type in a new set of addresses/domains one at a time. You wouldn't want to convert a list of address from which you *refused* mail into a list of addresses from which you'd *accept* mail!

Figure 3-17. Mail controls can keep nefarious messages from spoiling your day.

The first three options don't require special elaboration: they allow *all* e-mail, allow *all* AOL e-mail, or block *all* e-mail, respectively.

The last three options give you the ability to accept or deny messages from *specific* AOL or Internet addresses and domains. (An example of a domain is aol.com; you can read more about domains in Chapter 9.) In the list on the right, you indicate the addresses (or domains) from which you want or don't want to get mail. Allowing mail only from certain addresses is fairly restrictive; it might block access to worthwhile mailing lists, for example, or compels you to change the list every time your child makes a new friend.

The six choices are mutually exclusive; you can choose only one. For any of the six options under Mail Controls, however, you can also block e-mail with file attachments or inserted pictures, both of which are discussed in Chapter 9. File attachments can contain viruses, while inserted pictures can be offensive. To block such files, put a check in the box shown at the bottom of the window shown in Figure 3-18.

Newsgroup Custom Controls

Newsgroup controls are fairly stringent. In recent years, newsgroups, as the Internet's most public forums, have been overrun with spam, porn, and completely off-topic postings. On the other hand, you don't have to look hard for highly specialized and extremely useful newsgroups on subjects of narrow professional interest. Parents need to learn the value of newsgroups and perhaps identify ones for their kids.

Newsgroup controls offer many choices:

At Keyword: **Newsgroups** you can set more specific newsgroup preferences, including filters to remove junk postings. See Chapter 11.

Another solution for parents is to do the research, identify the good resources, and put specific newsgroups (with filtering turned on) into a child's Favorite Places folder.

▶ **Block all newsgroups.** The effect is pretty obvious. Why block them all? Over the years, spam (garbage or offensive postings) has flooded many newsgroups, so it can be hard to find good content.

▶ **Blocking Expert Add.** Disallows access to newsgroups whose specific names kids happen to know, newsgroups that otherwise might not be included in AOL's browsable list of newsgroups. (AOL's Expert Add allows members to go directly to any newsgroup whose specific name they know.)

▶ **Block file download.** Intended to prevent kids from downloading obscene images.

▶ **Block "adult-oriented" newsgroups.** Means that a youngster could not browse AOL's listing of newsgroups for the titillating ones likely to offend their parents. AOL has already identified such newsgroups and allows you to keep the list off limits to your children. You can supplement this list by specifying newsgroups or parts of newsgroup names you want to block (see next two items).

▶ **Blocking newsgroups whose titles contain these words....** Lets you selectively prevent access to newsgroups with *sex* etc. in their name.

▶ **Block the following newsgroups....** Lets you prevent a child from hanging out in certain newsgroups that, in your opinion, have no value or are dangerous for them. You must, of course, know the full names of such newsgroups.

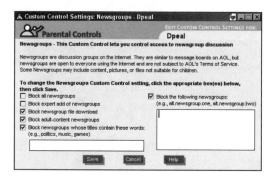

Figure 3-18. Newsgroups represent several possible threats to children, hence AOL offers several types of control.

A Quick Look Back

AOL 5.0 greatly extends the ways in which you can customize AOL to work the way you prefer. This chapter reviewed these preferences, organizing them into four big categories:

- ▶ **Online destinations.** Keep track of, and make it easy to access, your favorite online places on AOL and the Internet with Favorite Places, My Places, Shortcuts, and My AOL.COM.

- ▶ **People.** Use Buddy Lists to find out whether friends and colleagues are currently online; use the AOL Address Book to store and quickly retrieve their e-mail addresses.

- ▶ **Account information.** Keep track of your personal AOL account information (billing info, screen names, passwords).

- ▶ **Online safety.** Yes, there is a fair share of garbage and offensive material on the Internet. AOL's Parental Controls lets you adjust children's level of access by tool and by screen name, so they'll stay out of harm. In AOL 5.0 Parental Controls have been redesigned for much greater ease of use.

There's more: every Internet tool you get with AOL — the Web browser, e-mail, FTP, newsgroups — can be modified in many ways. The chapters on those tools show how to make them work for you.

ESSENTIAL DESTINATIONS: USING THE WORLD WIDE WEB TO PLAN, IMPROVE, AND ENJOY YOUR LIFE

Chapter 4

Essential Destinations: Using the World Wide Web to Plan, Improve, and Enjoy Your Life

IN THIS CHAPTER

A whirlwind tour of the most useful ways to use the Web to do anything useful

Planning your future and making big purchase decisions

Enjoying the moment: books, movies, gardens, and travel

Getting through homework with less pain and better results

Buying hardware and software online

Can't Live Without It!

In one recent hectic week, I put the Web through a workout. I needed specific information right away, and didn't even think of opening the Yellow Pages (the old-fashioned paper kind, that is). Finding information on the Web is instinctive by now. It's also fun. Here's what I quickly found on the Web, in little time and at no cost:

▶ The five-day weather forecast for Pittsburgh, to know what to pack for a weekend family visit
▶ The cheapest airfares between Pittsburgh and Baltimore (for someone else)
▶ A road map, with turn-by-turn driving instructions, between my city and a small town a couple of states away

▶ A directory of piano technicians in my area, five of whom I contacted by e-mail, one of whom turned out to be exactly the right person for the job

The Internet and the Web can support, simplify, and improve countless daily activities. It "improves" the day-to-day by automating tiresome tasks, helping you remember what you need to do and when, and quickly providing routine or specific information that helps you plan for the weather, for retirement, or for something else. This chapter attempts to convey the many ways you can use the Web in your daily activities.

AOL's Info Malls: Web Centers

A Web Center is not your standard "directory," like the many popular listings of selected sites. The big categories are the same: Entertainment, Family, Personal Finance, and more than a dozen others (see Figure 4-1), but you won't find a mere listing of Web sites and blurbs about them. Instead you get *extracted* information, beautifully organized into familiar categories. After all, you don't care about this or that *site*, but about this or that *question*. The latest insurance supersite, for example, is less interesting to you than finding the lowest life-insurance premium for your age bracket. AOL links you to the specific pages of a huge number of sites where you can answer your pressing questions. You don't have to guess which site might meet your needs.

For those highly specific questions, try AOL.COM's Shortcuts (Internet ⇨ Shortcuts). They'll help you find a recipe for spicy potato samosas, figure out where to go for Sunday brunch in your town, research an illness, or discover how much a mortgage at a specific interest rate will set you back every month.

One thing you'll see throughout Web Centers and Shortcuts: interactive fill-in-the-blank forms, which allow you to give personal information (birthdate and assets in a personal finance planner, for example, or dates and destinations of airline flights in a trip planner).

Another benefit of being an AOL member: you can follow a link from a Web page to AOL content—a specific channel or area, for example. Anyone on the Internet can use AOL.COM and Web Centers, but only members can follow links to both AOL's own content and to Web content. To tell the difference, hover your mouse over a link; links to AOL read Only On AOL.

AOL.COM's Shortcut pages (available at Internet ⇨ Shortcuts) bring together some of the most useful services in one compact page, where you'll find cheap airfares, find a new house or apartment, plan a night out, and do today's crossword puzzle.

4

Essential Destinations

AOL has a strict privacy policy on its Web site, meaning it won't share or sell any data you voluntarily enter. Have a look at AOL's policy at http://www.aol.com/info/privacy.html, which explains exactly why AOL needs personal information and what it does with it.

Figure 4-1. AOL's Web Centers: Start browsing here.

AOL's Personal Finance Web Center gives you access to more than 70 Web-based calculators for doing everything from saving the right amount of money to figuring out the mortgage you can afford. Go to keyword: Calculators.

Planning Your Life: What You Have, What You Need

Here's one of those subjects that matters to everyone: creating a financial plan, also known as thinking about the future. In creating such a plan, you need to think about where you are now and where you want to be in the future (at retirement, say). Or, you look at your situation and plan to buy a dream house or finance a college education. To do such planning requires that you provide enough information for the Web-based tools to run some quick calculations.

You get your answers in seconds. Applying these answers, adapting them, tweaking them — that will require some work on your part, but less work than if you did the calculations yourself.

From Web Centers, click Personal Finance, which is closely integrated with its counterpart on AOL (see Figure 4-2). Doing stock research on AOL, for example, invariably takes you to the Web, for a vast collection of frequently updated reports on thousands of publicly traded companies. In fact, you can think of an AOL channel as the central place from which to find both AOL and Internet information about a subject. First thing to notice here: you can customize the Personal Finance Web Center by adding (currently) up to ten stocks or mutual funds that you want to track whenever you see this page.

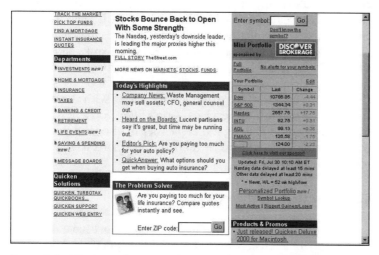

Figure 4-2. AOL's Personal Finance Web Center, with news, stock portfolios, tools for planning and tracking your savings, investments, and life events

Much of the information in AOL's Personal Finance Web Center comes from Quicken.com, an online personal-finance network with which AOL cooperates in providing a complete set of financial planning tools for AOL members.

Just want to see how you're doing? The Quicken.com Financial Health Checkup helps you with a range of daily activities like managing money, investing, finessing your taxes, paying for college, and planning for retirement. You'll need to supply a good deal of information about your situation to use this feature, but the path you take from here might differ as a result of what you find out.

Find It Online

AOL's Interests channel is one of AOL's most useful, in its focus on the day-to-day realities of home, food, autos, pets, and hobbies. Calculators can be found throughout the channel.

Find It Online

The Debt Reduction Planner, directly available at http://quicken.aol.com/ saving/debt/, uses a path-breaking Internet technology called Java, developed by Sun Microsystems, to review your debts, savings, and income in order to generate an action plan to reduce debt.

On the Web you stand a good chance of protecting your own interests, because you're not subject to a sales person's low-key, high-pressure tactics.

Banking Online

Home banking once required special software and a lot of patience; it never got people very excited — before the Web, that is. Now, banks are making more and more services available through the Web. Everything, it seems, but using your PC as an ATM. My middle-sized bank, for example, provides access to balances and allows transfers between accounts. I can tell which checks have cleared and which have bounced. If I had the time and was more systematic, I could download this information to the Quicken personal-finance software. Other banks allow (for a fee) bill-paying online and loan applications. Bank of America, for example, provides insurance quotes online and helps you choose the best checking plan for your needs. With the Web, any bank can offer such services — providing you a new level of choice and also making it much easier to choose a new bank when you move to a new city (contact your bank to see if they offer these services).

Wanna Buy a Car?

In the few times that I've had to buy a new car, I have usually felt at a disadvantage. Not knowing which specific model to buy, what a car is really worth, who's offering the best price, what the car will cost in long-term maintenance, what I can expect to recoup in resale, and how to pay for that mobile heap of chrome and metal. Feelings of intimidation in the dealer showroom come from not knowing what your adversary (the sales person) knows. Used cars are worse. Markets are thinner; there's less choice. It's hard to know what a car has been through and what it's worth, and it's much harder to know whom to trust.

Surprise! The Web can make life easier for you as a car purchaser as well. At the Autos Web Center at AOL.COM, you'll find everything you need to walk into that showroom with confidence — and crisp information. (Eventually the showroom will be electronic, but we're not entirely there yet.) What makes AOL stand out from the crowd of "portals" is the highly selective presentation. AOL's arrangement of services reflects your needs, so you click Used Cars, for example, instead of looking for a specific site on that subject in some long directory listing. In AOL.COM's Autos Web Centers (shown in Figure 4-3), you can do anything from getting the specs and pricing for any new car to find out how to change the oil in the vehicle you have.

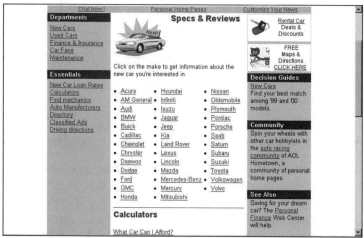

Figure 4-3. A small section of the Autos Web Center on AOL.COM: decision-making guides, complete specs for all new cars, calculators for figuring out what you can afford, plus (if you scroll down a bit) links to *Car and Driver*, *Road and Track*, and *Edmund's Buyers Guides*

Download Your Dream House

A recent TV commercial showed two suburban neighbors comparing the cool stuff they bought on the Web. One showed off an antique Pez dispenser, the other an old house; both items were bought on the Web. There's a bit of hype in the comparison, and more than a touch of suburban one-up-manship. But it is possible to do your house-shopping from AOL and save money in the process.

Houses and cars are the kind of things that cost so much that you probably don't *want* to buy them without seeing them. What you *can* do on the Web is learn about financing a house, compare rates, provide complete personal information in order to prequalify for a mortgage, investigate second mortgages or refinancing (next time rates dip), balance rates and points, and compare offers. The rate I recently got from a national mortgage broker, for example, was better than anything being offered locally. The real-world tasks included several

Find It Online

The next best thing to buying a house is seeing a picture of it, and Realtor.com (http://www.realtor.com) brings you descriptions, prices, and pictures, they say, of more than a million houses.

4

Essential Destinations

overnight-express deliveries and a short trip to a lawyer. The savings made the whole experience worthwhile.

Use Realtor.com's service to plan the entire moving process, from choosing a neighborhood to finding existing homes for that neighborhood. If you don't find a house, you will probably find a realtor who can help you settle in the neighborhood of your dreams. AOL's Real Estate Web Center pulls together everything from finding a house to finding a loan, closing a loan, moving, and settling in.

Making It All Happen: Finding a (Better) Job

Right up there with planning for a future is finding a job, or a new job, *now*; a regular income may be all that stands between you and the imaginary future typed into a personal-finance calculator. The place to start is your own community, if that's where you want to work, and Digital City (Keyword: **DC**) offers classified listings of local jobs, which you can search or browse. For your city or the city where you want to work, DC also offers listings of employment agencies and companies with Web sites.

AOL.COM's Timesaver is devoted to finding job links to the very best Web resources for job seekers (`http://www.aol.com/timesavers/findajob.html`), including:

> ▶ The Monster Board (`http://www.monster.com`), one of the oldest job-searching sites, offers free access to a searchable database of some quarter-million jobs. Leave your resume here for prospective employers.

> ▶ Careerpath.com (`http://www.careerpath.com`), too, provides access to a quarter-million jobs, drawn in this case from city newspapers.

One site not mentioned is a specialized service for people on the lookout for federal government jobs: the Office of Personnel Mangement's useful, searchable USAJobs (`http://www.usajobs.opm.gov/`).

You've Set Your Goals, Now Have Some Fun!

With a plan and a job, you can start enjoying the Web as a place to shop and have fun. Let's start with some efficient and fun ways to spend your hard-earned money.

Shop@AOL

The first serious Internet stores in 1994-95 had the clever idea of joining together to form malls, so that, like real-world malls, they could share overhead, generate traffic, and provide something for every customer. The first such malls lacked "anchor tenants" and attracted few shoppers.

AOL has finally made the online mall a reality. Shop@AOL (Keyword: **Shopping**) brings together online and Web vendors in a one-stop shopping experience that real stores cannot match, with their confusing maze of displays that never have your size or style. Shop at your own pace in some very big online stores as well as smaller specialty shops. You'll find on-line shopping faster and usually cheaper. It's also a good way to do last-minute shopping and find bargains. AOL's long list of Certified Merchants guarantees secure transactions and a high level of customer support.

The Shop@AOL (see Figure 4-4) service was just being rolled out as this book went to press. In the near future, look for a range of Shop@AOL online services, including catalogs, AOL Wallet, AOL Quick Checkout (to simplify smaller purchases), and personal buying guides to help you find and buy what you want, not what the stores happen to have. This megamall will be available to AOL members as well as to visitors of Netscape's Netcenter, AOL Digital City, and Compuserve.

Movie Gossip, Showtimes, Reviews

AOL's new Web service, Moviefone (Keyword: **Movie**), saves you time in finding movie show times and locations. Figure 4-5 shows some of the extra value Moviefone provides. Enter your Zip code, and Moviefone tells you the specific movies or

Tip

Use AOL's Reminder service (Keyword: **Reminder**) to be reminded of birthdays and anniversaries.

Tip

Consider this: more than 400,000 people shopped at AOL's 300+ stores during the last holiday season of the 20th century. With such numbers, some AOL merchants were able to offer benefits such as special sales, free shipping, online gift certificates, guaranteed 48-hour delivery, and post-holiday sales.

4

Essential Destinations

movies of a specific type (art or sci-fi) playing in your area (or broader area if you want) with reviews, plot synopses, and relevant links. You can also order tickets on the Web.

Figure 4-4. Shop@AOL: the comprehensive, safe shopping experience that won't tire you out

Other sources of movie information:

▶ City dwellers can get local listings at AOL's Digital City (Keyword: **DC**).

▶ Obsessed movie fans get gossip, edgy reviews, polls, video trailers, and other movie bric-a-brac at AOL.COM's Entertainment Web Center, courtesy of AOL's own Entertainment Asylum (`http://www.asylum.com`). Asylum gives the chance to chat about movies and to sound off in a Web-based message board.

Book 'em

Web visionaries like Nicholas Negroponte think books are a lame-duck medium, sure to yield to the obvious advantages (he says) of reading anything, anywhere, as long as it's on a screen. Occasionally trenchant, Negroponte got this particular prediction flat wrong.

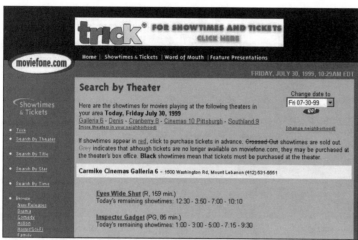

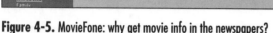

Figure 4-5. MovieFone: why get movie info in the newspapers?

AOL works with two huge online booksellers to make book searching and buying as convenient as possible for AOL members. Barnes and Noble (Keyword: **BN**) is the official AOL bookstore, while Amazon.com is AOL.COM's vendor of choice. Buying from either vendor gives you access to a vastly bigger selection of books than the largest superstore, often without sales tax, and at a discount to boot. Figure 4-6 shows Amazon.com.

Amazon.com pioneered the online solicitation of readers' reviews. Readers familiar with a book give it a rating (number of stars) and a chance to pan or praise the book, or show off critical acumen or superior depth and taste. The Entertainment Web Center's Books presents a selection of Amazon.com's interviews, best-seller lists, and reviews, plus opportunities to buy books. For any title in its indexes of in-print and out-of-print books, Amazon.com lets you know what other titles were bought by people who bought that title. Lots of search opportunities are available, and the purchase process takes place through a quick and secure computer — much faster than the line at my local superstore.

Tip

Amazon.com recently purchased Bibliofind (http://www.bibliofind.com), a source of more than nine million used and rare books. They've shown interest in many other businesses as well, including CD sales and online grocery shopping!

4

Essential Destinations

Figure 4-6. The standard for electronic commerce, Amazon.com has everything except a coffee bar. Amazon now lets you buy toys and electronic gadgetry as well as books and CDs.

CDs, CDs for Sale

CDs, like books, lend themselves to online sales. Online, shoppers can search for exactly the right CD in a fraction of the time it takes to find a store that has your CD in stock, drive there, find a parking place, and so on and so on. With CDs, content (the music) is usually more important than the plastic packaging, so it's often less important to see the CD before buying it. CDs, like books, can be readily shipped anywhere. Finally, at the big CD vendors you can usually listen to snippets from a CD before buying it, so you know the CD has the particular Sinatra tune or Scarlatti sonata you really want. (Or want to give as a gift: buying a CD or book online simplifies gift-buying, and most vendors offer cards and gift wrapping, and send it directly to the lucky recipient.) CDNOW (Figure 4-7) is a great site to do all this.

Figure 4-7. CDNOW, the place to buy CDs, whatever your taste

Cross-Reference

RealAudio and MPG are types of audio files. Read about both in Chapter 5.

Searching has gotten easier at CDNOW. For any CD you usually get track listings and notes, plus (sometimes) RealAudio or MPG clips. Aficionados find production information, release dates, and technical specs. My CDNOW, like AOL's My AOL.COM, gives you a personalized view of CDNOW: your wish list (CDs you want to buy some day), your order history, and a record of the points you've earned for your purchases, which can entitle you to free gifts.

Hey Mr. Handyman

Now that the rent's paid or the mortgage financed, use the Net to make your house into a place where you want to live. I've found North Carolina furniture makers on the Web, and California trellis builders. AOL's partner, Garden.com (available via the Home & Garden Web Center or directly at `http://www.garden.com`), helps you plan gardens, take care of indoor plants, and set up a greenhouse for any weather condition or time of year. If you're not the do-it-yourself type and need a contractor, Digital City offers a searchable guide at `http://aol.digitalcity.com/homeimprovement/` (the Digital City Directory makes use of the AOL.COM Yellow Pages, discussed in Chapter 7). If you are the do-it-yourself type, use an encyclopedia such as Better Home & Garden's at `http://www.bhglive.com/homeimp/`, whose Carpentry section is shown in Figure 4-8.

4

Essential Destinations

Tip

Gardens, houses, cars, movies, books: for every interest there's a neighborhood at AOL Hometown, a collection of Web sites created by AOL members and devoted to specific interests and hobbies. Such sites usually have links to an array of Web resources. Read Chapter 14, and join the block party.

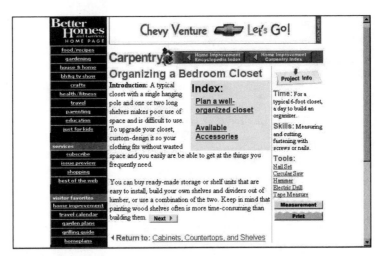

Figure 4-8. Learn how to hold a hammer and hit a nail squarely on the head, using the World Wide Web.

Two important Web destinations offer advice, tips, and deals for anyone with some work to do around their dream house. HouseNet (`http://www.housenet.com`) grew out of an online forum formerly available only on AOL and now open to the entire Web. Today, the attractive and easily browsable Web site offers gardening, design, roofing, and every manner of fix-it advice. If you're prone to applying too much mulch to the rhododendrons, use the Organic Mulch Calculator. You enter the length and width of the area to be covered, and the calculator figures out how much mulch to apply (in cubic feet). Also fun: the ceramic tile calculator (how many tiles to lay in that bathroom), the wood floor calculator (how much planking to buy), and the paint calculator (how many cans of paint for that overdue paint job). These handy tools are shown in Figure 4-9 All these valuable Project Calculators are currently available in HouseNet's Home Improvement section. (Remember that Web sites change all the time!)

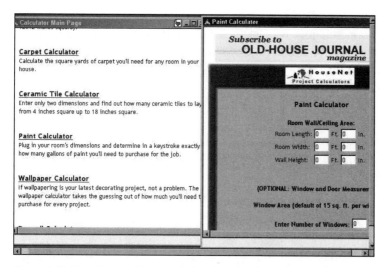

Figure 4-9. HouseNet's useful paint calculator helps you buy only as much as you need.

Home Depot, the Atlanta company that's conquering the 'burbs with its football field-sized warehouses, has its own site with hundreds of how-to projects in the fix-it, build-it, grow-it, decorate-it, and install-it categories. Learn to replace a doorbell, install a toilet, lay out a garden. A box-load of calculators can ease your life here, too.

Away from Home: Web Tips for Frequent Fliers

Personal and business travelers have benefited in many ways from travel sites offering more and more services. Since traveling is expensive and often involves spending time in strange places, travelers need all sorts of guidance, which can now be found on the Web. Preview Travel (Keyword: **Previewtravel** and at http://www.previewtravel.com/) is the place to start.

Through Preview you get access to Fodor's online Destination Guides. Choose a place like Guadalajara (Mexico) for a short description, current weather conditions, today's exchange rate, lowest airfares, local maps and restaurants, and other useful items. For anything *off* the tourist trail, do a Web search (Chapter 8) to find exactly what you need.

Find It Online

A newer service, Bid.com, offers auctions through AOL at Keyword: **Bid.com**. The Web site is available to the world. Bid.com is to other auction services what chat is to e-mail: you bid "live," in an auction environment, instead of over several days of intermittent bidding. Start at Keyword: **Bid.com**. In addition to these "Dutch" auctions in real-time, Bid.com offers auctions in which bidding takes place over several days.

Also, start at Preview Travel to get rates for flights and to book hotel and auto reservations. Or, use Preview to book a cruise, the perfect way to combine travel and lodging if that's your style. Preview's Business Travel section offers similar listings, with discount offers and links to releases from business newswire.

Other popular travel supersites: **Travelocity** (http://www.travelocity.com), **Trip.Com** (http://www.trip.com), and **biztravel.com** (http://www.biztravel.com).

Going Once, Going Twice: Online Auctions

Today, the idea of using networks as marketplaces has much broader appeal because the Internet population has grown to more than 150 million people. The idea is simple. Say you have a thing of value — that is, it's valuable to you, collectors might want it, or it is *really* valuable (Babe Ruth's autograph). How do you find a buyer and ensure payment? Many companies have answered that question, all in the same way: an online auction.

At an auction site, potential buyers and sellers first register by providing contact information and, often, a credit card number to ensure their seriousness and to identify them. Registration is usually free.

Here's how it works, in general. To sell that recently retired Beanie Baby, someone posts information about it, with a picture, using the auction site's form. Items are entered into specific categories, so potential purchasers can easily find them. (They can also do searches, of course, for those items that could wind up in more than one category.) Potential purchasers browse categories, on the lookout for good stuff at good prices. The actual bidding process varies by auction service, but you will usually have a chance to choose an item, type in a price you're willing to pay for it, and commit to buy the thing if you bid the highest price in a given period of time (a week or so). Often, you'll get to ask the seller questions by e-mail. Along the way, you can view the number and level of other bids. If you do win an auction, you'll be notified by e-mail, given an e-mail address of the seller, and the two of you can exchange payment and mailing details (whether you can pay by check, where that rare rug is to be sent, and so forth).

The biggest auction company, E-bay, boasts over 1,000 categories and a million auctions a day (`http://ww.ebay.com` or keyword: **Ebay**). E-Bay does nothing but auctions. Figure 4-10 shows what is probably the world's biggest auction house.

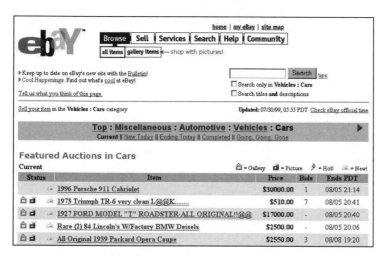

Figure 4-10. A publicly traded company, E-bay serves millions of people buying and selling thousands of things, from pins to trucks. Here are a couple of cars for sale. If you bid successfully for one, you'd have to discuss with the owner how you'd pay and have it delivered.

Acquiring Knowledge and Skills through the Web

Why not use the Internet as a gigantic memory support, like a portable reference library where the books are always shelved in the correct place? Where else can you quickly get simple answers to questions such as the definition of *detente*, the population of Norway, and the gestation period of whales? As with a reference library, it can also be fun to browse simple facts you have no real use for. One person's facts are another's trivia, after all.

Two reference resource "umbrella" sites (think of them as virtual reference libraries) bring together hundreds of Internet-based reference resources. Make the sites listed below AOL Favorite Places, as spelled out in Chapter 3, and they'll always be at your fingertips. Both sites have been around for years. If particular dictionaries, converters, and other sources are not available, return to one of these places for the most up-to-date references.

▶ Refdesk.com (`http://www.refdesk.com`), shown in Figure 4-11

▶ Internet Public Library (`http://www.ipl.org`)

Figure 4-11. RefDesk.com, a world-class reference resource

You Could Look It Up

The Web of Online Dictionaries, an awesome creation of Bucknell English professor Robert Beard, brings together in one place more than 800 dictionaries of over 160 languages (`www.facstaff.bucknell.edu/rbeard/diction.html`). If you must write, like to read, want to travel, or otherwise need to look anything up in any language, Mr. Beard has created a destination in which to spend all the time you can afford. Starting with English, you'll find the online versions of standard dictionaries, dictionaries of jargon and dialect, specialized dictionaries of railroads, sports, real estate, and whatever you need to know. Figure 14-12 shows one of the many useful ways in which these dictionaries are arranged: by language.

Figure 4-12. Pick a language, any language. Looking it up has never been easier ((c)*Robert Beard. Used by Permission*).

Baby on the way? The Etymology Of First Names dictionary can help parents decide on a meaningful (and of course unusual) name for that baby-to-be, with some ideas about how to pronounce it (`http://www.pacificcoast.net/~muck/etym.html`). Egg on your face? The Phrase Finder can reveal the origin of phrases like "Generation X" (the tenth generation of the American republic) and "never the twain shall meet" (*twain* comes from the Old English for two). See for yourself. The Phrase Finder's Web address is `http://www.shu.ac.uk/web-admin/phrases/go.html`.

Where in the World: Maps and Atlases

In Chapter 7 you will find out about the Web's services for planning auto trips. With such services you plug in a starting address and a destination address, and the Web site provides turn-by-turn driving directions, with mileage and the location of all the hamburger restaurants along the way.

But say you want to find maps of Serbia over the last five or six hundred years, in order to follow history and the current events that impact that part of the world. The place to find images of authentic maps, both historical and current, is the Perry-Casteñada Library Map Collection of the University of Texas (`www.lib.utexas.edu/Libs/PCL/Map_collection/Map_collection.html`). Each image is the digital rendering of an actual map. Some of the images are big (200-300K). More than 2,000 maps, from every period and part of the world, are available at this site, a small sampling of the PCL's holdings of nearly a quarter million maps.

Weights, Measures, and More

The Web boasts hundreds of converters of different kinds. Digital Generation, shown in Figure 4-13, packs dozens of converters into a very compact Web presentation, using something called Java, discussed in Chapter 5. First, choose a category such as area, length, temperature, or weight. Then simply choose the unit you have (such as degrees Fahrenheit) and the unit into which you want to convert (such as degrees Celsius). You don't even have to click: the calculator shows the answer automatically in the Results box. Note: try reloading this calculator if you find that units are not being listed. To reload, click the clockwise-turning arrow on the AOL navigation bar.

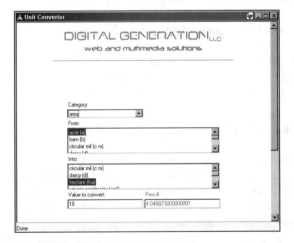

Figure 4-13. How hot would it be in Halifax? A converter for turning Fahrenheit into Celsius (http://www.webcom.com/legacysy/convert2/convert2.html)

What Happened on This Day in History?

Many individuals and organizations have created this-day-in-history sites. One of the snazzier examples comes from the History Channel, which provides a multimedia profile of a person who in history — recent history, usually — did something of consequence on today's date. For a bit more depth, the Library of Congress's today-in-history site offers pictures and other elements from the LOC's growing digital collections (`lcweb2.loc.gov/ammem/today/today.html`), shown in Figure 4-14. The Farmer's Almanac Today in History site (`www.almanac.com/`) engagingly combines what happened today in general history with what happened today in weather history, if you're a trivia buff or just sentimental about droughts and tornadoes.

Tip

The Farmer's Almanac includes five-day interactive weather forecasts for any of 900 cities around the world.

Tip

For AOL's latest educational initiatives start at Keyword: **AOL@School** (http://www.school.aol.com/).

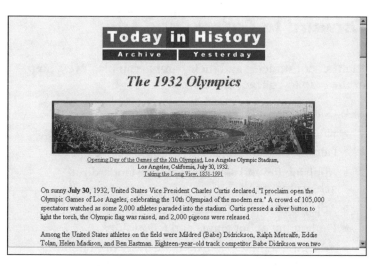

Figure 4-14. What happened on today's date in history, courtesy of the Library of Congress

A Word about Homework Helpers

With such high-quality reference resources, why would kids need any of the Web's numerous "homework helpers" — collections of Web resources of use to kids? One reason is that the homework helpers tend to be organized into curricular areas such as English and Social Studies. Another reason: many of the sites are written for children, and have supporting ask-an-expert services and the like.

Note

A new service called AOL@School gives students, teachers, parents, PTA chapters, and administrators a single safe Web destination where they can find school-related resources and services. Go to Keyword: **AOL@School** to take advantage of original Internet content, AOL services tailored for the K-12 community, and a large number of carefully chosen links to educational Web sites.

A *downside* to homework helpers is that kids can help themselves to what they find there, thinking that the Web is public and that no one will know the difference. Both assumptions are false; kids need to know that the rules of good research apply in any medium. Everything should be considered copyrighted and fully cited.

Of the many homework helpers, StudyWeb contains approximately 100,000 resources rated for their visual appearance and their grade level, and organized into familiar school subject areas. Brian Pinchbeck's collection of links, while not enormous, is distinguished by the fact that it was created in 1996 by a nine-year-old in the Pittsburgh area. Brian still maintains the site, which has won many awards. Now he even has his own domain name (www.bjpinchbeck.com).

Onward to College and Life

High-school students and their parents can plan every step of the road to college on the Web:

> ▶ Comparing college programs and costs
> ▶ Finding out what others say about different colleges
> ▶ Getting college details by visiting their Web pages
> ▶ Applying for, and studying for, the standardized achievement test
> ▶ Applying for college itself
> ▶ Finding out about grants and fellowships
> ▶ Adjusting to new realities of life away from home
> ▶ Learning about distance learning, so you needn't leave home to study at college

Different Web sites help you at every step.

> ▶ To get an overview of the process, start at the non-commercial Mapping Your Future (http://mapping-your-future.org/).

- ▶ To get some sound advice, try the award-winning College and Career Information for Counselors (www3.dist214.k12.il.us/guidance/index.html).

- ▶ To visit colleges and universities on the Web, start with a well-maintained list such as the University of Texas's (http://www.utexas.edu/world/univ/).

- ▶ To apply online, try (among others) CollegeNet (http://www.collegenet.com).

Computers Make All This Possible

The Web and Net were invented by technical people for technical purposes. It quickly became apparent that techies, too, like to play games, tell jokes, swap recipes, and socialize online.

When the Web went mainstream in the last few years, it became evident that most people are not technical. Unfortunately, non-technical people have to be technical enough to use a PC, and must also buy new hardware and software — all the time, it seems. If things don't get out of date or out of synch with other things (software not working with other software, not running on older hardware, and so on.), they get replaced by newer and faster things.

Buying anything computer-related can be even more intimidating than buying a car. Do I need that "fast bus" in a new PC? Is a flat-screen monitor worth it? Which vendor should I choose for a digital camera? Can I *trust* online vendors and distributors? Do I need that new operating system or program? Where can I find the lowest prices? When does shareware or freeware make sense?

In all these cases, you need specific information related to your actual needs. Two resources provide this data and simplify the process of buying computer gear:

- ▶ AOL's Computer channel
- ▶ CNET's Buying Guide, specially offered to AOL members

4

Essential Destinations

Tip

CNET provides detailed help with individual products — including AOL's ICQ, a communications program you can read about in Chapter 11. Help includes instructions, downloads, related Web sites, reviews, newsletters, and message boards.

Should I Buy Online, or Off?

Many people have good experiences buying online. It's a way of getting products that aren't available locally. It's also a way of getting a good price. You do give up the chance to see and use stuff before buying it, but you can get around this by trying something *similar* in a local store before buying it online. Buying online doesn't mean giving up service. Some PC vendors will make it easy to send products back by overnight express and get them back to you in a day or two. Some vendors even come to your site or home to fix things. Finally, like all computer transactions, buying online has become safe when you use a secure browser and purchase from a reputable vendor. When you buy from an AOL Certified Merchant, all you have to consider is whether you like or need a certain product. (See Keyword: **Certified Merchant**.)

CNET's Buying Guide

CNET, creator of computer-related programming for cable television, runs some of the Web's most authoritative computer-related sites. The Buying Guides are organized by type of product and also by type of user (student, home office, mobile professional). CNET's Buying Guides are available at Keyword: **Buying Guide** (see Figure 4-15). If you know what you want and what you're doing, start searching or browsing right away. The closest competitor, ZDNet, is also available to you on the Web, if you ever want to compare notes on any product (http://www.zdnet.com). ZDNet provides access to a huge set of reviews from the ZD magazine world.

If you want some background information first (you've never used a scanner, for example, and want to know which features to look for and what to pay), start in the Decision Maker category. Here you'll read expert CNET product surveys and general overviews, which often show you how things work and what features count.

Once you start looking for a specific product, CNET gives you options for finding what you want. The easiest way is to start with its categories. If you're less sure of what you're looking for, available products are sliced and diced in useful ways: by vendor, by price, by feature availability.

Take the example of digital cameras. At CNET you can use the criteria that matter to you (for example, price and vendor) to identify the cameras that make the most sense for you. At CNET you get reviews, filter out cameras that aren't PC compatible, and compare online vendors' prices for the best rate. For the camera I was researching I found more than two dozen online vendors, selling at a very broad range of prices.

Computing and Shopping Channel

AOL's Computing channel (available from both the Channel screen and the Channels menu) provides ready access to the CNET Buying Guides. In fact, you can search the guide from the channel's opening window, shown in Chapter 2 (Figure 2-20).

Satisfaction Guaranteed

Look for the AOL Certified Merchant Guarantee. When you buy on AOL from a certified vendor, AOL promises total satisfaction and offers a money-back guarantee (which also covers merchant return policies). AOL's certified merchants include computer companies such as Egghead.com, CNET, Beyond.com, and many more. Transactions are secure, and AOL says that since 1996 "the Shopping Channel has never received a report of a credit card that was compromised during a shopping transaction with Certified Merchants on AOL."

To support your buying decisions, AOL offers additional resources. At the online Computing Superstore (the keyword's the same as the name), you can browse and order products in the customary hardware and software categories. AOL members frequently get popular products at reduced prices. The Computing Superstore is a joint undertaking of vendors such as CNET, Beyond.com, and Bid.com.

Other big computer stores available through AOL include the Shopping channel's Computer Products (at that keyword), which links you to other vendors, including Egghead.com, PCMall, and Cyberian Outpost. If you don't mind getting used software, Egghead.com does auctions, as does the general auctioneer E-bay, discussed in the section "Going Once, Going Twice." I recently found a half-price CD-ROM on the American Sign Language using CNET's auction service.

AOL provides layers of value when you're in the market for computer products. A directory of tech companies (Keyword: **Companies**) can help you get more detailed information about any particular product. Also, at a software or hardware maker's site, you will get phone numbers so that you can ask your questions directly.

The Computing channel's mega-message boards can assist at any stage of the process. Before you've purchased, you can ask members what they like. In the Hardware message boards, you can discuss experiences with different vendors. Many technical people frequent these boards, so ask hard questions.

Once you have your hardware set up or software installed, AOL offers support through chat and message boards, but also through lessons. At Keyword: **Online Classrooms**, you can take classes on HTML, PaintShop, and office productivity applications (some of the classes will have a fee).

A Quick Look Back

This chapter provided a tiny sample of the ways you can use AOL and the Web to support your day-to-day activities: buying a car, a CD, or a modem; planning a night out or dinner at home; looking for a better job or bigger apartment; looking up obscure facts or helping your child with homework.

▶ The place to start for useful information is one of AOL.COM's Web Centers or AOL's Internet Shortcuts.

▶ The place to start a shopping trip is AOL's Shop@AOL, the one mall where you can count on the selection, price, convenience, and service at every store.

As a reference resource, the Web has the most to offer the most people, with its countless dictionaries, encyclopedias, map collections, and time/weight/currency converters. The best way to experience the Web's world of possibilities is to ask a question and start searching, perhaps beginning with a few of the resources in this chapter.

BEHIND THE WHEEL:

USING AOL'S WEB BROWSER

Chapter 5

Behind the Wheel:
Using AOL's Web Browser

The World Wide Web, or *Web* as everyone calls it, has become so much a part of daily life for millions that it's hard to believe it was invented only a decade ago — by physicists in Switzerland! This chapter has everything you need to use AOL's Web browser — the AOL tool that brings the entire Web to you.

Ten Long Years of Web History in a Minute

For decades, far-seeing scientists had long felt the need for a global "web" of knowledge, because of the real difficulties of accessing and keeping track of rapidly increasing scientific knowledge. Faced with the growth of electronically *networked* knowledge, Tim Berners-Lee, at Geneva's European Center for Nuclear Research (CERN), had the historic opportunity and clever insight to develop a simple way of linking bits of information across computer networks. In 1989 he came up with the broad outlines of such a web.

The Web is not the same as the Internet. The Internet consists of lots of kinds of information made available using lots of different tools (see "Your Browser: A Tool for Using Other Tools"). The Web was originally a way of accessing and *linking* all these research papers, data files, and messages using a single tool. It quickly became a way of publishing new information. Since 1989, the definition of "new information" has broadened from text (words) to multimedia of every sort (animations, graphics, animated graphics, video, sounds, and much more). What makes the Web a true web are the links between related documents across the Internet.

What a Browser Does

A browser is software that downloads and displays pages; click a link, and it downloads and displays another page. The clever thing about pages is that they're made of pure text in tiny files that zip across the Internet as fast as networks can carry them. Browsers take these little files and display them as formatted text, graphics, animation, musical accompaniment, and all the glitz and wonder we've come to expect on the Web.

When you type in a Web address in AOL's Address Box, the AOL browser requests a copy of a page from the computer where the page is stored. Pages, again, are just simple text files, so they *download* (are transferred) to your computer quickly. These text files consist of special tags that make text a certain size and font, or display a particular image or multimedia file. The system of tags and linked files is called HTML, or hypertext markup language.

What's Special About the Web?

Marc Andreessen, who was part of the group that developed Mosaic in 1992-93 while a student at the University of Illinois at Champaign, later helped create Netscape — both the company and the browser. Currently he's a strategic advisor for AOL.

Microsoft got its start in the browser business by licensing browser software *based* on Mosaic. The competition between the Netscape and Microsoft browsers, which both companies currently distribute free, plus the vast improvement in what a browser can display and *do,* has made the Web a revolutionary publishing medium. What makes it revolutionary is not only the multimedia stuff, but also the dramatic simplicity and the fact that *anyone* can create pages on the Web. Both the Netscape and the Microsoft browsers are readily available to AOL members, as you'll see in this chapter, and the next one (on Netscape).

A Word About Web Addresses

A URL (Universal Resource Locator) identifies *every* piece of information on the Internet. A Web URL such as `http://www.aol.com` has several parts.

▶ The **protocol** identifies *what* you are requesting, for example a Web page (http:// means hypertext transfer protocol). Protocols are languages spoken only by computers to help them exchange different kinds of data.

▶ The **computer** (server) identifies *where* the information is (its computer's domain). In *www.aol.com*, the computer is called *www* and its domain is *aol.com*. Chapter 9 ("A Word About E-mail Addresses ") goes into domains in more detail.

▶ A **page** indicates the specific *file* you want to use on that server. A page might have a name like beach.htm or baby.html. Often, you'll see a long URL

like `http://hometown.aol.com/milesdavis/`
`myhomepage/bluenote.html`. *Milesdavis* and
myhomepage, in this case, are the names of the folder
and subfolder in which the page, *bluenote.html*, is
stored on the computer. When no page is given in
the URL, such as `http://hometown.aol.`
`comstevecase/`, the default is *index.htm*.

Sometimes the URLs that display in the Address box with
a page are different and more complex than the ones you
typed in. This change in URL sometimes occurs when a
Web server routes a request to a specific computer in a
bank of computers. (Many sites these days use vast numbers of computers to meet the demand for pages.)
Sometimes, the URLs displayed in the Address box are
very long because of the site's use of dynamically created
pages. And when you do Web searches, you'll see funky
URLs with your answer pages.

Definition

In this book I'll say "AOL
browser" just to distinguish
the integrated browser from
the stand-alone browser on
your desktop. Both are based
on the same technology, and
share home pages and other
preferences.

Seeing the World Through AOL's Browser

On AOL you have everything you need to start browsing
the Web. The AOL browser is based on the latest version of
Microsoft Internet Explorer (MSIE). When you install AOL, you
get an integrated browser providing MSIE's power without its
complex interface; on your Windows 95/98 desktop you get
the full-blown, stand-alone MSIE browser, a separate application. The MSIE browser is available on your desktop by clicking the Internet Explorer icon.

One thing to get used to about the Internet: There's usually
about six ways of doing anything. And, you can do them all at
once. On AOL, you can use several browsers at the same time
and can have multiple AOL browsers open at the same time.

Pages of Multimedia Madness

Cross-Reference

Chapters 14 and 15 introduce the subject of using graphics on Web sites. AOL makes available the software, images, and image-editing software you need to get started.

Cross-Reference

On slower connections or older computers, you may want to prevent graphics from downloading when you use the Web. This feature can be set using the Advanced preferences of the stand-alone MSIE browser.

As you explore the World Wide Web, you'll see an amazing variety of Web pages, ranging from simple pages of simple text to multimedia creations featuring photographs, animation, video, sound, and interactive games.

Here are some of the things you can expect to run across when you download a page, with examples. Your browser knows what to do and how to display these things. Knowing what you're looking at can be an enormous help if you're trying to learn to make pages yourself — or just want to know what's going on when you're browsing.

▶ **Text.** The most basic page element, and for many purposes the most important. When I search for articles by certain writers in my field, I don't look for pictures but do try to find as much text as possible. It doesn't even have to be all that well formatted. It's a mistake to think text is not visual: good designers can vary font type, font color, and font size; they can play with the length of the line. They can also create graphics files consisting of words (as in Figure 5-3). In short, the Web has created a whole new field of design, and as standards rise, we can all enjoy better-looking pages that convey messages more effectively. AOL's Entertainment Asylum, shown in Figure 5-1, uses almost every element in the book.

▶ **Pictures.** Pictures can *support* text by illustrating a concept or reference in the text. Some audiences expect pictures: kids, for example.

▶ **Links** make the Web a small-w web, and a global web at that. Links display the strands connecting one idea to another. Click a link such as spiders to get more information about spiders or about a particular spider, or see a picture of one, or watch a video clip of one crawling up someone's arm, or a virtual reality simulation of one crawling up your arm. It all depends on the connections that the author or designer wants to create.

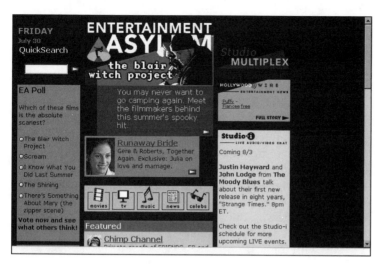

Figure 5-1. Entertainment Asylum, available at http://www.asylum.com/, uses every element: engaging text, tables, graphics, text as graphics, an animated GIF or two, interactive forms and polls, bright and varied backgrounds, links everywhere, and Web-based chat via plug-ins.

▶ **Tables** display text or pictures (or anything) in neat rows and columns (see Figure 5-2). You'll probably be most aware of tables of text, which look like what most people think tables look like; but in fact, even pages that don't appear to have tables may be full of them.

Learning HTML...from the Web

Resource	Comments
ABCs of Creating Your First Student Web Page	A simply designed and *long* page created for students of Women's literature at the University of Texas, with enough information about the basic tags for students to create their own course-related pages. http://www.cwrl.utexas.edu/~gsiesing/314/siesing/webhandouts/
Barebones Guide to HTML	Strictly a reference guide to HTML 3.2, *translated into almost 20 languages,* including Russian, Danish, and Chinese. Tags are usefully grouped into functional categories such as "lists," "forms," and "tables." Includes an HTML FAQ. http://werbach.com/barebones/
A Beginner's Guide to HTML	Originally written by Marc Andreessen, a creator of Mosaic and founder of Netscape. One of the best designed of the HTML sites, it requires use of a Java-capable browser. A PDF (Adobe Acrobat) version of the tutorial is available, as is a single long document (print it out and it's all you need!). This is the guide to which GWU sends students for advice in creating student pages.

Figure 5-2. This Web page includes plain text and links (the underlined bits of text) to present structured material. This page lists and annotates Web resources for learning HTML (http://members.aol.com/davidpeal/recommend.htm).

Tip

How do you tell where the links are? Move your mouse pointer over a Web page, and when it changes from an arrow to a pointing finger — you've found a link. The link's URL can be see in the browser's status bar at the bottom of the browser window.

Definition

At its simplest, Web *interactivity* means that a Web page doesn't just present information but has buttons and fill-in-the blank boxes for you to add information (as when you use MyNews at AOL.COM to create a custom newspaper — see Chapter 3). An interactive Web site responds when you type or press something; a non-interactive page cannot do anything.

Note

Java is a programming language that takes effort to master. It is used to create small programs that do things. JavaScript is a simpler (but still complex) text-based language that you drop right into the HTML of your Web pages. Both Java and JavaScript let designers incorporate games, moving images, clocks, drop-down menus, and visually enhanced links into their Web pages.

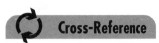

Cross-Reference

You can find large libraries of *scriptlets* to use on your own Web pages. Chapter 15 points you to some of the Web's best JavaScript resources.

▶ **Forms.** Forms add interactivity to Web pages by allowing you to enter information that can then be used in some way by an Internet computer (or *server*).

▶ **Frames.** A feature Netscape invented and made hugely popular on the Web, frames allow more than one Web page to be displayed at the same time, in different windows in your browser. Sometimes they're obvious, complete with thick borders and standard Windows scrollbars; sometimes they're invisible, with neither borders nor scrollbars. A typical use of frames: to display a navigation page (table of contents) on every page in a complex site. Links to all the other pages on the site show in one frame, the actual content shows up in a second, larger frame. Figure 5-3 shows a Web site with frames.

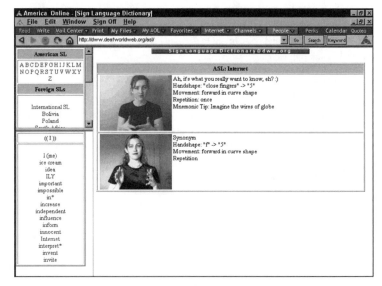

Figure 5-3. DeafWorld includes an illustrated dictionary of the American Sign Language. Choose a letter from the windows (called a *frame*) in the upper left, then a word from the frame below it. In the big frame, the simple animation (whose movement cannot be shown here) indicates how to sign the word.

▶ **Video.** Presenting video clips is a way of showing a little activity on a Web site. Over a modem connection, the experience is usually not great, since an adequate frame rate (of 20-30 frames per second) is difficult to achieve. Resolution is often blurry and the motion jerky. There are two kinds of video, *non-streaming* and *streaming*.

▶ **Java.** Java applets (small programs) let you do simple things like converting a temperature from Fahrenheit to Celsius, to complex things like entering numbers to represent a planet's orbit and seeing an animation of the results.

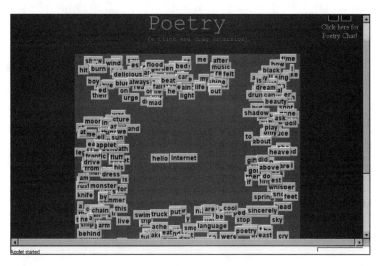

Figure 5-4. Make your monitor as useful as your refrigerator door; drag the words around to make new poetry at http://prominence.com/java/poetry/.

The AOL Browser in Action

To see the browser in action, you need to open a Web page. To do so, type a Web address — for instance, `www.aol.com` — into the Address box, and click Go (or press Enter). A page displays: AOL.COM, in this case.

The AOL browser is an ordinary window, with buttons in the upper-right-hand corner to make it smaller or larger, and to close it. Like any window, you can click the title bar to drag it around the page as you see fit. What goes on inside it is subject to the AOL navigation buttons, shown in Figure 5-5, grouped to the left of the AOL Address box.

Note

Something else to make you nuts . . . Netscape and Microsoft are competitors in the browser business, with different stakes in the development of Java and JavaScript. Different versions of their browsers support different versions of JavaScript. This fact is aggravated by the difficulty of programming in JavaScript. You'll occasionally see a message that says "An error has occurred in the script on this page," and you'll get a choice of whether to continue using scripts or not.

Tip

Web pages often display so much information that you need to maximize them by clicking the second of the three boxes in the window's upper-right-hand corner. To see even more, minimize the AOL *toolbar,* as explained in "Customizing the AOL Toolbar" in Chapter 3. Any part of a long page that can't be displayed in a browser window can be displayed by using the vertical scroll bar along the window's right side.

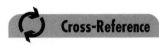

Cross-Reference

With AOL 5.0, you can put search words or AOL keywords into the Address box; click the Search button or the Keyword button to do the search or visit the keyword. On keywords, see "A Word About Keywords" in Chapter 2; on search words, see "Searching from the Address Box " in Chapter 7.

Tip

Usually, Web addresses begin with *http://*. The AOL browser assumes that you're looking for a Web page, so you don't have to type in the http://. Just type in the latter part of the site's address, such as www.aol.com.

Telling Your Browser Where to Go: The Address Box

The Address box is where you type the Web address, or URL, of the page you want to visit. Actually, URLs refer to much more than Web pages, as you'll see in the section "Your AOL Browser: A Tool for Using Other Tools." Once you've typed in the address, click Go or press Enter.

Telling the Browser How to Get There: Navigation Buttons

Figure 5-5 shows the AOL navigation buttons. They're quite simple, but like everything in software there's more to them than you'd think. One thing to consider up front is that the controls keep track of AOL screens as well as Web pages, so when you go forward and backward you'll often re-trace your paths through both the Web and AOL. Note that the Web pages display in the same browser window; the AOL areas open in separate windows.

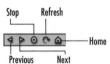

Figure 5-5. Navigation buttons. Note that this figure shows all the buttons; usually, at least one of them will be grayed out.

▶ **Previous.** This button takes you back to the last page or AOL area you viewed. You can continue clicking this button to backtrack through all the pages you've seen in the current session (or longer, depending on your preferences). The keyboard alternative is Alt-left arrow.

▶ **Next.** Once you've backed up, if you want to move forward again through the pages you've viewed in this session, click Next. Note that the button is active only if you've already used the Previous button. Keyboard alternative: Alt-right arrow.

▶ **Stop.** If a page is taking longer to arrive than you'd like, or you change your mind about viewing it before it's finished loading, click this button to stop it. Keyboard alternative: Esc.

5

▶ **Refresh.** This button reloads the current page. If you're viewing a page that is constantly updated with fresh information, using the Refresh button ensures you're seeing the latest version of the page and not one that you viewed previously that has been stored by your browser. Or, if a page you're downloading from the Web is taking all morning (it seems), it may have encountered some Net turbulence. Refreshing it can sometimes do the trick. Keyboard equivalent: F5.

▶ **Home.** This button takes you to the Web page you set as your home page. What's a home page? Skip ahead to "Your Home Page, a Personal Point of Departure" for the details (and for instructions on how to set one up), but the short answer is that a home page is simply the page your browser opens to — it can be a personal page you build, or a search site (like AOL Search), or an online bookstore where you spend half your time on the Web, or the online syllabus for a course you're taking, or anything else you like.

Some pages have their own, built-in navigational buttons showing arrows or words like *Next* and *Previous*. For navigation within a Web site, use the site's own controls.

Buttons are grayed out and indistinct if they are unavailable on a particular page.

Your Compass: The Status Bar

Along the bottom of the AOL browser window you'll find the status bar, which tells you what's going on as you're downloading a Web page. Point to a Web link with your mouse, and the status bar shows the page's address. Click the link, and the status bar shows you each step of the process (see Figure 5-6):

▶ Whether you've successfully connected with the server where the page is sitting

▶ Which items (text and graphics files) are being downloaded from the server to your browser

▶ How much of the page has been transferred (as indicated by a blue bar meter in the lower right corner)

Keeping an eye on the status bar may not help ease your frustration when the browser seems to be taking forever to do something, but at least it will show you what it's trying to do! If nothing is happening, it may be time to click Stop, then Refresh.

Figure 5-6. The status bar shows you what the browser is up to. Once a page has arrived, you'd see the word Done on the far left of the status bar. If you were just moving your mouse over links, you'd see the pointed-to URLs in the status bar. Here it's opening (downloading) a specific Web page, 17% of which has arrived.

Seize the Page: Right-click!

Right-clicking a Web page being displayed in the AOL browser offers you many useful ways of understanding the page and capturing information about it (or directly from it). These options change somewhat depending on where you click.

Right-clicking part of the page where *nothing but the background is displayed* — that is, where no picture is displayed — opens the menu in Figure 5-7.

Figure 5-7. Right-clicking a Web page brings up this useful little menu.

The menu is divided into several sections, each containing related items. From top to bottom, those commands are

> ▶ **Back, Forward.** These work the same as the Previous and Next buttons on the browser toolbar, taking you either back to the last page you viewed or forward to the page you viewed before you backtracked (in practice it's much simpler than it sounds). Unlike the AOL navigation bar, these buttons apply only to Web pages you've visited, not to AOL areas you've visited.

> ▶ **Save Background As** saves the background image (if there is one) to your hard drive under a name you select. **Set as Wallpaper** makes the background image your Windows wallpaper — the Windows desktop

Note

Right-clicking brings you face to face with the Microsoft browser, on which the AOL browser is based. Some of the choices (Back, Forward, Favorite) use the terminology of the Microsoft browser, which differs slightly from that of the AOL browser. You can take advantage of this situation by tapping the power of both sets of features.

5

Behind the Wheel

background you see with all the icons on your Windows desktop. **Copy Background** copies the background image to the Clipboard, allowing you to paste it to other programs. **Set as Desktop Item** makes the image part of your Active Desktop — if you like something so much that you have to appropriate it for use on your own Windows desktop.

▶ **Select All** highlights all the text (not the pictures) on a Web page; right-clicking after items are highlighted brings up an additional menu which gives you the option to **Copy** (Ctrl+V) the highlighted text in order to **Paste** it (Ctrl-V) into another application.

▶ **Create Shortcut** puts a link to this Web page on your Windows desktop. To visit the page again, all you have to do is click the link. If you're not online and AOL is your default Internet application (Chapter 2), AOL opens, signs you on, opens the page. When you click the desktop shortcut, either the AOL browser opens (and prompts you to start AOL if you're not yet signed on) or the Microsoft Internet Explorer opens, depending on which you define as your default Internet application (see Chapter 2).

▶ **Add to Favorites** adds the page to the list of favorite sites the browser maintains. This list is *not the same as your Favorite Places* list; it's a Microsoft thing, and as such is available from the Start Menu's Favorites list or the MSIE browser window's Favorites button.

▶ **View Source** displays the HTML skeleton of the page. This is a tremendous way to learn the ins and outs of HTML and find out how certain effects were achieved. If it's your own page, it's a tremendous way to troubleshoot things that don't work quite right.

▶ **Print** sends the current page to your default printer. Pressing Ctrl-P and clicking AOL's Print button have the same result. However, Ctrl-P brings up a dialog box that gives you some more control over what is printed and how.

▶ **Refresh** reloads the page, which, in the case of pages that change frequently, ensures that you're looking at the latest version, not an earlier version that your browser stored in its *cache* (something discussed

You can select all of a Web page—all the text, at least—or use your mouse to select a bit of it. This is a fast way of copying quotes, contact information, etc., from a Web page. For just about everything else, you're pretty close to copyright infringement whenever you use other people's words for your own purposes. Keyword: **Copyright** has sobering information.

Creating a shortcut can function, on your desktop, as a second home page, a sort of Web beach cottage.

Tip

To save a copy of a page or entire site, with all associated images and other elements, use a program like WebWhacker, profiled in Chapter 17.

below in "How the Browser Keeps Track of Where You've Been").

▶ **Properties** provides you with basic information about the page, such as its address, size, and when it was created and last modified. Why should you care? Sometimes (as when frames are used), it's not at all clear which URL you're viewing; the Address box can stay put at a site's top-level address. The properties box tells you which particular page, deep within a site, you're viewing. Sometimes, on AOL, a Web page will be displayed as an AOL keyword but without a URL; to get the URL and explore the site, you can copy the URL from the Properties box (Ctrl-C), and paste it into the Address Box (Ctrl-V).

Right-clicking a picture or link in a Web page brings up a different menu:

▶ **Open Link** opens the page or file the object links to, if it's a hyperlink, in the current browser window, replacing the page you're currently browsing.

▶ **Open Link in New Window** opens the link in a *new* window, so that the current page is still displayed — a helpful way of keeping a page of links open while exploring linked-to pages one at a time.

▶ **Save Target As** saves the page or file the link points to on your hard drive (do this if you're doing some serious study of others' pages or are troubleshooting your own page and don't have the original file handy). Note that you'll only be saving a page's HTML, not any of the embedded graphics or linked-to pages. **Print Target** prints the page or file the link points to (in other words, it'll print without you even visiting the place!).

▶ **Save Picture As** saves the picture to your hard drive. Watch out for those copyright infringements.

▶ **Set as Wallpaper** makes the picture your Windows desktop wallpaper.

▶ **Copy** a *picture* to the Clipboard, from which you can paste it into another program. Right-click a *link* and choose **Copy Shortcut** to copy the picture's Web address in order to paste it into another page, document, or application.

▶ **Add to Favorites** puts a picture or link in your list of Favorites and provides more information about it, respectively.

Making the AOL Browser Work Your Way

AOL's browser and Microsoft Internet Explorer allow for customization, but the process is a little different with each one. The things you might want to tinker with include

▶ Your home page

▶ Your history and temporary files

▶ Your browser's readability, colors, and fonts

Your Home Page, a Personal Point of Departure

The *home page* is the page that your browser brings up automatically whenever you click the Home button on the toolbar. When first installed, AOL 5.0 starts at the AOL.COM home page, an especially useful point at which to linger and return to (see Chapter 4, which is about to AOL.COM).

What should you look for in your home page? Consider using a site that contains information you look for every day or that can link you to a wide variety of information. AOL.COM (`http://www.aol.com`) is a good example of a home page that can lead quickly to every corner of the Web. Some people use a search page such as AOL Search ; others use a site they're building as a starting point. A specialized search site (described in Chapter 8) makes a good choice if your profession requires this kind of focus. Lawyers, for example, might start at FindLaw. Finally, if you work for a company that has its own Web site, you might want to make its home page your home page. At the very least, it will impress your boss.

To change your home page in AOL's browser

1. Choose My AOL ➪ Preferences ➪ WWW.
2. In the Internet Options dialog box, click the General tab.
3. In the tab's **Home page** section, type the URL for the page you want as your home page into the box labeled Address (see Figure 5-8).
4. Click OK.

If, in your Web travels, you come across a page you'd really like to make your home page, you can do so by bringing up the Internet Options box (Step 1) and clicking Use Current in Step 3. If you'd prefer to start your browser with a blank page, click Use Blank, instead. Why would you do that? For one thing, it opens up very quickly.

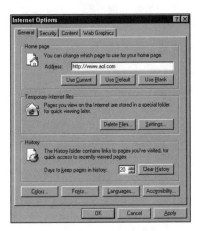

Figure 5-8. Finding a new home for your AOL browser

How the Browser Keeps Track of Where You've Been

You may notice that when you return to pages, they often load more quickly than when you first visited them. That's because your browser has stored them in its *cache*, a cubby hole on your hard drive where it squirrels away frequently used files from Web sites. So, if a site uses 20 small pictures in a bulleted list (for example, a stylized pebble in GIF format), the browser only has to download it once; subsequent references to the same small image are retrieved from the cache. Windows calls these cached items *Temporary Internet files.*

Fetching files from the cache is faster than downloading them from the Web. However, cached pages have a way of getting out of date. Web pages change over time, so to avoid seeing an older version that was stored on your drive instead of the newer version on the Internet when you revisit a site, you need to make sure your browser visits the actual page from time to time. You can customize how your browser does that, as explained below.

All those stored files take up disk space, and if hard drive space is at a premium, you may want to get rid of them, or at least limit the amount of space devoted to them.

Here are some ways to manage your history and temporary (cache) files:

▶ To delete your temporary files, click Delete Files in the Temporary Internet Files section of the Internet Options dialog box. You'll be asked to confirm your choice.

▶ To delete your History record, click Clear History in the History section of the Internet Options dialog box. Click the little spinner gizmo (with an arrow going up and an arrow going down) to tell Windows how many days worth of history you want to wipe out.

▶ To change the way your browser deals with temporary files, click Settings. This opens the dialog box in Figure 5-9.

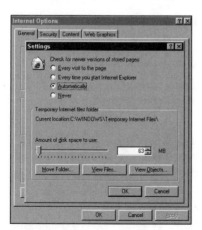

Figure 5-9. Customize the way your browser deals with temporary files using this box.

Note

HTML supports three kinds of links: links that haven't been clicked; links that have; and links on the fence — when you're moving your mouse over them but not yet having clicked (*hovering* is the preferred, Microsoft term). The color of each can be set.

- At the top of the dialog box, select how often you want the browser to check (on the Web) for updated versions of pages stored as temporary files. The options are to update the page (1) every time you want to see the page, (2) every time you start the browser, (3) automatically (meaning the page is only checked if you visited it in a previous session, not if you previously visited it in the current section), and (4) never. "Never" puts you at risk of relying on out-of-date, cached files. Always updating removes the value of having a cache. Something in between is a good idea.

- Specify how much disk space you want to use for storing temporary Internet files. The more disk space you specify, the more likely it will be that a page you're visiting has been stored, and will therefore load faster.

- Below that, you can click Move Folder to change the folder to which temporary Internet files are stored (if, say, you need more space for your cache but your hard drive is running out of free space).

The Web Is for Everyone

Sometimes, the true usefulness of software features is not evident. Take the ability to set font colors and sizes.

A text's readability can depend on text size and font, and the readability of text of one color against a background of another color. For the millions of people with visual impairments of any kind (whether congenital, or accidental, or a result of aging), being able to adjust the size and colors of text and backgrounds can make browsing *possible*.

Microsoft has been in the forefront of companies that support the needs of the disabled. The WWW Consortium (consisting of all major vendors, including Microsoft) recently issued a set of guidelines for designing Web pages accessible by the broadest possible audience (http://www.w3.org/WAI). The consortium's director, Tim Berners-Lee, the same person credited with inventing the Web, puts it as follows: "The power of the Web is in its universality." Browser features like being able to choose colors and fonts make the Web that much more universal.

Changing How Things Look (Colors and Fonts)

In the AOL browser, you can specify how your browser inter-prets the HTML coding in the pages you visit when it comes to the colors and fonts used for text.

Click the Colors button in the Internet Options dialog box to open a small box. These choices determine what colors you will see in your browser if no colors have been specified by the page's designer. You can set text color, background color, and link color.

Ordinarily, the colors chosen by the page user (you) are over-ridden by any colors specified by the page designer. However, you can change that, too, by clicking the Accessibility button in the Internet Options dialog box (see Figure 5-10). The first choice, *Ignore colors specified on Web pages,* ensures that all pages display using the colors you have specified, as explained previously.

Figure 5-10. In the Accessibility dialog box, you can tell your browser to ignore color and font commands specified by the Web page designer and use the default choices you have made instead.

Note the other two options at the top of the Accessibility box: *Ignore font styles specified on Web pages* and *Ignore font sizes specified on Web pages.* If you choose one of these, Web pages display only the font you specify using the Fonts button at the bottom of the Internet Options dialog box. Click Fonts to see the box where you choose the font that works best for you, as shown in Figure 5-11.

The older the version of the browser you're working with, the less likely it can properly display certain files. Since browsers are free, get yourself the most recent version of Netscape Navigator or MSIE that you can run on your computer.

Chapter 16 has the steps for adjusting the way Windows associates files with the specific programs (for example, plug-ins) required to play or display them.

Figure 5-11. Explorer lets you choose the type of font you want to use for displaying text on the pages you visit.

Through the Looking Glass: The World of Plug-Ins

The most recent versions of Microsoft Internet Explorer and Netscape Navigator can handle all the latest multimedia razzle-dazzle.

The good news is that the latest browsers can handle some very exciting sounds, video, and animation through the use of *plug-ins,* small programs designed to *automatically* open files. When you install a plug-in, Windows 95/98 learns that whenever it sees a certain type of file, the browser should open up the plug-in (a small program), which plays or displays the file.

It used to be, you'd need to get a special program to do multimedia: first you'd download the sound or audio or video file, then open a *helper application* to play it. Now, plug-ins *integrate* multimedia effects — either directly into the page or by automatically launching an unobtrusive player. Figure 5-12 gives you an idea of what RealVideo, considered the Web's most popular plug-in, looks like — a bit of video playing in a small window, but memorable and absorbing, nonetheless.

AOL has its own small helper application that can play MIDI, WAV, and AU sound files. For just about everything else (RealVideo, Shockwave, and PDF, for example) special plug-ins are required, the most important of which are included when you installed AOL.

Find It Online

AOL's Multimedia Showcase (a Web Center available at http://multimedia.aol.com/) has links to places where you can get the latest plug-ins, and it also guides you to the best examples of multimedia content. AOL.COM also brings a selection of daily news, business, and weather briefings; all require RealPlayer (http://www.aol.com/mynews/av/).

Figure 5-12. The Motley Fools, financial analysts who got their start on AOL, now have a huge following, with a big Web site and several books. Here's an interview they recently did on ZDTV (Ziff Davis's cable channel).

How do you get plug-ins? The most important ones are included with AOL 5.0; you don't have to do a thing. Usually, if you encounter a file for which you don't already have a plug-in, you'll be asked if you'd like to download the appropriate plug-in right away, and provided with a link to do so. They're downloaded and installed in the right place for you.

How do you get the *latest* plug-ins? Plug-ins evolve rapidly. Some, like Apple's QuickTime, provide a method (using the plug-in itself) to get updates. Some, like RealAudio, have commercial versions of higher quality than the free versions, or with additional features. Commercial versions ensure that you'll be informed by e-mail when new versions become available. When you use Netscape's Smart Update (Chapter 6) you can automatically find out which of your plug-ins have been updated, then easily get the newer versions.

If you don't update your plug-ins regularly, you might miss out on some of the latest features and improved performance and even find your plug-in unable to handle the files being posted in the format it's supposed to deal with.

RealPlayer Brings Radio and TV to the Internet

RealNetworks was one of the first companies to integrate sound into the Web experience. The company started with a product called RealAudio that made streaming sound hugely popular in the past few years, and both the quality of the sound and the features of the plug-in player have improved enormously in that time. RealNetworks extended their capabilities to include streaming video, and now you can get RealPlayer, a plug-in that plays both audio and video (called RealVideo). You can download the latest plug-in from `http://www.realplayer.com`.

Animating the Web with Shockwave and Flash

Macromedia's Shockwave adds strong imagery, movement, and animation to a Web site without making the user download some gigantic file and play it on some helper application. Instead, dramatic effects can be integrated into Web pages. Many of the graphics effects you enjoy on CD-ROM software were created with the same program used to created Shocked content for the Web.

Shocked pages bring you games, Dilbert cartoons, physics experiments, and simulations of every sort (like how hard you'll hit a truck at 30, 50, and 70 miles per hour when the truck breaks suddenly). Macromedia's Flash is used to make simple, elegant, fast-downloading animations, such as the highly visual map through the application process at ThinkQuest (`http://www.thinkquest.org`).

Hi-Fi for the Web: MP3

In the short time since the last edition of this book, MP3 has stormed the Net and established a new standard. This new sound format delivers music at a higher degree of fidelity than all traditional, popular formats. It delivers CD-quality music in relatively small files; a megabyte file plays for about a minute. Small bands and artists without a big name use MP3 to make their work known to a broad audience, without the record companies blocking their way or taking a cut. MP3 has become so widespread that many artists are promoting their records by releasing songs in MP3 on the Web. Portable

Find It Online

Broadcast.com's regular e-mail newsletter provides up-to-date listings of live RealPlayer programs available on the Internet — concerts, press conferences, earnings announcements, sports events, and more. For a list of hundreds of radio stations with live RealAudio programming on the Internet, check Broadcast.com (http://www.broadcast.com/radio).

Find It Online

For cool Shocked pages, start at http://www.macromedia.com. For fun, do a Web search for **examples Shockwave** to see the amazing stuff out there. Flash examples are available at http://www.macromedia.com/software/flash/leadingedge/.

players let you play downloaded MP3 files while jogging or on the way to work.

To play MP3 with AOL, you'll first need an MP3 player. Both Microsoft's new Media Player and the RealPlayer, just discussed, play MP3 files. Special-purpose plug-ins such as WinAmp give you more options. Figure 5-13 shows you why Winamp is so popular — it has an interface similar to most people's home stereo systems. Next, find and download those MP3 sound files, starting at a place such as `http://www.mp3.com`. Chapter 17 looks at WinAmp and Spinner.

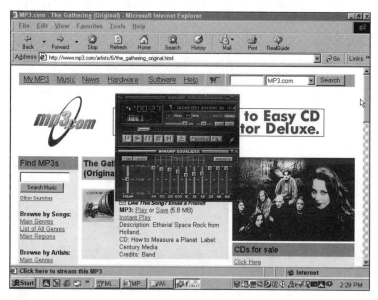

Figure 5-13. WinAmp, a popular plug-in that plays CD-quality MP3 files and sports a wizzy interface

Publishing *Real* Documents on the Web with PDF

Plug-ins are meant to help browsers read and display any kind of information; they support a browser's ultimate purpose of displaying everything on the Internet in a consistent and transparent way. When your AOL browser downloads a page posted on the Web with a **DOC** file extension (a plain-old Microsoft Word document, in other words), the document displays fully formatted, with a Word toolbar at the top, *inside* the AOL browser. Use this trick to post your resume online us-

Find It Online

CNET offers a gigantic MP3 Help center, with software, info about audio gadgets, questions and answers, and a large number of links (http://www.cnet.com/Help/Downloads/Multimedia/Audio/MP3). ICQ's Cool Links page also takes you to several MP3-stuffed sites (http://www.icq.com/coollinks/).

Cross-Reference

See Chapter 17 for more on MP3 shareware.

Tip

Where to start? NetCenter has a long list of MP3 directories (http://home.netscape.com), and Lycos's MP3 Search lets you search an index of half a million MP3 songs (http://mp3.lycos.com/).

ing My Place (explained in Chapter 16). Netscape Navigator handles DOC files by opening Word instead of displaying the files in the browser.

Adobe's PDF (short for Portable Document Format) gives publishers a way of distributing documents in their word-processed form, complete with page numbers and complex formatting — no HTML required! When you use a PDF file, you can print selected pages in longer documents, a kind of selec-tivity unavailable with Web pages. Company reports, scholarly papers, and thousands of government documents are available in this form, like the government document shown in Figure 5-18. To view them, you need the Adobe Acrobat Reader, which is free from `http://www.adobe.com`.

To *publish* PDF files, you'll need a commercial product from Adobe called Adobe Acrobat Writer (now up to version 4.0). This useful product works as follows: first you print a word-processed document *to a file* (instead of to a printer); then you upload the file to AOL (using My Place, as described in Chapter 16).

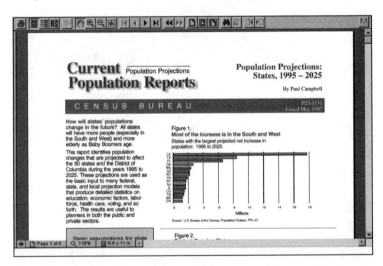

Figure 5-14. The government makes various reports available in PDF file to pre-serve accuracy and quality, and to avoid wasting time reformatting them in HTML.

Other Video Formats: MPG, AVI, QuickTime

AVI and QuickTime are the standard video formats for Windows and Apple computers respectively. Apple now makes a sophisticated QuickTime player for Windows. This player offers new features plus the ability to display many types of files, including ordinary graphics (PICT, a Mac graphics file) and sound (MIDI). Windows built-in Media Player can handle both AVI and the older MPG format, which is now available in a streaming version.

Sounds of Yore: WAV, AU, MIDI

MP3 may be the most popular format for music on the Web, but over the years a huge reservoir of sound has been preserved in older formats. WAV and AU files are digital recordings of actual sounds, while MIDI files play electronically simulated music. (WAV is the default sound format used by Windows.) WinAmp, RealPlayer, and Windows Media Player all play WAV and AU files. WAV and AU files, though capturing the fidelity of the original, tend to be quite large and play for a short time. MIDI files, as digital creations that merely simulate music, are smaller and play much longer. Huge MIDI archives have been created for specific types of music, like the Classical MIDI Archives at `http://www.prs.net/midi.html`.

Your AOL Browser: A Tool for Using Other Tools

The Internet isn't limited to the World Wide Web — by a long shot. The Web was invented to make the whole Internet more accessible, and each generation of browser (every year or so) brings you a bigger swath of the Internet. If your browser doesn't let you use other Internet resources, it will at least call up the special tools required to do so. You'll encounter these "other" tools and resources when you click a link leading to them.

A Quick Look Back

Your browser is your dashboard on the Internet. The more you travel, the more you're likely to push one or another of its buttons, which AOL makes as unobtrusive as possible. At the same time, the more you realize where your AOL browser can take you, the more places you will want to go.

AOL provides a simple-looking version of the Microsoft Internet Explorer browser (subject of this chapter) and a powerful-looking version. Both use the same technology, and many settings apply to both the AOL and the stand-alone browser.

The AOL browser gives you

- ▶ A complete set of preferences, so you can empty your cache; define colors and fonts; and create any home page of your choosing.
- ▶ Beautiful integration with AOL, so your Web and non-Web Favorite Places are kept in the same place (Favorite Places folder). Likewise, the toolbar's navigational controls apply to both AOL windows and Web pages.
- ▶ Support of all multimedia effects and plug-ins.
- ▶ Support of other protocols such as news and mail, as you should expect from any browser.

Later chapters explore other aspects of the Web: using Netscape on AOL (Chapter 6), searching the Web (Chapters 7 and 8), and building Web pages and sites (Chapters 14 and 15).

CHAPTER

6

ALL-PURPOSE VEHICLE:

NETSCAPE NAVIGATOR

Chapter 6

All-Purpose Vehicle: Netscape Navigator

IN THIS CHAPTER

Why use Netscape as a second browser?

Getting, installing, and updating Navigator and plug-ins

Getting around Navigator

Using Navigator to get around the Web

Bookmarks

Making Navigator work the way you want

Netscape-on-the-Web

AOL's browser makes the Web an effortless exten-sion of everything you do on AOL. When AOL is your default Internet application (Chapter 2), it's the browser that automatically comes up when you click a link, whether you're offline or online. From time to time you may want to browse the Web using a different browser. AOL gives you the flexibility to use any browser you want, including the Netscape Navigator.

Why Use a Second Browser

Why use Netscape Navigator when you have the easiest-to-use and most unobtrusive browser built right into AOL?

▶ You might want to use several browsers at the same time. On the Web you can download something time-consuming (like a Java applet) in one browser while looking at ordinary Web pages in the other. You could do a search with one browser and download software in the other, and so on.

▶ Some sites look best when viewed by a particular browser; that's just how they were designed. Usually, they'll tell you that right up front, with a message such as, "Page best viewed with..." and then the name of the browser the Webmaster thinks you ought to be using to look at his work. In practice, that means they look best with Netscape Navigator (subject of this chapter) or Microsoft's Internet Explorer.

▶ You might want to use Netscape simply because you're familiar with it. If you're using Netscape at school, for instance, you might find yourself more comfortable with it at home. Many colleges and companies have standardized on Netscape products, so you may want to use the same browser at home as at work.

▶ Or, you just like some of Netscape's features: the Related Sites button (to see pages similar to the one you're viewing) or Netscape's built-in Composer, a powerful *HTML editor*, used for building your own Web pages and sites.

Cross-Reference

Chapter 15 introduces Netscape Composer, a free part of the Netscape Communicator software suite.

Tip

Because an Internet connection is not "dedicated," you can do several things at once. Running several Internet applications at the same time often comes in handy, as when you play MP3 music with Spinner.com while downloading a file using FTP (Chapter 16) while actively reading your e-mail.

6

All Purpose Vehicle

Getting and Installing Netscape

Getting the latest version of Netscape's Internet software requires a visit to Netscape's home, also known as Netcenter, at `http://home.netscape.com` (see Figure 6-1). This site counts as one of the busiest Web sites on the planet. For now, try to avoid NetCenter's many distractions. You can also come back!

Note

Navigator is the name of Netscape's browser. **Communicator,** the name of Netscape's suite of Internet programs, including a browser (Navigator), an HTML editor (Composer), and an e-mail-and-news-group reader (Messenger). If you just want the browser, click Download (shown in Figure 6-1), then select Netscape Browsers from Departments. The version number for Navigator may lag behind that for Communicator as a whole (this is because the software is always being updated to a newer and fresher version). The exact order and actions of the procedure for getting Netscape may vary from the way it's described here.

To download Netscape, click this button

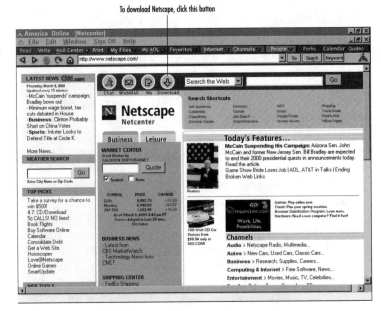

Figure 6-1. Netscape's Netcenter. Start here to download Netscape.

1. At NetCenter, click the Download button at the top of the page, Download, to start the process.

2. On the page that comes up, you'll get the choice of downloading either the Windows 95/98 or the Mac PowerPC version (also available are Unix versions, making Netscape truly cross-platform). Click the one you want. This will take you to a new page (see Figure 6-2).

3. Click the Download button. From the dropdown list, select a location near you from which to retrieve Netscape.

Remember what you're trying to do — *download* Netscape Communicator or Navigator, for a specific *operating system* (e.g., Windows 98), from the Netscape site closest to you, using *SmartDownload*.

Click to get the Smart Download program, which handles the rest of the process for you.

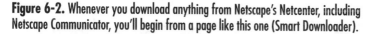

Definition

Downloading in this context simply means copying a file from an Internet computer to your PC. In this case, you're downloading Netscape Communicator, which you install on your PC and use to surf the Web.

6

All Purpose Vehicle

Figure 6-2. Whenever you download anything from Netscape's Netcenter, including Netscape Communicator, you'll begin from a page like this one (Smart Downloader).

4. You'll see a box that asks if you want to *Run this program from its current location* or *Save this program to disk.* Save it to disk, a geeky way of saying "on your hard drive."

5. When the Save As dialog box opens, choose Desktop or other location, then click Save.

6. The small Smart Download program downloads quickly. When done, the Download Complete box gives you the option of opening (running) the program you just downloaded. Click Open.

7. The Smart Download program now downloads the remaining files it needs to install Communicator. Be prepared to wait, especially if you have a modem connection! Make a note of the folder in which the file is saved.

8. Once downloading is complete, go to the folder where the file was saved, and double-click the Netscape file to run it. Follow the onscreen instructions. When offered the choice, choose the Typical installation, to install the most commonly used elements of Communicator and most commonly used plug-ins.

If you're slightly technical or a geek wannabe, you can set up the plug-ins and helper applications Navigator uses automatically when it encounters certain file types. To create associations between different files and the programs for viewing or launching them, visit Edit ⇨ Preferences, and (under Navigator) click Applications. You'll be asked for a MIME type, but you can usually leave that field blank.

At AOL's Multimedia Web Center (http://multimedia. aol.com) you can link to some hot sites for different kinds of multimedia requiring plug-ins.

How to Use Netscape as a Second Browser

Whatever reason you might have to use a second browser, AOL makes it easy.

1. With Netscape downloaded and installed as just described, sign on to AOL as you usually do (over a modem, network, or ISP — it doesn't matter).

2. Open the Netscape browser program by clicking or double-clicking its icon, wherever you've placed it: on the Quick Launch toolbar, or Windows desktop, or program folder (Start Menu ⇨ Programs ⇨ Netscape Communicator).

Now you can browse 'til the cows come home.

Plugging in, with Netscape Plug-ins

A *plug-in* is an additional piece of software your browser uses to let you view or do things on the Web you otherwise might not be able to view or do. Some plug-ins let you listen to music saved in a particular format (like MP3), others let you experience full-motion video and animation, and still others let you explore three-dimensional simulated landscapes. To see a complete list of the plug-ins installed in your copy of Netscape Navigator, choose Help ⇨ About Plug-Ins from the menu bar. The Microsoft browser lacks a simple way of viewing the plug-ins you have installed.

When you download Communicator and choose the Typical installation, four plug-ins are automatically installed (all are discussed more fully in Chapter 5).

> ▶ **RealPlayer** lets you hear and see "streaming" audio and video. You can hear FM-quality sound over a 28.8K bps connection, AM-quality sound over a 14.4K bps connection, and near-CD sound over a high-speed connection. Video quality varies similarly, depending on the speed of your connection, but it takes a broadband connection (Chapter 18) to use video effectively.

▶ The **Shockwave Flash** player lets you view quick-loading cartoons, games, and animations. Comedy Central, Sony, and Disney have all created Web sites that really come alive with Flash.

▶ The **Beatnik** plug-in lets you play back audio files in a variety of formats, including Rich Music Format (RMF), MIDI, MOD, WAV, AIFF, and AU. Sites that use Beatnik can play sound not only in the background as you browse, but when you move your mouse to a specific location — adding a fun touch of interactivity.

▶ Netscape's general-purpose **Audio/Video Player** plays most common audio and video formats you might encounter on the Web.

Software That Never Sleeps: Updating Netscape

Just because you've downloaded Netscape Communicator doesn't mean you'll never have to touch it again. No, Netscape is continuously evolving, especially since Netscape (the company) made the code available to the world's programmers to enhance and play with. The plug-ins you add, too, are frequently updated, to support more advanced multimedia features and browsers. So how can you be sure you've always got the latest versions of your Netscape software?

It's easy: use Netscape's SmartUpdate.

To access it, choose Help ⇨ Software Updates from the Netscape menu bar while you're connected to the Internet. This takes you to the SmartUpdate page on Netscape's Netcenter (see Figure 6-3).

Updating your Netscape software is a four-step process and is clearly labeled as such in Smart Update itself.

1. **Select Software.** Click the big number 1 at the right of the SmartUpdate page to start. Choose the updates or additions you want by clicking on their associated check boxes.

2. **Review.** In the second step, you review the software you decided to update or install. In addition, SmartUpdate may recommend additional software related to what you already have.

Definition

Streaming rocks. Actually, it does what it says: flows. Files are called streaming if, instead of downloading completely to your computer and then being displayed or played, they're displayed or played *while* downloading. RealAudio in particular lets you enjoy audio clips after a brief period of "buffering." You'll find them in music stores such as CDNOW.

Note

You'll have to register to use this useful service. Make sure to keep your username and password somewhere you won't forget them.

Tip

Keep an eye on the download process. If you're ever prompted to permit SmartUpdate to download something, click Grant. Browsers don't readily permit the downloading of unknown file types or files you don't explicitly request, so keep an eye on the upgrade window.

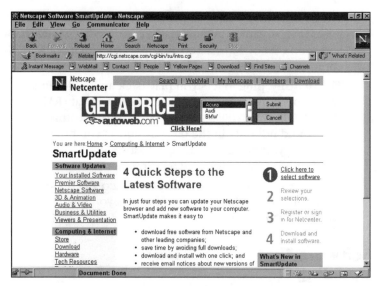

Figure 6-3. Smart Update: the easy way to fetch new versions of Netscape Navigator or Communicator

3. **Register or Sign In for Netcenter.** In order to use SmartUpdate, you have to register. It's free. If you're already a Netcenter member — you might have joined by registering your copy of Netscape when you first set it up — sign in here.

4. **Download.** You'll see a list of the items you chose to download. Click each one in turn to download it. Follow the instructions provided. Each one is separately downloaded and automatically installed.

Navigating Navigator

Navigator is similar in many ways AOL's browser, but it looks a bit different. Figure 6-4 shows you what AOL.com looks like when displayed in Navigator. I've labeled Navigator's main components.

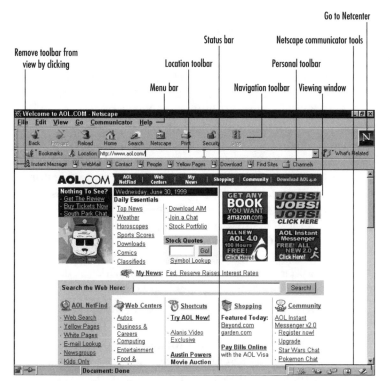

Figure 6-4. Navigator has the same basic components as the AOL browser, but they're arranged a bit differently.

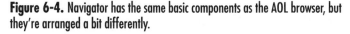

> All these toolbars take up space from the Viewing window; some toolbars you'll use more than others. To remove any toolbar from view, click its knobby-looking left edge. Click it again to restore it to view.

6

All Purpose Vehicle

▶ The **menu bar** controls your browser as an *application* — opening and closing files, printing them, working with bookmarks, and so on. *File* lets you open files (including HTM files on your computer) and save pages as your own HTM files. *Edit* (among other things) gives you the Find command, for finding a single word on long Web pages. *View* lets you increase and decrease the size of type on a page and refresh pages. *Go* provides a keyboard version of the navigational functions (going back, forward, home, etc.).

▶ The **Navigation toolbar** combines toolbar features like Search, Print, Security, and MyNetscape and the buttons that take you round and about the Web: Back, Forward, Reload, Home and Stop, just like in AOL.

An annoying feature with the address box on *all* browsers: you can't always enter a new URL to visit until the current page is finished downloading, which can take longer than you think. Press the Stop button before entering a new URL. Until a page has completely downloaded, it can still preempt the display of the new URL you're typing in.

Want to see where a link goes without actually clicking on it? Just point your mouse arrow at it. The address is displayed in the Status bar.

▶ The **Location toolbar** combines a bunch of functions to help you get to, and keeping track of the pages you like. In the address box (called Location field), you can type in Web addresses, find pages similar to the one you're viewing, and keep track of sites you like (*bookmarks,* they're called in Netscape). See "Bookmarking Sites You Like" for this important Netscape feature.

▶ The **Personal toolbar** has links to your favorite sites, plus some sites Netscape would like you to visit — sort of like Microsoft Internet Explorer's Links toolbar. When you first install Netscape Communicator, the toolbar contains links to Netscape sites such as New & Cool and the Yellow Pages. It also contains a button for AOL's Instant Messenger service, which is included with Communicator. For more information on AOL Instant Messenger, see Chapter 11. You can edit this toolbar at Bookmarks ⇨ Edit Bookmarks, as described in "Bookmarking Sites You Like."

▶ **Viewing area.** This, as you'd guess, is where Web pages appear.

▶ **Status bar.** The status bar provides information about the page you're currently visiting, including its progress as it downloads and whether it's a secure page (one to which you can safely send information). It also contains a handy little toolbar that provides one-click access to the other programs included in Communicator, if you've installed them.

▶ **Go to Netcenter.** Click the famous Netscape N in the browser's upper-right corner to jump to Netscape Netcenter. This particular link does not take you to *your* home page (see "Changing Your Home Page" for that); it's hard-wired to *Netscape's* home page, Netcenter.

...and Navigating *with* Navigator

Except for the different location of the buttons, browsing the Web with Navigator essentially does not differ much from browsing with AOL's browser. Type in the address of the page you want to visit (you don't have to type the *http://* part). Click Back to go to the previous page you visited and Forward to return to the page you visited after that. Stop halts a page from loading, and Reload reloads it. Home takes you to your home page (see "Making Netscape Work Your Way").

Another way to get back to a page you visited earlier in your current Navigator session is to use the Go menu. As you visit pages, this menu expands to list the last 10 sites you visited. Just highlight the one you want to return to go back to it. This feature compares to what you get in many word-processors and other Windows applications, which list the last several documents you used, so you can call them up immediately.

Just as with AOL's browser, you can also return to sites you've visited previously by clicking the down-arrow just to the right of the Location field (address box). This drops down a list of everywhere you've been recently. Choose the site you want to return to, and back you go.

Click the small triangle to the upper-right of the Back or Forward button to see your trail of Web pages backward and forward from the current location. Select any site on either trail to skip to that place.

6

All Purpose Vehicle

NetWatch: Netscape's Version of Parental Controls

Netscape gives parents a degree of control over what their kids can do online, but their solution is not more satisfying the Microsoft Internet Explorer's solution. Both fall short of AOL's Parental Controls in two respects: reliability (Parental Control sites are selected, not merely filtered out) and flexibility (Parental Controls apply to e-mail, file downloads, chat, newsgroups, and not just the Web).

Netscape's NetWatch can be set up at Help ➪ NetWatch. This filtering program works by comparing any page a child (or other Navigator user) wants to view against a decency standard *you* select; if the page fails to meet the standard, it can't be viewed. Parents can define decency in terms of the Net's two prevalent content standards, RSACi and SafeSurf. The hitch for both standards: they only work if Webmasters go to the trouble of rating the level of obscenity, sex, violence, and general nastiness on their sites. Many sites do *not* have such ratings. A more stringent filter, such as NetNanny (see Chapter 17), can filter out sites with certain URLs or certain words you specify.

Playing It Safe with Online Transactions

Wondering how safe a purchase at a particular site might be — how safe a credit card transaction would be? Worried about downloading a virus? In addition to NetWatch, which safeguards kids online, Netscape provides a way for you to safeguard your credit-card transactions. (See the "NetWatch" sidebar.)

View any page and click Navigator's Security button to find out how secure the page is. This button displays the same page of information as you get when clicking the icon of the open or closed lock in the lower-left corner of the browser window (see Figure 6-5).

Figure 6-5. You can get basic security information about any site you're visiting just by clicking the Security button.

The menu down the left side of this window leads to the security settings you can alter.

> ▶ **Security Info.** Find out whether a page was scrambled, or *encrypted* (possibly of interest if you are visiting your bank online to check your balances). If it was encrypted (as most commercial sites are), it will have a *certificate* showing which authority stands behind the site and until when the certificate is valid. In the Verification section, you get *authentication* information, too: does the page in fact come from the site you requested, or is it a fake? For big transactions or small

transactions with obscure sites, it's worth answering the question before proceeding.

▶ **Passwords.** Set up a password to prevent others from using your copy of Communicator (and changing security settings).

▶ **Navigator.** You'll want to enable SSL (which scrambles credit card and other transactional information). If you work for a company, you may want a warning before entering or leaving an encrypted site. Why? Using an encrypted page automatically decrypts it, leaving a decrypted copy in your cache (a big vat of recently used Internet files kept on your hard drive for quick re-display next time you visit a place). In theory, anyone with technical savvy can steal these decrypted pages. If you're a home user, you can safely choose not to get a warning when entering and leaving an encrypted page, because life is difficult enough without getting warned all the time.

Tip

Using this password to keep younger children from using Navigator and perhaps circumventing Parental Controls.

The rest of the security choices may be of interest network administrators.

Bookmarking Sites You Like

Navigator's bookmarks can be compared to AOL's Favorite Places. These are the online favorites to which you want to return.

While you add to your Favorite Places on *AOL* by clicking the heart button in any window's upper-right corner, you add bookmarks in *Netscape* by pressing Ctrl-D. Meant for use with your AOL account only, Favorite Places include e-mail messages, AOL areas, and message-board postings, as well as Web sites. Netscape's bookmarks keep track of Web pages only.

Even before you've added any bookmarks, you may find an extensive collection of the suckers: Netscape installs a number of them automatically. To see bookmarks (yours and the ones Netscape chose for you), click the Bookmarks button on Navigator's Location toolbar. Click any folder of interest to see what's in it. If you see a particular bookmark that looks interesting, click it and Navigator takes you there.

Tip

Put your most-used book-
marks in your Personal
Toolbar folder, so they're
available on the Personal
Toolbar, just above
Navigator's viewing area.

If you use Navigator, you'll soon find many other sites that
you'd like to be able to access with a single click. To bookmark
a site you're viewing, just press Ctrl-D or click the Bookmark
button and choose **Add Bookmark** from the menu to include
the Web site in your list of bookmarks.

Like AOL's Favorite Places and MSIE's Favorites, folders bring
a little order to your Navigator bookmarks.

> ▶ To create a new folder, choose Bookmarks ➪ Edit
>   Bookmarks.... In the Bookmarks window, select File ➪
>   New Folder. Give the folder a name, and click OK. Back
>   in the Bookmarks window, you can drag bookmarks
>   into folders, and folders into other folders, so that
>   things are just right for you.

> ▶ To remove a bookmark from a folder or from the
>   Netscape Bookmarks file, select Bookmarks ➪ Edit
>   Bookmarks.... Highlight any folder or bookmark. Right
>   click and select Delete Bookmark (use this trick to
>   delete anything, including folders and separators).

> ▶ To add a displayed site to an existing folder, choose
>   Bookmarks ➪ File Bookmark, then choose a folder from
>   the drop-down list.

> ▶ Still not orderly enough? Create a *separator* (thin line
>   separating two groups of bookmarks or folders) in the
>   Bookmarks window (Bookmarks ➪ Edit Bookmarks...)
>   to clump together similar bookmarks and folders. It's a
>   useful visual way of remembering related bookmarks.

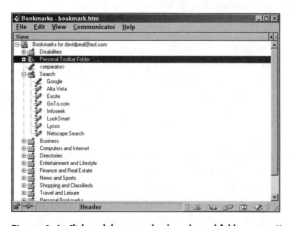

Figure 6-6. Click and drag your bookmarks and folders using Navigator's Bookmark
window, until everything's in the right place.

Making Netscape Work Your Way

You can customize Netscape in a number of interesting ways by choosing Edit ⇨ Preferences from the menu bar. This brings up the Preferences window, shown in Figure 6-7.

Changing Your Home Page

Your Home Page, as you'll recall from working with the AOL browser, is the page at which your browser starts when you open it. When you first install Navigator, the browser's home page is all set to take you to Netscape Netcenter.

You can change your home page using Edit ⇨ Preferences (see Figure 6-7). In the Location box in the Home Page area, type the address of the home page you want. If you're especially enamored of the page you're viewing, click Use Current Page to make it your home base. You can also open the browser to a blank page. Why do something that dull? Because *it* opens fast and *your* needs vary. Unique to Navigator is the useful option of being able to dynamically set your home page as the *last page you viewed in the previous session.*

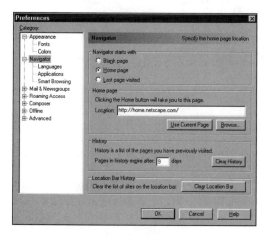

Figure 6-7. Navigator's Preferences window (Edit ⇨ Preferences). Click a plus sign to see two levels of choices in the panel on the left; you set all preferences in the larger panel on the right.

A cache stores copies of pages you've downloaded automatically in the course of browsing the Web. Clear your cache to keep it from slowing down your system — and slowing down browsing. Navigator puts cache-setting and -clearing in the Preferences window's Advanced tab, shown in Figure 6-10. Under Cache preferences, you can change the space devoted to your disk cache (hard drive) and memory (RAM) cache, and you can also clear them. Usually it's a good idea not to let your memory cache get too big: A memory cache temporarily stores pages in precious RAM; a disk cache stores stuff for a longer time in less-expensive, but slower, hard-drive space.

Netscape on the Web

As an AOL member, you begin your Internet surfing with the AOL browser at the best portal of them all, AOL.COM, but you still may find much at Netcenter to repay regular visits there. Like all great sites, Netcenter's appearance changes all the time. Currently it looks something like it does in Figure 6-8.

Figure 6-8. Grand Central Netscape takes you to new destinations on the Web.

Oh Netscape, My Netscape

You don't have to look at the same Netcenter start page that everyone else looks at; you can customize it to suit yourself. With My Netscape you can create a customized newspaper to show you only the news that you're interested in, as you can with AOL's My AOL.COM, which you can read about in Chapter 3. You'll only see My Netscape when you fire up Navigator.

Click the My Netscape button to set up your personal start page. If you haven't yet registered as a Netcenter user, you'll be asked to do so, then you'll see a start page like the one in Figure 6-9.

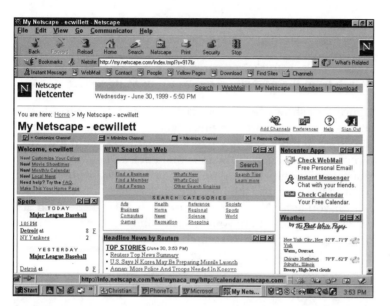

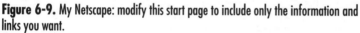

Figure 6-9. My Netscape: modify this start page to include only the information and links you want.

The page is organized into a series of *channels*, any of which you remove by clicking its Close button (the **X**) in the upper right corner. You set preferences for each channel by clicking the button in the upper right corner with the profile of a head in it. Add additional elements to the channel and specify where in the start page you want it to be located. A preview area shows exactly what the channel will look like when displayed on the start page, with a brief description. Click Save when you're happy.

Set preferences for the entire start page by clicking the Preferences link in the upper right corner, positioning various channels wherever you wish, naming your page, choosing English or metric measurement units, etc. To add channels or tools, click the Add Channels link, choose the channels and tools you want from those listed, then click Save.

Searching the Web

When you set out to search the Web, you'll probably want to use AOL's Search, which is always at your fingertips on AOL. Chapter 7 is devoted to AOL's search solutions. When using another browser you might want to try another search

Tip

If you are fonder of one search engine than another, tie the knot by clicking the box labeled *Keep (name of search engine) as my search engine.*

engine, since each one turns up sites that other search engines miss, a strange phenomenon discussed in Chapter 8.

Netscape Navigator's NetSearch makes searching easy. Click Search from the navigation toolbar to use this service.

Figure 6-10 shows Netcenter's search page, which provides access to several search engines, each of which has its own directory (see the first few pages of Chapter 7 about indexes, directories, and such). To search, first click an engine (such as HotBot or Google). Then type the word, words, or phrase you want to look for into the box, and click Search. Once you click Search, you leave Netcenter and are whisked to the search engine's home site, where you'll usually find yourself in a thicket of choices for refining the search, plus all the ancillary services you find at any search site.

Figure 6-10. Navigator points you to one of several Web search engines whenever you click the Search button.

Finding People and Businesses

NetSearch includes tools that can help you find individuals, businesses, products, and services. You'll find links analogous to those you find in AOL.COM, including links for folks seeking their long-lost college roommate or the best place to buy a hubcap for their 1954 Studebaker.

Finding a Business with the Netscape Yellow Pages

In the Netscape Yellow Pages, you have more ways to search than that. By filling in the form, you can search by category or company name, city, and state. In my case, I'm looking for the name, address, and phone number of the newspaper in Bismarck, North Dakota, so I put **newspaper** in the category box, **Bismarck** in the City box, and chose **North Dakota** from the State list.

Clicking Search, in this case, brings up a whole list of Yellow Pages categories related to *newspapers*, from Advertising-Newspaper to Publisher-Periodical. I choose Newspapers (Publishers) and get a list of five, including the *Bismarck Tribune* and *Farm and Ranch Guide*. Some include a link for more info; all include a link labeled About. Clicking that finally brings me the information I want, in the form of a page that also lists other businesses in the vicinity and provides links to more information about the community. The whole process took only a few seconds — far less time, expense, and hassle than finding the same information by calling directory assistance.

Finding an Individual with Netscape People Finder

Using Netscape's People Finder is similar to using the Yellow Pages. You enter the information you have about the person — first name, last name, city, state, country, then search for either a phone number and street address or an e-mail address. (AOL.COM's person finder provides separate tools for finding real addresses and e-mail addresses.) You may retrieve a bit more information than you were banking on, and even view a map of the area around the person's address (see Figure 6-11)!

Tip

You're much more likely to be able to find a person's phone number and street address than you are his or her e-mail address; phone numbers and addresses are freely published in phone books, while e-mail addresses aren't. In general, the e-mail address will only show up if the person you're looking for has taken the trouble to provide it to Netscape for publication in the People Finder database.

6

All Purpose Vehicle

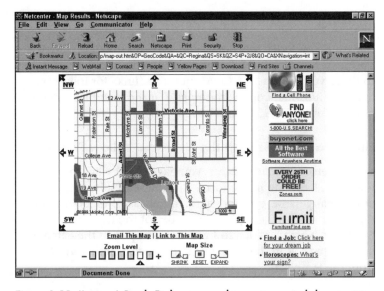

Figure 6-11. Netscape's People Finder can even draw you a map to help you get to a friend's house.

Resources for Web Site Builders

If you're building a Web site, you can trust Netscape: they created the most popular browser and created Web standards like frames and JavaScript. These people take the Web very seriously.

You'll find one powerful tool right in Netscape Communicator itself: Netscape Composer. This full-featured Web-page HTML editor makes creating a great-looking Web page almost as easy as using a word processor.

To access Composer, choose Communicator ⇨ Composer or click the Composer button at the far right end of the Navigator Status bar at the bottom of the browser window. Composer opens a blank Web page, into which you can type text, insert tables, images, links, and more, using the toolbars and menus (see Figure 6-12). With Composer, as you create your Web page you're seeing exactly what it will look like in the Navigator browser. Make sure to view it in AOL and MSIE, too, just to be sure it looks like the one you want.

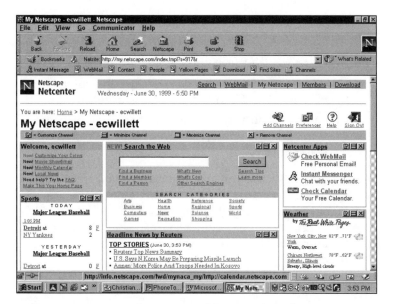

Figure 6-12. Netscape Composer is a powerful program that makes creating Web pages easy. A friend of mine created this page in two minutes.

For more detailed information on using Netscape Composer, choose Help ⇨ Help Contents from the menu bar, then Creating Web Pages from the directory of topics at the left. See also Chapter 15 for more about Composer.

If you are looking for background images, buttons, clip-art, animations, plug-ins or other tools to make your pages come alive, Netscape Netcenter points you in the right direction. At Netcenter, click Computing & Internet to find links to a bushel basket of Web-page tools, whether you're a small business owner looking to establish a beachhead on the World Wide Web or a family trying to celebrate a child's birthday.

A Quick Look Back

This chapter tries to shoe-horn a huge piece of software into a single chapter. Netscape Navigator, the subject of entire books (including Paul Hoffman's *Netscape Navigator for Dummies,* also from IDG Books Worldwide), is a large feature-packed piece of software. This short tour began with some reasons for using a second browser and then got down to business:

- ▶ How to download, install, and upgrade Netscape
- ▶ How to navigate the Net with Netscape, including how to get plug-ins and bookmark those favorite sites
- ▶ How to find your way among Netscape's vast metropolis on the Web, including NetCenter, My Netscape, and Netscape Search.

Elsewhere in this book you can read about Netscape's pathbreaking Open Directory — the most Net's ambitious project to date for building a popular, comprehensive directory of Web sites (Chapter 8). In Chapter 15, read about Netscape's HTML editor, Composer, which you can use to build Web pages.

Chapter 7

Finding Your Way: Internet Searching Made Easy with AOL

Everything is searchable these days. Your computer. Your favorite Web site. Your public library. Your favorite Web-based bookstore. A shelf-full of electronic dictionaries and reference books, even the massive holdings of the Library of Congress. And of course, you can "search the Web."

When you really need something, however, where do you start? How do you ask your question in a way that makes sense to a computer? How do you know which search results to trust? AOL, as you'll see in this chapter, cuts through all this complexity with AOL Search, an easy-to-use set of tools that can greatly simplify searching the Web, AOL, and much more

(Keyword: **Search**). In this chapter you'll learn how to make the best use of AOL Search. This chapter does *not* show in detail how to search for a newsgroup posting or find a mailing list to join; see Chapters 12 and 13 for those things. In the next chapter, you'll find out how to use other Web-search engines and how do *specialized searches*.

Web Searching, Sometimes a Pain

Today, when you search the Web with one of the many standard "search engines," you're first confronted by the sheer number of the world's Web pages — close to a billion according to one recent estimate, and growing at about 1.5 million pages a day by another estimate. With the current technologies, no single tool can possibly keep track of them all. Also, pages come in many languages, most of which are probably unfamiliar to you and thus not easily searchable. Even within the universe of English-language pages, many synonyms are used (Great War, World War One, WWI, and the War to end all wars, for example). In addition, the average page is only on the Web for a month or two, making even (or especially) the largest databases of Web pages out-of-date from the get-go. Some pages (all the online news services) change daily; Tuesday's front page of BBC Online differs from Wednesday's. Now, with the profusion of search engines, there's the new difficulty of where to start your search.

AOL Search: A Searchable Directory of the Web's Best Sites

To get the main idea in a book, most people will start with the Introduction or Table of Contents, then flip to chapters that sound interesting. When they want to retrieve an obscure fact — about gardenias, for example, — they turn, instead, to the book's index and look for appropriate entries, flipping back and forth until finding or not finding an answer.

Note

AOL Search takes the place of AOL Search, AOL's search engine since 1996. AOL Search is based on new technology and a simpler, more comprehensive approach to searching AOL and the Internet. It also replaces the various general tools AOL has provided for searching for specific AOL content. You now use a single page (Keyword: **Search**) to search both AOL and the Web.

7

Finding Your Way

Definition

A *search engine* is not a mechanical thing, much less an engine. It's simply a database (or *list* or *index*) made up of information about millions of Web pages. It provides a way of searching the list for specific pages. The kind of *structured* information in a search engine's list includes the Web addresses of millions of pages. For each Web address it includes the Web page's title, date, size, and so forth. In a search engine you search for words (like **auction**) and the "engine" gives you back (*returns*) the Web addresses of pages containing the term *auction* (like http://pages.e bay.aol.com). Search engines differ in their size, search speed, and syntax (how you ask your questions, or queries).

These two major search techniques, using the table of contents and using the index, correspond roughly to the popular techniques of searching a Web *directory* and searching a Web *index*.

Which do you use?

- ▶ If you just need an overview of a subject — choosing an insurance plan or learning about mountain bikes, for example — a directory, arranged by subject, can be the place to start. One such directory is Netscape's Open Directory.
- ▶ If you need to find information scattered across many subjects or to locate a specific fact, an index (search engine) can be the best place to do your search.

Online, the best search services provide a combination of both types of searches, allow you to alternate easily between browsing and searching. You can see the process in action when you use AOL Search, available at Keyword: **Search** and from AOL.COM (Figure 7-1).

AOL Search begins with a powerful directory based on the Netscape Open Directory (http://www.dmoz.org), which is discussed further in Chapter 8. The directory, simplified and made even more accessible as part of AOL Search, is being created by a volunteer army of more than 10,000 expert editors. These people select the best Web sites for their areas, and write short descriptions of them. AOL Search takes the Netscape Open Directory a step further by including AOL as well as Web content, letting you do combined searches of AOL and the Web.

With AOL Search you can:

- ▶ *browse the directory,* going from topic, to one or more subcategories, to individual Web site
- ▶ *search the directory,* going directly to specific Web sites and AOL areas of interest to you

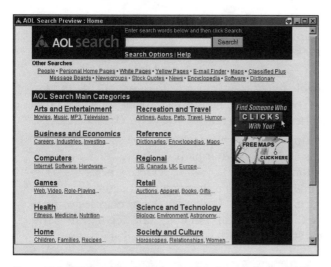

Figure 7-1. AOL Search combines the very best features of a topical directory with the flexibility of pin-point searching.

Suppose you want to learn about *tap dancing*. The AOL Search directory is arranged by topics with recommended sites and several layers of categories and subcategories. In the *Arts and Entertainment* topic, for example, you can click *Performing Arts*, then *Dance* (Figure 7-2) to find a special category devoted to *Tap Dancing* (Figure 7-3). The list contains, currently, nine sites–carefully selected by an editor in the Netscape Open Directory project and described in enough detail for you to choose the best sites for your purposes.

Your search retrieves either *Matching Categories* (folders *containing* sites) or *Matching Sites* (individual AOL areas or Web sites); sometimes you'll see Matching Categories *and* Matching Sites (see Figure 7-5). *Matching* means the categories and sites probably have what you are trying to find; they contain the word or words you indicated by clicking links or typing queries.

How would you know to begin in Arts and Entertainment? If you're unsure, start with a focused search (described in the next section). Your results will include both categories and specific sites. Choose likely categories to find collections of sites related to tap dancing.

Useful details help you as you drill down from topic to categories and their subcategories:

Tip

To keep up with search engines such as AOL Search itself, the Search Engine Watch Web site (http://www.searchenginewatch.com/) offers a monthly newsletter (available by e-mail, too), plus search engine facts, tutorials, and technical resources for users, searchers of all sorts, and Webmasters. The site itself is, of course, searchable.

Note

The right side of the screen gives you a list of related hot searches. You can see what others have searched — a great way to modify or further tailor your query.

7

Finding Your Way

Note

While AOL Search can be reached from both AOL and the Internet, links to AOL areas, message boards, channels, etc., are available only to members accessing AOL Search while signed onto AOL.

▶ In any category or subcategory, the *best* individual Web sites are denoted with a star — which means it is an Editor's Pick. These sites can be good places to start.

▶ On any page of returns, scroll a bit for information available only on AOL, such as message boards and forums (not shown in Figure 7-2). AOL resources (if available for your subject) are listed before Web resources.

▶ You can always see your path of topics and subcategories, and retrace your path. In Figure 7-2, for example, Home refers to Keyword: Search; Arts means you started in the Arts and Entertainment category; Performing Arts and Dance are the directories you traverse to get to the Tap Dancing subcategory. Any particular step in your path can be revisited at any time.

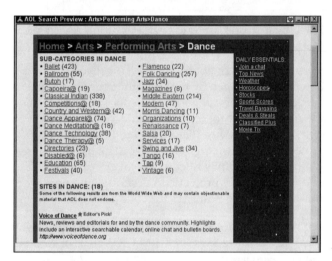

Figure 7-2. Browsing AOL Search provides clear orientation and rapid access to reliable sites on almost any subject.

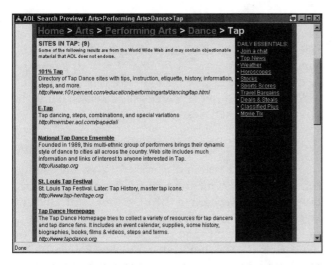

Figure 7-3. Hand-selected sites on tap dancing. Using an ordinary search engine would have netted many more sites, but no indication of the value of the individual sites. Many of these tap dance sites have their own lists of Net resources on tap dancing.

Searching AOL Search

Directories work beautifully — if every Web site dealing with (for example) *tap dancing* is contained in the single subcategory shown in Figure 7-3. But suppose such sites are scattered in many subcategories because they are not primarily focused on tap dancing. Such sites can nonetheless have essential information on your subject. AOL Search gives you the tools to browse a directory with well over a million hand-picked sites; it also lets you search for sites regardless of the categories they're in.

A search looks across categories, AOL content, and the Web for all the pages that contain certain words, or parts of words, or phrases. Searches tend to turn up more results than directory-browsing. However, the average quality of pages turned up through searches tends to be much lower than what you'll find when using a directory. Search engines also have the advantage of letting you search for a specific, even obscure fact (a tap dancer's birth date, for example).

7

Finding Your Way

Tip

A new addition to the AOL interface is the tiny search button to the right of the AOL Address Box. To do a search, type a search term in the Address Box and click the little Search button.

Note

Where did all those categories come from? AOL Search's directory includes regional listings of dance-related businesses and the arts.

AOL Search (shown in Figures 7-1 through 7-3) can help you pluck facts and knowledge from among the million or so quality Web pages contained in the Netscape Open Directory. What if your search leads you nowhere? AOL Search lets you effortlessly extend your search to AOL, to the Web as a whole, to an encyclopedia, and other resources summarized a little later in "Extending Your AOL Search."

To start a search, begin at Keyword: **Search**.

First let's *search* the AOL Search directory for Web sites about tap dancing or that at least mentioning tap dancing. This time you don't want to be restricted to the nine sites in the subcategory shown in Figure 7-3. From Keyword: **Search**, type **tap dance** and click Search. This time your search turns up 400 or so Matching sites in 24 Matching categories. See Figure 7-4. To see more sites or more categories, click the appropriate *next* > button. In "Making AOL Search Work Harder" you'll see how to further refine the search by searching for a phrase ("tap dance") instead of for two words (*tap* and *dance*).

Figure 7-4. A search for tap-dancing information turned up 378 sites in 24 categories.

Now let's try a search for specific data, such as the incidence and severity of earthquakes in 1999. An AOL Search for **earthquakes 1999** turns up approximately 900 Web sites in five subcategories, relating to regional events, engineering, and survivalism.

> **72% Earthquake Information- Recent Global Events**
> Near-real-time Earthquake Bulletin is provided by the National Earthquake
> Information Service (NEIS) of the U. S. Geological Survey.
> *http://civeng.carleton.ca/cgi-bin2/quakes*
> Show me more like this

Figure 7-5. Results of a search: a site, a link, a description, and the likelihood (in percent) of a good match.

Every matching Web site has several pieces of useful information, as shown in Figure 7-5:

> ▶ The percentage (72%) is a relevancy rating, AOL Search's estimate of the value of the site, given the information you provided. The ratings go from most valuable to least valuable. In general, the best sites are listed first. Often, the more specific information you provide, the more useful the ratings.

> ▶ The usually plain-English title of the page (*Earthquake information …*, in this case), *linked to the actual Web page.*

> ▶ The Web address (URL) of the linked page–useful if you print AOL Search's results for reference, and need to keep track of the URLs.

> ▶ *Show me more like this (a clickable link)*–one of the best features of the old AOL AOL Search. If one page in AOL Search's results is particularly good, click this link to find more such pages.

Extending Your AOL Search

AOL Search stands out primarily for the simple elegance with which it combines a large and well-organized directory with the capability to do specific searches across the web and AOL content. Because the entire world of networked information cannot be compressed into a million Web pages, AOL Search makes it simple to extend your search, in several ways.

First, at the top right of the earthquake search, for example, you'll see half a dozen similar searches run by other people (e.g., several variants of **turkey earthquake 1999**).

Second, and probably more useful, you can run the same query (**earthquakes 1999** in this case) through several other specialized content, including such things as message boards, Newsgroups, and the entire Web.

Definition

You ask questions, but computers understand only queries. A query is jargon for a formalized question constructed to get results from a computer database. Doing searches means tweaking queries to get the best results for your purposes from a given search engine. AOL Search gives you good results without fancy queries, but makes powerful search syntax available if you need it.

7

Finding Your Way

Tip

Say you've done a search for "covered bridges of Indiana" (AOL Search will ignore the *of* because it is so common). If you don't find what you're looking for on the Web, you can scroll down and choose another type of search, using the same query, so that you don't have to enter it again. You can search AOL articles, AOL message boards, Internet newsgroups, and encyclopedias.

You may see additional ways of extending your search on AOL Search, such as search AOL articles and news articles; the news, in this case, refers to the daily news, not to newsgroups. Note that most of these extended searches take you to different search sites, with their own techniques for refining your searches and doing new ones.

From the bottom of the page showing the results of any search, you can also click to "other searches," such as White Page and Yellow Page services, which are described later in this chapter.

Power Searching

Ordinarily, AOL Search lets you do powerful, focused searches without bothering with all this fancy stuff. AOL Search does offer two types of power features, which can be easily used in everyday searches if you want to do highly specific searches. These features require the use of operators, additional words that can specify the relationship between the words you use in your query.

▶ Some operators let you look for pages with certain words or phrases in *a particular order or proximity to each other*. Such operators lower the possibility of retrieving those many long pages containing all your words and phrases — but in completely unrelated contexts.

- ADJ tells AOL Search to look for words next to each other. ADJ differs from a phrase (in double quotation marks). Unlike phrases, with ADJ you can put together complex queries such as **(tony or anthony) adj blair**. The parentheses used in *(tony* or *anthony)* are also new to AOL Search; this query would retrieve pages about Tony Blair and Anthony Blair.

- NEAR tells AOL Search to look for pages with words close to each other, but in any order relative to each other. **aol near/5 andreessen** would look for pages where *AOL* and *andreessen* are within five words of each other.

Note that for both ADJ and NEAR, lowercase is fine.

▶ *Wildcards.* A wildcard is a character that stands for another character or characters. Note that wildcards cannot be used in phrases, since phrases look for exact matches of the words within the quotation marks.

▶ In AOL Search, a question mark (?) stands for any *single* character. To search for pages containing the acronyms ADSL or HDSL, for example, your query would be **?DSL** or **?dsl**. This particular search returned 70 categories with information about these networking technologies (see Chapter 18); choose any category of interest to zero in on what you need to find out.

▶ An asterisk stands for a *series of characters*: **gin*** looks for pages on *ginger ale* and *gingivitis*. A search for **tap danc*** netted 100 or so sites more than a search for tap dance.

For more information about AOL Search's advanced options, browse the appropriate Help pages at keyword: Search. In general, the first stop when learning a new search engine should be the Help button, usually located close to the search box.

Definition

Boolean operators are words such as AND, OR, NOT, NEAR, and ADJ that tell a search engine how to conduct a search when several words are used in a query. In AOL Search, AND is no longer necessary, and NEAR and ADJ have been added (see "Power Searching").

Tip

AOL Search's Help pages include sample searches to give you a sense of how different queries have different results.

7

Finding Your Way

Making AOL Search Work Harder

Traditional search engines required fancy queries just so you could filter out the millions of pages that merely appeared to match your interests. For example, if you're a World War I buff, you might want to inquire about the role of tanks in the war. Your query would read something like **tanks AND "Great War"**, meaning that the word *tanks* and the phrase *"Great War"* must be on the same page.

A *phrase* is a series of words that together have a specific meaning and must be adjacent, in a specific order. "Great War" has a very specific meaning. When not joined as a phrase, the words would retrieve many sites irrelevant to the World War I researcher, since many wars have been called great, and the

With AOL Search and all search engines, be as specific as possible, using several words in a query, from most specific to least.

When you do a search for something like *ice skating*, AOL Search lets you know the kinds of similar questions that other people have been asking (*ice skating toddler lessons*) and re-run their query if it's of interest to you.

words war and great can appear on the same page even if they have nothing to do with each other. The query, **tanks great war**, pulls up 396 pages, but **tanks "great war"** pulls up only 23.

AOL Search makes your life easier in many ways:

▶ It assumes AND when you use several words in a row, so you can say **tanks "Great War"** instead of **tanks AND "Great War."**

▶ It doesn't care whether you use uppercase or lowercase, so **tanks** and **Tanks** have the same results. The one exception is the phrase. "Great War" will not reliably retrieve pages with the phrase "great war."

AOL Search tends to return fewer sites, of higher quality, than traditional search engines. For every page of returned Web sites, the original query appears at the top of the page. For any search, you can refine the results by tweaking the original query. In particular, you may want to broaden your AOL Search query — something that never made much sense in the older engines, because they returned, as a rule, so many useless pages. To broaden a search, insert **OR** (the lowercase, **or**, is fine), as in **tanks or "Great War"** (which yields a respectable yield of more than 4,000 pages). You can also broaden a search by making it a bit less specific: drop words or edit them into terms with a more general meaning. Finally, avoid the NOT operator (as in "Mary Todd" NOT Lincoln) to avoid overly focused AOL Search results.

Fancy Queries Made Easier: AOL Search's Options

AOL Search's Search Options page gives you a way to construct fancy queries without worry about all those pesky Boolean operators. Figure 7-4 shows a prominent link to AOL Search's search options. Click the link to bring up the window shown in Figure 7-6.

Tip

Explore these searches, all available from a single place, and you'll be tempted to make AOL Search your home page on the World Wide Web, as explained in Chapter 5.

Figure 7-6. More powerful queries with less fuss about search syntax.

This figure shows a Web (not AOL) query that must contain *"Great War"* and *TANKS* and must not contain *WWII*. Here's what the query would have to look like, if done by hand: **("Great War" AND tanks) AND NOT (WWII)**. After running a query, the fields in Figure 7-6 clear and the Search Options defaults are restored.

AOL's White Pages, Yellow Pages, and E-Mail Finder

At Keyword: **Search** (Figure 7-1) you'll find two rows of "other searches" at the top of the page, just below the main AOL Search banner. In one place AOL gives you the opportunity to do all sorts of essential specialized searches on both AOL and the Web, including, the AOL Member Directory, classified listings, Hometown, message boards, and the Merriam-Webster dictionary or Comptons Encyclopedia.

In the following sections, I'll look only at a few of these resources, starting with AOL's electronic White Pages.

Using AOL Search to Find All Sorts of Addresses

Why search for a person's street address or e-mail address the old-fashioned way? On the Web it's usually faster, and you're never restricted to those heavy books with the torn pages. White Pages and Yellow Pages on the Net are merely databases of millions of names; as in familiar phone books, White Pages provide listings of individuals, while Yellow Pages provide listings of businesses. Unlike the phone books, the Web gives access to addresses for entire *countries* (not just your city or county). They also stay more or less up-to-date (unlike the white and yellow pages), since they are updated several times a year. And when you do find an e-mail address online, using e-mail saves you postage or a phone call.

AOL's Internet-based *people finders*, as they're called, help you track down e-mail addresses and street addresses. Both are available from the main page of AOL Search, shown previously in Figure 7-1. AOL's White Pages, powered by Infospace.com, is shown in Figure 7-7.

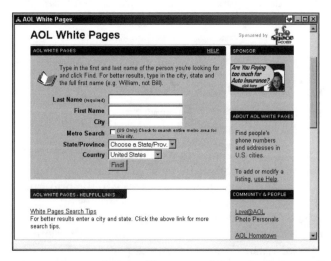

Figure 7-7. Here's where I would start to search for my brother's new address . . .

Because so much information can be dynamically retrieved on the Web, for anyone you find through the White Pages, you also find additional links such as driving directions to that person's house, a neighborhood map, and local pharmacies and pizzerias (Figure 7-8). You can send that person a message or greeting card, too, often at a small fee. Don't forget Keyword: **American Greetings**, mentioned in Chapter 10.

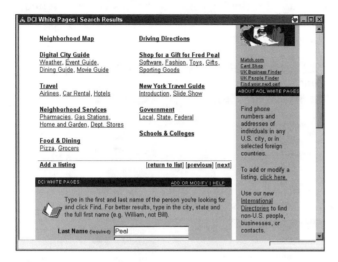

Figure 7-8. . . . and find out enough information to surprise him with a pepperoni pizza

Looking for someone overseas? AOL Search offers you a link to International Directories (you'll have to scroll down a bit), each devoted to a country and made available by Infospace.com or one of the national telephone companies. All the national directories are also available from a simple drop-down list when you use the AOL White Pages Directory.

AOL People Directory

The Internet White Pages are based on publicly available address listings, much like (often the same as) your phone book. Looking for someone on AOL? Just go to Keyword: **People Directory** and do a search. This directory can be searched only on AOL and contains profiles only for members who choose to create them.

As an AOL member you can make available your profiles, with info about your hobbies, computers, job, marital status, favorite quotes, etc. At Keyword: **People Directory**, click My Profile to create or modify your own profile. As always, it is unwise for minors to provide personal or contact information.

Finding E-Mail Addresses

Tip

Maps are available while doing White Page, Yellow Page, and e-mail searches; they're also available by simply clicking Maps (under Other Searches) at Keyword: **Search**.

AOL Search's tool for finding e-mail addresses can be fetched by clicking E-Mail Finder from AOL Search's main page (see Figure 7-9).

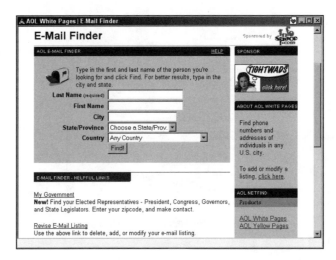

Figure 7-9. AOL's Maps & Directions: part of the driving directions for getting between two street addresses several hundred miles apart. Not shown are the beginning or ending points, or the overview map.

The e-mail finders are *not* based on publicly available databases. Instead, they collect people's e-mail addresses over several years, with the help of many people and companies. E-mail addresses can also be voluntarily added and electronically culled from other sources. In this catch-as-catch-can world of e-mail indexing, you may have less luck searching for e-mail addresses than you do searching for the real addresses of the same people. When you do find e-mail addresses, you may be finding old as well as new addresses, since the database has no way of knowing which addresses are new and currently in use. Like the White Pages, you can modify or hide your own e-mail address.

Using AOL Search's Yellow Pages

Online Yellow Pages offer all the advantages of white pages, and then some. While White Pages are always alphabetized by name, business pages tend to be alphabetized by category

(Insurance, Pets, etc.). As a result, you can do online searches for a category of businesses (like Pet Supplies or Pet Training) *and* search for a business by name, if you know the name. You can also screen businesses by location, so you don't get listings for three states' worth of businesses (as you can with the old, paper yellow pages) but only businesses of a certain type within driving distance from you.

Did someone say driving? It can be useful to get both a map of your destination and directions. With the maps provided, you can zoom in and out to get more local detail, or less. You need to play around to find the most useful view of a location. *Useful* depends on whether you need general orientation (planning the trip) or local intersections when you get close to your destination, or both. When you're satisfied with the perspective, click the appropriate link to get the driving directions. Use Ctrl-P to print the map. AOL's Yellow Pages come to you courtesy of both Big Yellow and Super Pages.

To see an aerial *photograph* of your destination, you can search for terraserver in AOL search. You'll find the official site in the list of recommended sites, which uses USGS data and declassified Russian images of almost every community and street in the U.S.

Roadmaps Have Never Been This Much Fun

It's also helpful to find a destination in order to estimate the time it will take to get somewhere or to do some route planning. This little tool is a godsend for those who are either wary of asking directions or can't remember directions when they have asked.

From AOL Search, Maps & Directions gives you a world of maps and driving directions. Figure 7-9, for example, shows every turn of the road between two addresses in different states (the starting and ending points are not shown here). You're not limited to your local area; you can get local maps for every square mile of the United States. It's easy to imagine the service being offered, someday, for the entire world.

A Quick Look Back

This chapter introduced the wonderful and indispensable subject of searching the Net (especially the Web). It looked at

7

Finding Your Way

► Why searching is a pain: there are too many pages, and most are in existence only briefly.

► Why AOL Search is a good solution: all the sites in the directory are hand-selected; the directory is searchable as well as browsable; your search includes AOL areas as well as the Web sites; your queries are easy to construct and easy to refine; power searches can be created in many ways; and you can extend your search, and do related searches, in many useful ways.

The next chapter introduces some of the non-AOL tools you can use to do both general and special-purpose Internet research. All these tools are available through AOL, of course.

C H A P T E R

8

FROM BREADTH TO DEPTH:
SEARCH ENGINES AND
SPECIALIZED SEARCHES

Chapter 8

From Breadth to Depth: Search Engines and Specialized Searches

The Web is literally crawling with excellent search engines. These sites comb millions of Web addresses and keep track of the words and other content contained at each address. These self-styled *portals*–gateways to the Internet–have all sorts of advanced search features, specialized directories, personal finance calculators, chat communities, and personalized Web services. Fierce competition among the portals drives them to do the same sort of things to attract subscribers and visitors, making for a certain sameness in what they actually do. Each engine does offer strengths and special features worth getting to know.

AltaVista

Once owned by computer maker Digital, subsequently a part of Compaq, now the latest subsidiary of an Internet investment firm, AltaVista has always featured a large, fast database–the most important features of any search engine. See Figure 8-1.

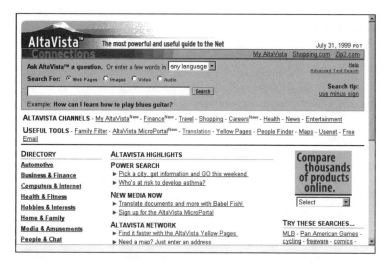

Figure 8-1. AltaVista features built-in Web filters, a translation service, useful advanced search options, and the opportunity to search for images, sounds, and video. (*Reproduced with the permission of AltaVista. AltaVista and the AltaVista logo are trademarks of AltaVista Company.*)

AltaVista also offers a number of novel services to enhance your search.

▶ AltaVista's translation service, available from its main window, lets you translate back and forth between English and (currently) five foreign languages. Why would you want such a thing? A translator can help you figure out the correct words to include for searches for non-English information.

▶ For normal searches, AltaVista tries to extract recognized phrases from the words you enter.

▶ AltaVista's Family Filter screens out inappropriate Web pages. With the filter turned on (by clicking a link), inappropriate or offensive pages can't be displayed.

8

From Breadth to Depth

Tip

Both Netscape Navigator and Microsoft Internet Explorer bring together many engines and simplify their use. See Chapter 6 on Netscape.

Cross-Reference

Netscape Navigator's Smart Browsing and Internet Keywords, discussed in Chapter 6, provide similar flexibility by allowing you to use *your* terms to frame a search instead of a *computer's* terms. In other words, you ask questions instead of queries.

▶ AltaVista multimedia finder, offered in cooperation with Corbis (a commercial service), lets you search for 15 million image, audio, and video files. Some of these files can be used free; others require a licensing fee. Click the Images, Audio, or Video buttons just above the search box on AltaVista's opening page.

AskJeeves

No fancy queries are required to get good results from AskJeeves. Of the non-AOL engines, only Google, described in a few pages, makes searching easier. AskJeeves fields about a million *questions*, a day, according to a newspaper story published when the company recently started trading on Wall Street.

AskJeeves, shown in Figure 8-2, encourages you to ask questions in plain language, instead of converting them into the terse and finicky questions only a computer could love. For example, I asked Jeeves "Where can I buy hats online?" AskJeeves' answers usually come back in two parts. The top part attempts to fit my question into familiar, sometimes already-asked questions. (Jeeves doesn't always do well with this kind of shoe-horning.)

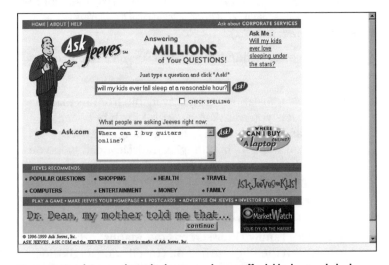

Figure 8-2. AskJeeves, the Web's best trained, most affordable, least surly butler

In this case, the second set of results, lower on the page, points me to some shopping sites. This part of the window shows the results after your question is run through several search engines, including Excite and AltaVista. Because engines vary in so many ways, the ability to compare the findings of different sites gives you a broader range of sites from which to choose than if you had just chosen a single engine. It's amazing to see how the same question will produce such different results in different engines–and a good reason not to settle quickly on an alternative to AOL Search.

Excite lets you exclude adult content (like AltaVista's Family Filter) to keep the kids from searching for materials that parents might object to.

Excite

Excite offers what you expect from a self-respecting index: easy-to-use directories, easy-to-browse maps, white and yellow pages, and news stories, plus AOL-style messaging tools.

One good reason to use Excite is the collection of advanced Web-searching options. You can specify what is searched (Web titles or summaries), how many pages are displayed per window, what kind of domain to search (COM, EDU, etc.), and in what language to search. I also like Excite's joint search of its directories and its index. For any query you get a small set of Excite's hand-picked resources (directory) and less-selective set of "Web results" (index). Another bonus: Excite's advanced options also let you use drop-down lists to construct complex queries, with numerous ANDs, ORs, AND NOTs. AOL AOL Search, essentially the same as Excite, supports all this fancy stuff, but you need to type in the ANDs yourself.

Google Breaks the Mold

Google is an experimental search engine that will probably be better known by the time this book is available. Netscape Netcenter (http://home.netscape.com/escapes/search/) now offers Google as one of its major search options. Most engines automate the process of going page to page and keeping track of what words are used at which Web sites. When you do a search for a word, the engine returns the Web page's name and address. Simple–when it works.

Google's approach is different. Do a search, and Google returns not just pages that contain certain words. It also returns only pages *that are linked to by other pages*. Instead of working mechanically, it begins with the human reality that the

Note

A *google*, by the way, is the number one followed by 100 zeroes, the probable market valuation of the company in a few years.

Tip

Notice the funky *I'm Feeling Lucky* button? Click that button to forget all the search stuff and go directly to the first item that would be returned by a Google search in response to your query. That's how confident they are.

Note

HotBot uses a research-based database technology offered by a company called Inktomi. AOL has announced plans to offer an Inktomi-based search service that will provide specialized multimedia and foreign-language searches; it will also allow users to personalize searches by setting preferences, which the system will remember.

good, authoritative, and useful pages are the ones that other people point to in their pages. It also looks for pages that serve as hubs–the most popular pages *from which* people browse to related pages. The approach makes sense because it's based on the actual browsing habits of millions of people.

Figure 8-3 shows the results of a Google search for "assistive technology."

Figure 8-3. Google helps you identify the pages that others visit (*Google, Inc.*).

With Google, you use quotes to indicate phrases, but you don't have to use ANDs or plus signs. Google currently always assumes you're using AND–an intelligent assumption. When you get results, you can click the bar (see Figure 8-2) to see a list of pages linking to this page.

HotBot

Recently acquired by Lycos and offered as part of the Lycos Network, HotBot still has its own URL (www.hotbot.com) but now can also be found on Lycos's home page as well. Lycos is described later in the chapter.

A large number of useful and some unusual services is available from HotBot's top level, including an FTP search (see Chapter 16 for more on FTP and Lycos's Search FTP). At the window's bottom, look for other the Wired Web sites also sold to Lycos, like HotWired (an Internet classic), Wired News (for edgy politics), and WebMonkey (devoted to Web development).

Infoseek

Infoseek is part of a larger web of partnerships, with Disney at the center. Its Web holdings now go under the moniker "Go Network," a bundle of sites that includes ESPN.COM (sports), Disney.com (family), Mr. Showbiz (entertainment), and ABCNews.com (news).

Like AltaVista, Infoseek now has its own filtering system to protect children from obnoxious content (GoGuardian). Like HotBot, it offers a large number of filters for specifying the Web sites you want, letting you slap together complex searches and specify where to search (what domain), how many pages to show, what countries to search, etc. New to Infoseek is an AltaVista-like translator, letting you turn a query in one language into another. You can even translate entire foreign Web sites into English!

LookSmart

Looksmart creates custom directories, which it licenses to other companies, Internet service providers, and even search engines (such as AltaVista). LookSmart provides an attractive window on its million or so hand-picked and well-categorized Web sites. While the Netscape Open Directory Project (below) encourages anyone to select and rate sites, LookSmart encourages Web builders to submit their URLs directly.

Lycos

Like AltaVista, Lycos offers a special area if you need to search for multimedia files, including MP3 files. With some 80,000 images of its own, Lycos can also search the Web's tens of millions of image files. Also like AltaVista, Lycos has its own built-in filter (SearchGuard–no, it's not for protecting new sofas), to keep kids from viewing nasty stuff.

A feature that sets apart Hotbot is its support of searches for different kinds of media and files, such as images, video, JavaScript, Shockwave, RealAudio, and even MP3. For some of these you'll have to use Advanced Search (which just means more detailed filters).

Say you do a search and pull up a Web page. At first the page appears to have nothing to do with what you were looking for. *Does* it have anything to do with what you were looking for? To find out whether it even *contains* the word you were searching, use AOL's Find box, always available by pressing Ctrl-F. Type in the query word and click Find. The stand-alone Netscape and Microsoft browsers also support Ctrl-F.

Netscape Open Directory

Netscape's answer to Yahoo, the Net's big directory, is the new Open Directory Project, whose "goal is to produce the most comprehensive directory of the Web by relying on a vast army of volunteer editors." Currently more than 15,000 editors contribute site reviews to Open Directory's more than 100,000 categories.

Using a group of widely distributed volunteers fits very well with the Internet culture: it's a large project, based on volunteer effort, whose goal is to contribute something clearly better than existing resources yet free to everyone in the network community. If you have the time and want to share your expertise, you can sign up to be an editor at the Netscape site by following the links from the home page (http://www.dmoz.org). Editors exercise their judgment in both their choice of sites and in the few words used to characterize those sites.

Open Directory has a fairly deep hierarchy of sites. The at symbol (@) indicates a subcategory of sites; a plain link indicates a site. At the bottom of every window, in good ecumenical Internet fashion, you can run the same search on another engine, such as Excite.

Northern Light

Two things set Northern Light apart. First, you can search specific data collections (as opposed to the entire World Wide Web). Second, Northern Light presents results in a highly usable format. Results are grouped in special folders, arranged by subject, data type (e.g., press release), source (e.g., Web), and language. This makes it easier to get an overview of your results than in other engines. Arrangement into resource types acts as a power filter, helping you quickly identify the best resources.

Yahoo

The first popular directory is today probably the biggest such service. This large and professionally compiled directory — they won't reveal their exact size or growth rate — can be searched as well as browsed.

Among Yahoo's services: two dozen international subject directories; special icons for new, reviewed, or cool sites; intra-category searches; a (real) magazine; advanced searches of the Yahoo directory so you can string together complex queries and specify how recent pages must be (from a day to three years).

Find It Online

For a single page, with a ton of useful and a few weird links, check out ICQ's Cool Links page (http://www.icq.com/coollinks/).

The Art of Asking

No matter which engine you use, the following general tips can help you get good results. In AOL AOL Search, AOL Search, and in every search engine, look for a **Help** link to get tips for using that particular service; they all differ in required and recommended search "syntax," the rules for stringing together queries. The noteworthy search-engine meta sites (www.searchenginewatch.com and www.not-ess.com/search) include excellent comparative reviews of sites, with comparison of features and estimates of their size as measured by pages indexed. Here are some general guidelines for asking good questions:

▶ **What do you want to know?** Be clear about what you want to know and whether the Web is the best place to start. If you want to tap opinions and expertise (for example, get advice on buying a piano or choosing a college), perhaps a newsgroup or mailing list search makes more sense–a place where you can ask detailed personal questions of others, and then ask follow-up questions (Chapters 12 and 13 on lists and newsgroups).

▶ **What specific words convey what you want to find out?** What series of specific words convey your topic? Use all these different words in the same query, from most specific to least specific.

▶ **Use ANDs.** Most engines recognize AND, which requires a pair of words or phrases, or word and phrase, to be present. Some recognize the plus and minus signs that require a single word or phrase to be present (or, in the case of the minus sign, insist on its absence). Others interpret a space between words in your query as an AND or an OR. Each engine's Help page can tell you who supports what.

8

From Breadth to Depth

Tip

The meta searches support engines with different syntax--they differ, for example, in whether they take AND, what spaces mean, and how they handle capital letters and common words. Your queries must thus be a bit simpler if you want to use the meta-searchers effectively.

▶ **Avoid empty words.** *The, and, in,* etc. are ignored by many search engines, even in phrases like "The United States of America."

▶ **Check spelling.** Some engines give you some latitude if you've misspelled something; others take you at your word and give you just what you asked for.

▶ **Refine, review**. Run another query. When you finally start to turn up valuable sites, use a "Show more like this" link if it's available (as in AOL AOL Search and Excite). If your search didn't turn up anything at all or anything relevant, think of synonyms and also think of additional words or painfully specific words.

▶ **Still not successful?** Try your luck with another engine–or several, using a "meta" engine, as described in "Doing Many Searches at Once." Or (my personal choice) look for a specialized site devoted to your topic (see "Specialized Searching").

Doing Many Searches at Once

Famous for letting you ask questions in "natural language," AskJeeves does its work by feeding your query to many search engines at the same time (see "AskJeeves" above). Notable for its personality and ease of use, AskJeeves is just one of many *meta* search engines out there, referring to sites that search several engines at once.

Meta-searches exploit the fact that search engines differ. They crawl the Web differently, keep indexes of different size, and rank words differently. Searching several at once amounts to scattershot, but still tends to turn up something valuable.

The following meta search sites differ in the engines searched, the options (filters) provided, and the way results are presented. Just as in the case of the individual search engines, the meta search engines require that you play around with them until you've found one that works for you.

DogPile

With its endearing name, DogPile, shown in Figure 8-4, has some pretty formidable advantages (www.dogpile.com).

Currently it searches 25 engines of all kinds. The process is simple: choose *what* to search (Web, Usenet–i.e., newsgroups, FTP, White Pages, etc.) and type in your *query* for that type of resource. DogPile relies on the biggies, as well as less well-known Web searchers like Thunderstone. In addition to the Web, DogPile rifles through FTP sites looking for files to download (more about FTP in Chapter 16), newsgroup postings, and a lot more. The custom search lets you pick the engines you want, in the order you want. Results are presented in a continuous list rather than within a separate window for each engine.

Figure 8-4. DogPile presents an admirably simple view of a wide range of search tools.

MetaCrawler

One of the oldest meta searchers, MetaCrawler is now part of Go2Net, Inc., a Seattle Internet company (www.go2net.com/). MetaCrawler scours the major search engines (such as Lycos, Infoseek, Excite, AltaVista, Looksmart, and Yahoo) on your behalf. *Minicrawler* is a conveniently tiny window for entering your queries (*convenient* because MetaCrawler's home page is overcrowded with directories, yellow pages, ads, and other distractions).

MetaSearch: All4One

MetaSearch differs from the DogPile and MetaCrawler in presenting results of multiple queries in separate frames in a

Specialized search sites used to be (and still are) a labor of love, often undertaken by experts; such is the origin of the WWW Virtual Library, discussed below. Specialized search sites have been so expensive to do and maintain that they have become commercial undertakings or at least accept sponsorships. As with any information resource, with *collections* of resources, make sure to find out who is behind the effort, how current it is, and whether it is comprehensive.

window (http://all4one.com/). Although these frames make for a cluttered appearance, it can be a big help to know exactly where a result came from and to refine it *within* that engine. Frames can be easily maximized, or resized by clicking and dragging.

Web Sleuthing

For research at school or work, or for searches that require authoritative results, it can be useful to search specific databases, directories, and sites otherwise devoted to your topic. Here's how they work: instead of doing your search within the world of *all* Internet resources, they narrow the scope. You don't start with mechanically harvested, blindly indexed pages, but with resources selected by experts and often based on real-word library resources. Some such services are, in fact, created by libraries, hence sensitive to serious information needs. The best ones consist of searchable and browsable collections of resources, in any format, usually compiled by experts and arranged in a way that makes sense for the audience and the subject matter.

Specialized Search Collections

Just as the meta-search engines like MetaCrawler let you do multiple searches, a number of sites have sprung up to collect and search specialized sites.

Here are three awesome collections of this kind, two non-commercial directories of hand-picked and authoritative sites, and a commercial site that pulls together thousands of searchable specialized Web sites.

A Collection of Special Search Engines

From the Library of Leiden University in the Netherlands comes **A Collection of Special Search Engines**, a very long listing of "discipline- or subject-specific" and even a few "national or regional search engines" (www.leidenuniv.nl/ub/biv/specials.htm). Not elegant in appearance, its content is gold. The Collection is organized by subject. Some items include a few descriptive words highlighting unusual features; most don't. Clicking links opens pages in a separate browser, so the Collection itself is always available.

Don't assume starchy and academic listings. Included in the Leiden Collection are more than a dozen specialized sites for people looking for MP3 resources (a music format discussed in Chapters 5 and 17), and there's a Games category as well. The Collection includes a thorough overview of Internet resources dealing with searching itself.

Digital Librarian

Digital Librarian is the one-woman work of Margaret Anderson, a librarian in Cortland, New York (`www.servtech.com/~mvail/`). With its 100 or so categories arranged into a conveniently compact interface (Figure 8-5), the Digital Librarian avoids the commercial directories with more layers than a wedding cake. Instead of burrowing down five levels, you choose from the longish list of librarian-vetted main categories and get longish lists of choice resources for that category. Each list is alphabetized, of course, and almost every individual listing is sufficiently annotated to give you a sense of what's there. Ms. Anderson uses a special icon to denote new resources as she adds them. She maintains the site almost daily.

Figure 8-5. Digital Librarian, a heroic effort to catalog the most useful resources in more than 100 subjects © *1996-1999. A Librarians Choice of the Best of the Web. All rights reserved. May not be copied or mirrored without written permission.)*

iSleuth

Note

Families are not the only group with their own mega-sites. Women, for example, have communities such as Electra (Keyword: **Electra**), Women's Wire (www. women.com), and iVillage (www.electra.com). Seniors have Third Age (www. thirdage.com), AARP (www.aarp.org), and SeniorNet (Keyword: **SeniorNet**).

This commercial site brings together more than 3,000 searchable (hence *big*) Web sites that can be each searched from this site (the new address is www.bighub.com/). For example, under Recreation at iSleuth, you can get direct access to the searchable Web sites, Juggler's World and Skating the Infobahn. ISleuth also lets you do general Web search using any (or all) of the huge engines, or do newsgroup searches using DejaNews.

Many categories contain subcategories. Under News you can do specialized searches of specific *magazines* (*Atlantic Unbound, Life, the Nation, Wired,* etc.) or *newspapers* from many states in the U.S. For every resource you can link to the home page (of the magazine or newspaper, say) and putter around there. Or, do a search *from within iSleuth.* The results come up within the pointed-to database, not iSleuth. In other words, iSleuth is a starting point. You continue and refine your searches in the pointed-to megasites.

Family-Friendly Finding

One type of specialized search resource focuses not primarily on content but on the needs of a particular audience. Families, for example, are increasingly well served with their own search sites. Central to the family is the appropriateness of what kids can view.

How can young people learn to integrate the Internet into the worlds of fun and learning without being exposed to obscenity, Nazism, and other obnoxious stuff on the Web? The industry has grappled with the core problems of child safety in many ways:

▶ By devising technologies for offline browsing (such as WebWhacker, discussed in Chapter 17)

▶ By controlling what children can retrieve from the general-purpose engines (filtered searches)

▶ By creating hand-picked directories of kid-appropriate sites

Schools are grappling with the issue by teaching kids, earlier than parents might prefer, how to distinguish for themselves to identify and avoid trash and to learn the difference between opinion and fact. Here are a couple of kid-friendly search sites:

▶ **Searchopolis** (www.searchopolis.com/), an Inktomi-powered engine that offers special features, an inviting but not childish design, and filtered search. The major search engines also offer filtered searches: **AltaVista's Family Filter, Lycos's SearchGuard,** and **Infoseek's Go Guardian** ™ (see Figure 8-6).

▶ **AskJeeves for Kids** (www.ajkids.com/) wins the charm award in its Jr. edition. Nasty queries can't even be entered, and the sites searched do not include any included on the list of sites blocked by SafeSurf, a major filtering service. Another kid-friendly feature: entries can be spell-checked.

▶ **AOL's Search for Kids Only**, a click away from AOL Search (http://www.aol.com/aolsearch/kids/home.html), combines an engine that searches only safe sites and a directory of top-quality sites arranged in categories like Explore, Sports, and Interact.

▶ A relative newcomer is the compelling bright searchable directory created by the Information Please people, the **Infoplease Kids' Almanac** (http://kids.infoplease.com/).

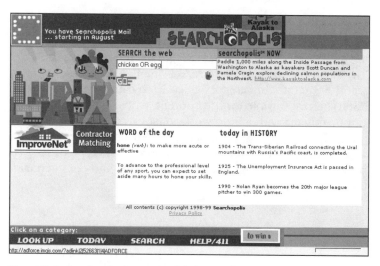

Figure 8-6. Searchopolis: Designed with kids in mind

The Most Authoritative Specialized Directories

Does "authoritative" sound dull? Think of it this way: do you want doctors making surgical decisions based on literature that is not peer reviewed? Highly subjective introductions to major disabilities? Lawyers engaging in fuzzy thinking about law? Illogical and unreadable introductions to HTML and Web design? Yesterday's political news? Probably not. There are in fact times when you must have reliable, authoritative information.

The WWW Virtual Library (VIRTUAL LIBRARY): Subject Matter Experts Weigh In

The Virtual Library (Figure 8-7) calls itself "the oldest catalog of the Web." This brain-child of Tim Berners-Lee, the creator of the Web, is "run by a loose confederation of volunteers, who compile pages of key links for particular areas in which they are expert; even though it isn't the biggest index of the Web, the Virtual Library pages are widely recognized as being among the highest-quality guides to particular sections of the Web." The Virtual Library, which has always been a little hard to find, has finally secured a simple URL (www.vlib.org) and set up a series of mirrors in other countries–identical sites designed to make this important resource easy to access by people in other countries.

The Virtual Library consists of both a newer *subject* list, an up-to-date and compact arrangement, and an older, more detailed list of almost 300 lower-level *categories*. In searching the Virtual Library, make sure to search the links database, and not just the database of category titles. Each category has a "virtual librarian" responsible for the content, whose e-mail address can be dug up with a little work; most categories claim to be regularly updated. A special benefit of Virtual Library is the arrangement of resources by both content and type of resource and the pulling together of scholarly and commercial information resources.

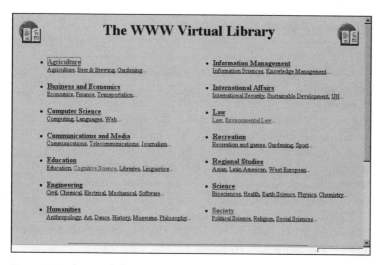

Figure 8-7. The Virtual Library: Dog-eared and worth your time

Argus Clearinghouse: Librarians Rate the Net

Easier to navigate and more cleanly designed than the Virtual Library, the Argus Clearinghouse grew out of a collective project undertaken in the early 1990s by library science students of Louis Rosenfeld's at the University of Michigan (www.clearinghouse.net/). Each student or researcher (and the countless people who have kept the project going) would prepare a guide to all the Net resources about a specific topic.

Since the early 1990s the Clearinghouse staff has been evaluating *those* guides, using a 1 to 5 rating scale applied to several factors. A special strength of both the Virtual Library and the Clearinghouse is the attempt to include all types of Net resources: not just Web sites, but also mailing lists and newsgroups (and more). Today, as with the Virtual Library, anyone can take part in the Clearinghouse and submit a guide to Internet resources on a well-defined topic. Less than 10% of guides submitted to Argus are accepted, however, and all accepted guides are rated before they're published at the Argus site. For you this means that the guides are top-drawer, selective guides to the best Internet resources about highly focused subjects.

8

From Breadth to Depth

Specialized Search Sites

Start your health-related voyages at AOL's Health channel, which guides you to the major specialized health resources. DrKoop.com, the Web venture created by the former Surgeon General, is AOL's authoritative source of health information. See Figure 8-18.

AOL has long offered Medline at Keyword: **Medline**. Many health-related Web sites now offer this authoritative resource as well. Medline consists of a searchable database of information *about* medical journal articles published in the last few years. You don't find the articles themselves online, and those articles tend to be written for specialists, not consumers. On AOL, Better Health, and IntelliHealth, you can order medical articles retrieved through Medline, but a fee often applies. For any serious medical research, Medline is indispensable.

The next two sections look at Health and Legal resources, two very practical areas where it can be extremely expensive *not* to be informed. Being informed is not just digging up a Web site or two, but also having access to experts, people with experience, access to the resources of leading organizations, and a context for understanding *your* information needs. Net resources on health and the law can also help you choose the lawyers and doctors who make the most sense given your needs and budget; without the Net, it can take luck and time to choose the right professionals. With this kind of Internet information, you'll be able to ask the right questions and know what is happening to you.

Health: Specialized Resources

Most people have concerns about their own health, or at least the health of their kids, spouses, and parents. Focused medical resources proliferate on the Web, and the following examples serve only to point to trends in such resources, not necessarily make recommendations.

Johns Hopkins' IntelliHealth site (www.intellihealth.com) provides another one-stop source of solid information, from one of the world's leading medical centers.

HealthAtoZ (Health A to Z) has been another strong contender in the increasingly crowded Internet health field for several years (www.healthatoz.com). HealthAtoZ provides many examples of the advantages of the Internet over traditional information sources: it's always available, of course; it claims to be, and seems to be, up to date; it provides services that supplement the value of the rich data it makes available; and it's interactive, meaning that you can take part in message boards and chat to learn things from other people. In its Health Center, for example, articles for certain groups (like expectant moms) put Web sites in context. More than 50,000 health-related Web sites are recommended or rated at this site.

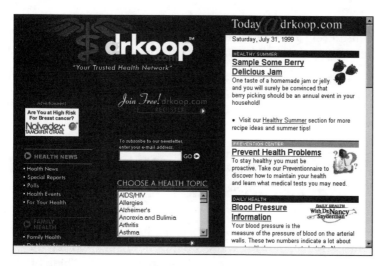

Figure 8-8. DrKoop.com, the authoritative guide to health.

Law: Specialized Resources

Law, like medicine, is one of those areas of life where expertise is often well-rewarded and professional service can be unavoidable and expensive.

Many consider FindLaw the hands-down best place to start looking for law information (www.findlaw.com). A winner of Argus Clearinghouse's Digital Librarian award for outstanding information guide, FindLaw has grown so big, so fast that it has come to serve a broad range of users, including consumers, law students, paralegals, small businesses, and law firms of all sizes.

Consumers can find very thorough guidelines for finding and interviewing lawyers, then formalizing an agreement with one. Included on FindLaw is an online copy of the Consumer Handbook, a compendium of useful information about your rights as a consumer (credit, lemon laws, phone fraud, "distance shopping," etc.).

If you are a small business, FindLaw gives you free information about such issues as employee benefits, intellectual property, credit and collections, unfair practices, and dealing with the government. Selected Web sites throw light on every aspect of forming, running, growing, and dissolving a business.

Tip

Places like HealthAtoZ don't try to take the place of your healthcare specialist. Instead, you can get information about disorders, get advice for staying well, and gather the facts you need to ask the questions that can help you get the best medical care, whether you want traditional oncology or alternative medicine.

Tip

FindLaw seems to be everyone's favorite, but the Virtual Library provides guides to an even broader spectrum of legal resources on the Internet. Indiana University's law school hosts the Virtual Law Library, and IU continues to maintain this rich resource (http://www.law.indiana.edu/law/v-lib/lawindex.html). Its list of search tools and comprehensive legal sites numbers around 40 items, of which FindLaw is just one. What sets FindLaw apart is the number of people using the service, which creates the framework for an active and knowledgeable community supporting informative chats, mailing lists, and message boards.

Note

If you're not a lawyer and have no idea how a case travels through the system and up to the Supreme Court, you'll find basic information about the U.S. legal system at FindLaw.

Find It Online

The non-legislative branches of the federal government and all levels of government make aggressive use of the Internet in their efforts to cut costs and communicate with their various publics. For the federal government's executive branch, start at FedWorld (http://www.fedworld. gov/). For state and local government, start with the Library of Congress's directory (http://lcweb.loc. gov/global/state/stategov. html).

Tip

AOL does more than provide directory and search directories. It has created its own specialized directories such as Government Guide (http://www.government-guide.com). This well-arranged, annotated guide to federal Internet resources is a click away from AOL Search.

If you are a lawyer yourself, or a paralegal, or legal librarian, or considering a career in law, turn to FindLaw to learn about law schools, connect with others, or get a more challenging job.

Start with FindLaw to learn about online copyright issues and other aspects of the emerging law of the Internet.

From Libraries on the Web to Digital Libraries

Hundreds of years of book publishing have made the library indispensable. In many ways, the Internet has supported the work of libraries and made books more accessible. Think of Amazon.com, for example, or the hundreds of libraries whose catalogs are now searchable on the Internet (increasingly over the Web). Some visionaries anticipate a flood of books being published in an electronic format, with multimedia enhancements, globally searchable, and accessible from anywhere.

Library Catalogs on the Web

Where the Net can't retrieve books and documents, it can make short work of your library searches, letting you search libraries in your hometown or practically anywhere. You can't actually take out books in most case, yet, but you can

▶ Create a bibliography for school or work

▶ Find out what's current in any field

▶ Find out who wrote what, when

In addition to all this book research, you can, of course, buy books still in print and many books out of print, using an online bookstore like Amazon.com or Barnes and Nobel (Keyword: **BN**). Amazon's recent purchase of Bibliofind, a massive database of used books, will make it simpler and considerably faster to find rare, old, and out-of-print books.

Searching a library's Web catalog is easier than searching the entire Web, because you're searching one place only for a special kind of thing, a book, and a book has some standard features (such as author, title, and subject).

Figure 8-9 shows a search of the National Library of Medicine for information about Alzheimer's disease. A search for books alone uncovered almost 400 items. I could also have searched for authors who have written on the disease or journals devoted to it. Using such services is a great way to save time *before leaving home*. Such searches indicate which libraries have what you need and whether particular volumes are currently on the shelf and ready to be used.

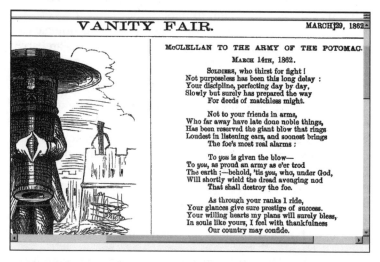

Figure 8-9. Results of a library search on the Web. Click an item to see whether it's on the shelf!

It's not just the big government libraries that offer free services like this. A public library in Cape Cod has created a list of more than 500 U.S. libraries that can be searched by the Web (`www.capecod.net/epl/public.libraries.html`); there's probably one such library close to where you live. Many library search sites include many useful searchable databases, as well as online catalogs. Loitering and whispering are not discouraged.

Digital Libraries

The first publishing ventures on the Internet involved the re-publication of the text versions of out-of-print, public domain books. **Project Gutenberg** goes back to 1971, when the project grew out of some unique circumstances and a brainstorm by a gentleman named Michael Hart. (You can read the remarkable history and find out how to volunteer for the ongoing project at `http://promo.net/pg/`.) The project's purpose has been to publish text versions of classic books in their original languages. Herman Melville, Edith Wharton, Anton Chekhov, Agatha Christie, Omar Khayyam–at the end of the millennium the list is closing in on the 2,000th free electronic volume.

The same sort of project, with heavy underwriting, is **Project Perseus** at Tufts, which aims to publish the classic texts of ancient Greece and Rome in both English and their original languages (www.perseus.tufts.edu/). Of course, they're searchable. The texts are heavily annotated, so you will be able to click any unknown word to track down definitions and allusions.

Archives, too, are very slowly beginning to make the world's record available online. The **University of Michigan's Making of America** (MOA) digital archive, for example, currently holds more than *600,000* individually scanned pages of 19th century American magazines and books. Access to original documents can bring the excitement of discovery to students and history buffs who have never had access to archives. Nothing can better grab the imagination of the most hopelessly bored students of the Civil War.

Major libraries like the **Library of Congress** are beginning to create digital versions of their holdings (the best-known example is the American Memory project). The **Smithsonian Institution** has recently put together a very long list of public libraries that are digitizing their rare holdings and making them available on the Web (`http://www.sil.si.edu/ SILPublications/Online-Exhibitions`). An easy-to-search digital library — a library system for the planet — remains one of those grandiose dreams best left for the 21st century, but the dream may come true sooner than you think.

A Quick Look Back

The Net's not much good if you can't find what you need. This chapter provides some guidelines for finding what you need on the Web. For help finding mailing lists, see Chapter 12; for newsgroups and newsgroup postings, Chapter 13.

The biggest Internet resource, with close to a billion pages, the Web also presents the biggest search problem. No single search engine (list of information about Web addresses and Web content) comes close to indexing all of it.

This chapter provides strategies for making the best of the situation. It included the following:

▶ Reviewed the major non-AOL search engines, emphasizing their specific strengths. **AltaVista**, for example, offers a large index and strong foreign-language support. **HotBot** lets you search for types of content such as Shockwave and RealAudio and provides easy-to-use filters. **Google** restricts the scope of your search to pages that other people seem to consider worthwhile. The **Netscape Open Directory** is building a directory of well-organized sites selected and described by volunteers across the Internet; you can count on a search retrieving valuable resources.

▶ Presented exemplary mega-sites and search sites created just for families, such as **Searchopolis** and **Ask Jeeves for Kids**.

▶ Looked at the specialized sites that successfully provide depth of coverage about a specific area, such as FindLaw and DrKoop.com. You could also get some resources that compile specialized resources, like the **Virtual Library** and **Digital Librarian**.

▶ Introduced the very exciting new world of searchable libraries and digital libraries.

CHAPTER

9

YOU'VE GOT MAIL:
WHAT TO DO WITH THE
E-MAIL YOU RECEIVE

Chapter 9

You've Got Mail: What to Do with the E-mail You Receive

Electronic mail, or e-mail, directly supports everyday communication between you and your colleagues, family, friends, and all the organizations you rely on for support, employment, education, and information. AOL makes it extraordinarily simple to get, send, manage, and embellish your e-mail. This chapter looks at *getting* mail (which is easy) and managing thousands of messages (which AOL *makes* easy). The next chapter turns to sending messages, which is fun: using signatures, smileys, and stationery (and other things) to write e-mail that gets the right kind of attention.

How E-Mail Messages Are Different from Letters

An e-mail message is often compared to a letter, in the letter's favor. However, the way to think of e-mail is not as the electronic version of a letter, but as a different and more flexible thing — something that can't replace the personal letter but can fill an essential communications need not met by letters:

Tip

More proof that AOL makes life easier: You can now buy electronic postage stamps on the Internet. Go to Keyword: **E-stamp** to find out how.

▶ The same e-mail message can be sent effortlessly to many people at the same time, which would be more expensive and even more impersonal by regular mail.

▶ Your AOL e-mail messages can have file attachments at no extra charge.

▶ E-mail is blazing fast.

▶ E-mail cuts your costs.

▶ E-mail can improve communication by allowing for the exchange of messages — a word or two, sometimes — that otherwise would not merit a paper letter but nonetheless do serve to keep lines of communication clear and open between any number of people.

▶ With e-mail, on AOL, you can automatically keep a copy of all messages you send and receive, for as long as you want.

▶ While it's true that e-mail lacks the personality of a letter, the online culture has generated a wide range of ways to express feelings, show off wit, and enhance your message with photos, colors, and other effects, as you'll see in this chapter. Ways of enhancing messages are discussed in Chapter 10.

▶ Finally, it's simply not true that handwritten letters encourage better writing than e-mail messages. Because of the relative starkness of electronic characters and the difficulty (usually) of taking them back, I have noticed a drift toward better and clearer writing in e-mail messages. Message writers often feel that each word counts in e-mail because of the relative absence of context. The words have to be more carefully chosen and the context more explicitly spelled out.

A Word About E-mail Addresses

A mailing list is nothing more than a list of e-mail addresses of people who share an interest of some sort. On the Internet, special software has been developed to automate the processes by which people join lists and by which messages get distributed to everyone else on the list. Chapter 12 has the full story.

To receive e-mail, the sender must know your e-mail address.

Your e-mail address on AOL is your screen name: milesdavis, horselady, vrbsgt, whatever it happens to be. Screen names set up under a master account (the account of the person paying the bills) receive e-mail under those screen names.

▶ If the person sending you a message is on AOL, that person can use the screen name alone, typing it into the Send To box of AOL's Write Mail window.

▶ Anyone not on AOL must add a bit of information to your e-mail address to ensure that it gets to you: an at sign (@) and **aol.com** — stevecase@aol.com, for example (see Figure 9-1). Non-AOL members will use a different e-mail program to send you a message, such as Eudora, Pegasus, or Outlook.

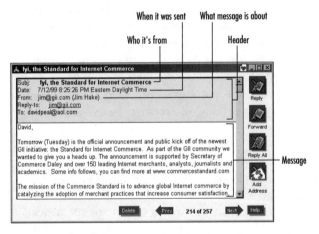

Figure 9-1. A simple message sent from the Internet, hence providing my full @aol.com address

Seen a little more abstractly (you'll see e-mail addresses in many contexts and use them in many ways), an e-mail address identifies both a *person* and the *computer domain* through which the person accesses the Internet.

Domains usually indicate the type of organization providing Internet access. There are all sorts of domains out there. Your domain, aol.com, says two things: your Internet access is

provided by AOL, and AOL is a company (the *.com* part). Other domains, with examples, can be found in Table 9-1.

The parts of a domain proceed from specific to general, from name of organization to type of organization. Each part of a domain name is separated by a period (the famous *dot*). Names of organizations can have several parts, as in listserv.aol, a mailing-list computer at AOL that manages mailing lists, as described in Chapter 12. Likewise, the most general part of the name can have levels, as in co.uk (a company in the United Kingdom) or ky.us (the state of Kentucky in the United States). Note that the major global domains have *three letters* (edu, com, net, mil, and org).

On the Internet, every domain name must be unique, so messages won't get lost in the shuffle. On a domain, every user name must be unique. That's why e-mail from one AOL member to another doesn't require the @aol.com; the message doesn't leave the domain. Within other domains, the same pattern applies.

Doing Mail on AOL

AOL has its own solution to electronic mail: you can read and write e-mail directly from the main AOL window (Figure 9-2).

Write a message

Mail Center Address Book ;
Mail waiting to be sent ; Automatic AOL ; etc.etc.

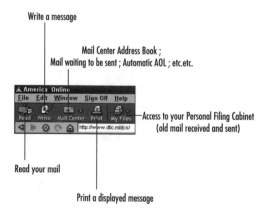

Access to your Personal Filing Cabinet
(old mail received and sent)

Read your mail

Print a displayed message

Figure 9-2. The AOL toolbar has buttons to press to do different things with e-mail messages.

Cross-Reference

Read about AOLMail and AOL Mail (via the PalmPilot) in "New Ways to Do Mail," at the end of this chapter.

Tip

If the icon showing a mailbox on the Welcome Screen shows a raised flag, you've got mail. You'll see this if you have mail you read three weeks ago and kept as new.

Figure 9-3. AOL's Mail Center (Keyword: *Mail Center*) answers those pressing e-mail questions.

With AOL 5.0 you get two additional methods for sending and receiving e-mail:

▶ If you're away from your computer or on the road without a computer, you can access your e-mail (send it and receive it) using just the Web. AOLMail lets a browser simulate the functions of AOL's built-in e-mail. AOLMail has a slightly different look, but the functions are almost identical.

▶ In version 5.0 AOL has allows users of the PalmPilot handheld computer to access their mail by means of a modem and phone line connection — through a special kind of Internet service.

You've Got Mail

How many workaday software features turn into the titles of major Hollywood movies? The You've Got Mail button on the AOL Welcome Screen and the famous voice telling you that "You've Got Mail" were already imprinted in many minds before Meg Ryan and Tom Hanks starred in a movie on electronic romance.

The best way to see if there's anything new, worthwhile, and unread is to open your New Mail list. You can do this in three ways.

▶ Click the You've Got Mail button on AOL's Welcome Screen

▶ Click the Read button on the AOL toolbar

▶ Use the keystroke alternative, Ctrl-R

Up comes an electronic mailbox like the one shown in
Figure 9-4.

Note

In AOL 5.0 you can keep up
to 1,000 messages in your
New and Old mailboxes — a
great many more than you
could before.

Messages new or kept as new

Messages sent in the past month or so

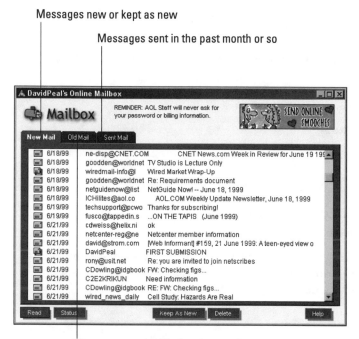

Note

You can keep a message in
your Old Mail list for up to
seven days. To do so, go to
MyAOL ⇨ Preferences ⇨
Mail, and use the "spinner"
(clicking the up and down
arrows to adjust the number)
to set the number of days
from 1 to 7.

Messages received in the past week
(up to seven days) that weren't kept as new

Figure 9-4. The AOL electronic mailbox

Since AOL 4.0, the mailbox has had three tabs. Click a tab to
bring up the corresponding mailbox: New Mail, Old Mail, and
Sent Mail.

▶ **New Mail**: Messages you have either not read or have
read, but decided to Keep As New (that is, kept as a
new message and left in the list).

▶ **Old Mail**: Messages you have read but have neglected
to keep as new and haven't deleted. Messages stay here
only a few days. As long as you opened the message, it
will be available in your Personal Filing Cabinet (assum-
ing you have the preference set up accordingly). This

Tip

As your mailbox starts to overflow, it gets harder and harder to find specific messages, to get the sender's address, to double-check whether you received the message, to make sure you downloaded any attached file, and so on. In any mailbox, you can find specific messages by pressing Ctrl-F, typing in a word or two, and clicking Find. To keep searching, click Find again.

Note

In the New Mail list, your newest messages are at the *bottom* of the list. For your other two mailboxes, messages are listed from most recent at the *top* of the list to oldest, at the bottom.

process is described later in "Using and Managing Your Personal Filing Cabinet."

▶ **Sent Mail**: Copies of the messages you sent in the past month or so.

You'll probably be using the New Mail box most frequently, to keep up with your new messages. In companies, some people check their mail every couple of minutes throughout the day.

For any new message, you get the information provided in Figure 9-5.

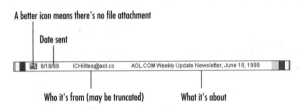

Figure 9-5. Anatomy of a message. Each line describes a single message (can be truncated).

Figure 9-6 shows the various types of messages — unread ones, read ones, ones with inserted figures, and ones with files attached.

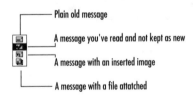

Figure 9-6. Interpreting a message's contents

▶ The next bit of information, to the right of the letter icon, is the *date* when the message was sent to you. Open the message to find out the exact time (Eastern time, usually) the message was sent.

▶ Proceeding to the right, you get the *sender's AOL screen name or Internet e-mail address*. (If you're on a lot of mailing lists — described in Chapter 12 — you'll get messages from something called LISTSERV, a piece of software that automatically distributes mail to the tens or thousands of people on the list.) Long e-mail addresses are chopped off at about 16 characters.

9

You've Got Mail

▶ Finally, the longest bit of information is the *message's subject*, as provided by the person who typed the message. Again, machine-generated messages will have distinctive subjects like *Finance - Internet Daily @ 10/10/99*, indicating in this case the name of the mailing list, the creative use of the at symbol (@), and the newsletter's date.

To open a message, either double-click it or select it and click Read at the bottom of the screen.

Reading Your Mail

Open any message in your New Mail list and you see, first, the *message header*, providing a somewhat fuller set of information than shown in Figure 9-5. Sometimes the person sending the message, when using a non-AOL mail program, can provide two addresses — the address from which the message was sent and the address to which you should reply, if necessary. Using AOL's Mail Preferences, you can make addresses appear as hyperlinks so that you can reply to a linked address by merely clicking it. You'll also see the names and addresses of other people who got the message (the "received a courtesy copy," or CC).

Scroll down to the bottom of the message for a much more complex header, which can provide useful information if you're having messaging troubles and someone at AOL needs to troubleshoot the problem. Otherwise, ignore this jumble of numbers, including a unique message ID (for troubleshooting) and the IP addresses of all the computers through which the message passed on its way to your mailbox.

Managing Your Mail

At home I get so much junk mail (unsolicited commercial stuff) that I usually go through the day's mail at the garbage can, throwing away much more than I keep. That's an example

Tip

At MyAOL ⇨ Preferences ⇨ Mail, you can tell AOL you don't want white headers. Uncheck that preference to set your headers against a grey background (as in Figure 9-1), making it easy to recognize them as headers.

Note

In messages you receive, you increasingly see blue underlined *links*. The meaning of the link varies depending on where you see it. In a header, a link can launch a Write Mail window in which you can reply to a different address than that of the sender's address. In the message body, a link can take you back to AOL content (if the link is in a channel newsletter, for example) or out to the Web. For example, the Scout Report, a weekly review of new Internet sites (see Chapter 12), links you from its weekly mailing to the HTML and PDF versions of the report. Pass your mouse over a link to see the URL.

Tip

Displaying a message is also the quickest way to add an e-mail address to your Address Book. Just click the Add Address button (Figure 9-7), edit the Address Book entry for that address, and click OK. See next chapter for the absorbing details.

Tip

A speedy answer to a message is more respectful than a reply that takes days. If you can't answer someone right away, say something like "I'll get back to you when I find out, thanks."

of *managing mail.* Fortunately, with AOL it's easier to stop junk e-mail than junk paper mail. Managing e-mail takes little work on AOL. You can, of course, keep messages as new, but keeping a lot of messages in your New Mail list means you have to download the entire list of headers from AOL every time you read your new mail!

Effective ways of managing your mail include:

▶ Replying to the person sending the message

▶ Forwarding the message to someone else

▶ Saving the message as a text file for ready reference in the future

▶ Deleting the message

Replying to a Message

The easiest and laziest way to *send* a message (the subject of the next chapter) is simply to reply to a message someone has sent you. This goes for messages sent to you by a friend or by some mailing list software.

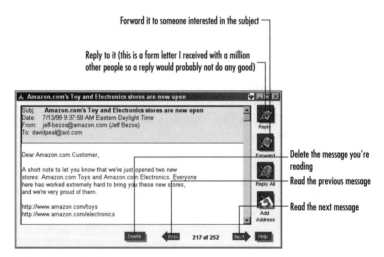

Figure 9-7. Now what? Ways to manage a message.

To reply to a message:

1. First decide if you want to include any of the original message in your response. You would do this in order to provide context for your reply. Use your mouse arrow to highlight any part of the message you want to appear in your reply. Selecting nothing means no part of the original message will be included in your response, which makes sense if two people have full knowledge of the context. Selecting everything keeps the original intact (as forwarding does). You can't select discontinuous passages (a word or sentence here and there), but you can choose a couple of paragraphs and break up the quoted material with several replies of your own.

2. Next, decide who to reply to. To reply to a message someone sent just to you, click the Reply button in the upper right-hand corner of the mail-reading window (shown in Figure 9-7). If you were one of many recipients of the message, as in an informal mailing list for your team at work, click the Reply All button instead of Reply. In either case, if you first selected some text, it will appear "quoted"; each line will be preceded by a greater than sign (> like this) and a space, or the entire selection will be surrounded by AOL quotes (<<like this>).

3. Add a greeting (Hi Jack, for example) if you wish. Type your message: an introduction if you wish (at the beginning) and a reply (after the quoted stuff). If you've selected some text in Step 1, put your words after the quoted material (Figure 9-8). Most people seem to do it that way.

4. Do something with the Subject line if you wish. Doing nothing means the original Subject line will be picked up automatically, preceded by *Re:*. Keeping the Re: retains the message's character (a reply); in brackets or parentheses, you can add a word or two indicating the content of your reply.

   ```
   Re: Able to play volleyball Sat. AM? [you
   bet]
   ```

5. Done? Click Send.

Note

Use your mail preferences to choose "AOL style" quotes (<< >) instead of "Internet style" quotes (preceding each quoted line with a greater than sign and a space (>): MyAOL ⇨ Preferences ⇨ Mail. The difference: Internet quotes set off *each* line but can mess up spacing in some mail programs; the AOL messages enclose the entire quote but can get lost in long quotes. Your choice!

Tip

Use *Forward* to reply to a message when you want to capture the entire original message and also want to avoid mucking up your reply with quote marks. See "Forwarding a Message." Unlike a reply, no e-mail address is automatically picked up in the Send To box in a forwarded message, so you'll have to fill in the sender's address (from memory, the Address Book, or by copying and pasting from the original message).

Re: automatically precides the reply's subject line

Original Subject

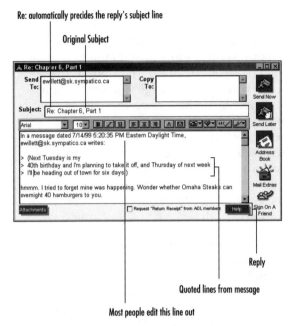

Reply

Quoted lines from message

Most people edit this line out

Figure 9-8. A quoted reply with a follow-up message

Forwarding a Message

In real life, as it's sometimes called, you forward a *postal letter* to someone who used to be at your address but has moved on.

Forwarding an e-mail message isn't quite the same thing. You'd forward a message

▶ To *share its contents.* With nothing in the original message selected, clicking Forward sends the entire message — without quotes — to someone else.

▶ To *reply in a way that retains the entire message intact.* Just remember to type in the address of the original sender in the Send To box.

To forward a message, first display it, then

1. Decide on content. *Select nothing* to forward the entire message. *Select part of the message* to send just that part to someone else. You can't select discontinuous parts of a message. In this scenario the entire forwarded message gets appended

2. Click Forward. Your new message picks up the received message's Subject line, preceded by Fwd: and a space. Edit the Subject line as you see fit. In the body of the message, you'll see nothing if the entire message is to be forwarded (yes, you read that right), or just the passages you selected if that's all you want to forward.

3. Add some words of your own, if you wish, to provide context for the forwarded message. Click Send Now (again, check out the next chapter to read about the strange Send Later button).

On AOL, a forwarded message has two headers: one belongs to *your* message; the other, to the message you are *forwarding*.

Saving a Message as a Text File

Your Personal Filing Cabinet, described later in this chapter, can be set up to automatically save all the messages you receive or send. Sometimes, you may want to save an individual message as a separate file. I do this all the time when I read particularly good contributions to mailing lists or stumble across a list of URLs someone is sharing with other members of the mailing list.

To save a message, display it and then

1. Select File ⇨ Save As.
2. Give the message a name and find a folder in which to keep it. Watch how the title bar of the message changes from the name of the message (that is, its subject) to the name of text file you just created.
3. Click Save.

You can now retrieve the saved message at any time using File ⇨ Open and navigating to the place where the message was saved.

Want to save a part of a message? I do this all the time with my mailing list messages, in order to select a single message

Tip

Mailing lists often include rich information about new Web sites or other info worth saving. Such messages can be saved as separate text files and dropped into a handy folder on your PC for quick reference later (if you remember where they are, of course). Chapter 12 is devoted to mailing lists.

Note

Once upon a time, a message deleted was gone forever. In AOL 5.0, you can restore messages up to 24 hours after deleting them. Go to Mail Center ⇨ Deleted Mail, and from the list of deleted messages, select a message to resuscitate and click the Keep as New button. Next time you open your mailbox, look for the message in your New Mail box.

Tip

If you're reading today's mail, deleting the message you're looking at brings up the next one. Use the Next or Prev key to read the next or previous message.

Note

Any message that is itself greater than about 28K is automatically turned into an attached file on AOL. Most messages are 2-3K. The messages routinely turned into files are mailing list digests, the daily compilations of a list's messages. If a digest has more than about ten messages, it'll exceed AOL's limit. Such attachments usually arrive as simple text and can be read in AOL's text editor or a word processor.

from many messages in the day's digest (Chapter 12 has everything you need to know about digests). To do this trick

1. Select part of a long message, using your mouse. Copy it by pressing Ctrl-c or by right-clicking and selecting Copy.

2. Select File ⇨ New to open up a new document window in AOL's built-in text editor. Paste it by pressing Ctrl-c or by right-clicking and selecting Paste.

3. Give the new document a file name and find an appropriate folder in which to stash it. Keep track of where you store files!

Deleting Messages

You can delete messages you don't want to read, or have read, or are reading and don't want to waste your time with.

To delete a message, highlight it in any of your mailboxes (New, Old, Sent), and click Delete (you can Shift-Click to select many messages in a row or Ctrl-Click to select messages scattered all over the place. Deleting messages is a good way to prevent your mailbox from getting leafy and attracting the unwanted attention of rodents.

Getting Files

What's a file attachment?

Look again at Figure 9-6. The picture of the computer disk clipped to a letter indicates that the e-mail message contains both a message (to read right away) and a file of some kind (to use by downloading the file and using it). Open a message with an attached file, and the header shows you the name of the attached file (including the all-important file extension, which tells you what program you'll need to use the file); the size of the file; and the approximate time it'll take to download (*DL*) the file, given your connection type and modem speed. Figure 9-9 shows these lines of info in a typical message header.

Subj: **Special Event Update and Reminder**
Date: 7/10/99 1:50:03 PM Eastern Daylight Time
From: danielr@early.com (Ronald D. Daniel)

File: panel.doc (33724 bytes)
DL Time (TCP/IP): < 1 minute

Figure 9-9. You've got a file to download; this one is 33,724 bytes (33K) and will take under a minute to download (DL).

To download an attached file

1. With the message displayed, click Download Now. A window comes up warning you about the dangers of downloading files from unknown senders. The informational window is actually worth reading, so check it out. Click Yes to continue with the download. If you have downloaded the file before, a message will ask you whether you want to do so again. Use Download Manager to look for that file. Go to MyFile ⇨ Download Manager, and click the Show Files Downloaded Button. Look for your file (with Ctrl-F if necessary). Select it and click Locate to find out where it is and whether it is still available. Download it again if you want it and it's no longer available.

2. Confirm where you want to save the file and what you want to call it. In Download Manager, you can change the default folder into which files are downloaded. Click Download Preferences. A File Transfer box tracks the file's transfer from AOL to your computer, using both a percentage and a block thermometer box. When the file is on your computer, a little window says "file so and so has been transferred." Click OK.

3. Retrieve the file. It's in the folder where you downloaded it, of course, but in Windows 95/98, a simpler way to get it is from the Start Menu ⇨ Documents list.

Using Downloaded Files

Anything can be attached to a message: a picture (JPG or GIF), a word-processed document (DOC, TXT), a compressed file, several files zipped up in one file (ZIP), or something weird like MIM (a MIME file).

▶ Image files are pretty easy to handle. Usually AOL displays its built-in image view to display an image being downloaded. AOL or Windows displays a simple media

Cross-Reference

Click Download Later to do a "batch" download of several files at once, either on demand or at the end of an AOL session. AOL's Download Manager (MyFiles ⇨ Download Manager) gives you control of this neat little utility. Chapter 17 has more to say about Download Manager; Tom Lichty's AOL Tour Guide goes into much greater detail.

Caution

It's true: don't download files if you don't know their source. Become familiar with the virus information at Keyword: **Virus**. Even DOC (Word) files can contain a so-called Macro virus, which can mess up the way Word displays files.

Tip

You can download only one attached file at a time.

Tip

Mailing list digests usually have the same name, day in and day out. Change the file's name to avoid overwriting (replacing) the last digest you downloaded from the list. (On the other hand, you'll quickly eat up hard-disk space by saving all those large digests.) Try saving digests and individual messages one at a time as separate files, as described above in "Saving a Message as a Text File." Attachments won't be retained forever in your Personal Filing Cabinet.

Note

On AOL, you can now send as well as receive zipped files. See Chapter 10.

player when you're downloading a standard sound file (WAV or AU).

▶ DOC and text (TXT) files can be easily opened in a word processor. Windows 95/98 is usually set up to open a text or word processor when you try to open up these files. Figure 9-9 shows that a DOC file is attached.

▶ You'll frequently see zipped files attached to messages. These files are reduced in size and zipped up into a single file for speedy downloading. First download the file, as normal. If you have a utility like WinZip, double-clicking the file launches the program and shows you a list of the files contained in the zipped file. (If you don't have WinZip, don't worry; Chapter 17 shows you how to get it.) AOL's Download Manager can be set up to automatically unzip files when you sign off, another groovy option discussed in Chapter 17.

▶ Oddball formats like MIM can be handled by WinZip as well. (MIM is an old Internet standard for digitizing binary files in order to transmit them quickly as text over networks.) WinZip can also handle UUencoded (used in newsgroups) and BinHex (Mac) files. Chapter 17 tells you how to get WinZip 7.0.

▶ A PDF file requires Adobe's Acrobat Reader, which is free. Chapter 5 has more to say about these files; they can be used to publish highly formatted documents online, without recoding them in HTML.

Using and Managing Your Personal Filing Cabinet

Your Personal Filing Cabinet (PFC) is your, well, filing cabinet: space on your hard drive to store all your messages, both the ones you've read and ones you've sent — for as long as you want. It also keeps automatic track of downloaded files and newsgroup postings you've downloaded using Automatic AOL (described in the next section). Your PFC is always available, online or offline, at MyFiles ➪ Personal Filing Cabinet.

▶ To activate your PFC, you need to fiddle with your Mail preferences (MyAOL ➪ Preferences ➪ Mail). The fourth and fifth options shown ask whether you want to keep the mail you get and send in your PFC. Make sure there's a check in the boxes, and click OK.

What is PFC? Have a look at Figure 9-10.

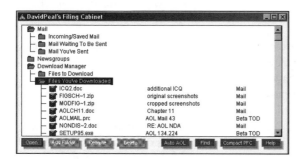

Figure 9-10. Your Personal Filing Cabinet keeps all your messages, files, and postings on your hard drive.

In Figure 9-10 I've closed all the folders just to show PFC's folders. Notice that PFC keeps track of postings and downloaded files as well as messages. Whenever I use Automatic AOL to download mail or newsgroup/board postings, those items go into the appropriate PFC folder, and can be accessed there, online or offline.

PFC has three mail folders in which to store your e-mail messages automatically.

▶ *Incoming/Saved Mail* contains copies of all messages you've received and *opened*; deleted messages won't show up here.

▶ *Mail Waiting to Be Sent* consists of messages you've written but not sent (you've clicked Send Later instead of Send Now from the Write Mail window).

▶ *Mail You've Sent* corresponds to your Sent Mail list.

In all three folders, messages are represented by a single line of information, exactly as in your New, Old, and Sent Mail boxes. As Figure 9-5 shows, for each message you can see whether there's a file attached, when it was sent, who it's from, and what it's about. The one difference between the "live" mailboxes (whose messages are sitting on AOL's comput-

Note

PFC has its own set of preferences, controlling how much space to use (in Mb and in percentage of your hard drive). You can also say whether you want to confirm your decision to delete anything from your PFC (a message will prompt you for the second-guessing). The preferences are tucked away at MyAOL ➪ Preference ➪ Personal Filing Cabinet. Turn off the size limits if you have a large hard drive and want to avoid getting annoying prompts.

Tip

You are not restricted to these three folders; they're just the ones AOL uses automatically to store your mail on your hard drive. To create a new folder for particular messages, click Add Folder at the bottom of PFC.

Note

PFC won't keep track of the messages you exchange using Instant Messages or AOL's Instant Messenger (see Chapter 11 about these features).

While reading an e-mail message, you can now have the individual message saved in your Personal Filing Cabinet. That way, you don't have to save all your incoming messages — every single message you open — to your PFC, which can consume a good chunk of disk space. (You'd save everything by setting your Mail preferences to "Retain all mail I read in my PFC.") With the message open, select File⇨Save to Personal Filing Cabinet⇨ Incoming/Saved Mail. These selected messages are always available, whether you're online or offline, at Mail Center⇨Read OfflineMail⇨ Incoming/Saved Mail.

ers) and your PFC, or dead letter box (whose messages are on your PC): a read message you've read in your PFC *will* be marked by a check mark but *will not* be removed from the PFC when you close the PFC window.

When you read a message in your PFC, it comes up in the same window you use to read your daily mail. From this window, all the buttons work the same, so you can reply, delete, or add the sender's address to your Address Book.

Figure 9-10 shows you the buttons at the bottom of the PFC. They do pretty obvious things like opening, deleting, and renaming messages and folders. Auto AOL (discussed in the next section) takes you to the AOL window for setting up automatic downloading of messages and such. Compact PFC keeps your PFC from getting too large, which can slow down AOL as you load up the program each day.

E-Mail on Auto Pilot

Through your Personal Filing Cabinet, you always have access to all mail you've written and sent. How does mail get to your PFC in the first place? Two ways: when the preference is set and you open a message, a copy is made and placed in the appropriate PFC file. The other way is through automatic downloads of mail. (Files get into your PFC when you download them using AOL: over FTP, from e-mail, from the Web.)

Automatic AOL lets you download e-mail, message board, and newsgroup postings either on demand or by clockwork — on a set schedule. If you do the downloading automatically, AOL automatically signs on for you, fetches messages, and signs off.

Here's the procedure:

1. Select Mail Center ⇨ Set Up Automatic AOL (Figure 9-11). Use the set of check boxes on the right side to tell AOL what to download (you can check any or all): mail waiting to be read or sent; message board and newsgroup postings waiting to be read or sent; and files marked for downloading later. Use the buttons on the left to tell AOL *for which screen name* to schedule

a download (Select Names) and when to do the down-loading (Schedule Automatic AOL).

Figure 9-12 shows the scheduling window

Do it now: An alternitive to regularly scheduled automatic AOL

Automatic AOL

Schedule Automatic AOL

Run Automatic AOL Now

☐ Send mail from the "Mail Waiting to be Sent" folder
☑ Get unread mail and put it in "Incoming Mail" folder
☐ Download files that are attached to unread mail*
☐ Send postings from the "Postings Waiting to be Sent" folder
☐ Get unread postings and put in "Incoming Postings" folder
☐ Download files marked to be downloaded later*

Select Names

Walk Me Through

*NOTE: Downloaded files will be placed in the directory specified in the "Download Manager."

(No sessions scheduled)   Help

Select what to download (messages, postings, etc), when, for what screen names, step by step

For which screen names should activities be carriedout (make sure to provide passwords for sign-on purposes)

Figure 9-11. Tell AOL to retrieve all sorts of messages automatically.

Tip

If you don't like the idea of automatically signing on, or don't need the regular pick-ups, just run Automatic AOL whenever you need it. Referring to Figure 9-13, click Run Automatic AOL Now. Or, from the Mail Center menu, select Run Automatic AOL whenever the spirit moves you.

2. Tell AOL for which screen names you want to download messages. Click Select Names and put a check by the screen name or names, supplying the corresponding passwords, so AOL can sign on automatically.

3. Tell AOL when to download messages for the screen names selected in Step 2. Click Schedule Automatic AOL to bring up the scheduling window (Figure 9-12). First, put a check in Enable Scheduler. Then set a frequency at which you want to schedule message pick-ups (How Often): from every half-hour to daily. Then specify the days you want all this to happen: any day or the days of the week you want. You have less flexibility in setting a time. The minute is specified for you, alas. You can't have quite everything, even on AOL.

4. Close the Automatic AOL window to put your new schedule into practice from now on.

5. Read your mail. You can read your "incoming/saved" mail using either MyFiles ⇨ Personal Filing Cabinet or (the same thing) Mail Center ⇨ Read Offline Mail ⇨ Incoming/Saved Mail.

Make sure to check this box

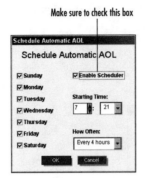

Figure 9-12. Automatic AOL's scheduling window tells AOL when to sign on and do the things requested in Figure 9-11.

AOL Anywhere: New Ways to Do Mail

For the next few years, most people will continue doing AOL mail at a PC or laptop, signed onto AOL and hooked into a phone line and electrical outlet. Two new ways of doing mail point to new habits to learn in the near future:

▶ AOLMail, which gives you access to your AOL mail when you're using a browser but not signed on to AOL

▶ AOL Mail, for use with a handheld PalmPilot

AOLMail

For a long time AOL has let you sign on as a guest, if you're at someone else's computer and that person has AOL installed. You can't do everything as a guest — you can't do anything involving the person's hard drive, for example, such as using Personal Filing Cabinet. You can, however, do e-mail.

Since the release of AOL 4.0 you can do AOL e-mail at a computer *even without AOL installed on it.* When would you want to do that? At computer labs, conferences, relatives' houses, kiosks, and other places and occasions that you will quickly discover. The only requirement: the computer you're using must have a recent Netscape or Microsoft browser (Netscape 3.02 or higher or MSIE 3.0 or higher). Any operating system will do: Windows 3.1, NT, 95/98, Mac OS. And, the computer must have an Internet connection.

AOLMail is Web-based e-mail. To use it all you need is your web browser to display your AOL mailboxes and let you send and receive your mail. Here's what to do

1. Log on to the PC using the person's network connection or Internet Service Provide connection.

2. Go to the Web address: `http://www.aol.com/aol-mail`. Also, from AOL.COM, there's a link to AOLMail.

3. You'll have a hoop or two to jump through the first time, like filling in AOL's registration agreement. When you're ready to go, just click Read My AOL Mail Now you'll go directly to the sign-in window for AOLMail. Otherwise, the plug-in will be downloaded for you, and then you'll sign in. The AOLMail sign in window will look very familiar to you.

AOLMail itself is shown in Figure 9-13. Notice the similarities to your ordinary AOL mailboxes. You've got three mailboxes: New Mail, Old Mail, and Sent Mail, each identical to the mailbox you use in AOL. For each message, you get four pieces of information: whether a file's attached; when it was sent; who sent it; the subject.

Tip

With QuickBuddy, you can also use AOL Instant Messenger — without AIM being installed. QuickBuddy and AOLMail together let you communicate live and by e-mail, without being signed on to AOL! See Chapter 11 for more.

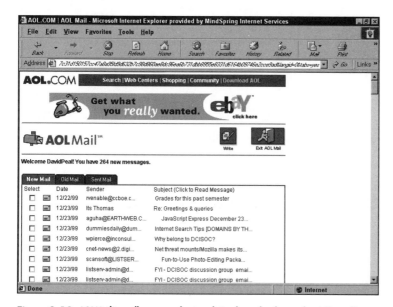

Figure 9-13. AOLMail's mailboxes: as clean and simple as the day-to-day AOL mailboxes

To write a new message

1. From the main AOLMail display, click the little Write button.

2. The message box is nearly identical in layout to AOL's Write Mail window, with the exceptions that you don't get Mail Extras or Send Later or your Address Box, and formatting capabilities aren't available for AOLMail yet. You can, however, attach a file (if you have one on a floppy, say) and request a return receipt.

To leave AOLMail, close the browser or (more gracefully) click the Exit AOLMail button in the upper right corner of most AOLMail windows.

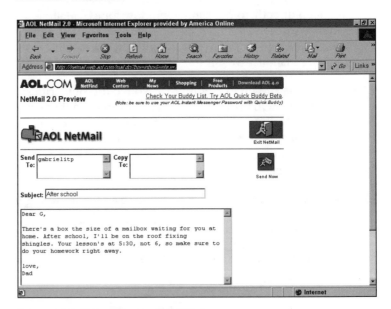

Figure 9-14. Writing a message in AOLMail

You've Got Unwanted Mail

Every Internet Service Provider (ISP) has been plagued by the swarms of unsolicited messages that find their way into subscribers' mailboxes. AOL is not your standard ISP, and AOL has the resources to combat these so-called *spammers* (senders of unsolicited mail) through technology and in the courts.

However, you will get unwanted mail from time to time. Such mail includes make-money-fast schemes, adult/obnoxious advertisements, and the occasional chain letter. Ignore them all! Delete them without opening them. If you do open them in error:

Cross-Reference

Chapter 12, on mailing lists, concludes with a lengthier description of what to do about unwanted mail.

▶ Forward e-mail messages (with no files attached) to TOSEMail1

▶ Forward e-mail with files attached to TOS Files

▶ Forward unsolicited commercial e-mail to TOSspam

Or, go to Keyword: **Notify AOL** and follow the instructions for handling different kinds of online nuisances (not just the mail-related ones). Keyword: **Junk Mail** reviews the tools you can use on AOL to minimize spam and provides an overview of what AOL's doing in the court and with other companies to combat spamming.

This chapter covers e-mail essentials: reading, responding to, and managing your AOL e-mail. If you're new to e-mail, start using it today, but don't forget to write an occasional letter; they're all the more meaningful because so few people still write them. The next chapter digs into the creative side of e-mail: adding flourish, photos, stationery (graphic design), signatures, and other effects.

A Quick Look Back

"What's your e-mail address?" has become a standard part of social protocol, up there with "nice to meet you." Reading mail involves more than exercising the basic skills you learned in primary school. It involves

▶ Knowing what messages to read (interpreting the message headers shown in your AOL mailbox) and what messages to delete without reading.

▶ Responding to mail (replying to the sender or forwarding the message to someone else); and saving or printing the message. Or, you can not respond to mail — delete it after reading it.

▶ Managing the mail on AOL's computer (such messages are available for about a month) and on your own computer (AOL's Personal Filing Cabinet).

▶ Downloading and using files attached to (or pictures inserted in) a message.

AOL in recent years has been making it possible to read mail when you're not signed on to your own personal or work PC. All you need is a browser, these days, and AOL's AOLMail Web site. If you use the Palm Pilot personal digital assistant, and have a Palm modem, you can read and send mail, too. Look for the capability of reading AOL mail wherever you happen to be.

Chapter 10

Sending Mail: What Do You Have to Say for Yourself?

Creating a Message

Sending messages, like creating Web pages, is your way of taking part actively and creatively in the world of the Internet. In this chapter you'll find what you need to get started as quickly as possible. I'll also show you the fun stuff, too: signatures, greeting cards, funky stationery, smileys and emoticons, and more.

The last chapter, on reading and managing your e-mail, covered the easiest ways to send a message: replying to or forwarding a message someone already sent to you. To generate a message from scratch requires a shade more creativity, and is that much more fun to do.

To create a new message, start by clicking the toolbar's Write button to use the Write Mail window (Figure 10-1).

Message

What message is about

E-mail address of recipient

CC's, if any

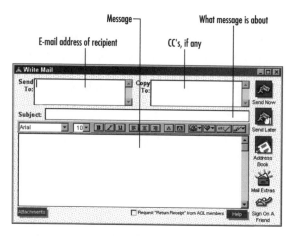

Figure 10-1. A clean slate: here's where you make your mark.

Where the Message Is Going (E-Mail Address)

Sending a message requires at least one piece of information: an e-mail address. See "A Word about E-Mail Addresses" in the last chapter for the low-down. In the Send To box, enter an AOL screen name (without @aol.com) or, for friends not on AOL, a full Internet e-mail address (for example, friend@suchansuch.com or mypal@thisandthat.net).

Your main recipient is the person for whom your message is intended (*John* in a *Dear John* letter, for example). A CC used to mean *carbon copy*; now it means courtesy copy — which is more accurate. The main recipient (in the Send To box) will be aware of anyone CC'd. A BCC is a blind courtesy copy, a courtesy copy of which the main recipient is unaware. To send a message to several direct or indirect recipients, separate the names by commas. Your recipients can be on either AOL or the Net.

Want to send your message to several people at once? AOL gives you many ways to take advantage of this opportunity:

▶ To reach *several main recipients* at once (a work team or PTA subcommittee, for example), enter all their

Note

You don't have to be signed on to AOL to write a message, only to send it. So, you can draft messages offline, and then click Send Later to reread and send them once you're online.

Tip

You can send a message with only an address—and no subject or message! You might do this to send yourself a file from work to use at home. You'd be expecting the message at home, so you wouldn't need to add any extra information.

10

Sending Mail

Note

Messages can go to people with either an AOL or an Internet e-mail address, in any order, in either the Send To or Copy To box.

Caution

BCCs can be risky—if the main recipient finds someone else was privy to an exchange, it can seem like a breach of confidentiality. BCCs do make sense in some private mailing lists in which you don't want members to know each others' address for one reason or another.

e-mail addresses in the Send To box, separated by commas. Don't worry if the addresses break in weird places. Maximizing your Write Mail window often takes care of that.

▶ To send someone a courtesy copy (CC) of your message (your boss, for example, if you're writing someone in another department or outside the company), place that person's e-mail address in the Copy To box. Again, for multiple CCs, make sure to separate the addresses with commas.

▶ To send someone a blind courtesy copy (BCC) of your message, enclose the e-mail address in parentheses in the *Copy To* box (there is no special BCC box). For multiple BCCs, separate the enclosed addresses with commas.

What the Message Is About (Subject Line)

The e-mail message improves on the letter (but also removes the anticipation) by allowing the recipient to tell at a glance what the message is about. Using the Subject line, the sender describes what's in the message and can characterize the message's purpose or spin. In a few words, you can say enough about your message to entice the recipient into reading it.

Entice is not pejorative in this case: people get so much mail these days that unless your Subject line is specific and concrete, and clearly from you, your recipient(s) might delete it without bothering to open it. Short, punchy, communicative, and descriptive subject lines are likely to get positive attention. (*Short,* because anything long is likely to be truncated — shortened into a meaningless phrase by the recipient's e-mail program.)

Something That Must Be Said (Read This!)

In past editions of this book I have volunteered lots of tips about how not to ruffle feathers, make yourself clear, demonstrate respect, and in general show what a nice person you are. Since then I've become more aware of the many purposes e-mail serve just short of the fully developed thought. In some messages, a single word (*yes*) or simple number (for example, a fax number or zip code) can be perfectly sufficient and a good use of e-mail. A fully formed message ("Dear so and so . . .") is often not necessary when the context is well understood by both the sender and the recipient; in a family or ongoing work situation, everything doesn't have to be spelled out.

In messages to mailing lists and strangers, however, the old rules apply: be explicit; be polite; check your spelling and grammar; avoid unnecessary terseness; avoid humor that could be construed as rude; respect differences that might exist between you and the recipients.

Many people read the first paragraph or two of a message and then respond. Some people, like me, make the mistake of asking several questions in one message. One subject, one message can help ensure the response you want.

Sending That Message on Its Way

Sending messages is not rocket science. With your recipient(s) and anyone CC'd or BCC'd, a subject line, and the right message for the purpose, just click Send Now.

Send Later is a genuinely useful option. Say you're writing a particularly sensitive message or a message in the heat of the moment, to a boss or employee, spouse or child, and so forth. Draft the letter, then let it sit for a while by clicking Send Later — giving yourself time to reflect or cool off. For me, this sort of bottom-drawer treatment is usually a good way to get some distance on something I've written and to do a better job proofing when I do look at it. Just to make sure the message doesn't inadvertently get sent, put your own screen name in the Send To box. (In fact, sometimes people CC themselves in e-mail just to have a record of what they sent and to see it from others' perspective.) Note that you can't send the message later unless it has a valid e-mail address in the Send To box. Another reason to Send Later: if you're sending one huge file or several files of any size to different people, you want to wait until you sign off before starting that slow process.

One more thing before sending that message. For any recipients who are on AOL, you can get a return receipt — an automatically generated message sent back to you when that person opens the message. Place a check in the Return Receipt box at the bottom of the Write Mail window. Note

Unlike a letter, in a message you needn't bother putting a date in your message. Both the time (down to the second) and the date will be automatically inserted by AOL as your message wends its way through AOL's computers.

10

Sending Mail

Cross-Reference

Your Personal Filing Cabinet is discussed toward the end of Chapter 9; the Sent Mail box is discussed toward the beginning of that chapter.

that the return receipt merely registers a message being opened — not being read, or read in its entirely.

When you're ready to send the letter, sign on and go to Mail Center ⇨ Mail Waiting to Be Sent. You'll see the little window in Figure 10-2.

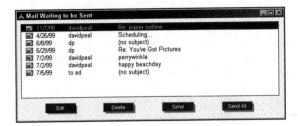

Figure 10-2. Messages waiting to be sent. From here you can edit further, send one message or all messages, and delete one or all messages. I address messages to myself or to a nonsense address to prevent accidentally sending them to the intended recipient.

Three of your AOL Mail preferences (MyAOL ⇨ Preferences ⇨ Mail) have to do with what happens when you send messages.

- ▶ **Confirm mail after it has been sent** causes a little message to pop up when it's been successfully sent.
- ▶ **Confirm when mail is marked to send later** serves to reassure you that the message *wasn't* sent and is thus available for editing.
- ▶ **Close mail after it has been sent** automatically closes the mail window once the message is sent.

After the Message Is out the Door

Here's one thing e-mail has over old-fashioned letters: You can keep track of a message in ways not possible with an old-fashioned letter.

- ▶ Rereading mail you've sent. Your Sent Mail list has all your recent e-mail messages for the last month or so. An even lengthier archive, in your Personal Filing Cabinet (PFC), extends back as far as you choose (as long as the preference is set).

▶ Notification of receipt of mail you've sent. Click the Return Receipt box at the bottom of your Write Mail window, and you can find out automatically whether any of your messages' AOL recipients got your message.

▶ Status of mail you've sent. Here's something you can do in Sent Mail but not in your Personal Filing Cabinet: Find out when a message you sent was read (opened) by your AOL recipients. In Sent Mail, select any message to someone on AOL, and click Status. You'll see a little window like the one in Figure 10-3, providing the Subject line of your message in the title bar (after Status of), who read it, at what exact time (if you are using auto-AOL this may only indicate when the message was downloaded).

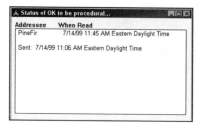

Figure 10-3. Mission accomplished: message has been read

Address Book

Released with AOL 4.0, the AOL Address Book found instant approval from long-time AOL users. To really appreciate it, use it actively with AOL 5.0. The Address Book lets you keep a lot of information about all your friends: their first and last names, their e-mail addresses, plus their postal addresses and other information in the Notes section (Figure 10-4). You can even keep a person's digital photo, just like you might carry around photos of kids, parents, girl friends, boy friends, and others. I use the Address Book for phone, fax, and address information, as well as e-mail addresses.

Note

AOL has no way of knowing whether any of your messages' recipients with Internet e-mail addresses got your message. Messages to the Net reliably get to their destination, but you'll never know that until you get a response. Usually, if a message is misaddressed, you'll get an obscure message to that effect telling you that the domain is wrong or the e-mail address doesn't exist on that domain. You won't, however, get anything like a return receipt.

Tip

Your Address Book is always available, offline or online, at Mail Center ⇨ Address Book.

10
Sending Mail

Note

The AOL Address Book orders items by whatever's in the First Name field if you use only a first name (as you might for a sibling or friend); if you fill in both first and last names, it orders by last name.

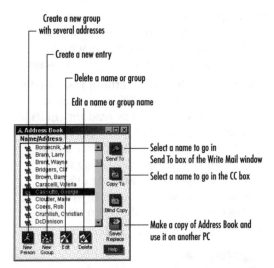

Figure 10-4. The AOL Address Book can be filled out manually (by typing in names and e-mail addresses) or automatically (by displaying a message from someone and clicking Add Address). Entries can then be updated at any time.

Adding a Name to the Address Book

You have two ways to add a new address to your Address Book.

▶ With a message displayed, click Add Address, to bring up a new page, with information filled in, based on the header information for the message you're reading (Figure 10-5). You'll almost always have to edit this information, providing a proper first and last name, and any notes. The Address Book often plugs the e-mail address into the First Name field. Copying and pasting is simple: select text with your mouse, right click, and select Copy; move to the place where you want the text to appear, right click, and select Paste. In the Notes section you can put anything. I often copy and paste signature information from the message's body, in order to gather a person's title, office address, and fax.

▶ The other way to add an address: display the Address Book (using the Mail Center window), and click the New Person button, shown in Figure 10-4. You'll see a window like the one shown in Figure 10-5, only it'll be blank. Type in a first and last name, e-mail address, and anything else you want. Click OK when you're done.

Figure 10-5. Add Address automatically creates a page like this in your Address Book. Feel free to provide actual first and last names, as well as any other information. You can even add a picture by clicking the picture tab.

Using the Address Book when you're writing a message is a piece of cake:

1. Open the Write Mail window. Click Address Book.
2. Select a name from the Address Book. You can select several names if you want, by pressing Shift or Control before clicking the names.
3. Click Send To in order to place the selected addresses in the Send To box of the Write Mail window.

   Click Copy To or Blind Copy To if you want to send these people copies or blind copies, as described earlier in this chapter.
4. Write your letter and send it (click Send Now).

Creating a Group (Mailing List)

An e-mail group has two elements: a name and a list of addresses. With the Address Book open, click New group.

1. Type in a name for the group — a single word or couple of words, such as Work Pals, Bar Mitzvah Team, or Bridge Club.
2. Type any AOL or Internet e-mail addresses you want in the group (Figure 10-6).

When you're writing an e-mail, you might want to add the address last, to avoid inadvertently sending a message before you're done.

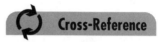

Chapter 12 is devoted to mailing lists, which, on the Internet, are managed by highly specialized software. Such software lets people add their name to the list automatically and distributes subscribers' messages to all members of the group.

10

Sending Mail

AOL 5.0 enhances attaching files by providing enough room in the Attachments window to see the entire file name, *with file path,* for each file you're attaching.

When you reply to a message that has a file attached, the reply doesn't include the attached file. When you forward a message that has a file attached, the file remains attached (it's considered part of what you're forwarding). In other words, if you're replying, it's assumed the original sender doesn't need to get the file she sent; if you're forwarding, the person you're forwarding to might want the file as well as the message.

When people in the group get a message you've sent to the group, they can copy and paste the group's e-mail addresses and create a list in their own mail program, or use the Reply All button, which all good mail programs have.

Figure 10-6. It's easy to create a simple mailing list with the AOL Address Book. Use AOL and Internet addresses, separated by commas.

Files to Go

Everyone can find reasons to attach files. For instance, I used them to submit chapters and screen captures (for this book), receive assignments in classes I teach, show samples of work to potential clients, share software with another person, send my mother-in-law pictures of the kids, etc.

Attaching One or More Files

With the Write Mail window open (Figure 10-1), click Attachments. The Attachments window comes up. Figure 10-7 shows the window listing several files that are to be attached to this message. (Remember that when you attach more than one file, the files are combined into a single, compressed file.)

For each file to attach

1. Click Attach.
2. In the Attach window (Figure 10-8), go to the folder with the file you want to share, and double click the file.

Click when you've added
the last file you want to attach

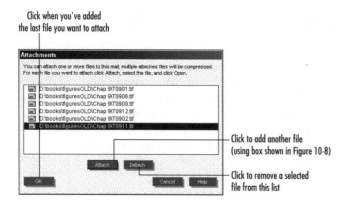

Click to add another file
(using box shown in Figure 10-8)

Click to remove a selected
file from this list

Figure 10-7. Include a file or two or six with your message

3. Repeat for each file to be attached.

   If you inadvertently add something to the Attachments
   window, select it and click Detach.

4. Click OK when you've selected all the files you want
   to send.

Screen for files of a certain type

Selected file appears here

Go up to another directory

Group to Windows 95/98 desktop

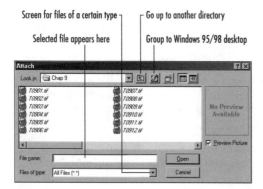

Figure 10-8. Select files to attach

When you send your message, it will take a bit longer than
ordinary messages, because your file must be uploaded. If you
are sending several files, they'll be compressed and zipped
before being sent. A progress box tracks the upload.

10

Sending Mail

Embellish Those Messages

Plain old text suits many messages perfectly. In a work setting, for example, you can live without your boss's photo emblazoning every message from his office. In messages to and from a diverse Internet audience, many great embellishments possible on AOL can't be viewed in the first place. For now, why not enjoy what you can do in your messages to other AOL members. Eventually, your messages will be able to cross all these boundaries.

Emphasizing Text

From the AOL Write Mail toolbar, you can apply any of the following type effects:

▶ Type style (bold, italic, underline).

▶ Type size, color, and face. (You may find more than one hundred type faces in the list, depending on the other programs you have installed. AOL itself does not come with any fonts, but it can use any of the fonts you have installed on your system.)

▶ Background color and tiling. *Tiling* is a single image repeated throughout a Web page. Such tiling can look like the ceramic tiles used on porch floors and kitchen and bathroom walls. Or, the tiling pattern can be seamless and appear continuous.

▶ Links to your Favorite Places and any hyperlinks you please; pictures inserted in the message or linked from the message; entire text files.

To apply a text effect, open a Write Mail window (click Write on the toolbar). Type anything in the body of the message (the big box). Select any words to enhance, and click the appropriate buttons, as shown in Figure 10-9.

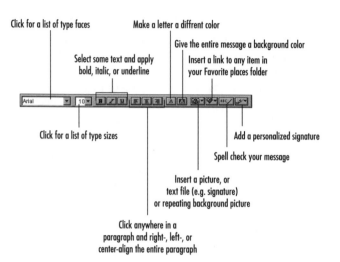

Click for a list of type faces

Make a letter a diffrent color

Give the entire message a background color

Select some text and apply
bold, italic, or underline

Insert a link to any item in
your Favorite places folder

Click for a list of type sizes

Add a personalized signature

Spell check your message

Insert a picture, or
text file (e.g. signature)
or repeating background picture

Click anywhere in a
paragraph and right-, left-, or
center-align the entire paragraph

Figure 10-9. No more boring text: the Write Mail's toolbar lets you add pizzazz.

Inserting Links, Text, and Images

To add a hyperlink to a message, so the person receiving the message can link directly to a Web page or AOL area that you want to share, you've got several choices.

▶ Use a Favorite Place. With nothing selected in a message, click the heart button on the Write Mail toolbar. A list of your Favorite Places comes up; select one. For Web sites, the site's name appears in your message, linked to the site. For Favorite Places, the text in your message will be the same as the Web address (URL); in this case select the linked text in the message and edit it into something English. You can also make it bold, larger, change the type face, or enhance it in some other way.

▶ Link to a site that's not yet a Favorite Place. With a Web site or AOL area open (but not maximized) *and* the Write Mail window open, select some text in your message. Drag the heart in the upper-right-hand corner of the Web site or AOL area's window onto the selected text.

Tip

You can create a "default" font that will be used in *every* message (and can be over-ridden in *any single* message, using the Write Mail toolbar). Select MyAOL ⇨ Preferences ⇨ Font. Choose any font you like: a default type face, color, and size; default style (bold, italic, underline); and default background color. The sample text in the window reflects your changes. Click OK when you like the type size, style, color, and so on. Reset returns you to AOL's default. Your changes apply to Instant Messages as well as e-mail messages.

10

Sending Mail

Tip

Right-click anywhere in the message body to see all your toolbar choices (change type size, style, color, and so on).

▶ Create a link from scratch — if you know the URL (Web address). With a message open and without anything selected, right-click and then select Insert Hyperlink. A window with two boxes pops up (note that Figure 10-12 shows a window with one box–to provide a URL). Provide both a description of the link (this is the link's descriptive text that will go in your message) and a URL, and click OK. Clicking Launch tests the link.

▶ Or, select words in the message, right-click, and select Hyperlink to see a one-box version of Figure 10-10. The selected text gets a link; in the window that pops up, type in a URL.

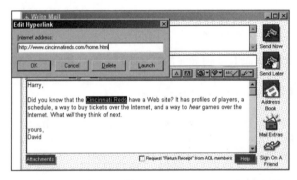

Figure 10-10. Select some text in your message as the clickable text, as in this figure, and all you have to provide is a URL. With no words in your message selected, right-click and provide both clickable text and a URL.

Worried about the impression a message will make? Before sending it, click the little ABC button in the Write Mail toolbar (Figure 10-9) to spell-check it. The spell checker compares each word to its list of words, and for each word that does not match, you can add that word to the checker's list, tell the checker to "learn" the word because it is correctly spelled, tell the checker to skip it just this time or all instances of it, or change it in the spell checker's Replace With box.

As an alternative to Send Later, create your message as a text file (using AOL's File ➪ New). Write it, edit it, and save it as a text file. Return to it later and tweak some more, sending it only when it's exactly right. Then, while signed on, click the Write button from the AOL toolbar. From the Write Mail toolbar, click the little Camera button and select Insert Text File. Find your message and double-click to insert it.

Inserting a text file into a message saves you from typing something again and again. Or, it gives you the chance to draft and edit as much as you want until it's ready to send. In either case, when you're done, a copy of the original remains on your hard drive, to use later. Text files must be just that: pure text (simple characters) — none of the formatting added by a word processor can be used in an AOL message.

Where do you get digital pictures to enhance your Address Book and to insert into your messages? Here are three easy ways to get digital pictures

In their AOL New Mail box, recipients of images you send will see a picture icon indicating an inserted message. Double clicking the message presents them with a warning message about opening unsolicited messages from unknown parties. Once open, your recipients can click the inserted image to display it in their AOL Picture Gallery, and from there to save it, edit it, etc.

▶ Using a scanner (to turn a paper photo into a digital one).

▶ Using a digital camera, to create digital pictures instead of paper ones.

▶ Using AOL's You've Got Pictures (YGP) service, to get digital pictures without owning a scanner or a digital camera. With this service, you take your traditional film to the photo store, and the print pictures are scanned and then posted directly to AOL. You can still get regular pictures. Click the new You've Got Pictures button on the AOL 5.0 Welcome screen for more info.

Inserting a picture into a message can illustrate a point or get attention. It's a less obtrusive and more direct way of sending a picture than attaching it, which requires that the other person use a graphics program to view the file. To insert a file, just position the cursor at the point in your message where you want the picture. From the mail toolbar, click the Camera button and select Insert a Picture. Find the picture and double-click. Small images can be inserted in text (in a sentence); the right, center, and left align buttons apply to the whole paragraph in which a picture is inserted (or the picture itself, if it's not part of a paragraph). If you insert a large image, you'll get a message asking you if you'd like to resize the picture to fit the document. If you choose yes, the picture is resized automatically; if you choose no, it's inserted full-size, which may require the recipient to scroll to see all of it.

Inserting a background picture (using that Camera button again) lets you create a tiled pattern (parchment or sandpaper, if you like).

Caffeinated Stationery and Other Mail Extras

With AOL's Mail Extras, you can borrow and adapt one of the bright and simple designs created by AOL's design gurus. You could create all this stuff yourself by playing with the Write Mail toolbar. Or, help yourself to them by clicking Mail Extras from any Write Mail window or select Mail Center ⇨ Mail Extras. You'll see the window in Figure 10-11.

Figure 10-11. Mail Extras: A source of classy effects at your fingertips

In Figure 10-12, I tried to create a message illustrating many of the things you can do with Mail Extras. The effects may be someone else's, but you can combine them in your own way and add a message that is absolutely your own.

Online Greetings takes you to an area where you can purchase a greeting card from American Greetings, personalize it, and send it by e-mail to anyone with e-mail, not just other AOL members.

Colors and Styles gives you small, colorful, simple pictures, made of characters, such as the coffee cups shown in Figure 10-12.

A *smiley* is a bit of text that represents a facial expression when you tilt you head to the left (see the grin in Figure 10-12). These Smileys, and many more, can be found at Mail Extras; click Smileys.

:-)~	Razzing Smiley
¦-D	Ha, Ha, Ha, Ha, Ho, Ho, Ho....
:-(	Bummer Smiley

:'-(	Boo Hoo, Crying Smiley
:-||	Snickering Smiley
:-[	Depressed Smiley
:-O	A surprised Smiley
=:-()	A Scared Smiley
:-/	A Stumped Smiley

Photos in Mail extras differ from inserted photos; they're links to existing AOL photos showing dogs, seagulls, shells, and other all-purpose images. The recipient of a message with such a photo gets a *link* to the photo.

Hyperlinks, too, are prepackaged links to AOL areas. To create your own links, see "Inserting Links, Text, and Images."

Stationery involves attractive designs. The stationery designs are mostly letterhead: patterns meant for the top of the message, where your name would go on fancy stationery (*greetings from ..., from the desk of ...*, and so on). When you choose stationery, you'll be asked to provide your own initials or full name. When the stationery is inserted into a message, you can change its size and position, even move its elements around.

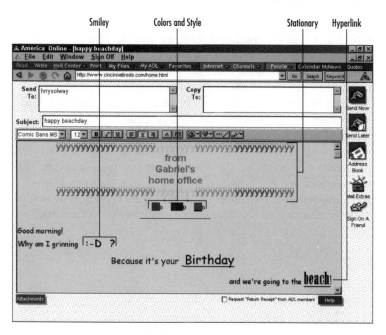

Figure 10-12. Create personalized stationery for your AOL mail using Mail Extras.

Note

Finally! New to AOL 5.0 is a feature that enables you to automatically add a *signature* at the end of your e-mail messages. Signatures can consist of any text you want to share. Also: you can create several signatures, each for a different purpose or type of recipient (serious, flip, and so on). Use signatures to share your URL, your business information, your motto, your favorite joke, or anything else fit to print.

Not included in Mail Extras is another form of online expressiveness called *emoticons*, short abbreviations that stand for common expressions. Here are some emoticons you might see:

▶ BRB	Be Right Back
▶ BTW	By The Way
▶ GMTA	Great Minds Think Alike
▶ LOL	Laughing Out Loud
▶ OMG	Oh My GOSH [fill in the expletive of choice]!
▶ OTF	On the Floor (laughing)
▶ ROFLWTIME	Rolling on Floor with Tears in My Eyes
▶ ROTF	Rolling on the Floor
▶ TTFN	Ta-Ta for Now!
▶ TTYL	Talk to You Later

Greeting Cards

Greeting cards are the latest thing on the Net. Web businesses create personalized Web cards, with animations and Java effects, whose URLs they send to others on special days. Graphics programs like JASC's PaintShop Pro and Adobe's PhotoDeluxe enable you to create custom cards and send them as attachments. On AOL you can customize thousands of professionally designed cards for any (or no) occasion, and send them to anyone on AOL or the Internet. All messages can be customized with your personal message. This commercial service comes from American Greetings; a small fee applies, but it's still less expensive than buying new software or running to the drugstore to get a two-dollar card.

Signatures

Signatures are bits of text automatically appended to the end of your e-mail messages. Before AOL 4.0, you had to add signatures manually. With AOL 4.0 you could insert short text files (already written) at the end of messages by clicking the Camera button and selecting Insert Text File. With AOL 5.0, you can create *up to 5* signatures and use whichever you want on any message, depending on occasion.

Tip

For signatures used on e-mail bound for the Internet, stick to text only; for your messages to AOL members, format all you want.

Creating a Signature

To create a signature

1. Click the last button on the far right of the Write Mail toolbar (Figure 10-9). Or, select Mail Center ⇨ Set up Mail Signatures. In either case, you'll see a window like the one shown in Figure 10-13 (mine already has a couple of signatures in it).

Figure 10-13. Create a signature to tell people about your latest achievements or share a joke.

2. Click the Create button. A signature has two elements: a name (which you choose) to identify the particular signature you want to use at the end of your message, and some text, which you can format any way you please.

3. Give the signature a name, as shown in Figure 10-13, and type in the signature, with the effects you want. Note the toolbar with different fonts, type sizes, styles, and colors — even backgrounds (click the A set on a square blue field button) and links (click the heart button). Click OK when you're done. Edit signatures by going to the Set Up Signatures window, selecting an existing signature, and clicking Edit.

A Quick Look Back

In this chapter I wanted to show you how you can use e-mail to communicate with anyone in the world who has an Internet account, including 20 million AOL members, give or take. Among other things, you learned about the following key features plus some good uses to which you can put these features:

▶ Creating an e-mail message

▶ Addressing your message and sending it on its way

▶ Writing effective e-mail

▶ Using the AOL Address Book to keep track of information about the people you regularly communicate with–not just their e-mail addresses

▶ Attach one or more electronic files to your messages

▶ Personalizing your messages with pictures, backgrounds, fancy fonts and colors, Smileys, and a custom signature.

Sending e-mail is the single most popular (and fun) use to which the Internet is put. With AOL, this indispensable form of global communication is at your fingertips.

Chapter 11

Live Communication: From Instant Messages to Internet Chats

Are you frequently frustrated by phone tag and unanswered e-mail? Do you and your friends have a hard time finding a time to meet? Would you like to keep in closer contact with parents and children? Or do you perhaps have a business and want to be easily accessible to your co-workers and customers?

With Instant Messages (IMs) on AOL and AOL Instant Messenger (AIM) on the Internet, you get quick, easy, *live* communication that bypasses all those teeth-grinding time delays. Think of it as real-time communication for real people.

ICQ takes live communication a step further to include chats, messages, voice mail, Internet Relay Chat (IRC), greeting cards, and, yes, e-mail itself. This hugely popular software, developed by a small company that's now part of AOL, is the focus of the second half of this chapter.

Chat usually refers to conversations between two or more people. AOL's Instant Messages support conversations between just two people. AIM is for chat *and* conversations, and ICQ is for every kind of communication, including chat and conversation, e-mail, mailing list, and newsgroups. They're all available to you on AOL — for simultaneous use, if you can't get enough of this stuff and are good at typing.

Cross-Reference

Chapter 3 shows you how to add buddies to your AOL Buddy List.

Tête-à-Tête with Instant Messages

All AOL members can use Instant Messages to have electronic discussions with their AOL buddies. The one condition of IMs: your buddy must be online when you send your message.

How do you find out whether a buddy or colleague of yours is online? It's easy:

▶ When you sign on to AOL, your Buddy List pops up automatically (see Figure 11-1). This little window lets you know immediately which of your AOL friends are currently online. Double-click a group to see which buddies are online. Double-click a name in the Buddy List to send an IM.

▶ The IM window (see Figure 11-2) itself is directly available by clicking Ctrl-I. To find out whether someone is online, simply type in a screen name and click the Available? button.

11

Live Communication

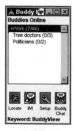

Figure 11-1. The Buddy List window appears when you sign on to AOL. If you should ever close the window, use Keyword: *Buddyview*.

If you're not starting from the Buddy List and don't know whether someone is online, you'll need, first, to type in the screen name in the To field and click the Available? button to see whether that person is online.

To see how messaging works, you don't need the screen name of a friend or relative; you can send a message to yourself.

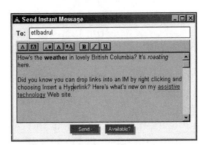

Figure 11-2. Composing IMs is like composing e-mail, except you can carry on a live conversation and don't always have much time to respond and make things pretty.

Using AOL's Instant Messages

To use your Buddy List to send an IM, double-click a screen name. Or select the name, and click the IM button at the bottom of the list. The Send Instant Message window pops up (Figure 11-2). The screen name of your buddy already appears in the To field.

Type your message in the larger box, and click Send. There's no spelling checker, but don't worry about that because people tend to be less fussy about spelling and grammar in IMs than in e-mail.

When someone sends you an instant message for the first time, a message pops up onscreen, accompanied by a tinkling sound. You can either accept the message (click Yes), decline the message (click No), or click Questions to get more information. Usually, you'll want to take messages from people you know and often you'll want to refuse them from people you don't. If you receive the message, you'll notice a Get Profile button on the bottom of the IM window; if the person has created a profile (keyword: Member Directory), you'll be able to read it by clicking the button.

Click Here If You Want Some Privacy

Work to do? Tired of communicating with people you don't know? Maybe you want to get a little break while online, and receive IMs only from a few people, or from no one at all. You have a number of options when it comes to limiting others' access to you via Instant Messages. To screen your incoming messages, click the Setup button at the bottom of your Buddy

List to display the Buddy List Setup window. Click the Privacy Preferences button to display the Privacy Preferences window (see Figure 11-3). You can also get at Privacy Preferences using My AOL ⇨ Preferences ⇨ Privacy.

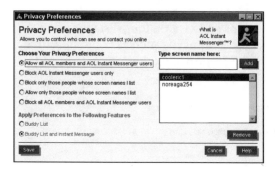

Figure 11-3. Adjust your Privacy Preferences to control other people's access to you.

You have a number of options when it comes to controlling who has access to you, and who is allowed to see whether you are online. You'll need to choose one of the following:

▶ Allow all AOL members and AOL Instant Messenger users to send you messages (in effect, allowing messages from everyone)

▶ Block AOL Instant Messenger users (in effect, blocking messages from the people on the Internet)

▶ Block specific users (in effect allowing messages from anyone except people sending unwanted messages)

▶ Allow only specific users (a good idea for kids' screen names)

▶ Block all AOL and AOL Instant Messenger users (when you want to take a cat nap or finish some serious work online)

Click to select the one option you want (the choices tend to be mutually exclusive). To allow access to specific users or to block specific users, type the screen names in the window at the right and click Add. Repeat the process to add as many users to this category as you want. Likewise, remove names by selecting them one at a time and clicking Remove.

The last option can be used to keep people from seeing you in their Buddy List (click Buddy List or Buddy List and Instant Message).

AIM has so many options, it's easy to lose sight of its simplicity in purpose and use, especially when compared to a popular Internet Relay Chat application such as mIRC (Chapter 17) or complex communications programs such as ICQ. If you ever do need help using AIM, it's available from the main AIM window shown in Figure 11-4 at Help ⇨ Help Topics.

Right click the stock ticker to see an intraday price chart for a particular stock or index.

Take It to the Internet with AOL Instant Messenger

AOL Instant Messenger (AIM) is a handy way to help you both maintain friendships and save on long-distance phone charges. AIM can meet serious needs such as communicating with business colleagues or providing quick facts to anyone who needs them.

List of your buddy groups; Click right-pointing arrow to see who is online now

Add and Create groups and buddies

Buddy Groups

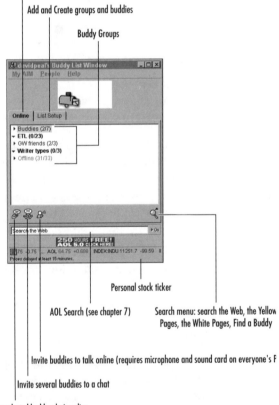

Personal stock ticker

AOL Search (see chapter 7)

Search menu: search the Web, the Yellow Pages, the White Pages, Find a Buddy

Invite buddies to talk online (requires microphone and sound card on everyone's P

Invite several buddies to a chat

Send a message to a selected buddy who's online

Figure 11-4. My AIM Buddy List already has a few entries. Click a folder (group) to see who's in it and whether they're online.

AOL Instant Messenger

▶ Costs nothing, for both AOL members and *anyone* on the Internet.

▶ Comes in versions for Windows, Macintosh, and Unix.

▶ Can be used (once you're registered) without the AIM software. See the "Quick, Buddy" section for the details.

▶ Enables you to chat, carry on two-way messaging, and even talk, at least if you and your buddy have microphones for your PCs.

▶ Provides a sophisticated and easy-to-maintain Buddy List of its own, which combines many features of AOL's Member Directory (see Figure 11-4).

▶ Can be embedded in your Web pages, so visitors can chat there or send you a message about the page, or anything else.

Tip

Select Save Password if you don't want to enter it again, and Auto-Login if you want AOL Instant Messenger to start automatically when you go online. Having AIM run automatically and start itself ensures that you won't miss messages.

Downloading, Installing, and Running AOL Instant Messenger

If you have Netscape Communicator on your computer, you probably already have AOL Instant Messenger, too; the programs are often bundled. Open Netscape Navigator and click the AIM button on the left-hand side of the Personal tool bar (see Figure 6-4). Or, double-click the AIM icon on the right-hand side of the Windows toolbar at the bottom of your screen).You may also be able to access AIM from the Communicator menu in Netscape (you'll launch the software if you have already installed it).

Here's how you can get AOL Instant Messenger if you don't already have it.

1. Start at http://www.aol.com/aim (or just look for the link within AOL.COM). Have a look at the features overview. Click when you're ready to go (you'll see a Click Now or similar button).

2. You'll need to provide a screen name, but on AOL all you have to do is confirm that you want to use your AOL screen name.Wait for AIM to send you e-mail confirming your screen name and password.When you get the message, you're ready to go.

3. Follow the prompts to indicate where to store the program on your hard drive, and *remember where you put it*.Write the directory path on the back of your hand if you must. Press Enter to start the download process.

Tip

Registration can seem complex. Once you have installed the AIM software, open the program and use its help system (File ⇨ Help) to find out about multiple screen names and much more.

Tip

Set up a profile about yourself at File ⇨ New User Wizard. You can also indicate whether and how you want others to find out about you.

Note

When you start AIM, you get a personalized news ticker in its own window (Figure 11-4). At the bottom of the main AIM window, a scrolling stock ticker shows you the current prices of any stocks or indexes you wish to display. Indicate your preferences using AIM's MyAOL⇨ Stock Ticker Detail and News Detail.

When the download is done, double-click the file to install it. You'll be asked some standard installation questions: where to install AIM, whether you accept their terms (Yes), whether you want to sign on using your AOL screen name right away (probably Yes, for simplicity's sake) or another screen name, and so forth.

4. Once registered and with AIM installed, return to the Sign On window and enter your new screen name and password if necessary. Your new (and still empty) Buddy List window appears. Like AOL's Buddy List (but more so), AIM's list is the hub of what you do in the program (refer again to Figure 11-4).

Finding a Buddy

While I was writing this chapter, AOL announced that 750 millions messages were being sent daily using IMs, AIM, and ICQ messages — more messages than the United States Postal Service was delivering daily!

With more than 20 million people on AOL and many millions more using AOL Instant Messenger and ICQ, there's a pretty good chance you already have friends on AIM. There's even a better chance you'll find people on AIM and ICQ who share a hobby or a career interest, or who live in your community. How can you find these people? Use the Find a Buddy Wizard!

From the main menu, select People ⇨ Find a Buddy Wizard to display the Find a Buddy window. Select one of the three options for finding a buddy: by e-mail address, by name and address, or (the best way to find *new* friends) by a common interest. Or, click the magnifying glass on AIM's main window, shown in Figure 11-4, and select Find a Buddy from the drop-down list.

AIM, like AOL, requires a screen name and password; for AOL members the two can be the same. Suppose you want to find the AIM screen name for a friend whose e-mail address is SkyCerulean@yahoo.com. Select By E-mail Address, and click Next. Enter the e-mail address in the box, and click Next. Find something else to do while AIM scours its lists of registered AIM users. I happened to find two AIM screen names corresponding to SkyCerulean@yahoo.com.

You can also search for buddies by interest. Suppose you want to find some AIM users who are gardening fans. Select People ⇨ Find a Buddy ⇨ By Common Interest ⇨ Home and Gardening ⇨ Gardening. Click Next.

Fellow gardeners who are registered AIM users and willing for strangers like you to contact them will show up in a list like the one shown in Figure 11-5. Highlight a name and click the Add Buddy button to add the name to your Buddy List. You can then IM them as you would anyone else when they're online. The results of this search are not saved, so if you do another search on even the same day, the results may differ because of the speed at which the AIM community is growing.

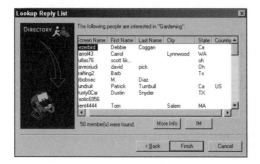

Figure 11-5. Search for fellow AIM users by a common interest.

For anyone you pull up using Find a Buddy, you can send an IM (select the name and click IM) or get more information, the equivalent of an AOL profile, if that person has made information available.

Adding Buddies to Your Buddy List

For your buddies on the Internet to use AIM, they'll have to get the program, too. From the main menu in the AIM Buddy List window, click People ⇨ Sign on a Friend to invite your friends to use AIM. Enter the e-mail address of a friend, and type a short message telling them about AIM. Your friend will receive e-mail explaining how to get AIM.

Once you obtain the screen names of some friends and acquaintances, your next step is to add them to your AIM Buddy List.

▶ To create groups for buddies who have something in common — your work group, your siblings, your accounting class, your investment club, and so forth, click the Add a Group button. With groups created, you can drag a buddy from one group to another.

Note

When you're on AOL and receive an AIM message, you carry on the exchange using the *AOL* IM window, even if you have AIM. Even when AOL members contact you by AIM (say they're inviting AOL and non-AOL folks to a chat), you'll take part in the discussion by IM.

Note

Everyone on AIM gets a screen name — even Internet folks used to the full regalia of an @ symbol and long domain name. As an AOL member, you can keep your AOL screen name on AIM, but non-AOL folks must choose a new screen name. In other words, you can't add an Internet address to your AIM Buddy List.

11

Live Communication

Note

If you subscribe to mailing-list digests (see Chapter 12), the Mail Contacts Online group usually includes the mailing list itself (in square brackets), but that means only that you can currently post e-mail messages to the list software.

Tip

You can use your Buddy List preferences to turn off the Mail Contacts Online feature. Here's how: From your Buddy List, click Setup. Then click Buddy List Preferences. Then uncheck the box "Show me the Mail Contacts Online Group...." Then save your changes.

▶ To add a buddy to your list, click the List Setup tab (see Figure 11-6). Select a group and then click the Add a Buddy button.

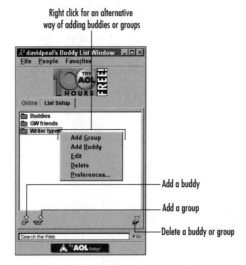

Figure 11-6. Add buddies and groups of buddies using the List Setup tab. AIM requires screen names even from non-AOL members, so you'll have to ask your Internet buddies for their AIM screen names.

AOL Mail Contacts: Chatting with Your E-mail Buddies

There's more than one way to respond to an e-mail message. You can respond by e-mail, of course, by just clicking Reply with the message displayed. Now, in AOL 5.0, whenever you open an e-mail message on AOL, your Buddy List window (Figure 11-8) indicates whether the message's sender, as well as any of the first seven recipients of the message, is currently online. These online buddies are listed in a new, automatically created Buddy List group at the top of the Buddy List. The new group is called Mail Contacts Online. (If you can't currently see your Buddy List, go to Keyword: **Buddyview**.)

The AOL screen names or Internet e-mail addresses of people who are online and can receive IM or AIM messages are listed in Mail Contacts Online. However, the address of anyone on-line who can't receive such messages is surrounded by square brackets. Bear in mind that AIM users can be online yet not signed onto AIM. In this case, their names appear in square brackets.

Sending Messages with AIM

Using your AIM Buddy List, you'll be able to see when your buddies are online. To send a message, double-click the online person's screen name. An Instant Messenger window pops up. Alternatively, in the Online tab select a buddy and click the Send Instant Message button at the bottom of the window. If your buddy is online, simply type what you want to say and click the Send button. As with AOL's IMs, you've got lots of formatting options to use if you want (see Figure 11-7).

AIM's most recent version (Figure 11-7) makes possible new or simplified tasks such as adding links, inserting images, dropping in graphical smileys, and sharing files with your buddies. To send an image, click the Images icon shown in Figure 11-7, and confirm that you want to create a special connection for exchanging images. Likewise, if you wish to talk with a buddy, using a microphone, AIM will set up a special connection for you. You can exchange files, too, with online buddies willing to receive them.

Select word in message; click this button to link word to a web site

Format text   Add image to your message

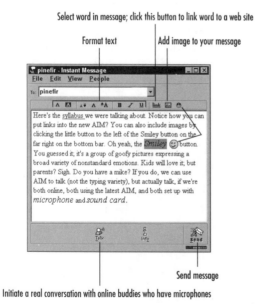

Initiate a real conversation with online buddies who have microphones

Send message

Figure 11-7. When you send a message such as this one from AIM, Internet recipients get the message in an AIM window; AOL recipients see it as an IM-type message.

Caution

Avoid IMs from strangers on AIM. Though you're on AOL, with AIM you are *not operating under AOL's Terms of Service* and lack TOS's guidelines and protections. Here's the AOL policy (from Keyword: **Notify AOL**): "Instant Message conversations with people using AOL Instant Messenger are not subject to AOL's Terms of Service. When you receive an Instant Message note from an Instant Messenger user, you will be asked if you want to accept or ignore the message. To further control who can send you Instant Message notes, use the Buddy List feature's Privacy Preferences. Go to Keyword: **Buddy**, then click Privacy Preferences." For more on these preferences, see "Screening Your Callers (AIM Preference)" later in this chapter.

Tip

Have you changed your e-mail address or AOL screen name? Go to My AIM ⇨ Edit Options ⇨ Update E-mail Address. Fill in the box and click OK.

11

Live Communication

Receiving Messages with AIM

You can receive IMs both from AOL members with AIM and Internet folks with AIM, unless you don't want to be contacted by people you don't know (see the "Setting Your AIM Preferences" section a little later for details on customizing AIM). When you're signed on to AOL and get an AIM-type message, you will be asked if you wish to accept it. Click Yes or No. Click Block to prevent the user from sending you any more messages.

Creating and Joining AIM Chats

AIM makes it easy for you to invite others to chats and to join chats yourself. Figure 11-8 shows the AIM chat environment, with a list of people present, the scrolling window where discussions takes place, and the box at the bottom to add your two cents.

To start up a chat, simply go to the Online tab and click the Send a Buddy Chat Invitation button at the bottom of your Buddy List window; type in buddies, with screen names separated by commas. When you click Send, you will automatically be transported to the chat window. Your invitees need only click a link to join you. Similarly, if you receive an invitation to a chat, you click a button to take part.

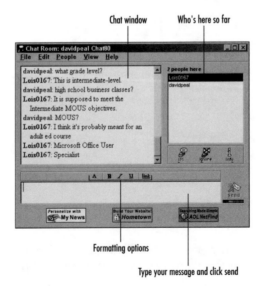

Figure 11-8. Join the growing communities of chatters who use AIM. Just click the Hyperlink URL button at the bottom of the AIM window (the button shows the picture of a cityscape).

Once you are in the chat room, you type your comments in the blank field in the center (see Figure 11-8). Click Send to transmit your message to the rest of the chat room participants.

Setting Your AIM Preferences

AIM preferences let you alter the look of your messages, the sounds that announce them, who can contact you, and all kinds of other things. Preferences are available by right-clicking the AIM icon in your "system tray" (at the bottom right of the Windows display). Select Preferences to view a window with more than a dozen, clearly labeled tabbed sections. Preferences always seem to look more complicated than they are. Why so many preferences? Because messages have to do with human communication — and impressions!

So much is possible with AIM that only a few of your many choices are highlighted here. AIM's truly helpful Help system (Help ⇨ Help Topics) can show you how to set up all the other preferences.

To edit any of your preferences, select My AIM ⇨ Edit Options ⇨ Edit Preferences from the Buddy List main menu. The Edit Preferences window appears, with different tabs on which you can change settings.

The General tab is especially useful for customizing AIM. You can

▶ Have AIM start up automatically each time you start Windows

▶ Change the fonts and colors used in the composing window to give your messages flourish

▶ Change the text magnification in the messages you receive so you can read them easily

The new Smileys button lets you insert one of the bright yellow expressions into a message (see Figure 11-7). You can turn them off by clicking the Disable Graphical Smilies box in the General tab. Similarly, you can make other minor modifications by selecting or deselecting the various options. When you have made the desired changes in the General tab, click OK to save them.

Tip

I know someone who swears by bold navy 11-point Arial on a light gray background. Try it, tweak it, and set up a distinctive text appearance that others will come to identify with you.

You can save all your AIM preferences to a text file, which you can then use with another copy of AIM running on another computer. Look for the AIM icon in your system tray (the far right end of your Windows 95/98 toolbar). Right-click. Select Save Buddy List. Give the file a name (e.g. *AIM*) and save it in a folder where you won't forget it (e.g., the America Online 5.0 folder). Copy that file to a floppy disk. While running AIM on another computer, reverse the procedure. Right-click the AIM icon in the system tray; select Load Buddy List; select the file (from the floppy); and follow the instructions.

Changing and Formatting Your Screen Name

AIM lets you change and format your AIM screen name. You might want to change screen names to suit your different roles (work and home) or to personalize access when several people in your house will be using AIM. To add a new screen name first register it at http://www.aol.com/aimand and then enter the new screen name over the old one at the AIM sign-on window.

Why would you want to *format* an AIM screen name? In a chat environment (or anywhere online), you may want to project a certain image — bold, serious, funky, whimsical, whatever (**GrLpowrz** with alternating, clashing colors, for example). You can alter the appearance of your screen name so that it uses the capitalization and spacing you like. Go to File ⇨ My Options ⇨ Format Screen Name. Enter your screen name, changing the capitalization and spacing so it looks the way you want it to look. All that matters is that the characters appear in the same order as your original AIM screen name.

You, Your Shadow, and Your AIM Profile

Your AIM profile says who you are, whether you're available for chatting, and anything else you want to share. By creating a profile, you can help friends and family find you online. Make your profile available for searching, and they can then use the Find a Buddy feature to look for you by interest, name, or e-mail address.

To set your profile, or to edit it, select File ⇨ My Profile from the AIM main window. See Figure 11-10. In the Create a Profile window, enter as much or as little information as you wish, and decide whether you want other users to be able to find

you — sort of like whether you want to have a listed or un-
listed telephone number. Once you enter as much personal
information as you feel comfortable with, click Next. You are
then asked if you are available for chat and, if so, what your
interests are. Make the appropriate selections, and click Next.
You can then enter a brief text description, formatted as you
want. Click Finish. You can edit this profile at any time by once
again selecting File ⇨ My Profile from the Buddy List menu.

The downside to having a profile is that strangers also have
access to this information unless you block all but a specific
number of users (which can be self-defeating). Like your profile in the AOL Member Directory, creating an AIM profile is
entirely voluntary. The two profiles are entirely separate.

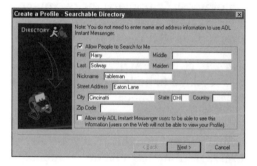

Figure 11-9. Edit your profile to reflect your personal information and
your interests.

Quick, Buddy

What if you're on the road, and can only manage a quick
hookup to the Internet? And what if you don't have AOL?
QuickBuddy provides the key features of AIM even if you
don't happen to have AOL or AIM at the moment. It's a small
program (a wonderful use of Java technology) that's delivered
over the Web and to your browser.

To use QuickBuddy, you must have already registered
with AIM. If you haven't already done so, go to `http://`
`www.aol.com/aim/` and follow the instructions. With
QuickBuddy, you use the same screen name and password
you use with AIM.

Once you have your screen name and password, go to
`http://www.aol.com/aim/quickbuddy/about.html`
and click the QuickBuddy button. You can be using the AOL
browser, Netscape, or Internet Explorer. A separate tiny

browser window pops up, where you can have a conversation (with two or more people) just as you would on AIM. When you finish chatting, just close the window. The full range of AIM features (file sharing, saving conversations, and so on) is not available using QuickBuddy, but as a simple device for chatting on the Web, it's brilliant.

groups@AOL

In the past, AOL members and their Internet brethren communicate with each other primarily by e-mail. AOL Instant Messenger has helped enormously in bringing the two otherwise close communities even closer together, because it enables one-to-one conversations as well as group chat.

New in AOL 5.0, groups@AOL gives the AOL and non-AOL communities all the tools required to build lasting virtual communities that include anyone who's online.

Groups@AOL gives AOL members the ability to create and control their own communities, and then invite anyone on AOL or the Net to join. An AOL group has a unique combination of features that, together, make it an ideal venue where family, friends, hobbyists, business colleagues, students, classmates, and anyone else can meet and share information.

> ▶ **Starting a group.** Any AOL member can start a group by simply visiting Keyword: **groups@aol** and providing the required information.

> ▶ **Joining a group.** The group leader can invite anyone on AOL or the Internet to join the group; people can't join unless they're invited. Leaders can also invite members to take part in leading the group.

Groups are meant to be more personal than traditional Internet communities. When people join a group, they ordinarily fill out a short personal profile and choose an avatar — a cartoon-like image that can be used to represent them in communicating through the group's message board. Unlike a newsgroup (see Chapter 13), an AOL Group can't be browsed by outsiders.

AOL members who are invited into a group and want to join are automatically admitted. Non-AOL members must first download and register the free AOL Instant Messenger software. They'll use their AIM screen names in communicating with group members.

Note

Groups are responsible for their own actions online. Any person invited to join a group that apparently engages in illegal activities can use Keyword: **Notify AOL** to file a report.

▶ **Better than chat**. Unlike chat rooms, a group persists and offers more than one way to communicate: e-mail and message boards as well as AIM-based chat and one-to-one live conversations.

▶ **Joint calendar**. Groups can maintain their copy of My Calendar (covered in Chapter 3) in order to keep track of group events. Individuals in the group can copy events from their group's calendar to their own copy of My Calendar. Birthdays entered into a member's profile (when they join the group) are automatically transferred to the group's joint calendar.

▶ **Group e-mail**. As people join a group, they are automatically enrolled in a sort of mailing list (see Chapter 13 on lists). By sending a message to the group's address (groupname@group.aol.com), the message is sent to the mailboxes of every member of the group. In addition, within a group, members can use a special e-mail form, available on the group's Web page, allowing them to send mail to one or more members.

▶ **Group Web page**. What gives groups a feeling of stability, compared to the more fluid world of chat, is the Web page that's automatically generated for each group. This page provides the group's tangible home, and the place at which the group's shared resources can be found — its calendar, shared photos, message board, and list of favorite things. The Web site shows which group members are online at any time.

▶ **Group message boards**. The Web page hosts a simple message board which members can use as the group's bulletin board. The board holds up to 200 messages. The most recent message appear on the group's private Welcome screen. Only group members, of course, can read and post messages.

▶ **AIM on steroids**. Group members can carry on live one-to-one or group chats using AOL Instant Messenger, with all of AIM's powerful features (see previous section for a summary of those features).

11

Live Communication

The next few pages and the accompanying figures illustrate the Advanced mode in order to show you what's possible on ICQ; I strongly suggest, however, that you start, as most people do, in the simple mode until you get the hang of ICQ.

Want to build a virtual community around a specific interest, consisting of your high-school classmates, fellow hobbyists, or anybody else? On ICQ you can create a virtual community that's held together by many different communications elements: chat, e-mail, the Web, files, and more. ICQ collects all resources you need as a site creator in one place (visit http://www.icq.com/sitecreator/). Searching for a community to join? ICQ's real-time answer to AOL's Hometown is the IRC Network (visit http://www.icq.com/networks/).

Check out *ICQ For Dummies* by IDG Books Worldwide.

▶ **Group favorites**. Individual AOL members can create their own Favorite Places (Chapter 3). Group members can do so, too, using their Web page to list them. The Favorite Things list is a jointly compiled list of favorite movies, books, restaurants, Web sites, jokes, and anything else the group wants to keep track of.

▶ **Group pictures**. Members can share pictures of kids, vacations, group functions, and so on., in a fashion similar to You've Got Pictures. The images will be linked from the front page of the group's Web page.

▶ **Parental Controls**. Groups are subject to Parental Controls (see Chapter 3), and the children on a master account can be given access to groups. However, to the extent other AOL features are integrated with groups (such as the My Calendar and You've Got Pictures), kids will be blocked from using those features.

Global Communications with ICQ

ICQ ("I Seek You") calls itself the "World's Largest Internet Communication Network." Is this true? Who knows? You'll just have to find out for yourself. Give yourself plenty of time to explore the huge number of options available with this amazing program.

Like AIM, ICQ lets you chat with others and also have one-to-one conversations. While AIM is an extension of AOL, ICQ is its own world — younger, more international, perhaps a bit less family-oriented, packed with communications tools of its own.

On ICQ you can

▶ Create your own ICQ home page from which to coordinate your communications — and through which others can communicate with you.

▶ Create your own ICQ chat room.

▶ Find a directory of Internet-telephone users, so you can actually use software such as Internet Phone (see Chapter 17 for a profile of this program).

▶ Keep your To Do list handy and create Reminders.

▶ Chat in different languages, with people from different countries, on topics of shared interest. Or, get a new perspective on anything of interest.

▶ Create a mailing list.

▶ Join chats on specific subjects.

▶ Get help with any aspect of ICQ, at any level of expertise, from ICQ's legions of volunteers.

▶ Use one of ICQ's Web's portals, perhaps as a home page.

These are *your* tools, designed so you can make your own communities, complete with Web chat, IRC, mailing lists, and other features. Keep in mind that you can build communities on ICQ, not just join others'. For an understanding of ICQ's diverse capabilities, you have to explore them. If it has to do with (live) communication, it's probably available through ICQ. The next few pages can get you started but don't come close to exhausting the program's possibilities.

Downloading and Installing ICQ

Download the latest version of ICQ from `http://www.icq.com/`. You might have to get ICQ from another site, however. Because of the chat program's popularity, the ICQ site is often busy. When that's the case you'll get some recommended alternatives at ICQ.com, such as TUCOWS and CNET, the download warehouses discussed in Chapter 17.

Once you have downloaded ICQ, find it on your hard drive, and double-click to install it. You're then prompted to register. Select a nick (nickname, that is) and password, and ICQ automatically assigns you a number. You're ready to go.

ICQ: Some Key Features

On ICQ, it can be hard to know where to start and where to go for help (a huge difference from AOL). Up front, be aware that ICQ takes place on both the Web and in the ICQ pro-

Note

Unlike AIM, ICQ allows duplicate nicks (screen names); some nicks are shared by dozens of users. The only way to tell apart two users with duplicate nicks is by their ICQ number and name, so make sure to search using two pieces of information.

Tip

Use the Invitation Wizard to invite people to use ICQ that you know aren't yet on ICQ (click ICQ on the main window — refer to Figure 11-13 — for the wizard).

Note

ICQ, for all the millions of people using it, is still under continual development. Don't be surprised to see features diverging from the way they're described here. And don't be surprised if you have to download and upgrade ICQ more often than other programs.

11

Live Communication

Note

Unlike AOL Instant Messenger, with ICQ you can communicate with ICQ people who aren't online; your message will be waiting for them next time they use ICQ.

Tip

Consider forming a group of your own for your family, company, Brownie troop, church, or synagogue fellowship group, whatever. Groups offer the power of ICQ without the great complexity of that software (see the next section for a surface review of ICQ's myriad features). AOL has exciting plans for groups@aol, including the close integration of You've Got Pictures, My Calendar, and the People Directory.

gram. One place that gives general orientation is the ICQ *Web* home page at http://www.icq.com (you'll see this later in Figure 11-18), which helps you get the software, get started, find friends, get help, and link up with other users. For general help, use the ICQ Site Guide at http://www.icq.com/products/webguide.html. To use the ICQ program itself (the thing you downloaded), start at the small window shown in Figure 11-10, which opens whenever you run ICQ.

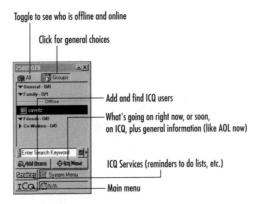

Figure 11-10. ICQ's main window (Advanced). The simple ICQ window has one tab on top, fewer communication options, and lacks the services and other features.

When you open ICQ, you start at the small window shown in Figure 11-13. This window has two "modes": simple and advanced. The simple mode keeps the window open whatever you're doing and provides a simpler set of choices (for example, not quite as many types of communications).

The ICQ window shown in Figure 11-10 (Advanced mode) has two tabs. One tab functions as a buddy list (the tab on the left, labeled All or Online). The other tab is a sort of control panel with some frequently used functions.

Finding and Adding People to Your ICQ List

You can find people in ICQ in several ways: by unique ICQ number (if you have it), by nick (if you know their ICQ screen name), by e-mail, or by profile details (if the person has made this information available).

Click the Add Users button on the ICQ window (Figure 11-10). In the search window (see Figure 11-11), enter any information you have: e-mail address in conjunction with a name, or just the first and last name. Click Search to begin. If the search is successful, the results appear in a new window with the user's ICQ number and corresponding nick. You can double-click the user information to add the user to ICQ's version of a buddy list. You will be asked which group you want to place the user in. Select the appropriate one, and click OK. Repeat the process to add as many users as you want to your list.

In the main ICQ menu the button at the bottom-right corner indicates your online status to others. Click to put out different signs on your virtual door: Do Not Disturb, N/A, Away, Free for Chat, and so forth.

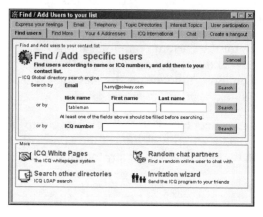

Figure 11-11. Finding someone on ICQ, using any information you happen to have

Throughout ICQ you'll find other ways of searching for people: from the window in Figure 11-10, for example, you can find a random chat partner. Or, click Add Users to get the big set of directories shown in Figure 11-11. Using these directories, you can find ICQ users accessible by Internet phone; users with specific interests; and users in different countries or speakers of different languages. ICQ's White Pages enable you to search by age, gender, interests, occupation, affiliation, location, and other criteria. In a few seconds I could find many ICQ users with my professional interests and in my town (none in both categories, though).

Not everyone you find using any of these methods automatically wants to take part in online communications with you. Their time, like yours, is limited. Their needs, like yours, may be highly specific. When you find the user's name in a search and then try to add it to your ICQ buddy list, a Privacy window pops up, asking you to send the user a request to be added to your list. Type in your reason in the box, making sure to clearly identify yourself and your interests. Click Request. When the user checks ICQ messages on the next login, your request will be among them. Once users respond affirmatively to your request, they'll be added to your list.

Security and privacy safeguards have been built into ICQ. Rather than ICQ protecting you and your children, it's up to you to protect yourself. ICQ provides the tools. Click the ICQ button at the lower-left corner of your ICQ window (again, see Figure 11-13), and select Security and Privacy from the pop-up menu. In the Security window, make and save your changes. Here you can password-protect your settings, make your online presence invisible to certain users, and ask ICQ to filter out any messages containing certain words.

11

Live Communication

Sending Messages

Find It Online

To keep up with all of the new ICQ features, visit the ICQ What's New page *frequently* (http://www.icq.com/products/news.html).

Messaging is at the heart of ICQ. In ICQ you can send your message to an entire group at once or to a single user. Unlike AOL's AIM's instant messages, with ICQ you're confronted at once with a broad range of ways and *things* to communicate. You can send a simple (or highly formatted) text message; a URL; a file; a greeting card; a voice message if you and your buddy are set up for sound; or, check this out, an e-mail message. See Figure 11-12 for the current communications choices. Also unlike IMs and AIMs, many of the choices are available offline and online; offline means the messages will be awaiting the user's next visit.

From the main window, select either an individual or group to send a message (select a group, and you get the option of sending a message to the whole group or any individual in it).

Figure 11-12. You have many ways to communicate in ICQ: e-mail, greeting cards, file-sharing, and more.

If the user to whom you want to say something is currently online, clicking and selecting the option Send Message to Username displays the Send Online Message window. If that person is currently offline, the Send Offline Message window appears instead, as shown in Figure 11-13. In either case, type your message and format it as you please. Once you've finished the message, click Send.

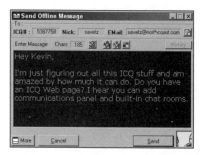

Figure 11-13. Creating an ICQ message is like writing an e-mail message.

Being Found

Just as you click Add Users in the ICQ window to search for someone (by his or her e-mail address, interests, name, or e-mail address), so can others find you in the same way — if you've taken the time to make information available about yourself.

If you are running a business and actively seeking new customers, you may want to make your contact information easily available, of course. And if you are living alone, you may want to hide your home address and phone number from the rest of the world. A good compromise on ICQ is to make a limited amount of personal information available, but to set up your options so that users who want to add you to their ICQ list must first request your permission.

Here's how to create a profile (called My Details) listing personal information and interests:

1. Click the ICQ button at the lower-left corner of the ICQ window.

2. Select Change My Details to show the personal information you have already entered, and to change it if you want. The ICQ Global Directory window pops up (Figure 11-14), with nine tabs on which you can enter or edit information about your affiliations, your phone contact information, your work, your interests, your picture, and so on.

Sending voice messages works best if both you and your caller have fast Internet connections. While a 28.8K modem may work well most of the time, eventually you'll want to move up to broadband, as discussed in Chapter 18.

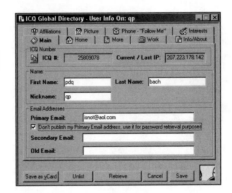

Figure 11-14. Provide as much or as little information about yourself as you want.

3. Add as much information as you like, and click Save when finished to save the changes. You can change this information at any time by returning to your profiles and editing them. Your details can always be viewed from the main ICQ window (click ICQ) or the ICQ White Pages directory (click OK when you're done).

ICQ's Important Portal

These days everyone's trying to create a *portal*, those virtual mega-malls from which you're supposed to set sail and at which you're supposed to drop anchor after your daily odyssey. ICQ plays this game, too, with features and a look designed to appeal to people eager to communicate with others. The ICQ Homepage provides a wealth of information on various topics, as you might be able to tell from Figure 11-15. If you need help with any aspect of this huge program, you'll find it here — including help provided by ICQ users such as yourself.

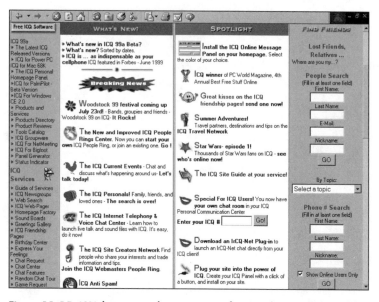

Figure 11-15. ICQ's home page; the starting point for more than you bargained for!

A Quick Look Back

This chapter introduced AOL's Instant Messages (IMs), the easy-to-use tool for holding one-to-one conversations with other AOL members who are online. I also gave a glimmer of what you can do with AOL's two great tools for communicating on the Internet:

- ▶ AOL Instant Messenger (an extension of AOL's Instant Messages)
- ▶ ICQ (the ten-headed version of the same animal)

AIM can be put to use right now to stay in touch with family, classmates, and others. ICQ, with its endless communication possibilities, takes a while to use to its full capacity. Use either tool to chat with others, organize your work time, save on long-distance phone charges, play games, find friends, and meet others with similar interests. Both programs are completely free — to AOL members and the broader Internet community alike.

11

Live Communication

VIRTUAL COMMUNITIES:

MAILING LISTS

Chapter 12

Virtual Communities: Mailing Lists

The Internet mailing list takes a great idea–electronic mail–and improves upon it. Many people consider these lists the Net's most useful resource and most effective community-builder. Lists can plug you into groups of novices and experts who share a strong professional or personal concern.

Here's how lists work. Say you work for a company in which many off-site workers are dispersed across the country. Or, you are taking an accounting class with people scattered throughout your metropolitan area. A mailing list gives you a way to stay in regular touch with everyone in the group. You'll know what's going on at work, and you won't miss anything that goes on in class. When you want to tell your work group about an upcoming meeting, or share a blinding insight with your classmates, you don't have to send the same message to each individual in the group or class; all you have to do is send a single message that goes to everyone in the group.

Definition

A mailing list is nothing more than a list of e-mail addresses, just like the lists you can create with your AOL Address Book. (To create such a list, click the New Group button in your Address Book, as shown in Figure 12-1. Give the list a name, and type in a bunch of e-mail addresses. The Address Book doesn't care whether you include the e-mail addresses of people on AOL or not on AOL.)

Subscribing to a list just means adding your e-mail address to a list of other addresses. There's nothing to pay, and you can quit at any time. Only subscribers can send a message to other subscribers.

Figure 12-1. A list of e-mail addresses; a single message to the group goes to every individual whose e-mail address is listed.

Internet mailing lists go beyond the capabilities of your Address Book, of course. Special mailing-list software lets the people who run lists automatically take care of chores such as making sure all the e-mail addresses are active and streamlining the process by which people join and leave lists. As lists grow and as list members change e-mail addresses, such chores can become very time-consuming.

List software means that a much greater number of people can take part, more effectively, with more options for customizing the way they receive and send lists messages. By making the special list software available on the Net, lists lose the strictly private feel of your Address Book buddies without becoming as public as newsgroups, which are discussed in the next chapter.

Lists have evolved in recent years to take advantage of the Web.

12

Virtual Communities

▶ E-mail messages to lists can now contain hyperlinks to Web sites. Lists have always been an outstanding method of sharing news of Internet resources with a group of people with the same interest; sharing discoveries is now more immediate. A great example is the AOL.COM Update newsletter, which each week brings site reviews to your mailbox. The reviews are linked, so you can visit the sites with just a click.

▶ Many lists now have searchable Web archives of list messages, so anyone (including non-subscribers) can find messages on particular subjects. Searching such archives is a good way to find out whether a list you're thinking of joining has what you want and is worth the daily effort of screening messages from the list.

▶ Many lists become the nucleus of dedicated communities, which have real-world meetings and create Web sites that form tangible, or at least virtual, community centers. Such sites also serve to share the community's resources with the larger Internet.

▶ On the Web you'll find more and more mailing lists that can be joined *on* the Web, rather than through the older, more cumbersome e-mail based subscription methods of the recent past. On such sites, all you have to do is fill in your name and e-mail address, sometimes just your e-mail address, and you'll be automatically subscribed.

▶ Likewise, Web fill-in-the-blank forms let you set your preferences and tailor the content you receive, rather than having to figure out the e-mail commands.

▶ Many Web sites use mailing lists to keep in touch with their communities–the people who frequent them and share the same interests. Such lists are very easy to join (usually you only have to type in your e-mail address and press Enter), and they can help you stay informed about additions to the Web site.

▶ Finally, a new crop of list providers (companies that set up and maintain lists for you) put everything on the Web — except the actual messages that subscribers send each other. You can create a list, and others can discover, join, and participate in the list at the list provider's Web site. See "Creating Your Own Mailing List" later in this chapter.

All of these new dimensions of the simple mailing list have powerfully extended its usefulness, and will be discussed later in this chapter. The next sections look at the two major types of mailing lists:

- ▶ The interactive kind, in which subscribers can send messages to the entire group
- ▶ The non-interactive kind, sometimes known as newsletters, which are sent from one person or organization to a list of subscribers

Mailing Lists You Can Take Part In

In their earliest incarnation (1975 in one account, 1981 in another), mailing lists were discussion groups. People started and joined them to stay in touch with other people.

E-mail has a lot of advantages over other types of communication, and by extension so do mailing lists. Most important, you're under less pressure to respond (no pressure, really) than if you were having a face-to-face conversation or finger-to-finger electronic conversation (Instant Message or chat). When you get a message you can respond at your own pace, thinking through each word and editing your own message. Or, you can choose *not* to respond. With mail and mailing lists, you can keep a record of these slow-motion, potentially thoughtful electronic conversations, and you can listen in (*lurk* is the term of art) to the conversations of the real experts (or big mouths) in your group or profession.

Discussion lists differ in three important ways.

1. How they're **managed**–the software used to keep them going. That's not your problem, but the business of the list's owner. However, it does affect the mechanical things like how you subscribe to a list and how you leave it, and which options are available.

2. The extent to which they're **moderated**. Moderation refers to the right of the person in charge of the list to screen all messages to the list, keeping out offensive or off-topic messages and also blocking messages they don't agree with. We're talking about a continuum here.

 Note

Not surprisingly, the first lists were on technical subjects. Telecomm Digest, still very active, claims to be the first list (1975). The list's digest and history, with a highly selective set of telecommunications links, can be found at http://hyperarchive.lcs.mit.edu/telecom-archives/.

Tip

To save any message to a file, open the message and select File ⇨ Save As. Give the file a name and put it in a convenient folder on your hard drive. The message will be saved as a text file.

Listiquette (Mailing List Netiquette)

It's okay to lurk on lists. That is, it's fine to listen to what others have to say without saying anything yourself. In any learning community, such observation is often the best way to learn how things are done in a group and to learn *about* whatever the list's active subscribers are discussing. There is no rule that you ever have to take part, and some expectation that you only take part if you have something to say (like a town-hall meeting or some classrooms, in that sense). At any rate, lists have their own cultural quirks, and lurking can help you respect them if you do eventually take part.

While it is fine to introduce yourself to the entire group in an e-mail message (in list-based support groups focused on a disease, for example), it is less appreciated if you ask basic questions. Less appreciated yet, don't ask people to do your homework for you. Least appreciated are responses to others' messages such as "right on" or "me too!"

Chapter 9 showed you how to quote e-mail messages in responding to them. On lists, such selective quoting is even more critical, since the quoted material goes into the mailboxes of dozens or perhaps thousands of other people. It's annoying re-reading messages quoted in their entirety, when a single word or two would have provided enough context for a person's comments.

Another bit of netiquette that carries over from e-mail: humor and irony can more easily backfire in a semi-anonymous environment than in a one-to-one exchange such as e-mail. Write clear subject lines. Respect the diversity of your audience in your messages.

Finally, on mailing lists, many people like to know who is behind a message. AOL 5.0 now lets you create signatures for your messages, several lines of text identifying you to the others. For Internet mailing lists, make sure to use text only (not formatted text). Provide enough information to give some idea of where you are coming from. Chapter 9 has some examples.

Substantive, useful, on-topic lists are moderated to keep them focused. Good lists also thrive on trust and sociability, and don't like one person silencing subscribers without a really good reason. Good list-owners will, however, also step in to prevent one subscriber from flaming or annoying another.

3. Most important, discussion groups vary in their **content**: the daily traffic, the ratio of "signal" to "noise" (good stuff to garbage), and the general spirit of the group.

Electronic Newsletters

A growing number of lists don't let you carry on discussions with the other people on the list. In fact, you usually can't even find out who's *on* the list. These non-interactive lists work like newsletters, with the same message and same information (of any kind) going out to a large number of people. They can also be compared to regularly posted mailings, with the difference that they are solicited and can usually be readily discontinued (wouldn't you love to turn off the junk-mail spigot that easily?).

AOL publishes a large number of such one-way newsletters, all of which can be joined at Keyword: **Newsletter** (Figure 12-2). Most AOL channels create weekly newsletters devoted to new AOL resources, new Internet resources, and relevant goings on in the channel. A few AOL newsletters are highlighted at the end of this chapter.

Different organizations offer mailing lists to keep members, donors, and other interested parties up to date. Such informational mailing lists can provide a key professional service while also promoting the organization's work. For example, I receive several mailing lists on learning disabilities, including the *LD Online Report,* which supports the leading Web site on the subject; you can join the list at the site.

Tip

Subscribe to **Net Newsletters** and receive about 20 of the Net's most informative electronic newsletters, such as Seidman's Online Insider, the Internet Tourbus, and Dummies Daily, IDG Books Worldwide, Inc.'s newsletter(s) on Net goings-on. Look for a subscription form where you can provide your name and e-mail address at http://scout.cs.wisc.edu/caservices/net-news/.

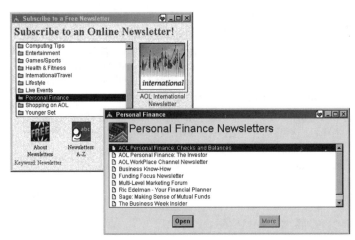

Figure 12-2. All of AOL's mailing lists, including this one, can be found at Keyword: *Newsletter.*

Some newsletters serve informational purposes, but the information is strictly commercial. For example, if you buy things on the Web, such as books, CDs, and software, almost all major vendors make it easy for you to subscribe to a regular mailing list. The purpose of many such lists is to bring special sales and offers to your attention.

More and more companies make it easy for you to subscribe to their lists and newsletters. They have a good reason: when you show interest in their products and services, they learn their market, and eventually figure out a non-intrusive way to offer products and services customized to individuals' preferences.

One popular newsletter genre plies you with something new every day. With a little effort using Liszt (as described later in this chapter), you can get lists that bring you a new word every day, a new recipe, a new Bible message, a new joke (clean or dirty, take your pick), a list of things that happened on this date in history, a quote, or just about anything else-a-day.

For example, A Word A Day (AWAD) features daily offerings on themes that change every week or so (Figure 12-3 shows a typical daily message). Each day's word includes a definition, a quote, and a link to an audio file in which the word is pronounced. AWAD's Web site includes browsable and searchable archives of words sent out through the list, going back to early

1994. At the Web site you can both subscribe to and unsubscribe from the list, and even send a gift subscription to someone else. A neat thing about AWAD is the monthly summary of who's subscribing and from what countries.

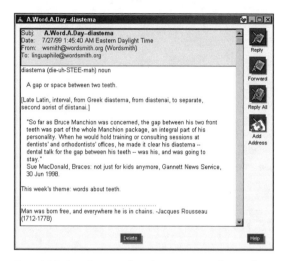

Figure 12-3. Today's word is...diastema. From the popular AWAD mailing list.

A popular informational newsletter for many AOL members is the Portfolio Direct Daily Report, which provides a personalized market wrap-up. Subscribers receive a review of each stock in their stock portfolios, with gains and losses, links to company information available on AOL, and business stories about those stocks compiled from Reuters and Bloomberg. Go to Keyword: **PDC** (Figure 12-4) to sign up.

At AOL's Personal Finance channel you can also subscribe to Multex's regular market newsletters, which go into more detail about certain market sectors. Many leading brokerages offer free or for-fee company reports, too.

Finally, in the same "daily" category, several big news services and Web sites bring the day's news to your mailbox — before the 6 o'clock news. Wired Daily is one such service, which you can customize to your interests (culture, finance, and so forth) (http://www.wired.com). Infobeat is another, which offers a range of types of daily business news, depending on your interests (http://www.infobeat.com).

12

Virtual Communities

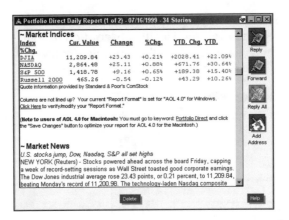

Cross-Reference

Chapter 6 goes into the difference between indexes (which are automatically created by software) and directories (which consist of hand-picked resources).

Figure 12-4. AOL's Portfolio Direct, where you can create a tailored daily report showing how your portfolio is doing

Finding Lists to Join

Searching for mailing lists is different from searching the Web. All you have to work with are the *names* of mailing lists after all. You can't (yet) search the content of mailing lists as you can search for words that appear on Web pages. Another difference (this one more positive) from searching the Web: with mailing lists, you don't have a hopeless profusion of search engines to choose from. Instead, you've got two major ones:

▶ Liszt, an automated list of lists, with some nifty features (similar to a Web *index*)

▶ PAML, a hand-created and well-organized catalog of mailing lists (similar to a Web *directory*)

I'll also look at some of the less well-known sources of information about mailing lists.

Liszt

Liszt (a friendly, gratuitous play on the name of the composer) is a searchable database of close to 100,000 mailing lists of all kinds. The number is impressive, but it includes its fair share of chaff. To make up for the uneven quality of lists, Liszt Select is a mini-directory of approximately 3,000 "public, general-interest" mailing lists. Searching Liszt means asking

Liszt to look for a word or several words in a database consisting of the names of mailing lists.

Notice that when you enter more than one word in the text box, you can specify whether to search for any of the words, all of the words, or all the words in the order you typed them (that is, a *phrase*). For example, if you're interested in *rock climbing* and search for *any* of those words, the search will root around and return a large number of lists having to do with rock and roll, perhaps, but not necessarily with rock climbing. Searching for the phrase "rock climbing" on the other hand, is too narrow because it assumes that everyone thinks of the subject the same way, with the same language, as you do. What worked best in this case was a less ambiguous but sufficiently broad search for the single word *climbing*.

Or, take MP3, the popular music format discussed in Chapter 4. A Liszt search for MP3-related lists turned up what seem like some useful lists (Figure 12-5). MP3 is known around the Internet world, and the search term *MP3* is unlikely to be confused with anything else.

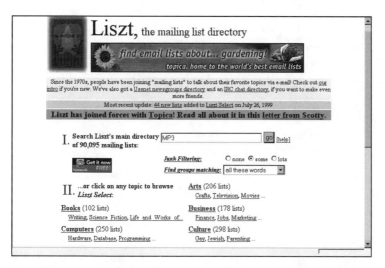

Figure 12-5. Liszt, where you can search for specific mailing lists and browse directories of lists recommended by others

For any results retrieved by Liszt, click an underlined list name, as in Figure 12-6, and Liszt takes you to a page of information. Unfortunately, the information is usually generic and concerns the type of list you're dealing with. That is, if it's a

LISTSERV-type list, you get instructions for subscribing to LIST-SERV-type lists, taking part in them, and unsubscribing from them (all of which information is summarized in "Mechanics of Joining and Taking Part in a LISTSERV Discussion List," coming up).

Liszt also gives you the opportunity to recommend a mailing list for Liszt Select, though if you're just learning about the list yourself, recommending it might seem a bit premature. For lists in the Select category, clicking the link takes you to a somewhat fuller description list, including a link to the list's home page on the Web, if there is one.

Liszt takes its search a step further. Say you're interested in MP3 but want to take part in larger, public discussion forums — that is, you don't want to join a mailing list. When you get your mailing-list results, scroll down to the bottom of the page to post the identical query (MP3) to other search engines that retrieve lists of MP3 newsgroups and IRC channels, Web-based discussion boards about MP3, and more, not all of which are equally useful–are you really interested in books and movies about MP3?

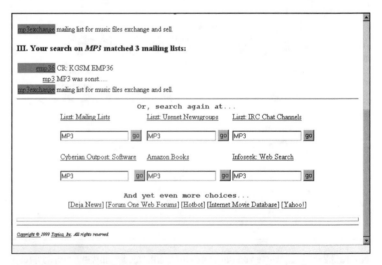

Figure 12-6. Results of the Liszt quest in Figure 12-6, including one list in Liszt Select. Look at the many follow-on MP3 searches you can conduct: newsgroups about MP3, IRC chat channels, books, Web-based message boards, Hotbot, etc.

Think of a newsgroup as a discussion group more public than a mailing list; there's no subscribing, and anyone can post. An

IRC channel is the real-time (live) version of the public news-group, they're freewheeling Internet chat rooms. As it turns out, this Liszt search turned up 35 newsgroups and more than almost 500 IRC channels having to do with MP3.

Publicly Accessible Mailing Lists (PAML)

An annotated directory of mailing lists, usefully organized into subjects, PAML goes back to the early 1980s, in the Internet's Mesozoic era. Since 1992 Stephanie da Silva has kept this Internet classic current (a heroic example of Net voluntarism). You can browse lists of either subject or names. In my experience, the search facility did not work reliably, but the purpose and size of PAML is such that browsing makes more sense.

Mechanics of Joining and Taking Part in a LISTSERV Discussion List

Different types of mailing list software (such as LISTSERV and majordomo) all provide a standard way to subscribe and unsubscribe. You'll encounter variety in how lists are administered, because of the wide variety of list-management software.

In this section I'll look at the mechanics of joining and taking part in a specific, common, well-established type of list, administered by a type of software called LISTSERV. Created in 1986 by Eric Thomas, LISTSERV was originally designed for old-fashioned IBM mainframe computers and a network called BIT-NET. That's all ancient history, and today LISTSERV is owned and licensed by L-Soft International, Inc.

Subscribing to LISTSERVs

Subscribing to any mailing list means adding your e-mail address to the list's other addresses. Subscribing to a LISTSERV list requires that you send an e-mail message to the list software saying that you want to join. For example, if you want to join ROCKCLIMBER, the name of a fictitious mailing list, you would create the e-mail message shown in Figure 12-7.

Cross-Reference

Newsgroups are covered in the next chapter and IRC in the previous chapter.

Tip

If you're a newsgroup person or want your personal copy of this list of lists, visit the newsgroups: news.answers or news.lists.misc. While not coming close to the *number* of lists you can search at Liszt, PAML does offer greater selectivity and more information about individual lists, with information files and Web sites (where available).

12

Virtual Communities

Figure 12-7. Subscribing to a LISTSERV list takes a simple e-mail message like this one — instead of ROCKCLIMBER, type in the name of the list you want to join.

To subscribe to a LISTSERV list, you send a message to the list's administrative address, as follows:

1. Open the Write Mail window by clicking the Write button on the toolbar.

2. In the Send To window, type **listserv@listserv. rockyhills.com**.

   For your list, the address will differ, but it will often begin with *listserv@*.

3. Leave the Subject box blank.

4. In the body, type SUBSCRIBE ROCKCLIMBER.

   Instead of ROCKCLIMBER, type in the name of the LISTSERV list you wish to receive.

5. Click Send Now.

Here are a couple of things to note about this very simple process:

▶ Use the ***listserv****@listserv.rockyhills.com* address for all your administrative mail (subscribing, unsubscribing, and so forth). For actual lists, you'll often see administrative addresses beginning *listserv@*....

▶ Use the actual name of the list (in this case, **rockclimber**@listserv.rockyhills.com) to send messages to the other people who have subscribed to the list.

   For actual lists, the addresses to send a message to people on the list begin the list's name, such as WWWEDU, DEOS-L, ITFORUM, etc.

▶ With AOL's mail program, you don't have to use the annoying uppercase LISTSERV@; lowercase is fine.

> ▶ LISTSERV (the software) doesn't care what's in the
> Subject line; it ignores it.

Very soon (often less than a minute or two) after subscribing,
you receive an e-mail acknowledgement of your request. In
some cases, you will then receive a welcome message almost
immediately thereafter. However, with most LISTSERV lists,
you will likely be asked to confirm your subscription by visiting a URL or sending back a confirmation message. To visit the
URL, simply visit the link to confirm your subscription. If you
do not have the option of visiting a URL, send a confirmation
message as described in the instructions you receive.

You will then receive, if you haven't already, an e-mail message
welcoming you to the list itself. You should keep this message.
In fact, it's a good idea to save all welcome messages in your
Favorite Places folder (explained in Chapter 3). The message
will tell you how to take part in the list, how to get a list of
commands for the list, and how to unsubscribe when
the time comes.

Posting to a LISTSERV List

Within minutes or hours, and at regular intervals (daily or
weekly), messages from the list start coming into your AOL
electronic mailbox. For *you* to post to the list, you can respond to another posting; this is called taking part in a *thread*
(as in the thread of an argument). Or, you can start a topic of
your own by sending an e-mail message to the list itself, rather
than to the administrative address (rockclimber@listserv.
rockyhills.com, rather than listserv@listserv.rockyhills.com).
Always use a brief, precise Subject line to clarify your
new topic.

In general, no fixed rules apply to posting, unless the list
moderator has created such rules. Many lists reject commercial postings and unsolicited mail. For example, a list for
English teachers is not the place for textbook salespeople to
make an unsolicited pitch for their new titles. Spamming a list,
sending unsolicited commercial messages without any rela-
tion to the list's purpose, is bad form and likely to have some
negative consequences. Some of these miss-steps can result in
flaming — nasty messages going back and forth. Flames add
to people's irritation. Sending spam can get people kicked off
the list, which is always the list owner's prerogative.

Note

Once subscribed to a list,
you might get random
administrative messages
asking you to confirm your
continued interest (which
you can usually do with a
simple reply) or to verify that
your address is active (you
can usually ignore these
messages).

Tip

If the e-mail address begins
LISTSERV@... or listproc@...
or majordomo@... or some-
thing similar, you're dealing
with an administrative address. E-mail addresses beginning with something
meaningful (like ROCK-
CLIMBER or ending in a *dash
L* (–L) (such as DEOS-L) indicate that you're dealing with
the list itself and can make a
contribution — if it's a discussion list, of course.

12

Virtual Communities

Tip

Watch that Reply button in AOL when you're reading your lists. Hitting Reply usually picks up the list's address as the recipient of your message, not the author of the message you're responding to. In the case of daily digests, discussed below, replying to the digest will *prevent* your reply from reaching anyone. In replying to digests and to individuals, you'll have to copy and paste e-mail addresses to make sure your message gets where it's meant to go.

Responding to the List Versus Responding to a Person on the List

Some messages will make you think of something personal that you want to share with the sender of the message, as when the sender asks for very specific information that you happen to know. Some messages will come from people you know personally, and will inspire a personal comment or aside. And in response to some list messages you will want to share a long tome. *Make sure to send these kinds of messages directly to the sender and not to the list as a whole.* E-mail headers (the *header* is discussed in Chapter 9 and 10) provide you with lots of information, so you can usually figure out readily enough the e-mail address of the person who sent the message; use that address, not the list's address, in such personal responses.

Making LISTSERV Work Your Way

LISTSERV offer a wide range of options for users to tailor how and when they receive messages. Many of these options are rarely used, I suspect, because their usefulness isn't clear or few know they exist. That's too bad, since commands can be useful.

At any time, you can get a list of LISTSERV commands available for a list by sending a message to a list's software (for example, listserv@wvnvm.wvnet.edu) saying **help**. In response you'll get a list of common commands. Send a message saying **info refcard**, and you'll get comprehensive LISTSERV commands. To use a command, you simply send it to a list's administrative address (for example, listserv@wvnetvm.wvnet.edu).

Leaving a LISTSERV List

You can leave a mailing list for many reasons: you don't like it; it's taking too much time; it's not what you thought it would be. A not-so-good reason to leave a list is that you're going away for a vacation or will be out of touch for a week and don't want to get flooded by e-mail while you're away. Use the SET *list* MAIL command to turn off mail temporarily, or use the SET *list* DIGEST command to get one message a day instead of several messages.

If you ever cancel your AOL account, first make sure to unsubscribe to all the mailing lists you've subscribed to. If you don't unsubscribe, the list messages sent to your account will bounce back to them, drowning them in unwanted mail and causing them extra work.

When you're ready to leave the list (unsubscribe), send a message to the LISTSERV address for the list, with the following in the body of the message:

```
SIGNOFF list
```

For example, if you want to leave the TOURBUS list, type **SIGNOFF *TOURBUS*** in the body of the message, substituting your list's name for TOURBUS.

Other Types of Mailing Lists

The most common lists you'll see are LISTSERV discussion and newsletter lists, which you'll see on AOL and many commercial vendors, where all you have to do is fill in your e-mail address to join a list; you leave by clicking an Unsubscribe list or something simple like that. (Many automatic lists, like AOL's, use LISTSERV.) Two types of lists you might encounter include the following (in parentheses are places to get more information):

▶ ListProc (http://www.cren.net/listproc/)
▶ Majordomo (http://www.greatcircle.com/majordomo/)

More and more, you'll see lists hosted on commercial list-providing services such as those mentioned in the "Creating Your Own Mailing List" section. Such lists strive for simplicity from the perspective of both list owner (so it's easy to set up and manage a list) and list user (so it's easy to find and join a list).

Creating Your Own Mailing List

If you have a special interest not met by an existing mailing list, or want to provide a simple discussion forum for a class you teach, or want to stay in regular touch with a group of

Tip

Whenever you see a reference in a book or on the Net to a mailing list, make sure to write down the subscription instructions. If there are no instructions, try to identify the list-software address (as in LISTSERV@LISTSERV.AOL.COM); send the message **help** or **info** to that address for subscription information. Or, do a Web search for the name of the list, in the likely event that the list (or the list's owner) has a home page.

co-workers, PTA buddies, or fellow hobbyists, you can create your own mailing list. The easiest way to start a list these days is to turn to one of the companies that do much of the work for you.

One such company, Topica, which recently acquired the mailing list search site, Liszt, lets anyone set up a mailing list for free. (They'll make money by selling banner ads and other promotions.) Existing lists can be transferred to Topica, and new lists created by just filling in a Web form with your name and address, the list's name and address, a description, and the associated Web site. Potential subscribers will be able to find the list in the Topica directory, subscribe to it by filling in a simple form, and take part using regular e-mail. Other companies offering this service include ONElist (`http://www.onelist.com`), Lyris (`http://www.lyris.com`), and Egroups (`http://www.egroups.com`), shown in Figure 12-8.

Egroups lets you browse and read messages on the Web. As with newsgroups (see next chapter), you can read and take part in any list (as long as it's hosted on Egroups, that is). Subscribing, in Egroups, means keeping a list of the mailing lists you like. You can also do everything by e-mail. List owners may exert any level of moderation they wish.

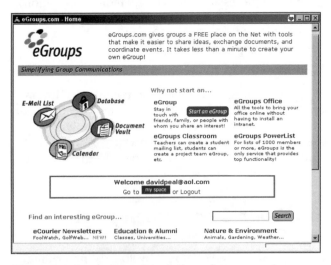

Figure 12-8. Egroups lets teachers, hobbyists, businesses, and *anyone* set up mailing lists. It also makes it easy for users to find and subscribe to lists.

In choosing a list provider, look beyond the price to see whether the list provider ensures security, offers technical support, allows your list to grow if (for example) it is business-related, and provides users with a range of options (relating to the degree of moderation and ability to get digests, for example). Lyris offers powerful features if you need security, scale, and support, but they're not free. Onelist and Topica are likely to appeal more to consumer mailing lists. Egroup offers both free lists and "powerlists," for larger numbers of subscribers. This corner of the Internet industry is changing quickly, so look for many changes, new services, and consolidation.

Just created a list? For advice on promoting your new mailing list, see Guidelines for Publishing and Promoting an Email Newsletter (http://www.trafficplan.com/newsltrtips.htm).

Likable AOL Lists You Should Know About

Many AOL channels use newsletters to keep AOL members in the loop as resources are added. Many of these newsletters have a strong point of view and give you a good sense of the channel's purpose and personality. The **Kids Only Newsletter,** for example, uses large colorful text, with background colors for highlighting and an easy-to-read typeface. Kids' poems and messages find their way into the newsletter as well.

The technical needs and interests of teen geeks, who are often more sophisticated in these matters than their parents, are addressed in **yt direct** (available online at keyword: YT, for Youth Tech). In addition to pointers to forum content at YT, the newsletter has quips, jokes, quotes, interviews, factoids, polls, and other good stuff.

The large, growing, and highly informative Computing channel, which caters to newbies and seasoned pros alike, puts out a newsletter, too, that does a good job conveying the breadth and coherence of the channels offerings. The **Computing Channel Newsletter** usually focuses on a theme such as graphics. A typical issue of the newsletter will identify forums, classes, download and upload areas, as well as the new Web-based buyers guides now being offered to AOL members by CNET. Live links take you directly to the forums and areas described.

Research & Learn's newsletter, **Know It All**, takes a personal view of the channel's and Web's rich reference holdings. Sometimes Dr. Dewey, the newsletter's author, pulls together links related to what's currently going on: the season, the holidays, the week's events, and the millennium. Other times she'll zero in on a theme such as books, and look at book-related

12

Virtual Communities

Tip

The **AOL Tips** newsletter provides occasional advice about AOL features you may not know existed. The irregularly posted tips come in two versions, advanced and beginner. Look for the newsletter at Keyword: **Newsletter**.

places on AOL, teaching kids to read, and the online Writer's Club.

Two Internet-related newsletters require special mention. **AOL.COM Weekly Update**, once known as IC-Hilites, offers a quirky set of Web sites and mini-reviews dealing with a theme or event (for example, the recent war in Kosovo or, for fun, the world of fashion). The author, Casey, also provides AOL and Internet tips such as how to use links in e-mail. Otherwise, she just lets you know what Web sites she likes these days. Several years' worth of newsletters are archived at `http://members.aol.com/ichilites/editions.html`.

AOL's other, newer Net-related list is Kevin Savetz's **AOL Hometown Weekly** (Figure 12-9). The newsletter supports AOL's new Hometown Web site, where members and non-members can add their Web sites to a fast-growing community of Web pages. AOL Hometown Weekly, one of AOL's most useful and best designed newsletters, looks at a single theme each week (for example Put Graphics on a Diet, Color Me Colorful, and Fonts of Knowledge). It offers a slew of tips for improving your page design, or color use, or fonts, or whatever. Especially useful are the links to related online HTML classes and to exemplary member pages.

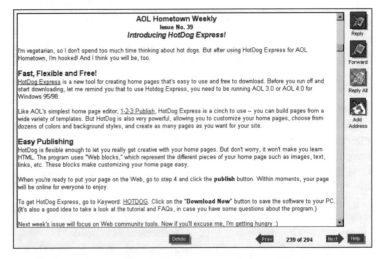

Figure 12-9. AOL Hometown Weekly gives you tips for smart Web design.

On and About the Net

The Net itself provides the best resources for keeping current on the Internet. Mailing lists in particular can let you know about Internet resources in the subjects that interest you particularly, as well as larger trends in the Internet industry.

Start with the **Scout Report**. Created by a large and well-established project team at the University of Wisconsin, the Scout Report is a weekly e-mail message containing information about and links to new high-quality Internet resources. The Scout Report comes as a plain e-mail or in HTML format; if you subscribe to the HTML version, download the attached file and save it with the extension HTM (for example, TheScout.htm). Now, open that file, and you'll see a Web page with links taking you first to detailed descriptions of the week's new resources and links to the actual resources (you must be signed onto AOL for the links to work). Figure 12-10 shows part of the HTML version of a recent weekly Scout-Report.

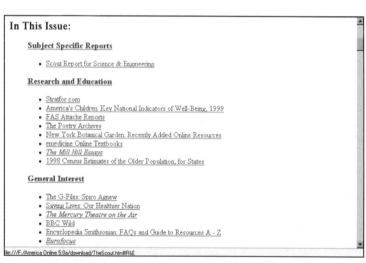

In This Issue:

Subject Specific Reports

- Scout Report for Science & Engineering

Research and Education

- Stratfor.com
- America's Children: Key National Indicators of Well-Being, 1999
- FAS Attache Reports
- The Poetry Archives
- New York Botanical Garden: Recently Added Online Resources
- emedicine Online Textbooks
- The Mill Hill Essays
- 1998 Census Estimates of the Older Population, for States

General Interest

- The G-Files: Spiro Agnew
- Saving Lives: Our Healthier Nation
- The Mercury Theatre on the Air
- BBC Wild
- Encyclopedia Smithsonian: FAQs and Guide to Resources A - Z
- Eurofocus

file:///F:/America Online 5.0a/download/TheScout.htm#R&E

Figure 12-10. Scout Report reviews some of highest-quality new Internet resources, selected and described in detail every week. In HTML format (shown here), the list is formatted and you can link directly to the resources reviewed!

In addition to the classic Scout Report, the Scout Project folks have created a KIDS Report and three specialized reports, including the Business & Economics report. You can search all

Tip

HTML e-mail messages? Sometimes you'll find links embedded in messages. Sometimes messages themselves are Web pages. In the latter case, save the entire message as a file with the **HTM** extension, then open the message (File ⇨ Open) inside a browser to view and use the page.

of the Scout Report's many thousands of detailed site descriptions at `http://scout.cs.wisc.edu/`.

The Internet Scout Project now manages two important Internet-related mailing lists. You can subscribe to any of the Internet Scouting Project's ten or so mailing lists from the main Web site at `http://scout.cs.wisc.edu/`.

 ▶ **Net-happenings** began life as a mailing list and newsgroup in the early 1990s, then migrated to the Web. The content has been consistently excellent: Net-happenings carries dozens of new Internet resources every day, all selected for their likely interest to the K-12 community of students, parents, and teachers. The annotations are thin, but sufficient contact information makes it possible to access the new list, newsgroup, or Web site.

 ▶ **New-List**, another classic resource now maintained by the Scout people, posts daily information about *new mailing lists* on all subjects.

IDG's Dummies Daily is a once-a-day mail message on any of a dozen subjects (shown earlier in Figure 12-2). Among the newsletters you can get for free: America Online, Computing Basics, Internet Search Tips, Web After Five: Reviews, and Internet Tips.

Exceptionally useful is the monthly **Search Engine Watch**, written monthly by Danny Sullivan, who analyzes the search-engine market, new features of the individual engines, and new developments in the frenetic search industry. A fee-based version of the newsletter offers more extensive analysis. To subscribe, just go to `http://searchenginewatch.com/sereport/` and fill in the form.

Yahoo, the large and popular directory of popular Web sites (described in Chapter 8), creates a mailing list called Picks of the Week, which takes an irreverent look at what Yahoo considers the best of the Web, without pretense of being serious or useful. It gives a good sense of what's fun and what's trendy on the Web. You can subscribe at `http://www.yahoo.com/picks/`, where you can also recommend sites and browse earlier weeks' offerings.

Bob Rankin and Patrick Crispen's **Internet Tourbus** brings you a deeper look into a special Internet topic every few days.

Topics may sound arcane but usually have a clear practical value, such as "sending a fax over the Internet," and "Net audio." Recently, the newsletter's authors discussed one of the hostile viruses making its way through the Internet as an e-mail attachment, and made useful recommendations for minimizing the threats from this virus. The very popular list has its own Web site, where you can read back issues.

The Tourbus LISTSERV is hosted at AOL. You can subscribe on the Web at `http://www.tourbus.com`.

Another list with a strong personal flavor stands out for its multimedia presentation. David Lawrence's **Online Today**, delivered each morning, contains a RealAudio file attachment. Download the day's file, then select it from your Windows 95/98 Start ⇨ Documents menu. Opening the file launches your RealAudio Player, which is included with AOL, and you'll hear David's stylish radio broadcast, which provides a human-interest view of Net industry news, new resources, and the like. Each file weighs in at more than 500K, so they can be burdensome to download and store. For more information, to access the archive, and to subscribe, check out `http://www.personalnetcast.com` (see Figure 12-11). It's a wonderful list; make it a habit.

Tip

Here's what e-mail can do that a Web site can't do. If you check your mail regularly, which most people do, and you subscribe to relevant e-mail lists or newsletters, you can't avoid such information about what's happening right now (whether in Belgrade or cyberspace). How would you know to do the appropriate Web search for "new virus" and then know which site to visit?

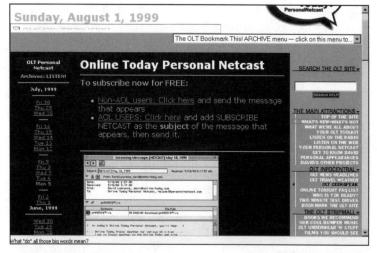

Figure 12-11. David Lawrence's Online Today list comes to your mailbox as a daily RealAudio file with the day's gossip, company news, and other Net developments. Follow the list daily and you'll be humming the theme song, chewing more gum, using Geekspeak, and speaking knowingly about Internet goings-on.

12

Virtual Communities

Spam messages are phony, and can usually be easily identified as such. Sometimes they cloak their purpose not in friendliness and come-ons, but in official-sounding requests — requests for you to download something, send some money somewhere, or provide your password. At AOL's Mail Center, you can read about particular scams and find out what to do about them. ***No one from AOL will ever ask for your password.***

Note

AOL takes legal and technical measures against anyone who (among other things) sends bulk e-mail to AOL members, uses fake addresses, and "harvests" addresses for the purpose of spamming. You can read its Unsolicited Bulk E-mail Policy at http://www.aol.com/info/bulkemail.html

Loathsome Lists and What to Do About Them

Simple ideas like the mailing list invariably attract fraudulent, deceptive, and annoying persons who see the potential for exploiting the idea for their own purposes. Take *spam*, or unsolicited mail. People who send these messages promising instant wealth (or at least rapid hair replenishment) compile or buy e-mail lists and send out messages without the recipients' approval and probably without any indication of the recipients' interest in goods and services they're hawking. Some such spam is itself toxic, as in the case of some AOL members who have received e-mail messages with links to adult Web sites. At keyword: **Notify AOL** you can report such messages.

What do you do when people treat your mailbox as a garbage can?

▶ Whenever you see a message from someone whose address you don't recognize or whose subject line contains a pitch or a teaser, consider simply deleting the message right away.

▶ Beware of the hyperlinks. Often, you'll find hyperlinks (blue, underlined words or phrases that link to AOL or Internet sites) in your e-mail messages. Beware of hyperlinks in e-mails from people you do not know!

▶ Were you unsure enough about the message's origins to open it anyway? Here's AOL's advice: "To play it safe, you can display the destination of the hyperlinks before you click them. Simply position the cursor over the hyperlink. AOL will display its destination. Links to Web pages will show the Web address or URL. Links to areas on AOL will say *On AOL Only*. Displaying the destination, before clicking a hyperlink, is helpful if you're not sure if you should follow the link."

AOL has fought the worst spammers using technology, education, and the court system. When you do open an offensive unsolicited message, play your part by *forwarding* the message to AOL using keyword: Notify AOL. Unsolicited messages coming from AOL violate AOL's Terms of Service (keyword: TOS) and can get spammers kicked off AOL. Don't hesitate to report them.

Use Mail Controls, as explained in Chapters 3. Spam e-mail addresses are often faked but you can often decode the domains
from which they are sent (keyword: Learn Domains explains
how). Remember that the domain in an address is the part
that goes after the at (@) sign. In the Mail Controls area, click
the button, "Block e-mail from selected AOL Members, Internet
domains and addresses." Enter a spam domain in the box in
the upper right, and click Add, repeating as necessary.

A Quick Look Back

Mailing lists provide a consistently high level of quality, along
with a clear focus on a specific topic. This chapter conveys
some of the tremendous diversity of this world. While the
word *community* is used just about everywhere on the
Internet, mailing lists have been supporting communities for
many years, with little fanfare.

This chapter highlighted some good lists on AOL and some essential lists for keeping up with the Internet. Use it as a reference when you need to know

> ▶ How mailing lists work
> ▶ How discussion lists differ from newsletters
> ▶ How to find e-mail lists that interest you, using Liszt,
>   the Publicly Accessible Mailing List directory, the LIST-
>   SERV search tool, and other resources
> ▶ How to join mailing lists
> ▶ How to create your own e-mail lists

12

Virtual Communities

GLOBAL BULLETIN BOARDS:
NEWSGROUPS

Chapter 13

Global Bulletin Boards: Newsgroups

Schmoozing, milling about, swapping stories. Many public places are designed for this sort of sociability–churches, coffee shops, restaurants, neighborhood organizations, conferences. *Newsgroups* serve this public, social purpose on the Net. The "news" they deal with has nothing to do with the evening news or local school-board politics, but with ongoing public discussions focused on any of thousands of topics; each topic has one or more newsgroups where people can read and post messages about the topic. Anyone on the globe with standard "news-reading" software can take part. On AOL, everything you need to find and take part is at your fingertips.

Because the messages posted to these bulletin boards can be archived and their collective wisdom condensed, they serve as "human knowledge bases" providing "one of the Internet's most effective methods for getting answers to tough questions and engaging in discussions on a variety of subjects .... Newsgroups are probably the largest decentralized information resources in existence," as someone recently wrote in ZDNET.

With AOL you have immediate access to this rich collective resource, the closest the Net has to a long-term memory. Read on to find out what newsgroups are about and how to find and use newsgroups of interest to you on AOL.

Tip

Many AOL members subscribe to both newsgroups and mailing lists on a particular topic, just so that they don't miss *any* valuable information. Outstanding information is available on both, but easier to find out about on newsgroups.

I Love Mailing Lists. Who Needs Newsgroups?

With so many focused, close-knit, and informative mailing lists out there, using such a reliable format, why does anyone read newsgroups?

- ▶ **Mailing lists are more personal, newsgroups more public.** With a mailing list, you have to go to the trouble of joining. Then, messages come to *your own* mailbox. The readership on lists tends to be smaller, too. Even large mailing lists usually don't have more than a thousand subscribers (with the exception of the monster newsletters, described in Chapter 12).

- ▶ **Every newsgroup is publicly accessible, and not subject to specific subscription procedures.** Newsgroups, on the other hand, are meant for easy access, and you can flit in and out of them as you wish. On AOL all newsgroups are always available using the same tool–AOL's newsgroup reader. You can read soc.culture.afghanistan today to get perspective on something in the news, for example, and then never return. Many newsgroups do have an established readership, of course, and some newsgroups have existed for more than a decade.

Note

No one controls newsgroups. Users alone are responsible for respecting the system and each other. While mailing lists are moderated and guided to some extent by list administrators, most newsgroups have no effective mechanism for focusing attention and preventing conflicts and unsolicited or off-topic messages. That's why *netiquette* matters more in newsgroups than other environments. See "Playing Nice" for the guidelines — most of which you can probably figure out!

Cross-Reference

Chapter 3 shows how to use Parental Controls to prevent access to newsgroups, to specific newsgroups, or to postings with files attached, and more. A program such as NetNanny (profiled in Chapter 17) can supplement Parental Controls.

Newsgroups: The Untamed Frontier

Without much by way of adult supervision, newsgroups are often abused by the folks who send the same lame commercial messages (spam) and lewd advertisements (pornography) to every newsgroup in creation. Such posts can make newsgroup browsing stomach-churning at times. Even the focused, informative newsgroups have their share of obnoxious, off-topic postings.

How do you minimize exposure to junk posts?

▶ AOL's new filters weed out junk, and you can also use Parental Controls (see Chapter 3) to keep kids from seeing the trash that makes it past the filters. See "Global Newsgroup Preferences."

▶ Keep your eyes on the positive reasons for using newsgroups: diverse perspectives on a myriad of subjects, and a rich source of collective knowledge, often embodied in compilations of frequently asked questions (FAQs). See "FAQs: Essential Reading," toward the end of the chapter.

Newsgroups on AOL

Take your pick of two easy ways to get to newsgroups on AOL; both take you to the Newsgroups window, shown in Figure 13-1.

▶ Keyword: **Newsgroups**
▶ Internet ➪ Newsgroups

When you first visit the Newsgroups area, you get a pop-up message telling you about AOL's *filtering options*. Don't ignore this message! It keeps popping up until you set your filtering options. The next section looks at these options.

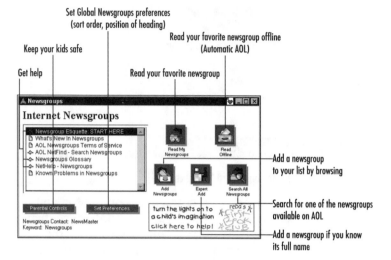

Set Global Newsgroups preferences
(sort order, position of heading)

Keep your kids safe

Read your favorite newsgroup offline
(Automatic AOL)

Get help

Read your favorite newsgroup

Add a newsgroup
to your list by browsing

Search for one of the newsgroups
available on AOL

Add a newsgroup if you know
its full name

Tip

If you're new to all this, use the help resources in the list box (see Figure 13-1): NetHelp, a Newsgroups glossary, and a set of guidelines that would please Miss Manners (Newsgroup etiquette).

Figure 13-1. Start here — AOL's Newsgroup window.

Newsgroups and AOL Message Boards: What's the Diff?

If a subject is timely, controversial, popular, or just interesting, AOL probably has a message board for it, such as the MTV boards (use Keyword: **MTVmessageboards**); the Grandstand Message Boards (in the Sports channel); and the Friends Message Boards (Keyword: **AOLTeens**). In researching Chapter 18, I found outstanding messages in AOL's various broadband message boards.

The following figure shows boards from the Travel channel, a source of excellent ideas for places to go and how to get to them. To get to the boards, just click Member Opinions in the opening window of the Travel channel. As a matter of fact, most channels make their message boards available from their main screen (the name of the collected boards varies from channel to channel, though).

Note

AOL cannot control what non-AOL people say in news-groups--that's why there are filters and Parental Controls, so *you* can control them.

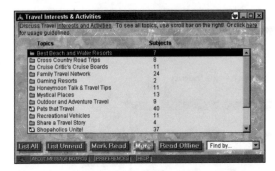

Figure 13-2. An AOL message board (Travel channel)

What's the difference between newsgroups on the Net and message boards on AOL? There's less and less difference than there used to be. AOL's boards have come to resemble the Net's newsgroups in the way they look and work, in audience size, and in breadth of subjects. Message boards, like news-groups, also have *threads*, and you can read them offline. Both let you mark messages as read and unread to simplify reading and responding.

You can set your preferences for message boards in much the same way you do for newsgroups. Click the Preferences but-ton on a message board and you'll see a window very similar to the Global Newsgroup Preferences window shown in Figure 13-3. You can create custom signatures and filter out messages from certain people and messages on certain sub-jects. Newsgroup preferences, however, give you much finer-grained control, as you'll see in the next section.

AOL message boards do, however, tend to have tighter con-trols. Offensive messages will be quickly discovered and deleted as violations of AOL's Terms of Service (see Keyword: **TOS**). However, the *uses* of newsgroups and message boards are converging, just as their interface is becoming more similar.

Global Newsgroup Preferences

Click Set Preferences to display the Global Newsgroup Preferences window, shown in Figure 13-3. Here you can de-cide to filter out certain postings, control how postings are listed (in which order), and specify how *your* postings appear (with a personal signature, for example).

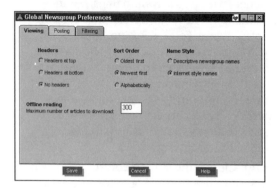

Figure 13-3. Control how you want to view your newsgroup messages in the Global Newsgroup Preferences window.

Newsgroup-Viewing Preferences (Viewing Tab)

Click the Viewing tab to control how the messages are displayed in the AOL newsreader.

- ▶ **Headers**: Headers provide more information than you probably want about a posting's path from one newsgroup computer to another, and then from AOL's to yours. You can choose to see these distracting headers at the top of the message or at the bottom, or not at all. If you aren't deeply interested in network routing, go ahead and place the headers at the bottom.

- ▶ **Sort Order** You can view the postings with the oldest shown first or the newest first. If you are viewing a current events newsgroup (such as alt.politics.clinton), you will probably want to see the newest postings first. If you are reading a personal interest newsgroup, such as rec.arts.books, less date-sensitive, you will probably want to see the articles in chronological order, so you can follow discussions as they develop over time. If you choose to view the postings alphabetically, you can quickly scan through the various subjects and quickly identify threads on subjects of interest.

▶ **Name Style:** If you have used other Internet providers besides AOL, you are likely used to Internet-style (actually, they're Usenet-style) newsgroup names. For instance, the Internet-style newsgroup, *rec.food.cooking*, has the descriptive name, *Food, cooking, cookbooks, and recipes*. If you haven't seen, or never felt comfortable with dots and terse/obscure naming systems, you can opt for descriptive style names. Note that "English" versions of newsgroups aren't available for all newsgroups and, outside of AOL, no one will know what a Descriptive name is, so it's sometimes a good idea to get comfortable with the Internet style.

▶ **Offline reading:** Clearly, the way to control the downloading of newsgroup postings using Automatic AOL, as described in "Using Automatic AOL for Your Newsgroups."

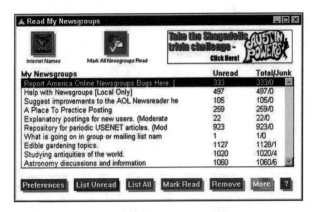

Figure 13-4. Internet-style newsgroup names tell you how the newsgroup is classified.

Posting Preferences (Posting Tab)

Click the Posting tab to set posting preferences, which have to do with how you want to be seen when you post. Do you want to use your real name? Do you want people to know your e-mail address? Or, do you want to provide some personal information about yourself, using a signature (yes, just like the sigs in e-mail, now possible in AOL 5.0).

▶ **Using Your Real Name:** If, when you post to a newsgroup, you want to be identified by your real name in parentheses after your e-mail address, enter it in the box. You can also use a nick-name, or alias, or provide no personal information.

▶ **Junk Block**: Senders of unsolicited e-mail regularly scour newsgroups, harvesting other people's e-mail addresses. They then send out thousands of e-mail messages to those addresses. One way to help defeat spammers is to add a junk block to your e-mail address. For example, if you put *applepie* in your junk block, the posting address would appear as, for example, PineFir@aol.comapplepie. Any attempts to e-mail that address would bounce. Enter whatever word you like. The drawback is that legit readers who want to e-mail you may have a more difficult time, since they won't be able to use the Reply To feature without editing the junk-block address.

▶ **Using a Signature**: A signature can be used to express your personality, tell a joke, display your insight, provide business contact information, or all the above. You type in a signature in the lower box. My signature block is shown in the box. See Figure 13-5.

Cross-Reference

A domain is the part of an e-mail address after the at symbol (@). See Chapter 9 for the low-down.

Tip

Filtering out the following words, numbers, and punctuation marks can reduce the trash: adult, ADULT, 18, 18+, FREE, free, !, !!, !!!. People who send this stuff try to get attention by using all capital letters, and one or more exclamation marks. The Filtering preferences make newsgroups a much better experience.

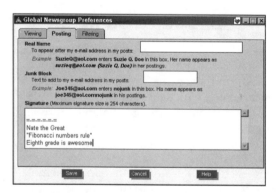

Figure 13-5. Got a sig? Use your signature to say something salient about yourself.

Filtering Out Garbage (Filtering Tab)

Here's a good way to supplement Parental Controls, described in Chapter 3, which provide the best first line of defense.

Your Filtering preferences let you block messages that contain a particular word or words in the subject line. You can also

Note

Somewhat more precisely, from left to right, each element encompasses and refines the preceding terms. Web addresses like www.aol.com are based on an entirely different scheme from newsgroup addresses like alt.showbiz.gossip.

Tip

The core, oldest, newsgroups can be found in the so-called Big Seven categories: comp, misc, news, rec, sci, soc, and talk. In numbers of newsgroups and popularity, the easy-to-set-up alternative newsgroups seem to have outstripped the Big Seven. *Alternative* refers to non-Big Seven categories in general and to the *alt* category in particular, a disparate category that includes newsgroups on everything from theology to scatology. Non-alt alternative categories focus on places (like Germany and Portland), universities, professions, and other less-general areas of interest. Though narrow, they're still publicly available to anyone in the world who has newsgroup access and whose ISP carries those particular categories.

block messages from particular people and domains. In message boards, all the messages are within the AOL domain!

For example, you may want to filter out all words containing the word *adult* in the subject. From the Select filter type list, select Subject Contains. Enter the word *adult* in the Enter New Filter box and click Add Filter. Add as many filters as you want. If you want to avoid all posts by the odious poster sending messages about sluts, use the Author Is filter, and enter the appropriate e-mail information. Or, if you notice that a particular domain seems to produce undesirable postings, you can filter that out as well.

A more benign use of filters: If you're an avid cook with enough time to read rec.food.cooking and don't like vegetarian food, just block messages containing that word or *tofu* or something else you find odious.

Buttons at the bottom of the Global Preferences window let you remove or clear your filters.

How Newsgroups Are Organized

A newsgroup is like a box containing messages. Every newsgroup is in turn stored in a bigger box called a topic, which is contained in a very large box called a category. For example, the *rec* category has topics on everything from autos to woodworking, each of which consists of many newsgroups; each newsgroups contains postings — the part that interests you.

Unlike e-mail addresses (with their domain-naming scheme), newsgroup names go from the general to the specific, from category, to topic, to newsgroup. The element to the far left is always a category, the element to the far right the newsgroup, and everything in between topics. For example

```
alt.showbiz.gossip
```

Alt (see the Tip) is the general category, *showbiz* the topic, and *gossip* the specific newsgroup, containing messages in which people share kind words about the Hanson Brothers and George W. Bush, Jr.

Most categories are further broken down into more specific topics, many of which have subtopics. Newsgroups like misc.education have only two parts to their name, category and newsgroup. Most newsgroups have a category, a topic, and a newsgroup (like misc.education.medical). The sharp-eyed will spot four-part newsgroups, such as misc.education.home-school.christian. Such newsgroups often grow out of other newsgroups.

Adding Newsgroups to Your List of Favorites

As with mailing lists, a subscription just means you're making it easy to keep up with your favorite discussion group. In newsgroups, you must add a newsgroup to Read My AOL.COMgroup if you want to use Automatic AOL and download (or upload) postings automatically. Not being subscribed doesn't prevent you from reading and taking part in a newsgroup — just from doing so systematically and letting AOL keep track of read and unread messages.

Sometimes you'll see reference to newsgroups you are *subscribed* to. The word suggests a discrete series of steps, as in mailing lists. Actually, it's easier to subscribe to newsgroups, and you always have immediate access to newsgroups to which you are not subscribed.

Read My AOL.COMgroups contains your favorite newsgroups, the ones you want to read regularly. This list may change as your needs change, particularly if you use newsgroups as a temporary research resource to get information about a financial, medical, or other problem, or if you are looking for specific information about an upcoming trip or event. Read My AOL.COMgroups also keeps track of which messages you've read in any newsgroup, so you won't have to reread messages. Or you can mark messages as new so you *can* read them again.

To add groups to Read My AOL.COMgroups, you use either Add Newsgroups or Expert Add.

▶ Use *Expert Add* if you already know the name of the newsgroup you want to add (for example, rec.pets.cats) to your list. Clicking Expert Add at

Find It Online

At Keyword: **Newsgroups**, click Add Newsgroups to see which categories AOL carries, and the topics, subtopics, and individual newsgroups available for every category.

Tip

To remove a newsgroup from your list, select it and click Remove.

Note

Names, notations, and such. Earlier editions of this book used the starchier word, *hierarchies,* to refer to categories and the older word *articles* to refer to messages. In this chapter I'll use categories, topics, newsgroups, and messages (or postings). Together, messages and their replies form *threads,* or *subjects.* An asterisk (*) in a topic's name, as in comp.dcom.*, refers to all the newsgroups in a topic. Newsgroup names are lowercase.

Note

No matter which way you subscribe to a newsgroup, you have the opportunity to select separate preferences applying to that newsgroup. These newsgroup preferences refine for an individual newsgroup any Global Newsgroup Preferences you have set for all newsgroups. If for example, in rec.creative-cooking, certain subjects simply don't interest you, use the newsgroups Preference button to filter them out. You can set individual newsgroup preferences both from the Read My AOL.COMgroups window (Figure 13-6) and within a newsgroup, with the messages displayed, using the button at the bottom.

Keyword: **Newsgroups** saves a few steps but makes sense only if you know a newsgroup's full name and don't want to know what else is available in the same topic. Make sure to enter the name exactly right (e.g., *not* rec.pets.cat).

▶ Use *Add Newsgroups* to browse categories and read a likelylooking newsgroup before subscribing to it. Suppose, for example, you want to subscribe to a newsgroup about old cars but aren't aware of what's out there. If you are familiar with newsgroup organization, click Add Newsgroups at keyword: **Newsgroups**. Double-click rec (that category that plays home to hobbies), then rec.autos (topics about old cars). Select your newsgroup and click Subscribe. The group now shows when you click Read My AOL.COMgroups at Keyword: **Newsgroups**. Repeat the process for any other groups you want to read regularly. See Figure 13-6.

If you don't know where to start, start with a search. At Keyword: **Newsgroups**, click Search all Newsgroups and do a search for **cars OR autos**, or whatever words concisely capture your area of interest. More information about searching can be found in the next section.

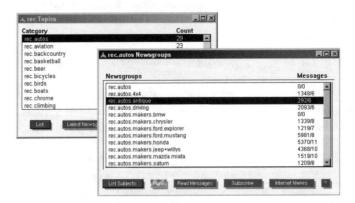

Figure 13-6. Adding a newsgroup: the bottom window (rec Topics) shows the *count* (number) of newsgroups in a topic; the top window (rec.autos Newsgroups) shows the number of messages in a series of related newsgroups. The proportion means the total number of messages over the number of junk messages — a rough measure of the amount of noise in a newsgroup.

Searching for Newsgroups

Using Add Newsgroup involves burrowing through levels and levels of topics and subtopics. This approach almost guarantees you *won't* find all newsgroups whose subjects span the often tersely and subjectively characterized topics.

To search for newsgroups containing certain words or parts of words in their names, click Search Newsgroups in the Newsgroups window to display the Search All Newsgroups window. Remember, you're searching for newsgroups (by name), not postings (by content). For that, see the next section!

Suppose you wanted to find newsgroups about gardening (with *gardening* in their name). Enter gardening in the box at the top, and click List Articles. You will see a list of newsgroups that contain articles on the subject. See Figure 13-7.

Tip

You can add either individual messages or entire newsgroups to your Favorite Places folder just by clicking the tiny heart in the respective windows' upper-right-hand corner. You might do this in order to create Favorite Places folders devoted to a specific topic like Tofu in History and consisting of all sorts of content — e-mail messages, newsgroups, Web sites, etc.

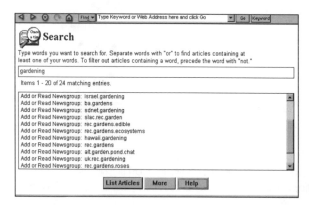

Figure 13-7. A fine crop of gardening newsgroups from the UK, Hawaii, Bay Area (ba), Israel, and elsewhere

Double-click the newsgroup you want to read. You get a choice of just *listing* a newsgroup's articles or of *subscribing* to the newsgroup (adding it to your favorites). Actually, clicking either *list* or *subscribe* has the same immediate effect: you can take part in the newsgroup *now*. Clicking *subscribing*, however, means you'll add the newsgroup to your favorites (Read My AOL.COMgroups) in order to read in the future.

When you uncover a good newsgroup at Deja, write down its full name. At Keyword: **Newsgroups**, click Expert Add. Type in the newsgroup's name to add it to your Read My AOL.COMgroups list.

Finding Newsgroups with Deja.com

Most newsgroup postings since 1995 have been archived by Deja (formerly DejaNews), a free consumer information site, available directly on the Web or as a link from AOL Search (Keyword: **Search**), which you can read all about in Chapter 8. The best search services use Deja when you do a "Usenet search." For extensive newsgroup use, start at Deja's Web site, http://www.deja.com, shown in Figure 13-8.

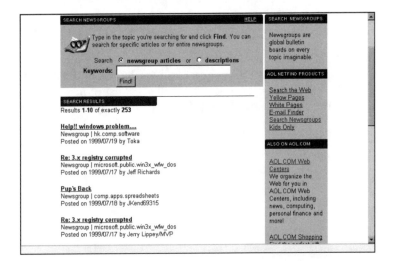

Figure 13-8. An awesome source of answers. Deja.com's search engine searches for newsgroups, searches for messages, and lets you take part in newsgroups — all from the Web! This figure shows messages from all newsgroups that have to do with a *corrupted Windows 95/98 register.*

With Deja, you're not just searching for newsgroup names, but can actually search for specific messages. You can also search for newsgroups.

Suppose you are having a problem with your Windows 95 computer. At Deja.com, type in something like **windows registry corrupted** in the search box. Click *newsgroup articles* (which searches actual messages) and not *descriptions* (which searches newsgroup names). Click Find to discover just how many newsgroup readers and Deja fans have the same problem. Click an underlined link to read a message. Here, too, you can browse other messages by clicking the More Headers link.

Similarly, suppose you want some advice on a particular illness or type of sailboat. Type in the name of the illness or sailboat, and search. In this case, you could use the name of the illness (or sailboat) to find entire newsgroups on that subject; before doing the search you would first click the *descriptions* button.

Deja returns only results from the last month or so. Use the Advanced Newsgroup Finder to do a search further back in time and take advantage of newsgroups' collective memory. Other advanced and really useful options include getting threaded results (so related messages from the same news-group can be seen together); seeing more results on a page; viewing results in different orders, and so on.

Best of all: Deja let's you browse newsgroups once you've pin-pointed specific messages. You can follow a thread, browse to the next and previous messages, e-mail the guy who wrote a message, and view that person's posting history. If you want to post through Deja, however, you'll have to register, which is free.

A Few Notable Newsgroups

You can find newsgroups for any taste, on any topic. The ones described below tend to have long-standing bonds among posters and thus a strong sense of community. Take the time to find newsgroups that support your interests.

- ▶ **misc.kids.moderated.** Formed after misc.kids was overrun by trolls (see "Playing Nice" for information on *trolling*), m.k.m. serves parents or anyone seeking in-formation or advice about children. The moderation is light but effective, and the quality of posts is high. Be sure to check out the misc.kids FAQs for the collective wisdom of this experienced crowd.

- ▶ **alt.folklore.urban.** Based on the work of folklorist Jan Brunvand, who coined the term *urban legends*. Designed for (and as a parody of) the gullible, this acer-bic, witty, and annoying newsgroup might turn you into a confirmed skeptic. Posters note the reemergence of old tales, and pick apart new ones. This old newsgroup has spun off a series of Web sites, including http:// www.urbanlegends.com/ and http://www. snopes.com/ (for newsgroup FAQs and background information). The newsgroup's "no smiley" rule has caused grief to some newbies; the rule about lurking before posting applies here (see "Lurk Before Posting").

▶ **misc.legal.moderated.** Although no substitute for legal advice from an attorney, this newsgroup can help you find out about possible legal remedies.

▶ **rec.pets.dogs.** You, too, can join this large community of dog lovers. Hundreds of FAQs on specific breeds are out there — plus general FAQs on breeding dogs, traveling with them, and caring for them, etc.

▶ **rec.arts.books.children.** This group is for people who love children's literature, as well as for those seeking to find the best books for their kids or students. The enthusiasm of the participants is contagious. The FAQ for this newsgroup is available by clicking through the hierarchy at `http://tile.net/news`.

▶ The **rec.food.*.** This family of topics contains many useful newsgroups for cooks and epicureans. See Figure 13-9.

▶ **rec.gardens.roses.** A newsgroup on cultivating roses is sure to attract interested posters. Casual and deeply committed growers alike will find useful advice.

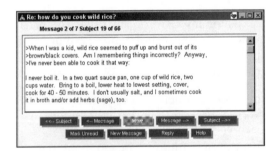

Figure 13-9. Remembrance of things posted. A message (reply) from rec.food.veg.cooking.

Ready to Read

Once you've added the newsgroups you want to read to your list of favorites, and set your preferences (globally and by newsgroup), you can actually proceed to read the messages.

Click Read My AOL.COMgroups to see your favorites. Click the newsgroup you want to read. If you want to see the posts you haven't read, click List Unread. If you want to see all of the posts, whether you have read them or not, click List All.

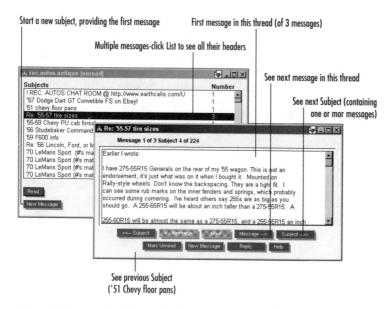

Figure 13-10. List of subjects (unique message subject lines) and a sample message from one of the most popular newsgroups for AOL members

The list of message subjects appears in the window. Click to select the subject you want to read about. To proceed to read the messages with this subject, click Read. The first message with that subject appears in the window.

Whenever the number of messages for a subject is more than one, you're looking at a thread — several messages about the same subject. To list all the messages with this subject (same subject line), select the thread and click List. The authors of posts with that subject appear in the window. Click a post you want to read, and then click Read Message. To proceed to the next message with the current subject (same thread), click Message ⇨ . To proceed to the next subject, click Subject ⇨ . The best way to learn this stuff is to try it!

Yep, just like an e-mail message, a newsgroup message (or posting) has a subject line and message body. Instead of an address it is posted to a newsgroup container (like rec.autos.antique); such containers are frequently distributed to other, neighboring computers, and outward from there until postings reach around the world.

If you want to print the article you're reading, just click the Print icon on AOL's toolbar.

Saving Newsgroup Articles

You can save newsgroup articles for future reference, a useful features for those long, informational posts with 17 URLs you'd never seen before. From the main menu at the top of your screen, click File ⇨ Save. Give the file a name and find a folder to keep it warm. When you have made the changes you want, click Save. Postings are saved as text, so you can later view them in Notepad or your word processor. Or, add a post to your Favorite Places folder by just clicking the tiny heart.

As always on the Net, be mindful of copyright laws and common courtesy. You can't redistribute a great posting or promiscuously borrow from it just because you like it. Ask the poster's permission.

Sending Postings

As in e-mail, the easy way to send a posting is by replying to someone else's posting. Another method: start your own thread by asking a question, making a comment, sharing new resources, whatever. However you take part, bear in mind some of the Netiquette guidelines outlined in "Play Nice."

Replying to a Newsgroup Message

To reply to a message you are reading, click Reply. The Post Response window appears, with the original message text in the Original Message Text box at the left (see Figure 13-11).

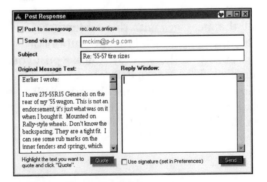

Figure 13-11. Replying to and quoting from others' messages is easy with AOL. The address has been removed to protect the innocent.

You can send your reply to the poster (click the Send via e-mail box) or to the newsgroup (click the Post to newsgroup box), or both. You can edit the subject line (but make sure it is relevant to your post). You may need to edit the e-mail address if you are replying by e-mail, since many posters have added spam blocks to their addresses.

In the Original Message Text box, be sure to highlight only the portion of the post necessary to keep your post in context. When you have selected the text you want to include, click Quote. The quoted text will appear in the Reply Window. You can quote bits and pieces of the original.

Type your response in the Reply Window box at the right. If you want your signature to be included in your post, check the Use signature box. (Remember, you create a signature using your global preferences, available at Keyword: **Newsgroups**.) Done? Click Send.

Note

In earlier versions of AOL, you needed a special utility, or a lot of copying and pasting, to properly quote a newsgroup posting. With the latest version of AOL, you can now selectively quote from the posting to which you are responding.

Composing a New Post

Click the New Message button in the newsgroup window if you want to post a message with a new topic (see Figure 13-12). Type the subject in the Subject field, and type your message in the Message field. If you want to include your signature in the post, make sure the Use Signature box is checked. Click Send after double-checking your message.

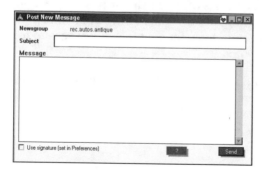

Figure 13-12. Starting a new message. If others reply, congratulations; you've started a thread!

Deleting Your Posts

New to AOL 5.0 is this ability to delete postings to newsgroups. No more desperate messages to AOL's Newsmaster to delete that hastily written or intemperate message!

Oops. When you post something you wish you hadn't, you can delete the message before anyone catches your blunder. There's no guarantee, of course; Deja may have already archived it for eternity. The faster you catch the mistake, the less the damage (if any).

Here's how: Click Read My AOL.COMgroups and select the newsgroup to which your message was posted. Open your message, and click Delete. Easy as pie, and another way AOL gives you control of your own online experience.

Playing Nice

Getting along in newsgroups is not much different from getting along with neighbors — in a very big city. One difficulty with newsgroups, mailing lists, or any written communication for that matter, is the absence of context: sighs, body language, and the countless visual cues that convey more or less unmistakable meaning.

Still, common sense serves as the best guide. If you were at a hobbyist meeting where the topic was goldfish, and this was your first time attending, would you shout out a question to the expert about the diseases of angelfish? Or pose a question so simple that any eight-year-old with goldfish would know the answer? Probably not. Hang out a bit in any newsgroup to find out what's appropriate.

Another way to get up to speed: Read the FAQ, the frequently asked questions document created by many newsgroups to distill the group's knowledge, point of view, and, sometimes, wisdom. See "FAQs: Essential Reading."

Flaming Hurts

To *flame* someone is to lash out verbally; it's an old, obnoxious Internet hobby, a male reflex mostly, inflicted piously and gratuitously by people who like to humiliate others in defense of the motherland. Flaming is discouraged in most Internet newsgroups (with the exception of alt.flame* and its more than 60 newsgroups); AOL's message boards usually have strict rules regarding flaming as well. If you aren't sure whether the message you are going to send is a flame, save it as a text file, and look at it tomorrow.

Flaming is often an aspect of a charming but abrasive style. You don't have to curtail your style completely, just use the same degree of discretion you would if you were speaking to an audience of thousands. That's sort of what you are doing in newsgroups.

Lurk Before Posting

Read messages for a few weeks before posting (or as the somewhat menacing lingo goes, "lurk") in order to get a good feel for the place before you post to it. Many newsgroups and mailing lists, in particular, have distinctive cultures, some more inhospitable to newcomers than others. As in any apprenticeship, stay on the outside of the circle until you're comfortable approaching the inside.

Post Appropriately

No spamming! Violating AOL's Terms of Services can get you kicked off AOL even if you're not on AOL proper, but rather using the Web or reading newsgroups. So, here are some don'ts you should know about.

▶ Don't post chain letters, get-rich schemes, multilevel marketing plans (even if you are convinced of their worth), or anything clearly unrelated to the newsgroup. Don't *cross-post* (send the same posting to many newsgroups).

▶ Don't post questions for which the answer is readily available elsewhere, such as in a FAQ.

▶ Don't quote excessively when responding to another message. It wastes space and time. Usually, this means don't quote an entire message if you're responding to a single item in the message.

▶ Don't troll.

> **Note**
>
> Unlike e-mail, newsgroups don't let you "send later." You've got to do your proofreading on the spot, or save your posting as a text file and look at it later.

Definition

Here's how *troll* is defined in the Newsgroup Glossary (available in Keyword: **Newsgroup**'s list box): "A purposely stupid, inflammatory, or downright wrong article (closely related to *flamebait*). Its purpose is to get people mad and make them look stupid and gullible."

Tip

AOL has its own newsgroup hierarchy — called *aol*, of course. The aol.newsgroups. help newsgroup, for example, is home to FAQs on subjects like newsgroup basics, handling files, and using your Personal Filing Cabinet. You can count on AOL's newsgroups to be junk-free.

Find It Online

Keyword: **Computing FAQs** takes you to informative FAQs developed on AOL for AOL members. They're devoted to topics like hardware, software, graphics, PDAs, home pages, etc.

FAQs: Essential Reading

The Internet tends to be very much a here-and-now kind of place. Hundreds of thousands of thoughtful people have created *FAQs* (lists of Frequently Asked Questions, with answers) on numerous topics, so that knowledge gained over time can be transmitted efficiently to newcomers. Most of these repositories are voluntarily created and (the time-consuming part) maintained. FAQs provide something like long-term memory.

Perhaps you know a high-school student who wants to post a question to a particular newsgroup, such as sci.math, asking about the status of Fermat's Last Theorem. Starting with the sci.math FAQ can save this kid from asking a question everyone in the newsgroup can answer. The fact is, lots of people out there don't play nice, so don't subject yourself to their ridicule.

Warning, Files

Sometimes newsgroup messages have files attached: MIDI sounds, for example. They do this by converting multimedia files into a text document that's unreadable to people but (as text) can move easily around the Internet. Problem is, such files have to be unscrambled at the other end. The file format of these files is UUE.

AOL's newsgroups use a feature called FileGrabber to simplify the unscrambling of files. Say you want to download a MIDI from alt.binaries.sounds.midi.rock or one of the alt.binaries.sounds.mp3.* newsgroups. Open the newsgroup as usual by adding it to Read My AOL.COMgroups (click Add Newsgroups and browse or Expert Add or use Search All Newsgroups). Look for the file you want to download. Click to read it as usual.

FileGrabber Automatically Unscrambles Those Files

When a file is attached to a newsgroup posting, you will see a message prompting you to Download File or Download Message. Click Download File, and you'll be prompted to save the file on your computer. If you don't want to accept the default folder, change it and click Save. Downloading starts; a progress indicator tells you how much has been downloaded. Most MIDI files download quickly, because of their small size. Images and MP3 files can take a longer time.

Once a MIDI file has been downloaded, it plays within AOL immediately. In the case of a graphic, the picture shows up automatically in a new AOL window. For other files, you might need to use another program to use the file (an MP3 player, for example).

Other files use a different encoding method (such as MIME). Sometimes files, particularly large ones, are distributed across several articles. Use WinZip for both MIME and ZIP files (see Chapter 17 for a profile of WinZip).

Caution

When downloading any file from the Internet, make sure you have state-of-the-art antivirus software from a recognized vendor such as McAfee or Norton.

Using Automatic AOL for Your Newsgroups

Downloading newsgroup postings, particularly if you subscribe to even a few high-volume newsgroups, can take a long time (yet another reason to start learning about broadband Internet connections — see Chapter 18). Fortunately, with Automatic AOL, you can automate this task by downloading the postings automatically, at times of the day and night when you're doing something else. Then, at your leisure, you can browse the posts in your MyFiles ⇨ Personal Filing Cabinet without having to sign on; they'll be in the Newsgroups folder under Incoming/Saved Postings. They're also available at MyFiles ⇨ Offline Newsgroups.

1. Make sure you add the newsgroups you want to read offline to Read My AOL.COMgroups at Keyword: **Newsgroups**. See "Adding Newsgroups to Your List of Favorites."

2. At Keyword: **Newsgroups**, click Read Offline. The Choose Newsgroups window appears, with the names of all of your subscribed newsgroups. Click Add All if you want to read all of the newsgroups offline, or select specific newsgroups and click Add to add the

newsgroups one by one. Remove All starts from scratch; to remove a single newsgroup, select it and click Remove.

3. Select Mail Center ➪ Set Up Automatic AOL.

4. Put a check by either or both of the options relating to newsgroups:

   a. Send postings from the Postings Waiting to be Sent folder. These posting are the newsgroup messages you wrote offline either as new messages or responses to other messages.

   b. Get unread postings from the Incoming/Saved Postings folder.

5. Click Screen Names. Select screen names whose messages/postings are to be uploaded or downloaded, and provide the password for them. Click OK.

6. Click Schedule Automatic AOL, and indicate when you want postings sent or retrieved; probably you'll want postings retrieved regularly but sent only when you have something to send. Make sure to put a check in the Enable Scheduler box. Click OK when you've got the schedule figured out.

7. Just close the window shown in Figure 13-16 when you're done. Make sure your computer is turned on and AOL is open during the time that you have scheduled automatic up/downloading.

From Newsgroups to Web Message Boards

AOL message boards are available only to AOL members. They tend to be moderated and many have a huge audience. Postings tend to be on-topic, and, although the standards may be loose, any posters who offend TOS get their postings deleted.

The latest thing is message boards on the Web, open to anyone on the Net, including AOL members. These boards vary in quality compared to AOL's boards. And while newsgroups have a uniform interface, greatly simplifying use, every Web message board differs a bit in interface, features, and registration requirements. Anyone can start a message board on the Web with no standards or topic restrictions. Such boards can contain garbage and gems. Their number almost guarantees a great deal of likely interest to you.

The Web format has advantages, too: it's a familiar format and allows for linking. Web boards usually support threading quite nicely, with a visual display that can show several levels of threading (people responding to each other) and instantly see who's responding to whom. AOL itself has been moving some of its boards to the Web.

For help, read the site's instructions for customizing your settings and for posting and managing messages.

Find It Online

The best place to find message boards on the Web is http://www.forumone.com/. This site lets you search (as this was written) over 300,000 Web forum discussions for postings about specific subjects.

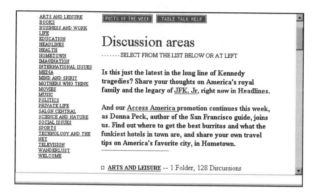

Figure 13-13. Salon's TableTalk Web message boards offer an almost inexhaustible array of topics. It helps to be highly opinionated.

A Quick Look Back

Through AOL you can take part in some 30,000 public discussion groups on death, taxes, and cable modems — every manner of subject. Here are a few postcards from our brief stay in the Net's noisiest province:

▶ You'll find it easier to take part in newsgroups than in mailing lists — you use the same window (Keyword: **Newsgroups**) for everything you do. More public than mailing lists, newsgroups are also less stable and a bit less friendly.

▶ Newsgroups are organized as boxes inside boxes — like those Russian dolls. An individual newsgroup consists of messages people send to the group; newsgroups usually belong to higher-level topics; topics belong to categories like rec, soc, and alt. For example: for the alt.folklore.urban newsgroup, *alt* is the category, *folklore* the topic, and *urban* one of many newsgroups.

▶ At Keyword: **Newsgroups**, you can search for newsgroups containing a certain word in their names or descriptions. To actually search for newsgroup articles (of which there are countless millions), start at AOL.COM's Newsgroup search.

▶ FAQs count as one of the Net's very best, most reliable, most informative resources. Many newsgroups generate and refine FAQs over many years.

▶ You never know who's reading your messages. Respecting others is a good way to avoid embarrassing yourself.

PART

IV

SPINNING YOUR
OWN WEB PAGE

Chapter 14

Contributing to the Web: Making a Page

I f you're like most people, you won't surf the Web very long before you get the hankering to put up your own Web page, or several pages, about the subjects that interest you. You might also be tempted to dismiss the idea, especially if you're new to computers and the Web. Perhaps it seems terribly difficult and like it would require all kinds of esoteric technical knowledge. It's not and it doesn't. AOL provides Web publishing tools so simple to use that all you really have to do is type on your keyboard, even if you only use one or two fingers to do it.

AOL makes each step easy:

▶ AOL's tools get you started in a few minutes.

▶ AOL provides every screen name a minimum of 2MB of storage space on its Internet computers for Web pages and associated files (digital pictures and sounds).

▶ AOL Hometown, made up of many different Web communities, provides both a home and a global audience for your pages.

▶ On Hometown and in the Computing channel, you'll find tutorials, images, advice, and tools.

This chapter shows you how to use AOL's two tools to create a simple Web page and how to add those pages to AOL Hometown:

▶ 1-2-3 Publish
▶ Easy Designer

1-2-3 Publish: A Web Page in Two Minutes Flat!

The easiest way to create a Web page on AOL is with 1-2-3 Publish. Just go to Keyword: **123** (see Figure 14-1).

Tip

Register your page with AOL Hometown by joining one of the online communities, and you can double your storage space to 4 mb per screen name — plenty of space even if you load your page with pictures of your grandparents, your children, your pets, and your trip to Hawaii. Registration is free. Any screen name on a master account can register a page as well and get the extra 2MB (megabytes). Register *all* pages in Hometown using the Add All Pages feature of Hometown, and you get 12MB of space per screen name.

14

Making a Page

Note

This chapter is about creating single *pages* on AOL. The next chapter is all about designing, building, managing, and marketing *sites*, consisting of many pages.

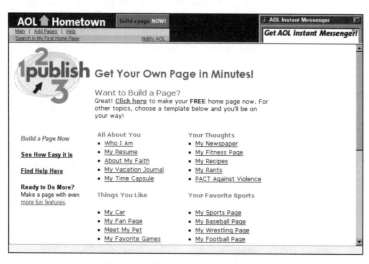

Figure 14-1. 1-2-3 Publish is the easiest way to create a Web page on AOL. Choose a template and you're off! Think of it as a way of creating a personal newsletter that won't cost a penny to produce or distribute.

Note

A *template* makes some decisions regarding the placement of elements and the possible color schemes. You just fill in the blanks with your own information.

Note

Your choices aren't permanent. Later in this chapter, you'll see how to make changes to your Web page.

Cross-Reference

Later in this chapter you can read about getting digital pictures. See "How Do You Get Digital Images?"

If all you want is a general all-about-you type of home page, click Who I Am. For a page that focuses a bit more on a particular topic, click a link to another of the dozens of available templates (see Figure 14-2).

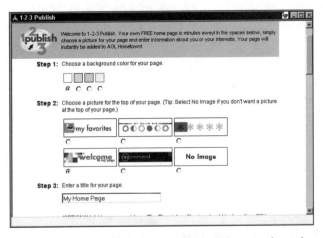

Figure 14-2. When 1-2-3 Publish first creates a Web page, it doesn't have any personalized information in it at all. That's for you to do, by filling in the blanks!

To complete this template and make it your own, just follow the steps. The exact steps vary by template.

1. **Choose a background color for your page.** Select the color you want to appear behind the text and images on your page. In this template, 1-2-3 Publish offers several attractive pastel choices.

2. **Choose a picture for the top of your page.** A banner at the top of your page can set the page's tone in an instant. 1-2-3 Publish offers five different banners you can place at the top of your page. You can also opt to use no image at the top.

3. **Enter a title for your page; insert a picture.** The words in your *title* (the technical term is *heading*, actually) appear below the banner, in large bold type. Type it into the blank provided. You can also insert a picture in this place if you have one handy on your hard drive, using the Browse button. Images must be in a format that a Web browser can recognize, typically GIF or JPG (meaning the file names have an extension — the stuff after the period — of *GIF* or *JPG*, for example, *nile.jpg*).

4. **Choose a divider style.** Dividers are thin horizontal images that separate one section of your page from the next. Again, you have five choices, plus the option to have no dividers at all.

5. **Enter your text.** 1-2-3 Publish provides you with three places where you can enter text. (On the finished page, each area is separated from the others by the divider you chose in Step 4.) Each area also gets its own title, in larger type than the body text but smaller than the main title. 1-2-3 Publish suggests sections titled "About Me," "My Online Life," and "My Interests," but these are only suggestions. Use any titles and any body text you want.

6. **Enter online links.** Links from one page to another are what make the World Wide Web a web. In this step you create a list of your favorite links (1-2-3 Publish lets you enter a total of three) to other sites on the Web. First type in a title for your list of links, and then type in a name for each link, followed by the address (for example, `http://www.asylum.com`). Make sure not to erase the `http://` part of the address, which is added automatically for you.

7. **Enter your contact information.** Finally, you're given the opportunity to enter your name and an e-mail address where visitors to your page can contact you. You can even add a link that enables AOL members who visit your page to send you an Instant Message note! (See "Giving Your Web Pages Something to AIM for" in Chapter 11.)

Once you've gone through each step, click the Preview button to see what your page looks like (see Figure 14-3).

Tip

People who are not AOL members can publish their pages on AOL Hometown, use the 1-2-3 Publish and Easy Designer tools, and receive free online storage space. If they use 1-2-3 Publish or Easy Designer, they automatically receive 12MB of free storage space on AOL. If they don't use one of these tools and join Hometown by adding a single page, they still get 4MB. If they opt to add all of their pages to Hometown, they receive the full 12MB.

Caution

Children creating a page should never provide their last name or any contact information, such as phone number and street address.

14

Making a Page

Text   Title

Section title   Image   Banner

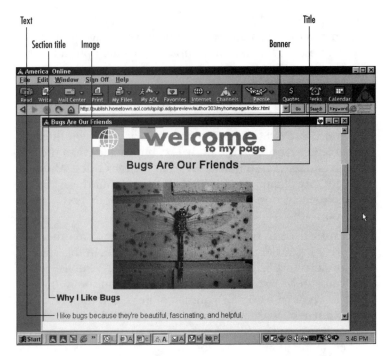

Figure 14-3. Here's the top of my new Web page, showing the banner, the title, a picture I inserted, and the start of the first section of text. It is still a little buggy.

Your Address

All pages created using 1-2-3 Publish and then registered at AOL Hometown have an address that follows this format `http://hometown.aol.com/YourScreenName/myhomepage/index.html`.

Here's a specific example: `http://hometown.aol.com/author303/myhomepage/index.html`. To access your page, people can leave off `index.html`.

If you're happy with the way your page looks, then it's time to move on to the next step, and publish it on the Web. To do so, click Save. You'll see a screen telling you that your page has been automatically added to the My Home Page community on AOL. Your new page's address is displayed in big bold letters. You might want to make a note of it and share it with friends.

That's it! Now anyone can visit your home page just by typing in its address. How will they know it's there? Tell them in e-mail, on your business card, and in your e-mail and news-group signatures.

By the way, it's not just individuals who are using 1-2-3 Publish to create home pages. Even businesses are getting into the act, as you can see in Figure 14-4. The pages may be basic, but they do establish your presence on the World Wide Web, and that's what counts. Sometimes, contact information, a simple mes-sage, and a strong image is all you need to publicize your business. Make sure to include a link for visitors to send you e-mail.

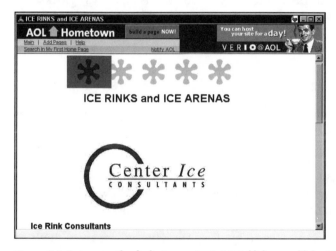

Figure 14-4. An example of a business using 1-2-3 Publish to establish a Web pres-ence. This page is at http://hometown.aol.com/icerinks/myhomepage/index.html.

Editing Your Hometown Pages

Whenever you view a page of yours in Hometown, or create a page and then click Preview, you'll see large buttons at the top of the page giving you the choice: Modify or Save. Modify gives you access, on one large page, to all the content of your page (similar to what you saw earlier in Figure 14-2). Click Preview, and then either Modify (again) or Save (on Hometown).

Cross-Reference

See Chapter 15 for sugges-tions on how to get the word out about your home page.

Note

Where are your actual files? 1-2-3 Publish pages (the HTML files) are stored in the *myhomepage* folder of My FTP Space, the space AOL gives you to store Web pages and other files. You can access these files directly using another HTML editor, but once you make any changes to them with another editor, you won't be able to use them in 1-2-3 again. See Chapter 15 for more about HTML editors and Chapter 16 on My FTP Space.

Tip

When you visit a page at AOL Hometown, you can e-mail a link to the page to anyone you think might be interested in the page. That person can then visit the page by simply clicking the link in the message. To e-mail a page, click the E-mail This Page link in the Hometown section (the top part of every AOL Hometown page).

14

Making a Page

Note

Personal Publisher is no longer available in AOL 5.0. If you have any PP3 or other HTML pages, you will not be able to edit them in 1-2-3 Publish or Easy Designer. To continue editing them, you may need to reconstruct them using Easy Designer. The benefit of switching to Easy Designer is greater control over content and layout, simpler publishing, and faster revision.

Tip

At AOL Hometown's Web-based message boards, you can ask questions and read answers to others' questions (http://hometown.aol.com/messageboard). Help is also available from the main Easy Designer window, shown in Figure 14-7.

Going a Step Further with Easy Designer

AOL's new Web publishing tool, Easy Designer (Keyword: **Easy Designer**), offers more control of layout, page elements, and content. Your Easy Designer pages can be published in Hometown AOL and viewed by anyone with access to the World Wide Web.

With a large set of fill-in-the-blank templates, Easy Designer makes it just as easy to get started as does 1-2-3 Publish. Unlike 1-2-3, with Easy Designer you can add as many text blocks and as many pictures as you want, and drag them around on your page so that they appear in exactly the right place, giving you greater design control.

Using a Template to Create a New Page

AOL's new Easy Designer goes far beyond earlier tools such as Personal Publisher. First off, everything takes place on the Web, so you can quickly go back and forth between the "edit view" of page you're designing and a view showing what the page will actually look like on the Web. Second, it's very simple to add words and pictures whenever you want, and then position these elements wherever you want.

1. When you first open Easy Designer, you're given the option of either creating a new page or opening and editing an existing page. Clicking Existing Page shows you a list of all the HTML files you've stored in My FTP Space. You'll be able to open up and edit any pages you've created with either 1-2-3 or Easy Designer. To start a new page, click Create a New page.

2. In creating a new page, the first thing you see is a list of available templates (see Figure 14-5). Select the topic and category that most closely match what you have in mind for your Web page — or, if you prefer to work from scratch and have pictures and text ready to use in your page, choose Blank Page. After selecting a template, click Next. If you're making a page from scratch (blank page), skip to "Adding Elements in Easy Designer."

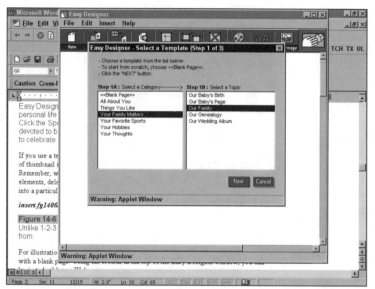

Note

Perhaps you've heard of Java, the innovative computer language invented at Sun Microsystems and used for creating small programs that can be shared on the Internet. Easy Designer is based on a Java "applet" (small application); as a result you'll see a message saying, Warning: Applet Window. With AOL's Java programs like Easy Designer and Quick Buddy (see Chapter 11), you can disregard all such messages.

14

Making a Page

Figure 14-5. Easy Designer, like 1-2-3 Publish, provides categories of templates (left) on your personal life, your family, your favorite sports, your hobbies, and your thoughts. Click the Sports category for individual templates you can use to build a page devoted to baseball, football, or another sport.

Definition

Think of an element as a block of text or a picture. You edit the text element in the Text Editor window and pictures in Picture Gallery window.

3. If you use a template, you'll next be offered a choice of page layouts, indicated by a series of thumbnail images (see Figure 14-6). Choose the page layout that appeals to you. Don't worry about getting locked into a particular layout. With Easy Designer you can later move elements around on the page, add new elements, and delete elements. After selecting a page layout, click Next.

4. You'll next be offered a set of color schemes for your template. A color scheme defines a combination of colors designed to work together: background color, text color, and pair of colors for your unvisited links and visited links. Click a scheme's name in the left side of the Select a Color window to see how the scheme looks in the right side. Click OK after selecting a color scheme. You'll see a filled-in template such as the one shown in Figure 14-7.

Note

Don't worry if you can't make a choice or if you later change your mind. With your page displayed in Easy Designer, you can at any time click the Color button on the toolbar to change the color scheme or create a custom scheme.

Definition

A visited link is a link to another Web page that a user has clicked already; an unvisited link has yet to be visited. On the Web, unvisited and visited links can be set in different colors to help your users realize where they've been and not yet been.

Tip

If you know HTML, you can add custom scripting, including JavaScript. From the Insert menu, selected Advanced HTML. Any code you add will not appear until you preview your page.

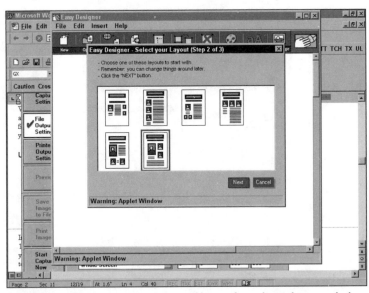

Figure 14-6. Easy Designer provides several layouts for each template. Once built, the layouts can be rearranged, and you can add new text and picture elements.

Color schemes are not just a matter of looks, but also of usability. Certain color combinations can make your pages difficult to read; others both look attractive and are easy read (the two go together). AOL's expertly matched schemes can greatly assist in improving your pages' appearance and usability.

Editing Text

The first thing you'll probably want on your Web page is a headline. Double click in the box where you see "Type a headline here" (or something similar). A text box comes up and lets you enter some text. If you wish, you can style the text (make it bold or italic), align it along the right or left side of the box, and change the font size and type. Click OK when you're done.

Whatever you're doing (adding or editing) and whatever you're making (text, list, headline): it all takes place in the Easy Designer Text Editor, shown in Figure 14-8.

Use your own digitized family photos here

Text boxes   Picture box   Your headline goes here

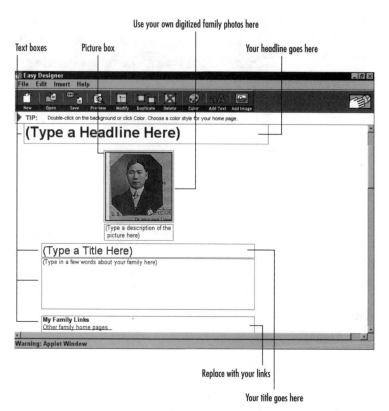

Replace with your links

Your title goes here

By resizing the text frames, you can create long skinny columns of text, wrap text around pictures, and more.

If you want to center the title of your page, clicking the Center button in the Text Editor is not enough; that action merely centers text in the box. You'll want to center the box as well, by simply selecting it and dragging it right or left.

Figure 14-7. An Easy Designer template. A template arranges text and images for you; you just replace template elements with your own words and pictures, resizing and moving around the boxes as you wish.

Notice how all the text and pictures live inside of boxes in Easy Designer? You can change the shape and size of a box by simply clicking any side or corner and dragging in the direction you want. Notice also how your mouse arrow changes shape as you pass it across different parts of the box.

To edit the contents of a box, double click inside any box containing text, as shown previously in Figure 14-7.

Delete the text (select and delete), then add your own, setting the font face, size, styling, and alignment. When you're done editing your text, click OK to close the Text Editor and return to Easy Designer.

Tip

Both the Text Editor and Picture Gallery window give you the ability to link your words or pictures to another Web page. This means that someone viewing your pages can click some text or a picture to jump to a related page. You have three different ways to add a link. You can type in the URL for a page anywhere on the Web; you can link to a page on Hometown AOL (if you've published one); or you can create a link to an e-mail address — your own, for instance, if you want your visitors to be able to send you comments by e-mail.

Note

If you find that your pictures appear on top of your heading (or other objects are in the same place), Easy Designer warns you with an Overlap warning message inside objects. Just drag the intruding objects so they're no longer overlapping other objects.

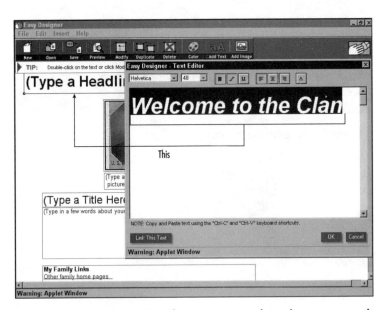

Figure 14-8. Easy Designer's Text Editor gives you control over the appearance and placement of text.

Editing Pictures

Editing an image also takes place in its own box, called Picture Gallery. Double click an image on the page to use the window shown in Figure 14-9. From here, you can either select one of the thousands of existing images (photo or clipart) provided by AOL or click Upload Picture to upload one of your own digitized family photos to AOL. The next section ("How Do You Get Digital Pictures?") can provide some guidance here.

You can resize images the same way you resize text frames, but be careful not to distort them by changing the height and width relative to each other. Move one side of the picture frame, for instance, and the picture appears squashed; move the other and it pulls like taffy. To avoid distortions, right-click the picture after you've resized it and choose Maintain Aspect Ratio from the pop-up menu. If you'd like to restore the picture to its original size, you can do so from this menu, too, by choosing Restore Original Size.

Now you're on your way! You can now start adding text and pictures, using the Add text and Add pictures buttons in Easy Designer's main window (Figure 14-7).

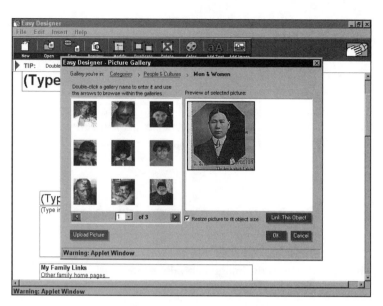

Figure 14-9. The Picture Gallery dialog box lets you choose the picture you want from either your hard drive or the clipart and photo collection provided with Easy Designer.

Adding Elements in Easy Designer

Here are some other useful tasks available from the Easy Designer toolbar when you're editing your page.

> ▶**Modify**. With an object selected, clicking this button opens the appropriate editing window. Use the Text Editor or Picture Gallery to make any changes.

> ▶ **Duplicate**. This tool is handy if, for instance, you want to use the same graphical divider several times on the same page or repeat a tiny GIF used as a bullet (in a bulleted list). Instead of clicking Add Picture for each copied image, just highlight the box containing the picture or text to copy and click Duplicate. A copy of the object appears, which you can then drag to the place where you want it.

> ▶ **Delete**. Use this option to get rid of an unwanted object. Select the object and click this button.

> ▶ **Color**. If you decide your template's color scheme doesn't quite cut it, click this button to select another

Tip

Every Easy Designer template-based page automatically includes AOL Instant Messenger Remote (AIMR) at the bottom of the page. AIMR gives visitors to your page the ability to send you e-mail, add you to their buddy list, toss you an instant message, and take part in a chat related to the topic of your site; the button bar is included at the bottom of your published page. In you're not using a template (i.e., starting with a blank page), use Easy Designer's Insert menu and select AIM Remote. Your visitors must have AIMR, a free program always available to AOL and non-AOL members from http://www.aol.com/aim (see Chapter 11 for more about AIM).

Cross-Reference

See also the "Registering with Hometown AOL" section in Chapter 15.

14

Making a Page

Caution

On the Web, *most pictures (and words, too!) are automatically protected by copyright law*. Someone else (not you) is entitled to reproduce them. Before you can use any material you find on the Web on your own Web page, try to obtain permission from the copyright owner. A good place to start is with the Webmaster of the Web page where you found the picture. Webmasters can usually answer such questions. Breaking copyright law can leave you open to legal action by the copyright owner, as more than one Web-page designer has discovered!

Find It Online

Keyword: **Web Art** offers an abundance of banners, bullets, buttons, bars, backgrounds (and more), all of which you can use in your Web page without copyright worries (read the fine-print anyway!).

scheme or to create your own custom scheme. You can also add your own background image to your page.

▶ The **Preview** button shows you the page as others will see it. The Save button lets you publish your page in AOL Hometown when you're happy with it.

Your new page's address will be `http://hometown.aol.com/YourScreenName/index.html`. You and your visitors don't have to type in the index.html part.

How Do You Get Digital Images?

To add text to your Web page, all you have to do is type. Finding just the right image can take more work. Here are four sources of digital images for your Web page:

▶ Pictures already on the Web.

▶ Pictures taken with a regular camera and then scanned.

▶ Pictures taken with a digital camera and then uploaded to your computer.

▶ Pictures taken with a regular camera and sent to the developer. Some developers can now provide the images on a disk or CD-ROM which can then be uploaded to your computer.

▶ The newest way to get digital pictures, You've Got Pictures, lets you get digital pictures without owning either a scanner or a digital camera. YGP makes your regularly developed pictures available as paper prints and as digital pictures; when the digital pictures are ready, you'll hear the "You've Got Pictures" message and click the You've Got Pictures button on the AOL Welcome screen.

Pictures Already on the Web

Browser software makes it almost ridiculously easy to copy digital images you find on the Web to your computer. All you have to do is aim your mouse pointer at the picture you'd like to copy, and then right-click. Choose Save Picture As from the pop-up menu, and store it wherever you like on your hard drive, ready to be used in your own Web page.

On the Web, graphics are low-hanging fruit. You can search for images at search engines such as Lycos (`http://www.lycos.com`), HotBot (`http://www.hotbot.com`), and AltaVista/Corbis (`http://www.altavista.com`).

Pictures Taken with a Regular Camera

One of the most popular pieces of hardware sold online at Keyword: **AOL Store** (click Hardware) is the scanner, and it's not hard to see why. A *scanner* is a device that turns photographs, drawings, and text into digital images. Scan a regular 4×6-inch photo, and the result is a GIF or JPG file you can edit, crop, and add to a desktop-published newsletter, greeting card, or Web page. Scanners have gone up in quality and down in price; you can probably find one for around $100.

Scanners have other purposes. I use my inexpensive Visioneer as a copy machine. Others use their scanning software to convert paper faxes into editable text. Converting paper documents in this way requires Optical Character Recognition (OCR) software, a standard component of scanning software.

Another way to get your pictures digitized is to bring your film a developer who offers the service of converting the film to digital pictures. The developer then saves the images to CD-ROM or disk. The images can then be uploaded on to your computer.

Pictures Taken with a Digital Camera

If you use digital photographs on your Web page, or love photography (and gadgets), or want to be able to send images over the Internet to friends and family without any

Cross-Reference

Chapter 10 has all the information you need to get started attaching and inserting images into messages.

Note

When you select pictures from your You've Got Pictures rolls to download, you can choose to download them at low, medium, or high resolution. Low resolution is generally fine for viewing online, and the smaller file size means that they'll load faster, too. Consequently, if you intend to use a picture on your Web page, stick to low resolution. Medium resolution is better if you're planning to print the picture. High resolution is best if you're planning to create a large print, but high-resolution pictures take longer to download and take up more space. You'll be charged extra for high-resolution downloads.

delay — even the 48 hours it takes for You've Got Pictures rolls to show up — then consider buying a digital camera. Like scanners, their quality, too, has gone up as their price has come down. They don't match the quality of a single-lens reflex camera (SLR), but for strictly online use the high quality of normal photographs still can't be represented on a standard monitor.

Digital cameras work pretty much like film cameras, except for one crucial difference: the photos you take are stored electronically from the very beginning. No scanning is necessary; instead, you download images from the digital camera directly into your computer, where they're immediately available for editing, e-mailing, or inserting into your Web page. Some digital cameras use 3.5-inch disks; others use special cards that fit into an adapter, which, in turn, can be used in your PC's 3.5-inch disk drive. Some digital cameras require a cable for uploading an image from your camera into the digital imaging software provided by the camera maker.

You've Got Pictures!

If you don't own your own scanner and don't plan to buy yet another piece of hardware, there is a way of turning pictures taken the old-fashioned way into digital pictures. It's called You've Got Pictures, and there's a link to it right on the main AOL Welcome screen, just below your mailbox on version 5.0.

To use You've Got Pictures, simply take your next roll of film into a photo developer who offers the service (the store must be part of the Kodak PhotoNet network). On the processing envelope, check the AOL box and fill in your AOL screen name. In a couple of days, your film will be developed. You'll still receive your photos and negatives as usual. In addition, digital versions of your pictures arrive for you at AOL. Click the You've Got Pictures button on the Welcome screen to view them. (You may have to type in a claim number provided by the photo developer to see them.)

You can arrange your pictures into albums for yourself, complete with customized layouts and background colors, create Buddy Albums to share with friends, or simply e-mail your pictures to friends. The pictures themselves aren't sent; instead, your friends are provided with a link they can visit to view the pictures online.

You receive 50 free online picture spaces for each screen name. If you need more, you can either purchase additional space for your pictures or download your pictures to your hard drive to free up your online space. If you're planning to use them in your Web page, you'll want to download them anyway. You'll also want to download them if you'd like to be able to share them with friends and family without having to go through the You've Got Pictures area. Once they're downloaded, you can e-mail them as attachments or insert them directly into your e-mail, as you would with any other digital picture.

Finding Digital Images on Your Hard Drive

Once you've got a few digital images on your hard drive, AOL 5.0 makes it easy to locate the one you want. You don't have to remember what you called it, because AOL 5.0 shows you a preview!

To find an image, choose File ⇨ Open Picture Gallery. Browse your hard drive for the folder containing the pictures you want to choose from, and then click Open Gallery. You'll see something like Figure 14-10. You can drag pictures directly from the gallery into an open e-mail window so you can e-mail them to a friend, or double-click to edit them using AOL's basic picture-editing tools, which let you adjust characteristics such as contrast, brightness, size, and so forth, and even crop, flip, or rotate images, such as the strange digital photo shown in Figure 14-11.

Find It Online

Keyword: **Gallery** spotlights notable member home pages.

Note

In addition to having your film developed and delivered to your AOL account, you will soon be able to upload images from your digital camera or scanner to use with the You've Got Pictures service.

14

Making a Page

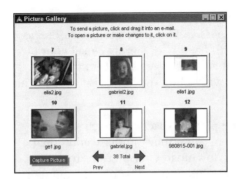

Figure 14-10. Once you call up a Picture Gallery of the pictures saved on your hard drive . . .

Figure 14-11. Double-click an image to edit it using AOL's picture-editing tools.

Finding Other Members' Pages in AOL Hometown

Like you, other AOL members have also been creating Web pages displaying their talents, interests, neighborhoods, kids, and *real* lives. With AOL Hometown it's easy to compare your page with others or to find like-minded people online.

How do you get home? Visit Hometown by going to Keyword: **Hometown** or choosing Visit Hometown from AOL's Internet and People menus.

Finding pages on any topic — that's the whole idea of Hometown communities. AOL Hometown also points you to interesting pages by frequently spotlighting members' pages.

Not only that, you can search AOL Hometown pages for key words or phrases, or for pages created by a particular member. The AOL Hometown home page puts all of these search techniques at your fingertips.

To search pages by keyword or screen name, type the words or screen name you want to search for in the box under the Search Pages banner. You'll get a page displaying a list of the pages that match your search terms. You can choose to either display all the pages, in a manner much like you see when you conduct a search with AOL Search, or display the communities they were found in. A search for communities having to do with science fiction retrieved about 200 communities and neighborhoods. Finally, you can browse AOL Hometown by going directly to the community that interests you, starting with the list of interests under the Explore Member Pages banner.

A Quick Look Back

On the Web, the best way to learn is from other people and their pages. Seeing the pages other AOL members — and non-members — have created can be fun, help you learn something new, and also help you create a more effective Web page for yourself. To help you choose a page and get started, this chapter told how to

- ▶ Create and publish web pages using different AOL tools–1-2-3 Publish (the absolutely simplest way to get a page) and Easy Designer (the most flexible solution).
- ▶ Find, use, and create digital images for your Web pages
- ▶ Locate the Web pages of other AOL Hometown members, to get ideas and find like-minded (or plain interesting) people

You won't be looking at other members' pages for long, however, before realizing how much is possible on the Web, and to what extent you can serve your professional and personal interests with a Web presence. The next chapter looks at how you, too, can move from a single page to complete site!

CHAPTER

15

CONTRIBUTING TO THE WEB:

MAKING AND

MANAGING A SITE

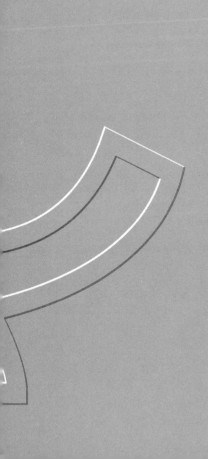

Chapter 15

Contributing to the Web: Making and Managing a Site

I n the last chapter you learned how to make a simple Web page. If all you want to do is tell the world about yourself and maybe post a few photographs for family and friends to get a kick out of, great; that's all you need.

If you want to move beyond the basic home page and provide details of your toy-car collection, or begin selling your home-made candles in global markets, or publish your own Webzine or your family's history over the last 200 years, you're going to need more than one page. You're going to need an organized collection of pages, or Web *site*.

Not only that, to hold the attention of fickle Web surfers, you're going to have to make that site stand out, which means using some new tools. And to make sure those Web surfers can find your site in the first place, you're going to have to do your best to ensure that people interested in your topic can readily find it.

Fortunately, the one topic the Web covers exhaustively is *itself*. There are hundreds of sites that provide how-to information, suggestions, tools of every kind, clip art, backgrounds, buttons, scripts, and utilities to help you make your site the best it can be. This chapter includes a selection of such sites. Above all, the Web offers examples — sites like the one you want to build, sites you want to differ from, and sites you just like.

This chapter takes a look at the process of moving from page to site, points you to some valuable resources on AOL and on the Web, and gives a few pointers on getting out the word about your wonderful site.

Definition

Script is programming code that your browser reads one line at a time in order to do something—like display a drop-down menu. HTML itself is a very easy-to-use scripting language for making Web pages. JavaScript and VBScript are commonly used scripts to make fancier, more interactive effects. Many Web sites let you help yourself to scripts to use on your own site, as you'll see in the "Adding Multimedia Excitement" section.

From Page to Site: Design Issues

The moment you move from one page to two. . .or sixty (and it happens faster than you might realize), you run into *design* issues. Design issues have to do with your site's purpose, audience, organization, and look. The following questions can help you generate the data you need to design your site thoughtfully from the ground up. Otherwise, you could find yourself wasting time making midcourse corrections.

Here are ten questions to ask yourself before setting pixel to monitor:

1. **Who is my audience?** If you're creating your Web site to please yourself, your job is relatively easy; just don't be surprised if you don't have many visitors. Otherwise, give some thought about who you want to visit your site. Just family and friends — or everyone on the planet who shares your interest in hairy-nosed Australian wombats? A site designed for your circle of

Chapter 7 covers AOL Search.

closest acquaintances will obviously be very different from one designed for strangers.

2. **What is my message?** Web pages are a form of communication, not just information. You're trying to share your thoughts on certain topics. Define a vision before designing your site, and the result will be better-focused and more engaging than if the information hops around from the antics of your dog to UFOs.

3. **What tone do I want to establish?** Web sites can be comic or serious or ironic, strident or laid-back, or some combination of expressive styles. Tone comes from the writing, the images, even the font colors and the design of dividing lines (horizontal *rules*). It's generally a good idea to make the tone match the image: a serious site detailing the inspiring stories of people who survived near-fatal car accidents, for instance, probably wouldn't work well with a background of multicolored balloons and clown faces. On the other hand, feel free to break the rules to achieve the effect you want.

4. **Has someone else created a similar site?** Do a little sleuthing. Use AOL Search and other search engines to find other sites on the same topic. Make notes on what you like and don't like about those sites. Take the good ideas a step further and adapt them. But be sure to also ask yourself . . .

5. **What can I bring to my site that's unique?** Sites on similar topics are going to have similar content. Surely, however, your perspective differs in some important way. You've probably got experiences and specific information no one else has, and, very likely, you can communicate your ideas more effectively in some way or another. What's unique about what you have to say and how you say it?

6. **How much storage space do I need?** AOL provides 2Mb of storage space for each screen name. Register with AOL Hometown, and you get 4Mb per screen name. Because each account can have up to seven screen names, you could have as much as 14Mb (or 28Mb) of storage space on Hometown. If you "add all pages" via the "add all" link in AOL Homtown's

Add/Manage pages screen, you get 12mb on that screen name. By adding all pages, that means that all HTML documents in your FTP space will appear in AOL Hometown's search database as well as under the AOL Hometown banner. The standard 2Mb is enough for dozens of pages if your pages are mostly text. Start adding lots of pictures, sound files, or animations, and both the number of pages you can create and the potential size of your site start shrinking. In order to get the information you need into your site, you might have to scale down your ambitions. The amount of storage space you have leads directly to some basic design questions, including . . .

7. **How do I want to balance text and graphics?** Do you want a site top-heavy with text and light on graphics, or vice versa? The former allows you to present lots of information, but may drive away the casual browser because it doesn't look inviting. The latter may be attractive but ultimately shallow, and will also eat up storage space in a hurry — not to mention make your page slower to load. You need to strike just the right balance to create a site that's attractive, informative, and quick-loading. It's a challenge. Again, look at the sites you really like and see how they strike this balance — especially if you don't have a staff of Web designers and technicians.

8. **What links do I want to provide?** *Links* make the World Wide Web a true web — links to other pages to which users can jump with a click of their mouse. Spend some time locating the best links related to your topic. How many links do you want to put in your text? How do you want to present links: on a separate page (like a directory), or embedded in your text, or some combination of the two? A link in the main text of your site can be an open invitation to visit someone else's site, which can be counter-productive. Perhaps you'll want to group your links on their own page (see Figure 15-1) or at least group links that take viewers to *other* sites, or indicate graphically or organizationally which links are external and which are internal.

When looking at sites for ideas, start with sites created by individuals, not multinational corporations, or you may get unrealistic ideas of what's feasible. Such sites require programming and computer resources often available only to Web sites with full-time staffs. With all the slick but shallow sites out there, a homey site with genuine substance can be a big success. Just make sure everyone who might care knows about the site (read on for tips to market your site).

Make sure to include a link allowing visitors to e-mail you (called a *mailto*). There's no better way to get feedback and suggestions.

15

Making and Managing a Site

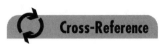

Cross-Reference

Later in this chapter, in "HTML in Five Minutes," you'll find an overview of HTML.

Definition

WYSIWYG: What You See Is What You Get (you will hear this pronounced wizzy-wig). That means that what you see in Netscape Composer as you create pages comes very close to what visitors will see once your page is published on the Web and viewed with a browser. (*Very close* means that differences in browsers and browser preferences make it hard to be completely sure how a Web page will look to visitors!)

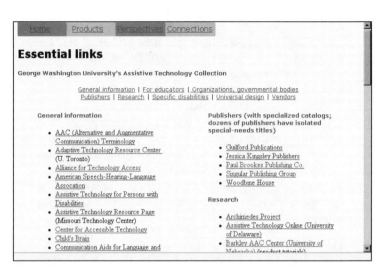

Figure 15-1. Many sites, such as this one, devote whole pages to links that might be of interest to visitors. If abundant, well-organized, and well-maintained, such directories can attract people to your site.

9. **Do I want to add multimedia?** Sound, video, and animation can be exciting additions to Web sites, but for most users they simply make the page load slowly; worse, they don't work with everyone's system. Sound files are useless if the viewer's computer doesn't have a sound card. Also, some formats of sound, video, and animation require special plug-ins that not everyone has. A rule of thumb: use multimedia when it supports your message, and use common formats (GIF, JPG). Multimedia files also hog storage space more than most pictures do.

10. **How do I want to relate my pages to each other?** With answers to the other nine questions in hand, this question leads you to the nitty-gritty of design. To answer it, you have to answer many other questions, such as what will the pages look like? Will they have a common layout and share a common background or other graphic elements? What fonts will I use? How will I allow visitors to move from page to page — a simple list of links down one side, or something more complicated?

Creating a Site with an Editor

Creating a site doesn't mean you have to learn programming; a working knowledge of HTML does help, however. There are plenty of programs available — free, as shareware, or commercially — that take care of the mechanics. This chapter looks at editing tools such as Netscape Composer, which is free (see Chapter 6). Netscape Composer is a *WYSIWYG HTML editor*, meaning that you can focus on the content (text and pictures) without giving thought to how the content is coded in HTML. If you do want to edit HTML, it's easy to do so (see "Using Netscape Composer").

If you've ever used Word's fancier formatting features or a desktop publishing program such as PageMaker, you'll know that you can focus on content and look, not on mechanics. Think of HTML editors as desktop publishing for the Web.

Using Netscape Composer

Netscape Composer is available free as a part of Netscape Communicator, which you can download from http://home.netscape.com. what link address will be used?Composer looks quite a bit like Netscape Navigator. To get to Composer, open Communicator and click the Composer button on the toolbar in the bottom right of the Navigator window.

In Composer, as in any word processor or desktop publishing program, you type text and edit it using the tools on the formatting toolbar. You add other items, such as lines (called *rules*), hyperlinks, images, and tables, using the large buttons above the formatting toolbar (see Figure 15-2). Most of them open a dialog box that you use to fine-tune the item you're entering. You can even do a spell check of your text.

Definition

HTML editor: You design your site and lay out your pages as you want them to look; the HTML editor creates the HTML for you, behind the scenes. All major editors give you direct access to the HTML, to make refinements and for troubleshooting. (Figure 15-6 shows what HTML looks like.)

Cross-Reference

Chapter 6 shows how to download Netscape Communicator using SmartDownload.

15

Making and Managing a Site

With any editor, you'll be working with files on your computer. Save them to and retrieve them from your hard drive. To simplify site maintenance, set up your local folder structure to mirror your intended site's structure.

Remember to upload any images when you upload the pages that embed or link to those images! Use your HTML editor to give images a size (in pixels), so your pages can download faster.

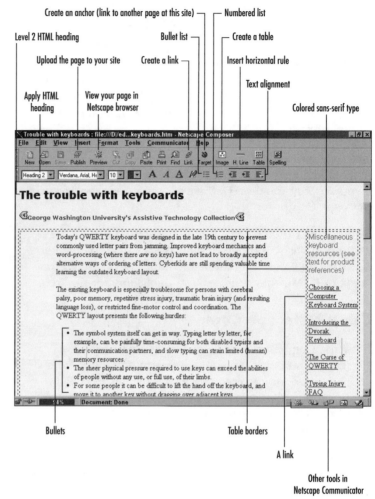

Figure 15-2. Netscape Composer simplifies page creation and site design.

Here are just a few of the point-and-click things you can do with Navigator, to get all your pages working together:

▶ **Insert a link.** Select some text, click the Link button, and provide a URL and some other information.

▶ **Create a target.** A *target*, also known as an *anchor*, is a link to a place on the same page or on a different page in the same site; you can use anchors in your navigational table of contents. Targets must have names, and links to them are preceded by a folder and file name (if on a different page), plus the anchor name preceded by a pound sign (for example, #birds).

▶ **Format text.** Select the text, then apply bold (for example), a different type size, or color, and so forth. For text that lends itself to points or items, create a numbered or bulleted list.

▶ **Apply an HTML tag.** Select some text, then apply a heading from the drop-down list in the right-hand side of the formatting toolbar.

▶ **Insert an image.** Click the Image button, and you'll be prompted to provide lots of information (do as much as you can or want): the picture's name and location, the size you want for it, any associated text and linking (making the picture a clickable link).

▶ **Add a table to present structured text or data.** In Chapter 5, Figure 5-2 shows a typical table. HTML tables were originally meant to present tabular data (numbers, mostly) in a grid of rows and columns, for clear presentation. More and more, they're being used to format data — using narrow columns to present "snaking text," for example, newspaper style. The latest version of HTML 4.0 gives Web designers more efficient formatting capabilities.

Power Tools: Graphics Tools, HTML Editors, Text Editors

You may eventually want special software for managing sites; creating and manipulating graphics; refining your color schemes; and creating and managing interactive, video, and animated content. A superb source of information about Web utilities, with reviews, is available at DaveCentral Shareware (`http://www.davecentral.com`).

The numerous commercial programs out there don't come cheap. FrontPage 2000 is the latest commercial version of Microsoft's HTML editor. If you use any other Office 2000 products, you'll feel right at home with it and may already have it as part of the suite. Heavy-duty products preferred by Web designers like Macromedia Dreamweaver run more than $200, and Allaire Cold Fusion, much more.

Find It Online

For commercial software, do a price comparison at Keyword: **CNET** (just search for the product of interest). You can buy any software at Keyword: **Software Shop** or Keyword: **Beyond**. Keyword: **Software** takes you to collections of both shareware and commercial software, with recommendations.

15

Making and Managing a Site

Tip

Shareware sites offer your best bet if you don't want to spend a lot of money. Start at any of the sites profiled in Chapter 17 ("Where to Find Internet Software"): Stroud, TUCOWS, ZDNET, CNET (please note that these aren't AOL Keywords). You'll find a wide choice of programs, with reviews, tips, links, and easy downloading.

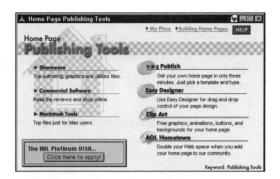

Figure 15-3. From Keyword: *Publishing Tools*, you get ready access to shareware, clipart, and both 1-2-3 Publish and Easy Designer. More advanced Web tools, including counters and guest books, are available on the Web at http://www.hemepagetools.com.

Web Utilities

Special jobs require special tools, especially in building Web sites. The following programs serve as essential utilities:

▶ GIFWeb lets you create *transparent GIFs,* images, which allow the background to show through. GIFs that aren't transparent don't blend with the background.

▶ GIFCON lets you create *animated GIFs* (a GIF containing a small number of separate images that, when downloaded, create the impression of simple movement).

▶ WS_FTP, profiled in Chapter 17, makes it much easier to upload your Web pages and related files to AOL, mainly because it lets you send a lot of files at once, instead of having to send them one at a time. WS_FTP simplifies management chores like deleting, moving, and renaming files.

▶ JASC Software Inc.'s PaintShop Pro (see Figure 15-4) is considered by many a full-featured alternative to the huge, expensive, and difficult industry-standard, Adobe Photoshop. It lets you paint your own images or manipulate just about every type of graphic file format, and comes complete with an animation studio.

Figure 15-4. PaintShop Pro, a shareware program, fine-tunes images for your Web site. This cropped picture, for example, focuses more closely on the main subject and reduces the size of the graphic.

15

Making and Managing a Site

HTML Editors: What to Look For

Most Web authoring programs support a range of tasks, from creating simple Web pages to managing complex sites and implementing advanced features such as layers and style sheets. All major commercial programs — HotDog, Dreamweaver, FrontPage, PageMill, HotMetal, and others — provide both a graphical interface and a way to view and edit the HTML script if you know HTML. Having access to the HTML gives you precise control over image placement, and helps you troubleshoot your pages when things don't work quite right. You'll *always* find something that doesn't work quite right, especially if you aim to have your page viewed by people using several versions of both the Microsoft and Netscape browsers; different browsers display the same Web page differently.

Continued

HTML Editors: What to Look For *(continued)*

Some things to look for in HTML editors:

▶ **Price.** Programs range in cost from nothing (for freeware) to hundreds of dollars; for around $200 you can buy an outstanding HTML editor. If you don't want to buy a program now, consider the shareware option; the well-respected HotDog Pro comes as shareware and can be downloaded at Keyword: **Hotdog**.

▶ **Ability to build relatively complex HTML elements.** With items such as tables, forms, and frames, how much do you do and how much does the program do? How easy is editing (for example, splitting a table cell or changing a table border or background, or making a frame's border seamless or scrolled)?

▶ **Quality of HTML generated.** Some WYSIWYG programs create clean and efficient HTML that can be easily imported into any other HTML editor. Others produce proprietary code, unique to the HTML editor, that is sometimes difficult to edit manually or use in another HTML editor. Is it easy to switch between the graphical and HTML views? Keyword: **CNET** provides plenty of reviews of HTML editors, to find out such things before buying.

▶ **Site management.** Some programs, like FrontPage and Dreamweaver, represent the links between your pages visually and allow you to alter these links easily.

▶ **Ability and ease in importing interactive content.** Is it difficult to import Java applets, JavaScript rollovers, and dynamic HTML animation?

▶ **Proofing tools.** Does the program check your HTML to make sure it conforms to the HTML standard (3.2, 4.0, or whatever is coming next)? Does it check your links to make sure they work? (You must be online to use link-checking, of course.) Does it let you do a spell-check? Does it let you preview your pages in different browsers?

▶ **Extensions and add-ons.** Is the product supported by additional utilities? For example, many companies provide utilities in support of Microsoft's FrontPage 98. Macromedia, for example, makes a product called Dreamweaver Attain that assists in creating Web-based training.

▶ **Complexity.** FrontPage requires the installation of server software on your PC and has a learning curve. Dreamweaver and HotDog have complex interfaces that can be intimidating — at first. Don't confuse real complexity with visual complexity. With Dreamweaver, you can clear away all windows, and do all your design work using the well-designed menus.

Even if you don't use an HTML text editor to create a page from scratch, they come in handy editing the output of the WYSIWYG HTML editors.

Text Editors: HTML the Old-Fashioned Way

Before WYSIWYG HTML editors, people still managed to create great Web pages. So can you, too — if you're a craftsperson with the time to learn HTML, to relearn HTML when the next version comes out, and to tweak your pages. You need nothing more than WordPad or Notepad, the mini-word processors built into Windows. Any word processor will do, as long as all your files are *saved as text.* You can even use AOL's text editor (File ⇨ New).

The fanciest Web pages contain, in fact, nothing but text, including the simple HTML *tags* that define how your words are to look, which images go where, what links you'll be using, and everything else people experience on your page.

Even if you're using a WYSIWYG editor, it's a good idea to have some understanding of HTML, the language in which Web pages are written. See "HTML in Five Minutes." Not only are you likely to find some very useful objects on *other people's* Web pages, but you are almost certain to want to tweak the HTML code of *your pages* if only to make sure they work in all browsers.

Of course, you can edit any page using WordPad or your favorite word processor; just make sure you save the file with an HTM or HTML extension so browsers will be able to recognize it as a Web page.

Fortunately, all major HTML editors give you access to HTML. A program like Netscape Composer gives you direct access to HTML, in order to view, edit, and save. You can also insert specific HTML tags into your Web page by choosing Insert ➪ HTML Tag. This lets you add a bit of HTML to your page without having to leave the WYSIWYG display.

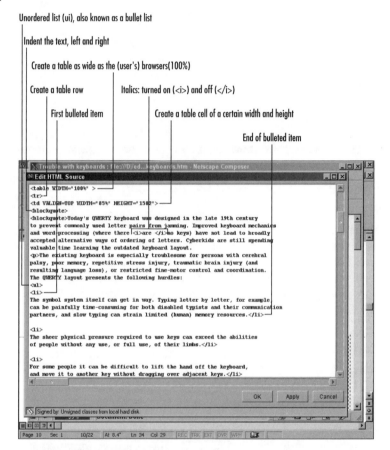

Figure 15-5. Netscape's Composer displays HTML in a cool Java text editor (Tools ➪ HTML Tools ➪ Edit HTML Source). This figure shows part of the HTML file on which Figure 15-2 is based.

HTML Text Editors

The difference between an HTML text editor and a WYSIWIG editor is that you build pages in raw HTML with a text editor (with lots of support and validation features), while you build pages as you want them to look in a WYSIWIG editor.

Several wonderful HTML editors give you the power of pure HTML and the control of an HTML editor. These products do require some comfort with HTML, but most provide reference links or resources so you can teach yourself what you don't yet know.

Allaire's HomeSite 4.0 comes bundled with many commercial Web products; otherwise it's fairly pricey shareware. NoteTab Light is the freeware version of a shareware program. Both are available from TUCOWS (`http://www.tucows.com`). For other editors, check out TUCOWS's collection of HTML Editors and Text Editors. With such programs, you type in the HTML with plenty of support from the editor; you also get the chance to view your developing page inside of a browser.

Figure 15-6 shows NoteTab Light displaying the underlying HTML used in the page shown in Figure 15-2.

Tip

Both HomeSite and NotePad are available at Keyword: **Publishing Tools**.

15

Making and Managing a Site

Figure 15-6. NoteTab Light. The HTML was generated by Dreamweaver.

HTML in Five Minutes

HTML "tags" tells the browser what to display; the browser decides exactly how to display the tagged content. Because the structure of every tag is identical (each one consists of a "less-than" sign, <, followed by a tag name, and then ending with a "more-than" sign, >), learning how to use HTML really means learning how to use various HTML tags. Figure 15-5, for example, shows several tags used in the page displayed in Figure 15-2.

Most tags appear in pairs, turning an effect on and off. Note the use of a forward slash before the text of the second tag, which turns off the effect. For instance, the following tags center and display in bold the words *ICQ Rules*:

`<CENTER><B>ICQ Rules</b></CENTER>`

HTML pages always begin with the tag <HTML>, which tells the browser that what follows is a Web page. The <TITLE> tag sets off the title of the page — which appears at the top of the browser — and the <BODY> tag designates the body of the page. All three tags must be turned off again. The Title tag gets turned off after the title itself (</TITLE>. The Body tag gets turned off after the page content has been presented </BODY>. The HTML tag gets turned off at the very end of the page </HTML>.

Table 15-1 shows some other, common HTML tags.

Table 15-1. *Some Frequently Used HTML Tags*

HTML Tag	Means . . .
<A>	Makes a link. Here's the link to `http://www.aol.com`:
	`<A HREF="http://www.aol.com">Visit AOL on the Web!</A>`
	HREF defines the Web address; *Visit AOL on the Web!* is what the user clicks; */A* closes the link.
<B>	Makes text bold

HTML Tag	Means . . .
<BGSOUND>	Triggers a background sound that plays as soon as the page is loaded into the browser. See the "Adding Excitement to Your Web Site" section.
<BLOCKQUOTE>	A very handy formatting feature that indents text from both the right and left margins, making for greater readability.

	Inserts a line break; see <P>
<CENTER>	Centers text and images
<EMBED>	Adds sound to a page by embedding a file that plays automatically when the page loads (for example, a MIDI file).
<FONT>	Set the font size, style, and color. At Keyword: **Building Home Pages**, you can learn about how to specify font, font size, and font color. For example: *Font type:* <font face="verdana, helvetica, arial, sans-serif">...</font> *Font color:* <font color="006699">...</font> *Font size:* <font size=-2>...<font>
<H1>	Main heading
<H2>	Second-level heading.
<H3>...<H6>	Lower-level heads.
<HR>	Inserts a horizontal *rule*, or line, as a separator, whose dimensions the browser determines. Alternatively, you can use a small, decorative graphic here; you determine its shape and other features.
<I>	Makes text italic
<IMG>	Inserts a graphic file. To embed an image called **mypic.jpg**, you'd type (for example): <IMG SRC="mypic.jpg">

Continued

Find It Online

On AOL, Keyword: **Build Your Web Page** also links to essential tutorials and references.

Table 15-1. *Some Frequently Used HTML Tags (continued)*

HTML Tag	Means . . .
<P>	Starts a new paragraph and automatically inserts space between itself and the previous paragraph. A leaves no space between lines, which you'd do to keep closely spaced the lines of a street address or the lines of a long heading
<U>	Underlines text

Online Resources for Web-site Developers

Start on the Web to get clip-art, buttons, dividers, images, JavaScript, WAV and MIDI sound files, background images, and software to create and edit all these things. You'll also get product reviews, tutorials, and design guidance at every level.

- ▶ **Creating a Home Page** (available on the Web at http://hometown.aol.com or on Keyword: **Hometown**; click **Help**). Visit this one first! This AOL resource leads you to a wealth of resources, including information and tutorials on HTML, DHTML (that's dynamic HTML, discussed a little later), and other scripting languages; libraries of clip art for your pages; collections of cut-and-paste HTML code; and instructions on how to add everything from counters to interactive forms to your site.
- ▶ **AOL graphics areas.** Many AOL areas live and breathe graphics, sound, and multimedia, including
  - ▪ Animation & Video Community (Keyword: **Multimedia**)
  - ▪ Photography Forum (Keyword: **Photography**)
  - ▪ Image Exchange (Keyword: **Image Exchange**)
  - ▪ PC Graphics Arts Forum (Keyword: **PGR**)
- ▶ **Web tutorials** (keyword: **Webtut**). Chat-based classes, chat transcripts, FAQs, message boards, and more.
- ▶ **Builder.com.** This site can be reached directly from AOL by clicking a link from the Building Home Pages window or going directly to http://www.builder.com. It provides an essential library on every topic from HTML, to multimedia, to e-commerce and security.

▶ **WebMonkey** (http://www.hotwired.com/ webmonkey). Published by HotWired, one of the first publications designed from the ground up for the Web, WebMonkey features thorough, informed, and up-to-date articles about graphic design, plug-ins, new products, and emerging technologies. The site itself showcases the latest technologies.

▶ **Vincent Flanders' Web Pages That Suck** (http://www.webpagesthatsuck.com/). You can learn a lot about making good Web pages by viewing bad ones — and you won't find any worse than the ones collected here. There's even a good book based on these bad sites!

Can't find what you're looking for on any of these sites? As they say in Australia, "No worries, mate!" Just fire up your favorite search engine and type in search terms such as **transparent GIF** or **JavaScript tutorial**. You'll soon find yourself up to your neck in useful sites.

Find It Online

Early on, choose a guide to HTML that includes all the tags and what they mean. The Beginner's Guide to HTML was originally published by the university where Netscape (Mosaic) was invented; it remains a wonderful primer (http://www.ncsa.uiuc.edu/ General/Internet/WWW/ HTMLPrimerP1.html). Browse CNET's Buider.com for other HTML references.

Adding Multimedia

It won't be long after you've created your Web site that you begin to suffer from Web envy. It's brought on by seeing sites that seem to have yours beat hands-down for visual design, cool effects, and perhaps even content. Maybe yours is static and theirs has sound and movement. Maybe you've only got text and pictures on yours, and they've got JavaScript rollovers and a Flash animation. (A *rollover* means that as someone rolls the mouse arrow over a graphic or text, that element moves, expands, shows a menu, or does something else.)

Adding Animation

"Animation" conjures up images of Bambi, Mickey Mouse, or, most recently, Tarzan surfing the jungle canopy. Don't worry. Web animation can be anything that moves on a page.

The simplest type of animation is probably the animated GIF. An animated GIF is really a series of individual GIFs that display rapidly, one after the other, in your visitor's browser.

Thanks to the persistence of vision that makes movies *movies,* and not just high-speed slide shows, your visitor sees movement. GIFCon, shareware for making animated GIFs, is available at Keyword: **Publishing Tools.** You can also achieve animation using some of the new Web plug-ins such as Macromedia Flash (the plug-in is free; the program to make animations for the plug-in can set you back some money).

Adding Dynamic HTML

One *free* way to liven up your pages is through the use of dynamic HTML (DHTML) tags in your page's coding. DHTML enables effects previously requiring special plug-ins to be achieved with scripting — that is, a bit of programming. Dynamic HTML requires a Version 4 browser (Netscape or MSIE), and it takes advantage of both JavaScript and the latest features of HTML 4.0 (layers and style sheets). Through scripting, DHTML lets you create moving images, scrolling marquees (see Figure 15-7), transition screens, special windows, and, in general, elements that are highly responsive to what a user does (at the mouse or keyboard).

Trouble is, there's no standard yet for DHTML, which means some tags you use may not achieve the same effects in all browsers. That's fine — as long as you say so explicitly on your page.

Adding JavaScript

A key piece of the emerging Dynamic HTML standard, JavaScript was originally developed by Netscape but works with Internet Explorer too (minor discrepancies notwithstanding). It's a scripting language, like HTML, meaning you insert JavaScript right into your HTML to achieve cool effects. If you have the smallest inkling to learn a little programming, start with JavaScript. You don't need anything more than an up-to-date browser, a Web resource, and a good book such as IDG Books Worldwide, Inc.'s JavaScript Bible, 3rd edition.

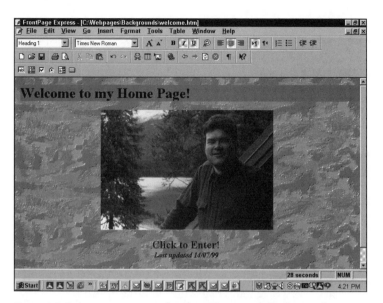

Tip

JavaScript, too, requires some programming, but at Builder.com you can have script generated for you. All you have to do is paste the script into your pages! JavaScript World gives away cool JavaScript for your pages.

Figure 15-7. A moving marquee (the title) adds action to Ed Willett's Web site.

JavaScript can be used to make words or pictures change when the mouse is pointed at them, or to pop up a special window over the regular browser window. You can use it to display the date, create a drop-down menu, or let your visitors choose your page's background color. Or, as in Figure 15-8, you can use it to do something as nerdy and complex as displaying the periodic table of the elements and providing information about each element!

15

Making and Managing a Site

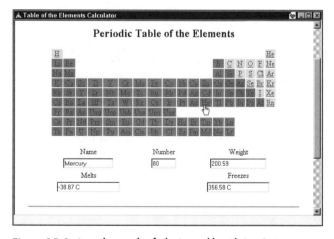

Figure 15-8. A good example of what's possible with JavaScript — an interactive periodic table of the elements. From JavaScript World (http://www.jsworld.com).

Most of the Web-building resources in "Online Resources for Web-site Developers" include information about JavaScript.

Adding Sound

The sounds you can easily add to your Web site come in two forms: digital recordings or MIDI. Digital recordings are based on recordings of real sound; MIDI files are simulated sound. If you'll be using sound in your site, make sure to test everything using a sound player such as Windows Media Player. This chapter does not look at the sounds requiring special plug-in software, such as RealAudio.

▶ *Digital recordings,* typical in the Windows 95/98-standard WAV format, are real sounds that have been digitized so computers can store, play, and modify them. Other files of this type, like the older AU and SND formats, were originally made for Unix computers.

In most cases, computers download and then play WAV files. You'll find some WAV files available in a *streaming* version (meaning the browser begins playing a file before all of it is received). The "download-then-play" method is probably more common simply because the streaming method usually requires a special plug-in for the browser plus special software on the computer where the Web page is stored.

▶ *Digital simulations* such as MIDI consist of music written for the computer. MIDI stands for *Musical Instrument Digital Interface.* MIDI files allow very long pieces of music to be transmitted quickly, even over slow connections. Such music can sound a little tinny, however. All of today's browsers can play MIDI files through the computer's sound card, and AOL plays such sounds using its Media Player.

A good way to add sound so that AOL's built-in browser, the stand-alone MSIE, and Netscape can all play it is to use the <EMBED> HTML tag. You'd type it into the HTML for your page like this:

```
<EMBED SRC="sound.mid" HIDDEN=TRUE
AUTOSTART="true" LOOP="true">
```

Tip

You can create your own digital recordings or MIDI files using whatever software you wish, or you can download digital files and MIDI files from sites all over the Web. On AOL, start at AOL's own Download Center (Keyword: **Download Center**), where you can find an entire Music and Sound library with files of all types. For WAV and MIDI files on the Web, start at the Daily WAV (http://www.dailywav.com). *All the sounds are copyrighted at DailyWAV,* but the Links page takes you to dozens of other sources of WAV and MIDI files, where you might find files you can use.

Note

By the time you read this book, MP3 sounds may be broadly enough available in streaming format to make them a worthy successor to WAV—and much more realistic than MIDI. Chapters 5 and 17 introduce MP3.

This *looks* complicated but isn't:

- ▶ You're embedding a MIDI file (sound.mid). In your own pages, just substitute your MIDI or WAV file for *sound.mid*.
- ▶ You want the link to be visible on the page (HIDDEN=TRUE).
- ▶ You want the sound to start playing automatically when the browser starts reading the page (AUTOSTART="true").
- ▶ You want it to play continuously, looping back to the beginning once it reaches the end (LOOP="true").

Viewing most Web sites is still a silent experience. By adding sound to your page, you can make your site stand out from the crowd — and keep impatient Web-surfers around a little longer. The wrong theme song could drive people away instead! Just imagine an endless loop of , say, "Ninety-nine Bottles of Beer on the Wall." Would you stick around? It's also a good idea to give the user a chance to turn it off.

Managing Your Pages

1-2-3 Publish and Hotdog Express, discussed in the last chapter, make publishing a single page to AOL as easy as clicking a button. Publishing more than one page, however, is a bit more complicated. Managing a multipage site, in which you may want to only edit a single page at a time instead of all the pages, is more complicated still. When you want to edit many pages (to correct a common misspelling, for example), you need to use a special tool.

When you publish a single Web page, as you saw in the last chapter, it's automatically called "index.htm" or "index.html." Browsers automatically look for this file first when they visit the Web address typed in by a user. Unless you specify a particular page when you type in a Web address, the browser tries to open *index.htm* (or *html*).

Cross-Reference

AOL's browser is the subject of Chapter 5, Netscape Navigator of Chapter 6.

Tip

Hotdog Express, discussed in Chapter 14, provides a very simple interface for adding sound to pages. Perhaps you'll want to generate pages in Hotdog Express, then refine them in another HTML editor.

Tip

15

Don't forget to upload any sound files along with your pages!

Note

If you scatter your site's pages across several folders of pages on *your* computer, make sure to create folders with exactly the same names at My FTP Space, or wherever you publish your pages.

Cross-Reference

See Chapter 16 on FTP, My FTP Space, and other fun FTP topics.

Name That Page

In creating Web pages, take special care to name them consistently enough that you can easily remember how to link to them from other pages on your site. Many people use short descriptive names: *links* for your links page, *photos* for your photo-album page, *resume* for your resume page, for example. Or, if your content changes daily, use a dating scheme like *19991231.htm*.

The larger the site, the more sense it makes to organize pages into folders. Suppose, instead of a single page of links, you had several pages of links, each related to different topics. You could create a folder called *links*, then place all of the links pages into that folder. Of course, every folder you add makes the address for the pages contained in it just a little bit more complicated. A single page of links might have the URL http://members.aol.com/yourname/funlinks.htm. Add a *links* folder, and the Web address grows a bit: http://members.aol.com/yourname/links/ funlinks.htm.

Some HTML editors give you a choice of how to make internal references within a site. Instead of providing a full (or *absolute*) path, as in the preceding paragraph, addresses can provide a simpler, *relative* path. Linking to a file in the same directory, for example, requires just the file's name, not its full path.

Publish That Site

If you're using 1-2-3 Publish, your job is easy; AOL does the publishing and managing for you. When you move from page to site, you can use the same storage space as that used by 1-2-3 Publish and HotDog Expres, but you'll need to directly access that space. The space is called My FTP Place (once known as MyPlace on AOL), and it's available at Keyword: **My FTP Space**.

The easiest way to upload files to My FTP Space is on AOL itself, at Keyword: **My Place** (as My FTP Space was formerly known). See Figure 15-9.

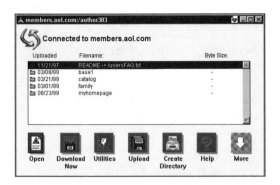

Figure 15-9. My FTP Space shows a list of all the folders and files you've currently stored in My FTP Space. (Your display will differ from this one.)

You can use FTP to upload new or revised pages to your Web site, rename existing files, or reorganize your Web space. For detailed information on using My FTP Space, see Chapter 16.

When you're using FTP to publish extra pages to your Web site, it's not enough to transfer the page itself to your FTP space. You must also transfer any graphics and other files linked from or embedded in that page, and you must make sure that you place them where the "referring" page expects them. For example, if the page expects all its graphics to be stored in a file folder called *graphics*, you must create a folder by that name in My FTP Space, then place your graphics files in that folder. Pages that can't find linked or embedded files will still download. However, instead of seeing graphics, visitors just see sad little X's or other placeholders where the graphics should be.

Note

Your 2M-per-screen-name storage limit (or 4-12Mb for each screen name registered at Hometown) applies to Keyword: **My FTP Space**. Visit there to get a quick sense of how much space your pages take up.

Getting the Word Out: Marketing Your Web Site

Build a better Web site and the world will *not* beat a path to your door, it's been said. No matter how good your Web site, with several hundred million pages currently available on the Web and more added hour by hour, you absolutely cannot expect people to just stumble across your site. You have to let them know it's there. How do you do that? Read on.

Tip

You can register any pages (or a site) with Hometown AOL, no matter what program you used to create them.

Tip

Add page lets you add a page at a time following the procedure in the text. Add all pages . . . well, adds all pages. Use this Add All option (moving all your pages from My FTP Space to Hometown), and you get a maximum of 12Mb of storage space in My FTP Space. In a master account, every screen name is entitled to this much space in exchange for adding all their pages to Hometown!

Registering with Hometown AOL

The first thing to do with that new page is register it with AOL Hometown. AOL has millions of members, and AOL Hometown is one of the first places those members look for people who share their interests. When you created a page with 1-2-3 Publish in Chapter 14, it was automatically registered with Hometown AOL in the My First Home Page community.

To add pages, go to the main Hometown AOL screen (Keyword: **Hometown**) and click the Add Pages link in the upper-left corner. This opens the screen in Figure 15-10.

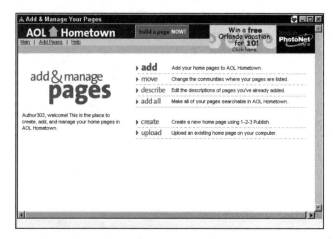

Figure 15-10. From the Add & Manage Pages screen, you can add your pages to Hometown AOL as well as move your pages to different Hometown communities and edit existing descriptions of pages.

To register the pages you've created with Hometown AOL, click Add. This opens the screen in Figure 15-11, the first in a series of screens that takes you step by step through the registration process.

The five steps in registering a page

1. **Select a page.** AOL shows you all the pages you have published to your AOL Web space (that is, uploaded to My FTP Space); select the one you want to add.

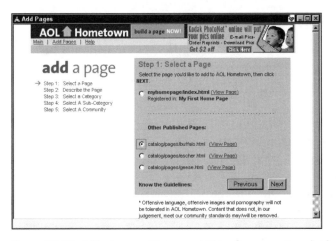

Figure 15-11. Adding pages to Hometown AOL is a five-step process that begins with this screen.

2. **Describe the page.** In 250 characters or less, describe the page you're registering with AOL Hometown.

3. **Select a category.** AOL Hometown currently has about a dozen categories under which you can register, on subjects such as business, careers, culture, education, entertainment, family, food, and hobbies. You can always change from one community to another using the Move option in Figure 15-11.

4. **Select a sub-category.** Each category is divided into subcategories. Pick the one that characterizes your page.

5. **Select a community.** Finally, select the community within that subcategory that best fits your page.

That's it! Your page has been added to AOL Hometown. Other people can now find it by searching or browsing Hometown.

To move pages to a different community, return to the Add & Manage Pages screen and click Move. Again, you're led through a simple step-by-step procedure. You can also edit the descriptions of your listed pages by clicking the Describe link on the Add & Manage Pages screen.

Tip

Make sure you register the index.htm page, since it has links to all your other pages. That way people who find your page on AOL Hometown will view it the way you intended. If you want all of your published pages to be searchable in AOL Hometown, even though they're not all listed individually, return to the Add & Manage Pages screen and click Add All. You can increase visits to your Web site by making all the pages in it searchable, thus increasing the likelihood that people seeking your information can find it.

15

Making and Managing a Site

Reaching the Rest of the World

Note

A recent study indicated that the Web is growing so fast that search engines are falling further behind in the effort to catalog everything, making it all the more important that you make the extra effort to draw their attention to your site.

Here are some other ways to get the word out about your wonderful Web site:

▶ **Register with online directories and search engines.** Many search engines let you add your URL to their list. If you don't register, it can be months before their automated systems find your site, if they ever do.

Most search engines have a link on their main page, saying something like Add Your Site, with a little box to enter your URL. On the AOL Search main page, look for a place to submit your site in the bottom-right corner. Clicking it brings up the Add Your Site form. You simply type in the URL for your site's index page, then provide an e-mail address and click Send. Inclusion in the database can take a couple of weeks, but then your site will be added to AOL Search and will begin showing up in the search results for people interested in your subject.

▶ **Use an all-in-one submission site.** Some Web services help you submit your site to several search engines at once. There are usually limitations on the number of search engines to which they'll submit for free. However, even the free services can save you a lot of pointing, clicking, and typing. Probably the best-known all-in-one submission site is Submit It! (http://www.submit-it.com). Submit It! lets you to add your URL to up to 400 search engines (for a fee); you can submit to up to 10 search engines by signing up for a free trial. Many such services are available.

▶ **E-mail.** You probably have many e-mail contacts, if you've been online for any length of time; make sure you send an e-mail announcing your new site to everyone you know who you think might be interested in your site. *Don't* send e-mail to complete strangers whose e-mail addresses you managed to get hold of; that's called "spamming" and it won't win you, or your Web site, any friends. Keep the word out there by adding your site's address to your e-mail and newsgroup signatures (as described in Chapter 10 and Chapter 13).

▶ **Arrange for mutual links.** Remember those Web sites you surfed when you first started planning your site? Now that your site is up and running, visit those sites again and post messages to their creators suggesting that they link to your site. You can return the favor with a link of your own. Building links with similar sites is a great way to get the attention of people who might be interested in your work.

▶ **Ring around the Web.** Web Rings are exactly what their name implies: collections of independent sites but from one to another in a big virtual circle. Each site in a ring has navigation buttons (usually at the bottom of the home page) that link to the next site in the ring or to the previous site. You can also view a list of the next five pages in a ring or go to a page at random. Anyone can set up a Web ring, find a Web ring on a specific topic, or apply to join a Web ring. Unlike Hometown, each Web ring has its own rules about who can join, and an administrator who approves or denies applications to the ring (for more information, visit `http://www.webring.org`).

▶ **Use offline publicity.** Just because your Web site is online doesn't mean you can't advertise it offline. Tell friends and acquaintances about it. Include it in letters. If it's a business site, include it in all your print advertising. Add it to your letterhead and business cards. Put it on your fax cover sheets. The more people who know about it, the more likely it is to garner visitors.

A Quick Look Back

For complex Web sites — organized collections of pages — you'll need to use some new software. In return, with today's tools, you can let your imagination take you where you want.

▶ **HTML editors.** An HTML editor like Netscape Composer, which is free when you install Netscape Communicator (Chapter 6), lets you focus on what you have to say, while it takes care of the HTML — the underlying language of the Web. *Simple text editors* (like Windows Notepad) and fancier *HTML text editors* (like Notetab Light) give you close control of everything on your page, if you're the do-it-yourself type and know

HTML. *Commercial HTML editors* like Dreamweaver offer real firepower. They make it relatively easy to create a large, structured set of pages (a site, in other words) and to graphically create complex effects involving layers, style sheets, and even JavaScript.

▶ **Resources.** AOL and the Web provide dozens of places to learn HTML, get tools, find help. Start at keyword: Building Home Pages.

▶ **Learning HTML and all that.** HTML itself can be learned on the Web or in an online AOL class. A good book or Web reference site, along with a good HTML editor, can help you build professional-looking sites to elicit the Ooh's and Ah's of others at Hometown AOL.

That wraps up Part IV, devoted to one of the Internet's favorite activities: making pages and building sites. Part V looks at the AOL tools and connections that provide for the complete (and fast) online experience.

P A R T

V

EXTENDING YOUR
INTERNET CONNECTION

Chapter 16
FTP, Telnet, and Such

IN THIS CHAPTER

Why you need to know about the file transfer protocol (FTP) and Telnet

Four main ways of transferring files using FTP on AOL

Searching for files

Using Telnet on AOL

FTP and Telnet once had a prominent place in books about the Internet, but the World Wide Web now takes center stage. It's not hard to see why. The Web provides instant gratification. You see and experience Web pages instantaneously, while FTP files and Telnet resources sit on distant computers, in a mostly non-graphical format. Or, you download resources and then open *another* program to use them.

So, why do you need to know about these dusty things? Because they're not so arcane as you might think. In fact, there's a lot on the Internet you can't do *without* them.

First off, FTP offers more than 100 million files to download, according to Lycos (see "Searching FTP Made Easy" later in this

chapter). FTP also gives you the most convenient way to upload files, including Web pages, in order to make Web sites
viewable by anyone. It also provides the cleanest way to
manage a complex Web site.

FTP stands for the Internet's *file transfer protocol*. FTP lets you
download files for your own use from across the Internet —
games, software, documents of every type. FTP also lets you *upload* files — make them available for others (as when you build
a Web site). Before the advent of the Web, FTP was the dominant
way of finding files and moving them from one place to another
on the Internet, and it remains very popular when you download files from software vendors and big shareware archives.

Telnet, one of the oldest Internet protocols, enabled researchers
in the 1970s to use large specialized programs on each others'
computers. Today, Telnet can still give you access to the processing power of a far-away computer in order to read e-mail, play
games, use libraries, and take part in interactive chat and games.
Some text-based games — from the interactive to the educational — still work only on Telnet. Some company and university
e-mail systems, too, run only on Telnet.

Definition

Downloading means copying
files from a centrally available location to your own
computer; *uploading* means
copying them from your
computer to a central place,
where they can be used
by others.

Four Ways to Use FTP on AOL

Through AOL you have a choice of four ways to connect to FTP:

▶ Through the AOL Web browser (for browsing and
   downloading)

▶ At AOL's Keyword: **My FTP Space** (for uploading files
   to managing them on AOL's computers — but only
   using *your* FTP space on AOL)

▶ Using AOL's built-in FTP program at Keyword: **FTP**
   (for browsing and downloading *any* FTP sites)

▶ Using a third-party application such as WS_FTP
   (for uploading, managing, and downloading on
   any computer to which you have access)

Cross-Reference

You can, if you wish, use any browser to access FTP, including Netscape Navigator (see Chapter 6) or MSIE.

Note

Downloading files can mean displaying them in the browser; Web browsing involves nonstop downloading!

Note

Using an FTP site opens a connection that is usually limited in duration. Most sites place a limit on the number of visitors who can be admitted at the same time. That's why you may not be able to access an FTP site. Try again later.

Using FTP Through the AOL Browser

Using FTP is like using your own hard drive. Both your hard drive and an FTP *server* (Internet computer) consist of folders containing either files or *more* folders.

Downloading a file from an FTP site while using a browser couldn't be easier — just click the file to download it. Notice in the next figure that both folders and files are old-fashioned, underlined, clickable links.

The AOL browser provides the simplest way to access an FTP site. To use it, type an FTP address such as **ftp://ftp.aol.com** into the AOL Address Box, and press Enter. For browsing and downloading, it's all you need.

Figure 16-1 shows the University of Kansas FTP site, which contains good articles on the early history of the Internet. Figure 16-1 shows three different folders at this site. Notice the different types of files. *HTML files*, for example, are Web pages, viewable as such if you click them. The files marked with a little question mark are just text files; click to read them on-screen.

To download a file: just click and it will display in your browser. To download a program file (such as the AOL program's **setup.exe**, at ftp://ftp.aol.com), click the file to download it to your computer.

The AOL browser is perfectly adequate for using public FTP sites and downloading files from them. The browser does have two important limitations, however.

▶ It cannot be used to upload files.
▶ It cannot be used with FTP sites that are password-protected, where you need to enter a log-in and username.

Text file

Folder Go up to ftp/pub/history (shown here) Web page

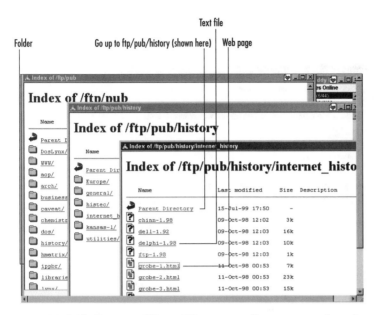

Figure 16-1. The University of Kansas FTP site, an excellent resource on the early Internet. (The text-based Web browser, lynx, was invented at this university.)

Using AOL's My FTP Space

My FTP Space has been around since 1995, when it was introduced to support AOL's new policy of giving every member two megabytes of space on AOL's computers. Keyword: **My FTP Space** takes you to your own space on AOL's computers for storing and sharing files, and making them available for anyone.

Why use My FTP Space? A Web page is no good until others can get to it, and they can't get to it until you've uploaded the page to an Internet-connected computer. On AOL, My FTP Space refers to the huge complex of Internet-connected computers known as members.aol.com. Here, you make your Web pages (and other files) available for others to use.

Figure 16-2 shows what you see at Keyword: **My FTP Space**. You might see some intermediary Hometown windows before you get there, so be prepared to wait a few moments.

16

FTP, Telnet, and Such

Note

With easy Web tools such as 1-2-3 Publish and Hometown Press, more and more of the uploading and downloading now takes place behind the scenes. The fancier your site, however, and the more control you want, the more you'll want direct access to My FTP Space in order to manage your growing family of files.

Tip

Register any page at Hometown and your screen name gets 4MB of space instead of just 2MB; register all your pages there and your screen name gets a total of 12MB. Chapters 14 and 15 have all the details.

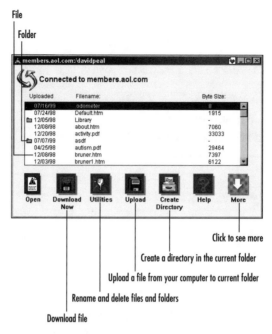

File

Folder

Click to see more

Create a directory in the current folder

Upload a file from your computer to current folder

Rename and delete files and folders

Download file

Figure 16-2. Welcome to My FTP Space; yours will show different files and folders.

My FTP Space goes beyond Web publishing. You can use My FTP Space to make files available to friends or coworkers. For instance, you can upload word-processed documents or PDF reports — anything that fits within the 2MB limit.

Uploading a File to My FTP Space

To upload a file to My FTP Space, follow these steps. If you have many pages to upload, you'll have to upload them one at a time using the following steps, because you can't upload several at a time:

1. Create your Web page and save it to your hard drive; remember this location. Likewise, for other files to upload, make a note of their locations.

2. Go to Keyword: **My FTP Space**. If you get an intermediary window, be patient. A list of files and folders in My FTP Space eventually appears. Figure 16-2 shows a bit of FTP space; yours will differ depending on the files you upload. This is *your* area, accessible only to your screen name.

3. Click Upload. The Remote Filename box appears. Provide the name ("remote file name") that you want for the file on My FTP Space. Yes, before selecting a file to upload you provide the name by which you want the file to be known after it's uploaded. Usually, you'll want to use the same name as the file on your hard drive. Often, however, your own naming scheme will require some tweaking to make your files recognizable by others. Make sure the Binary choice is selected; this setting helps FTP recognize *all* file types, including simple text. Click Continue.

4. Click Select File. In the file selection dialog box, find your file on your hard drive, and double-click (Figure 16-3). Click Send. A little box that looks like a thermometer tracks the progress of your file transfer. Next time you visit My FTP Space, your file will be there.

Caution

You can trust files downloaded directly from AOL's software libraries to be virus-free, but there's no guarantee regarding FTP files. Keep safe. Do a virus check and stay informed at Keyword: **Virus**.

Name of file once uploaded   File to upload

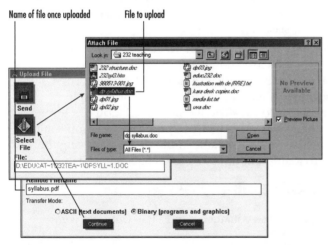

Figure 16-3. Select a file from your hard drive and send it. This file has a name meaningful to me, but the file name on FTP should be more generally meaningful. For simplicity's sake, many people use an identical name on both their computer and in their FTP space.

Managing My FTP Space

Any computer storage space (such as your hard drive or your FTP space) can quickly get overgrown with many files having unrecognizable names and forgotten purposes. When you need a specific file for a specific purpose, it's not clear where to find it.

Tip

If you do change file names, delete files, and move things around, make sure to change the links in your Web pages that refer to those files!

▶ **To delete a file or folder.** Highlight the file, click Utilities, and click Delete. You can only remove one file at a time. Note that you cannot delete a folder until all of its files have been removed; when files are removed, highlight the folder and delete it as you would delete a file.

▶ **To create a new directory.** Click the Create Directory button, as seen previously in Figure 16-2, and type in the directory name in the Remote Directory Name box. Click Continue to create another, or close the box (clicking the X in the upper-right corner) when you're done. Using forward slashes (/), you can create a subdirectory, such as /pub/work.

▶ **To change a file or folder name.** Select the file or folder, click Utilities, and click Rename. In the New Name box, type in the *full name* of the new file (all the folders and subfolders, separated by forward slashes).

▶ **To move a file or folder.** To do this, you change the name, as just shown. For example, to move a file, you first select it. Click Utilities and Rename. Then provide a different path to the file. For example: /davidpeal/README could be moved "down" a level by changing it to /davidpeal/pub/README. You can also change the file name in the process, moving the file to a different directory and changing its name.

Using AOL's Built-in FTP Program

My FTP Space gives you access to FTP — but only *your* FTP space on AOL.

To access other FTP sites, especially those that are password-protected, you'll need to use either Keyword: **FTP** (see Figure 16-4) or a third-party program such as WS_FTP, described later in this chapter.

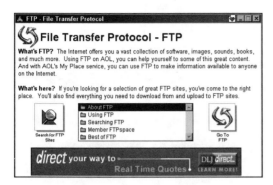

Figure 16-4. At Keyword: *FTP,* AOL gives you essential FTP features, including the ability to browse and download.

Downloading a File at Keyword: FTP

To download a file, you must first identify the site's exact address (for example, `ftp.aol.com`). It's best to know the whole directory path, with full file name and extension. Unlike the Web, on FTP (at least currently) you can only search for file names — not file content. Figure 16-5 shows one of AOL's Favorite Sites (MIT's `rtfm.mit.edu/pub`), with several open folders, any one of which can be added to your Favorite Places folder. (This great resource contains authoritative FAQ documents for hundreds of newsgroups, as you can read about in Chapter 13.)

Here's how to download a file using FTP on AOL:

1. At Keyword: **FTP**, click Go To FTP.
2. At the Anonymous FTP window, click Other Site.
3. In the Other Site box, type in the address. For Anonymous FTP Sites, leave the box unchecked. Click Connect.

   The site comes up. If it doesn't, it's busy — try again later.

Cross-Reference

See "How to Find FTP Files" later in this chapter for more information about finding complete file information.

Tip

When you find FTP sites with plenty of low-hanging fruit, such as rtfm.mit.edu, "Favorite Place" it by clicking the heart in the upper-right corner of the window. The FTP site, or the specific folder or subsubfolder, will be available in your Favorite Places folder (Favorites menu).

If you're used to tooling around the Web, you'll have to throttle back to enjoy FTP. Many sites have log-ins and passwords. The good news is that logging into *anonymous* FTP sites is automatic. Such sites permit *public* access, at least to the top-level /pub folder. Why *anonymous*? Your log-in name is "anonymous," and your username is just your e-mail address (for example, milesdavis@ aol.com). If you need access to a non-anonymous FTP site, you'll need a password and log-in. For this information, just ask the person who told you about the file you are trying to retrieve. Asking such a person is always the best way to get such information.

If you know the directory in which your file can be found, enter it, too. Include the file name, and you can go directly to the file and download it!

Place folder in Favorite Places, for direct access later (Favorites⇨Favorite Places)

Download selected files

Folders   Downloadable files   Folder names

Figure 16-5. From folders to files. Browsing from MIT's rtfm.mit.edu/pub to the FAQs available for the misc.kids newsgroups.

4. With a file displayed and selected, you can either download it (click Download Now) or, if it's a text file, view it online without downloading it (click Open, then View File Now). If you want to download, you'll be prompted to use the directory specified by AOL's Download Manager (see Chapter 17). Note that there isn't a Download Later option when using the Net's FTP sites.

Using Third-Party (Non-AOL) FTP Software

Several third-party FTP programs give you more features than AOL's browser or built-in FTP program. One of the best-known is WS_FTP, a shareware program available from keyword: Publishing Tools (click Shareware).

To use WS_FTP you must set up a session profile in order use My FTP Space on AOL, and thus streamline the maintenance of your Hometown AOL pages. Here's the information I use:

▶ Host name: **members.aol.com**
▶ Host type: **Unix (standard)**

▶ UserID: **Anonymous**

▶ Password: **guest@unknown**

▶ Initial directories:

■ Remote host: */yourscreenname*

■ Local PC: *any directory on your hard drive*

▶ Put checks in the Anonymous Login and Save Password boxes

WS_FTP uses a single window for all operations, which makes the program especially easy to learn and use. You see *your* PC's directories on the left side and the FTP directories on the right side, as shown in Figure 16-6.

Note

To use Internet applications such as WS_FTP, you need to find, download, and install them, and then figure out how to use them — all of which is usually pretty straightforward, or at least worth the expenditure of a little time. Chapter 17 has more information about WS_FTP.

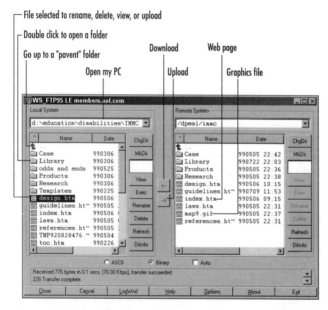

File selected to rename, delete, view, or upload

Double click to open a folder

Go up to a "pavent" folder

Download   Web page

Open my PC   Upload   Graphics file

Figure 16-6. WS_FTP: point-and-click FTP, useful in making a large Web site. Notice the parallel structure of the right and left sides. The left side shows my local files for a Web site I'm building; the right side shows the files in My FTP Space. Such parallel structures make Web sites simpler to maintain.

Here are the basic FTP chores with WS_FTP:

▶ To open a directory on either your hard drive or the far-away FTP space, double-click the folder.

Note

My FTP Space doesn't let you "write" folders — which means you can't create a directory in My FTP Space using WS_FTP.

Tip

If you need to make serious use of FTP, check out the somewhat old Anonymous FTP FAQ created by the FTP guru, Perry Rovers (find it at http://hoohoo.ncsa.uiuc.edu/ftp/faq.html).

▶ To upload, just select a file on the left, open the destination FTP folder on the right, and click the right arrow (between the two panels).

▶ To download, reverse the procedure: Select a file on the right, open the destination folder (on your PC) on the left, and click the left arrow.

▶ To upload or download several files, select them all (by Shift-clicking or Control-clicking) and click the appropriate arrow (right arrow to upload; left arrow to download).

▶ Likewise, you can delete one or more files on your hard drive or in your FTP space.

How to Find FTP Files

You must know what you're looking for before you set out to use Keyword: **FTP**, or get WS_FTP out of the garage, or fire up your browser. Often, *browsing* FTP just doesn't make as much sense as browsing the Web. On FTP you're dealing with file names only, and not with friendly English-language links, as on the Web. You're also dealing with countless files, scattered over countless FTP sites (identifiable only by their addresses), arranged in directory structure, like your dull hard drive — *not* in a more or less intuitive web of links, as on the World Wide Web.

File names have two parts: the part provided by a person, describing the *file contents* (before the period); and the file extension provided by software, indicating the *file type* and the sort of program required to use the program (the letters after the period). See the "Understanding File Types" section earlier for an overview of common file extensions. Here are some examples:

▶ **purchase.htm** — a Web page, which can be used in a browser or HTML editor

▶ **remove.txt** — a text file, while can be used in a word processor or text editor

▶ **tip.gif** — an image file, which can be used on a Web page or in any graphics program

> ▶ **census.pdf** — an Adobe Portable Document Format file, requiring the Adobe plug-in; can be used only in the appropriate Adobe products, such as the Acrobat reader

Downloading FTP files requires that you know the following:

- ▶ The FTP site where the file can be found
- ▶ The file's exact location (folder) on the FTP site
- ▶ The file's name and file type (extension)

How do you find out all this stuff? Read on!

Searching FTP Made Easy

The older method for searching for files required low expectation for success and high tolerance for frustration. You had to use e-mail, Telnet, and even the Web to get in touch with something called Archie, a distributed database of files available by anonymous FTP. However reached, Archie was usually painfully slow over a modem, if available at all. Archie often made no sense unless you knew exactly what you wanted in the first place.

This book focuses on FTP Search, available through the Web, a search solution created by a Norwegian company called Fast Search and Transfer, which is creating other tools for finding and transferring images, videos, and other types of complex data. You can access their FTP search engine at Lycos (`http://ftpsearch.lycos.com/`). Or, follow the link from the Lycos opening page at `http://www.lycos.com`. FTP Search is shown in Figure 16-7.

Remember the two parts of a file name — file contents and file type? FTP Search also lets you use a keyword as well as a file name. A keyword can be one or more words describing what you're looking for, such as "mamas and papas." File names needn't specify the exact format. *Sound*, for example, refers to *any* sound file, such as AU, MIDI, WAV, and MP3. Figure 16-7 shows a search for sound files, and Figure 16-8 shows the results.

Tip

Another new FTP search tool, France Télécom's FtpFind (http://www.ftpfind.com), lets you search by file format (sound, video, pictures) and operating system (Windows, Mac, and so on). If you don't find that MP3 file on FTP Search, try here!

16

FTP, Telnet, and Such

Tip

To play MP3 files, you'll need to find and install an MP3 player (see Chapter 17). Many MP3 files you'll find on FTP sites are pirated versions; the ones shown in Figure 16-8 were no longer available when I checked them out! Take the "100 million" files-on-FTP figure with a grain of salt.

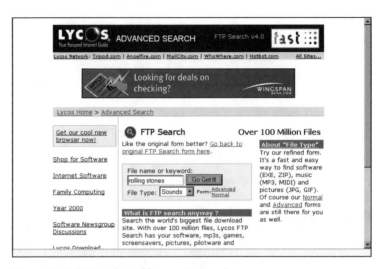

Figure 16-7. FTP Search simplifies your FTP searches.

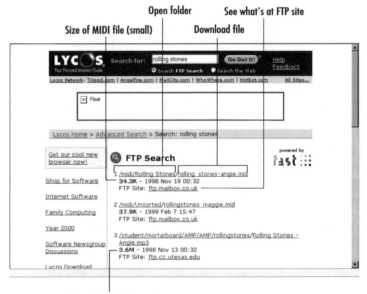

Figure 16-8. Results of the FTP search shown in Figure 16-7. Link from here to FTP sites, and individual folders and files.

Each entry in Figure 16-8 has several clickable pieces of information: the FTP site name; the folder containing the files you are seeking; and the files themselves. Click a directory to open it and see the files inside. You'll recognize individual files by their sizes and file extensions.

To download and play a file, just click it!

If you have experience with Archie, click the Normal and Advanced buttons. A benefit of this Web-based form for accessing Archie is the use of drop-down menus and extensive help for each field. The form can be used to search for files from certain domains (such as EDU) and certain dates (for example, the last year), as well as *part* of a file name (called a *substring*), without worrying about uppercase and lowercase. The more information you have about the file you are seeking, the better your chances of retrieving it.

Long Live Telnet

Telnet, like FTP, gives you direct access to far-away computers. While FTP lets you see and download files, Telnet lets you run the programs or use the services available at those remote computers. A Telnet screen might give you some idea of the Telnet experience. It's a world of characters and keyboards. Leave your mouse at home.

A few things to note about Telnet:

▶ Connecting does not take place instantaneously. For that matter, nothing takes place instantaneously on Telnet, but what's the rush?

▶ Imagine a cable connecting the keyboard on your desk to an Internet computer hundreds or thousands of miles away. That's what Telnet is about. Sometimes at the beginning of a session, you'll get a message asking what type of keyboard you're using. (Answering *VT100* or *VT 102* is OK for most of the remote systems you will access.) Sometimes, you'll have to say which keys you'd like to use to do certain things (such as using the Backspace key to delete a character).

From the Normal and Advanced forms at FTP Search on Lycos, there's a link permitting you to search one million file *descriptions* — not just file names. It's still not a lot better than Archie. My standard search for "aardvark" turned up 64 hits — many referring to obscure programs and small companies with *aardvark* in their names. Because you're still dealing with Archie, behind the scenes, expect delays and connections of short duration.

Illustrations in the next pages show NetTerm, a good-looking, easy-to-use Telnet program profiled in Chapter 17. A perfectly adequate Telnet program called HyperTerminal is included with Microsoft Internet Explorer and AOL's browser.

16

FTP, Telnet, and Such

Tip

Want a different Telnet program to come up when you use the AOL browser? Follow the procedures in the sidebar earlier in this chapter for "Telling Windows How to Handle File Types." Before you begin, make sure you've downloaded and installed the Telnet program you want to use as your new default. In Step 2, the Registered file type is URL: Telnet Protocol. In Step 4, find and double-click the Telnet program that you want to launch automatically when you enter a Telnet URL. Complete the procedure, and test it out.

▶ You're in a text-only world. Your graphical display has gone away, and the Telnet computer displays screenfuls of characters in response to what you do at the keyboard. Sometimes (as with certain games and opening screens) characters are arranged into neat graphical displays (ASCII art), but it's still a fairly airless environment.

▶ You might need a log-in name, but most resources are public, hence the log-in is either provided or not required.

▶ Just like FTP, the number of connections to Telnet sites can be limited, so you might not get on right away. Once you get on, things might be slow. The letters you type might show up on the terminal slowly; you might type too fast and not see the results of your typing or your corrections at all.

Using Telnet

A Telnet address is like any Internet address, except that it begins with **telnet:**. On the AOL browser, you visit a Telnet site by simply typing **telnet:** and its address into the AOL Address Box.

On AOL, you can do your Telnetting through your browser. HyperTerminal, a small program included with Windows 95/98. It's a separate application, with its own menus and commands. The commands you'll probably need are Disconnect (from the Call menu), Font (from the View menu, where you choose a large font size), and Capture Text (from the Transfer menu, where you can keep a text record of what you were doing).

If you've got serious Telnetting to do or want some flexibility and color in your life, you'll enjoy the additional features you get with a program such as NetTerm, profiled in Chapter 17. Other Telnet programs are available at keyword: **Download**; just click Shareware and search for one!

Why Use Telnet?

Telnet supports library catalogs, e-mail, and research databases, as well as game and other simulated environments, serious and otherwise. You'll also find some communities, especially in rural areas, where neighbors can remain plugged into Free-nets —

Telnet-connected networks that dispense school, government, business, and library goings-on while also connecting people to the wider world of the Web. The Web may be encroaching on all these domains, but Telnet remains vibrant in rural areas, small towns, and parts of the world without the latest Pentiums and browsers. In addition, many universities make their campus systems available primarily via Telnet.

As a text-based form of communication, perfectly acceptable over the slowest modems, Telnet is still used in much of the world, especially in libraries. The best way to find Telnet-connected libraries is HYTELNET. Hytelnet is a searchable directory of the many libraries around the world with public Telnet-accessible directories. Although not maintained since 1997, Hytelnet can still be accessed at `http://www.lights.com/hytelnet/`, and many links still work fine.

To support universal access to their resources, many U.S. government libraries make their catalogs available by Telnet, or by Telnet and the Web. The Library of Congress, National Institutes of Health, Lawrence Livermore National Library, the Smithsonian Libraries, and many other libraries all can be reached by Telnet. The Smithsonian, for example, gives access to a searchable record of a 300,000-piece art inventory compiled by the National Museum of American Art. See Figure 16-9.

Hytelnet (http://www. lights.com/hytelnet/) remains the closest thing to a directory of Telnet resources.

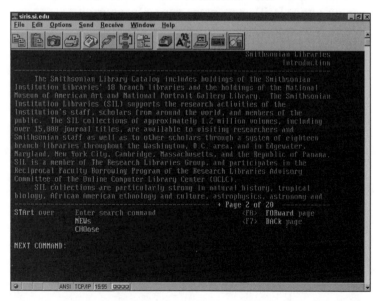

Figure 16-9. Using Telnet to search the Smithsonian's annotated catalog of art holdings

16

FTP, Telnet, and Such

Many MUDs encourage a level of violence, enacted in words, that parents won't be comfortable with.

A virtual environment can take some getting used to. You need to use special commands. You're in a space with many "rooms," and you need to figure out how to go from room to room. The words you type may not appear right away. When you've found a MUD to explore, join as Guest until you have the desire and skills to get a user name and take part. Many MUDs have beginner conferences. In Mud Connector's Discuss area (the message boards), you'll find boards called Mud Basics and Newbie Help.

In the United States, hundreds of universities and other institutions make their e-mail accounts and other services available by Telnet. In addition to my AOL account, for example, I use a program called Pine to access work and university e-mail accounts. The Pine program is used around the world to send and access e-mail. It dates back to 1989, just like the Web, when it was developed at the University of Washington. Still, it supports useful features such as named folders for saving all your sent and received messages.

MUDs and Other Diversions

If you're between 15 and 21 in age, or otherwise have a good excuse, try spending some time in the world of MUDs, short for *multiuser dungeons* (or dimensions). These old-fashioned, text-based worlds are constructed from the imagination. The best way to learn about them is the Mud Connector (http://www.mudconnector.com), the place to find reviews, listings, links to MUD Web sites, specialized MUD software, Java MUD software, and a large and clearly organized and annotated directory of MUDs. Most important, Mud Connector is the place to connect to them. Since the previous edition of this book, the number of MUDs has more than doubled.

Many action-oriented and talk-oriented MUDs encourage role-playing. Other MUDs encourage you to be yourself.

Particularly useful are those MUDs that support something in the real world, like TAPPED-IN, an online environment managed by SRI (the Stanford Research Institute) that supports teachers' professional development. TAPPED-IN says it's "patterned after a real-world conference center. Teachers with diverse interests, backgrounds, and skills can share experiences, engage in mentoring and collaborative work, or simply meet their colleagues."

When you visit a MUD, you'll call up your Telnet program (HyperTerminal, or NetTerm, or something else) just as you do with the AOL browser or MSIE browser. To play like a pro requires special MUD software, which shows colors, formats text nicely, and allows for automatically connecting to specific MUDs and keeping track of favorites. The popular ZMUD program comes in many versions and currently costs about $25 after a trial period.

ZMUD is one example of the dozens of Internet applications you can use with AOL. This and other Internet software applications greatly expand what is possible on AOL. Chapter 17 shows where to get additional applications and how to use some of these applications on AOL.

Tip

A Quick Look Back

This chapter covers a lot of ground. To switch metaphors, it also covers many layers of Internet history.

Tools like FTP, Telnet, and also e-mail remain indispensable even if they lack the flash and sex appeal of the World Wide Web; they are the tools on which the Net was built. FTP makes distant computers an extension of your own hard drive, so you can easily upload and download files. The ability to upload and manage files is essential when you build Web pages. On AOL you have, count 'em, four ways to do FTP: through the browser, at keyword: FTP, at keyword: My FTPspace, and using a third-party program like WS_FTP.

Telnet lets you use interactive programs on distant computers, for e-mail, library searches, games and MUDs, and other activities. To make the most of both FTP and Telnet requires third-party programs, a subject to which the next chapter is devoted.

MUD's future is in the browser if not on the Web. Mud Connector offers a Java Telnet client that supports mudding, and software vendor Zuggsoft makes a ZMUD plug-in for registered ZMUD users.

16

FTP, Telnet, and Such

Chapter 17

Internet Software and Where to Find It

This chapter helps you find and use *Internet software* — software that works over the Internet and gives you access to the files and resources of computers *on* the Net. I won't be looking at Internet-*related* software that runs on your own PC, such as graphics packages and HTML editors; a few such packages are discussed in Chapter 15.

Now, with AOL 4.0 and 5.0

- ► You automatically get Winsock; don't give it a second thought.
- ► When you download Internet applications, just make sure to get the software made for your operating sys-

tem (Window 95/98 or Windows 3.1). Of course, if you have a Mac, download only Mac Internet applications. Everything else is handled for you.

Software for the Asking? Hidden Costs and Free Lunches

Freeware means what it says; software with no financial outlay by you. The installation may be complicated and the learning curve steep, and you may want to buy documentation or a fuller-featured version of the software, but the freeware itself won't cost a nickel. Freeware products are often every bit as good as expensive commercial alternatives. For example, FreeAgent, profiled below, is free and very capable software for using newsgroups. The great browsers created by Microsoft (MSIE) and Netscape (Navigator) are good examples of freeware.

Shareware means what it says, too: the *author* (programmer) wants to make it broadly available by giving it away, but often under certain conditions. The most important condition, customarily, is that you can use the software free during a trial period (30 days, for example), but you must pay a nominal charge to use it after that period. Sometimes restricted use is enforced by the software itself; you can't use it after a certain number of days (WebWhacker and NetNanny work this way). Sometimes, continued use works on the honor system; you'll be prompted to register without being forced to do so (mIRC, NetTerm, and many others work this way).

Get It Right the First Time

How do you get the best piece of shareware or freeware for your preferences and needs?

1. Ask yourself what you want the software to *do*, starting with *your* needs. Does AOL already offer that functionality?

Tip

If you like software, pay the often nominal fee to register. In return you'll often get documentation, additional features, and notification of new versions.

Tip

The big download sites offer the most links to shareware and freeware in one place. The sheer number of products at such sites also makes them difficult to maintain. AOL's Keyword: **FileSearch** runs into the same difficulty, and often carries different versions of the same shareware, which can be very useful in maintaining older computers. For the latest version, however, visit the vendor's own Web site. There you'll also get details about specific changes from version to version, and you'll find out how to get documentation and other forms of support. To find the Web site, do a search for the product's name or its maker's name, or both.

Tip

How do you tell one version from another? In addition to the version number, usually included in the product's name (for example, Netscape Navigator 4.61), look for a *build* number (within a version number), which registers changes to the software that are too minor to warrant a new version number. *Beta* software is pre-release software, which may be incomplete or unstable. Support is usually not provided for beta.

Note

Network etiquette prescribes that, when you have a choice, you use a download site close to you. TUCOWS gives you a choice, and big companies like Netscape and Microsoft often give you a choice of the site from which to download.

2. Do you need every feature under the sun, or just the basic functions? At the big download sites described in the next section, you'll find toolkits that do many things at the same time, such as manage both FTP and Telnet, or e-mail and newsgroups, or bundle together Internet utilities of interest to more advanced users, like ping and whois.

3. Get the appropriate version for your operating system. If you have Windows 95/98, get something called *32-bit* software, because it's faster and often has more features. If you're strapped, on the other hand, look for special deals offering older versions of good shareware as freeware. If you're outfitting older machines (as in a school), don't assume the latest software is the best. Often newer software sprouts new features but little improvement in basic functionality. On the other hand, newer versions tend to perform better, have a brighter interface, and have fewer bugs.

4. Look at the various rating systems out there to see what experts and users consider best — ZDNET, Stroud, CNET, and TUCOWS have rating systems, all of which you can read about in the next section. Such systems are subjective but can be a good starting point. Also look (as in ZDNET and on AOL) for *number* of downloads; a high number of downloads can indicate software that users consider better, as communicated through word of mouth.

5. If you'll be downloading many programs, or a few large programs, wait until it's less busy out there — at the end of the day, or at least at the end of your day — so you won't encounter as much traffic or risk getting disconnected owing to very long download times.

Where to Find Internet Software . . . on the Web

It's not hard to understand why FTP is less and less familiar: it's simply not used as much for *directly* distributing shareware and freeware. Today, when you want Internet software, it's much easier to use one of several gigantic Web archives. These archives often use FTP, but in the background.

Here are four such collections of shareware and freeware of all sorts. You'll find the major applications available at all sites. These sites

- ▶ Make it easy to find Internet applications
- ▶ Have reliable performance
- ▶ Rate, review, or otherwise annotate programs

The list does not exhaust the mega-download archives. If you're looking for any of the programs mentioned in "Great Internet Software," start with these sites — and do a Web search (Keyword: **AOL Search**) for the software if you can't find what you need.

- ▶ **Stroud's Consummate Winsock Applications**, now a part of the Internet.com (Mecklar) empire of magazine and Web sites (`http://cws.internet.com/`). Internet.com also runs the popular Jumbo download site (`http://www.jumbo.com`).
- ▶ **TUCOWS**, a gigantic site with a large network of mirrors (alternate sites that contain the same information as the main site) so you can usually find a download site geographically close to you (`http://www.tucows.com`). See Figure 17-1. TUCOWS offers Mac, Linux, PDA, BeOS, and Java software — as well as the Window 98 software you expect. (In case you're wondering, TUCOWS stands for The Ultimate Collection of Winsock Software.)

Tip

From the Web you can download several files at the same time. AOL's Download Manager can do several downloads in a row at the end of a session, but not several at once.

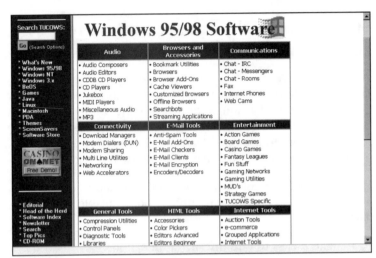

Figure 17-1. TUCOWS has a clear arrangement and offers ratings and reviews of all products. Here's a selection of Internet software available at TUCOWS.

▶ **ZDNET,** featuring reviewed software, with recommendations and related content from Ziff-Davis's large family of online and print magazines (http://www.zdnet.com).

▶ **CNET** has more than one site from which to download software, but I recommend Shareware.com (http://www.shareware.com), which boasts a collection of 250,000 downloadable files).

Downloading and Installing Software

You've done a few minutes of research, found the software, and checked the vendor's site for the most recent version: how do you get and install this stuff?

Downloading and installing have become easier with each passing year. The big commercial products like AOL and Netscape, in fact, combine the two processes, so all you do is start the download and answer some necessary questions during installation and you're ready to go. Usually, you have the option of using the newly installed software right away, so downloading software can lead quickly and more or less gently to its actual use.

Downloading Programs . . .

To download, just go to the Web site with the file and click a download link or button of some sort (reading something like *Download Now*). Respond to the Windows prompt asking where to download the software. As a rule, you'll only have to download one file, so you only have to make this decision once. It's a good idea to download software into a single folder reserved for the purpose and named accordingly (for example, /Download in the America Online directory).

Using Zipped (ZIP) Files

Downloaded software is usually zipped, meaning all the constituent files are reduced in size and packaged into a single file for more efficient transfer over networks. How do you unzip files? You have two choices.

> ▶ **Using a program like PKZIP or WinZip.** If you don't have a decompression program such as one of these, read on. WinZip is discussed in "Ten Awesome Internet Programs." If you do have such a program, double-click the downloaded zipped file (ending in the file extension ZIP) to automatically launch the decompression program. In the WinZip window, double-click a file called Install.exe or Setup.exe (Figure 17-2).

Tip

If you do forget where you've downloaded that new program, look for the file on the Start Menu's Documents menu after download is complete.

Note

Use these compression programs to install software right away (without signing off). Also, use them to make your own compressed files and to work with other formats you'll encounter from time to time, such as UUE.

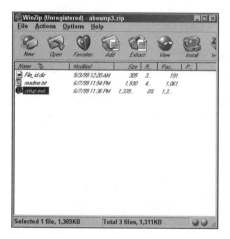

Figure 17-2. Start installation by running the software's Setup program, one of several zipped files here.

Tip

Program Folders, viewable from Start Menu ⇨ Programs, let you launch a program by its name, without regard to where (on which drive) it's installed.

▶ **Using AOL's Download Manager** (MyFiles ⇨ Download Manager). From the main Download Manager, click the Show Files Downloaded button to bring up the window shown in Figure 17-3. Select the file you want to install, and click the Decompress button. Download Manager can be set to decompress (unzip) files upon sign-off and to delete files automatically once they're decompressed. Click Download Preferences and uncheck those preferences if you'll be doing this stuff manually: if you use WinZip to unzip a package of files, the process might be repeated when you sign off.

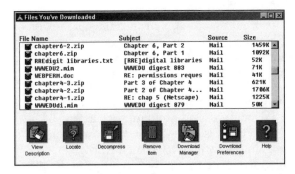

Figure 17-3. AOL's Download Manager: select a recently downloaded file and click the decompress button to unzip it. Notice that the DM lists files downloaded by any means: software libraries, e-mail, newsgroup, FTP.

. . . and Installing Programs

Start installation by running (double-clicking) the Setup or Install program that's included in the zipped file (see Figure 17-2).

Installation differs from program to program. More and more programs use a standard program called InstallShield, which makes the process practically identical no matter which program you're installing. With or without InstallShield, the process is automatic (the software installs itself, asking you for necessary information whenever necessary). You'll be asked the following questions, not always in this order: Do you accept the software's licensing agreement? (Click Yes.) Where do you want to install the program (make sure to choose a drive where similar programs are installed–or at least a drive with enough room)? Into which Program Folder do you want to install the various files (directories will always be automatically created for you)?

After the files have been copied into the specified folders and icons created, you usually get options to read a file explaining what's new in the program or some such thing, to register the program, and to use the program right away. Sometimes you'll have to restart your computer. The registration notice might pop up with each use until you register.

Once unzipped and installed, programs take up much more hard-drive space than you'd expect from the size of the downloaded file.

Ten Awesome Internet Programs

Most of the applications in this section are shareware; to use them after the trial period often requires that you pay a nominal charge. Free Agent and Bobby are notable examples of powerful and widely respected freeware. FreeAgent, the newsreader, assumes you access the Net through an Internet Service Provider under the Bring Your Own Access billing option. Since this book was written, new versions of these programs might have been released.

Keep an eye out for Java versions of the software you need. They're becoming more reliable or easier to use.

Bobby: Making Sure Everyone Can Access Your Web Site

Bobby provides a tool to enforce a new and important set of guidelines on the Web — the W3 Consortium's new Web Accessibility Initiative guidelines. The W3 Consortium, a "vendor-neutral" industry body that makes suggestions to improve the World Wide Web, estimates that 10-20 percent of the population has a visual, cognitive, or other disability that could be accommodated through Web design. For example, images (and all non-text Web elements) should have text labels (ALT tags), for the benefit of people whose browsers don't support the element. Video and audio clips should have text captions for the benefit of people who can't hear or see. The guidelines also recommend that links (the words you click) actually describe what will happen or where you will go when you click them. Such principles stand to benefit all users. The full set of guidelines is available at `http://www.w3.org/WAI/`.

FreeAgent

This great newsreader, from Forté, can be used to browse and read newsgroups. To use the program, you must sign on to AOL through your Internet Service Provider, under AOL's Bring

Cross-Reference

Chapter 13 is devoted to newsgroups, with a focus on AOL's built-in newsgroup reader.

Your Own Access billing plan. To use FreeAgent, you'll need to first connect to your ISP's News server; go to Options ⇨ General Preferences, and in the System tab provide addresses for your ISP's News server. You can also use FreeAgent as an e-mail program, in which case you must provide your ISP's SMTP (mail) server as well. Both addresses should be easy to get; just ask your ISP. Take a look at Free Agent in Figure 17-4.

Contributing to newsgroups and sending e-mail are controlled by numerous buttons you will quickly get the hang of. Just about all menu items have keyboard alternatives, and passing your mouse over buttons reveals their purpose in small text bubbles.

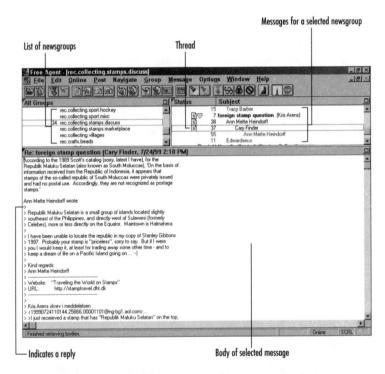

Figure 17-4. FreeAgent, for all its options, simplifies news reading by letting you see newsgroups, newsgroup message headers, and actual messages at the same time. This message shows a thread from the *rec.collecting.stamps.discuss* newsgroup.

Internet Phone

Internet telephone software includes many types of products. Some, like Internet Phone, let you talk from your PC to another person's PC (you'll both need a microphone). Others, such as Net2Phone (http://www.net2phone.com), let you use your PC to initiate an actual phone call or fax to any number around the world. The ideas have been around for years, but only recently have software, network capacity, and the number of participating users made Internet-based telephony a near-reality.

mIRC

This piece of shareware, developed over several years by Khaled Mardam-Bey, of London, has long been favored by Internet Relay Chat (IRC) aficionados. Think of IRC as chat on the Internet (see Figure 17-5).

Tip

If you want to use Internet telephone products, visit ICQ's Internet Telephony Center for both instructions and directories of ICQ members using different Internet telephone products (http://www.icq.com/telephony/telephony.html).

Tip

mIRC presents chat in pure, text form. You'll also find IRC as an integral part of other programs, such as ICQ and MP3Spy.

Caution

With few exceptions, IRC channels are not for children!

Figure 17-5. mIRC enables you to chat on the Internet.

Find It Online

For accessing IRC from AOL, see http://irc.web.aol.com/ to find out AOL's current IRC servers. You'll need this information when setting up your mIRC connection.

Tip

Many parents these days work closely with their kids so that they learn to evaluate materials by themselves, identify situations in which they are uncomfortable, and know some good, fun, safe, challenging places to play on the Web. Using AOL Search for Kids Only (Chapter 7) and a service like Searchopolis (Chapter 8), parents can quickly find hundreds of such places.

IRC is organized into tens of thousands of *channels* (chat rooms), organized in turn into a handful of *networks* with names like Undernet and EFnet. If you want to search a network for a specific channel, the place to start is Liszt (http://www.liszt.com), discussed in Chapter 12.

Unlike AOL chat rooms, IRC channels have no effective limits on how many people can join. Also unlike AOL chat, the person who starts an IRC channel, called the operator, gets certain privileges, to put it mildly — to name other channel operators, to kick out abusive people, to deny certain people access for any reason, to describe the channel for use in channel listings, and so on.

NetNanny

Statisticians have shown that the *proportion* of raunchy Web sites to all Web sites is trivial. Parents and teachers still have good reason for concern, however, since kids are curious, and the open Internet mirrors the world.

The browsers you can use with AOL, such as Netscape Navigator and Microsoft Internet Explorer, lack AOL's Parental Controls (Chapter 3). Web filters such as NetNanny can give parents some peace of mind when kids stray from family-sanctioned sites; exploration should not be discouraged, after all.

NetTerm

Telnet ultimately doesn't do much more than deliver streams of characters to your computer — slowly, since your keyword is talking to a distant computer, which is sending multitudes of characters back to your monitor (hence the delay when you press a key). See Chapter 16 for more information on Telnet and using NetTerm as your default Telnet program.

A good Telnet program needs to present text as attractively as possible — with the ability to alter font, size, color, and background color; it should be snappy, that is, connect quickly and have clear menu commands. It should also help you keep track of as many Telnet addresses as possible, so you can quickly use them. Adding new addresses must be easy, and the Telnet program should be able to double as a dialer, when you're using a BBS or similar phone-based system.

NetTerm does all that. It also lets you print screens and save sessions to text files for later review. If you know what you're doing, you can transfer files using the common modem protocols. NetTerm comes bundled with other programs, such as a simple FTP server.

Spinner and Other MP3 Paraphernalia

What the Web does for budding writers and publishers, MP3 does for musicians without access to the production, marketing, and distribution machinery of the big recording companies. At sites like Audiofind, you can find out about rising artists in your favorite musical genres.

Most Web plug-ins are Web-bound, and as such require that you view them through a big monitor chained to your desk — or a clunky laptop. MP3 is more than a plug-in, however. It's a new way of producing, distributing, and listening to music digitally. In quality, MP3 blows right past other plug-ins, even RealAudio. These high-quality sound files can be played not only by the browser, but also by special software players that can run around the clock on the PC and that let you create your own playlists. The downloaded files can also be used away from the computer, using new portable hardware devices.

MP3 is available in a streaming version called Shoutcast. *Streaming* means that these MP3 files can be heard right after they start to download. With MP3Spy you can choose a genre of music you like, then scan the Web for all the computers serving streaming MP3 in that genre. MP3Spy then plays the sound through AOL's WinAmp MP3 player. See Figure 17-6.

The first thing you'll need is an MP3 player (or a couple of such players), so you can hear the music on your PC. WinAmp and Spinner Plus (both recently acquired by AOL) play back your downloaded files, and give you the flexibility to create and enjoy your own mix-and-match playlists of CD-quality music throughout the day. WinAmp can even play streaming MP3 from Net servers.

Real Networks, the folks who brought you Real Audio, have their own MP3 player and recorder called Real Jukebox player, which lets you selectively record tracks of your audio CD to play back at any time and in any order.

Tip

Because of their quality and portability, MP3 files are worth listening to even when you're not on the Web, not online, and not at your computer! See Chapter 5 for more about MP3 as a browser plug-in.

Note

MP3 quality can be impaired by Net traffic jams — another reason to look forward to fast broadband connections and networks; see Chapter 18 for the full story. MP3 is also subject to other claims on your PC's resources; turn on the scanner (in my case scroll a Web page), and you'll interrupt that Bob Marley tune or Mozart aria.

Find It Online

Confused by the many MP3 technologies? One place to start learning is AOL's Multimedia Web Center (http://www.aol.com/ webcenters/computing/ multimedia.adp). Another is Snap.com's MP3 for Beginners, with its abundant and well-arranged resources (start at http://www.snap. com to find this area).

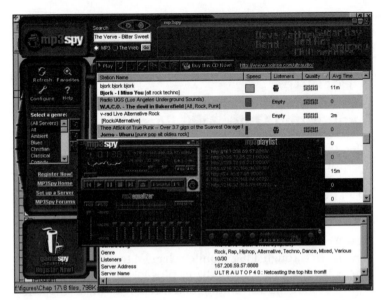

Figure 17-6. The WinAmp MP3 player (foreground window), against the MP3Spy channel selector. If you want, you can display an IRC chat room devoted to the genre of music to which you are currently listening (one of several options for that little window at the bottom of the screen).

Then, with a player or two installed, you'll want to get some MP3 files. Where? Here are three of about a million places to start:

▶ Lycos MP3 Search (http://mp3.lycos.com)

▶ MP3.COM

▶ CNET's MP3 Topic Center

MP3 files are in the multi-megabyte range, so be prepared to wait and to suffer a bit of sluggishness on your PC. In addition to the giant Web sites, you might want to look into one of the special search tools, like Abe's MP3 Finder (from a small Swedish company). Such shareware lets you do specialized searches when you're online. Abe's is notable for its fast searches for MP3 songs and its built-in FTP program, which (in theory) you use to download the songs you found. It's a good idea, but using an early version of the FTP client I found the program didn't reliably connect to and download from FTP sites with MP3 selections. Keep an eye on this program, because it gives you more control of your play lists than the programs that make selections for you.

You may want an MP3 portable player to take with you jogging and grocery shopping. Products like the Diamond Multimedia Rio let you transfer your downloaded MP3 files and play them anywhere. Other vendors with MP3 players include Samsung and Creative Labs. With such players you can listen to music when the radio signals are weak. Or, listen to CD-quality music put together from different online sources and CDs, in any order.

WebWhacker

A well-established program, WebWhacker, provides another solution for parents and teachers concerned about what kids can find on the Web. The program allows you to download a page or entire site (including all the image files) in order to view the page(s) offline. Since links to other pages are unavailable, kids can safely use Web sites with a clear educational purpose; they won't be able to wander away. It's the perfect program for classroom use and business presentations.

If you know the URL of a site you want to use offline, select URL ⇨ Add to bring up the Subscription wizard, which asks you how many levels of the site you want to store. If you stumble across a Web page or site you want to store you can also open WebWhacker and click Grab.

WinZip 7

Okay, this isn't exactly an Internet program, but you can't work with the compressed files you get from e-mail or download from software archives without it. Such files end in the file extension ZIP. Double clicking such files brings up WinZip, displaying the individual compressed files. Refer back to Figure 17-2 for an example.

To use any file, just double-click it. Any opened *archive* (WinZip's name for a zipped file) can be extracted — unzipped — and, if you want, moved to any directory.

To make your own archive file (ZIP file), click the New button (Figure 17-2). Give your ZIP file a name and location (folder), then starting adding files to it; the files you add can be from any folder — but make sure to keep track of the location of the ZIP you're creating.

Any business person who must give Web presentations will appreciate WebWhacker's ability to present sites in their entirety without a live link to the Internet.

With AOL 5.0, selecting more than one file to send by e-mail automatically creates a ZIP file.

Cross-Reference

For more information about FTP and about using WS_FTP, see Chapter 16, "Using Other FTP Software."

Note

The new Keyword: My FTP Space replaces the old keyword: MyPlace, which is not to be confused with My Places, the customized links to AOL destinations now available on the AOL 5.0 Welcome screen.

In pulling together all the files you want to zip up, WinZip reduces the size of each file; use this technique to create a zipped file with one (huge) file inside. I zipped a 1.4MB TIF graphics file for this book, with some other files, and the TIF file was reduced to 82K, a reduction of 94 percent! Unpacked, such files become outsized giants again, but you won't need all day to upload and download the files, nor will you waste network resources, nor will you waste the other person's time downloading.

WS_FTP: Don't Maintain Your Web Site Without It

Creating complex Web sites requires some familiarity with a program like WS_FTP, because you'll need to do some heavy-duty uploading and re-uploading of all those HTML files.

Chapter 16 introduced some of the ways you can access FTP: via the AOL browser, directly at Keyword: **FTP** (for download-ing), and at Keyword: **My FTP Space** (for uploading to and downloading from My FTP Space). The beauty of a program like WS_FTP is that it lets you upload to and download from *any* FTP site. The simple design gives you parallel views of your hard drive and the FTP server's directory structure, or at least the parts you have access to, as you can see in Figure 17-7. Like the traditional FTP programs you can also upload and download many files at once, a great time-saver.

Figure 17-7. WS_FTP, a powerful but simple FTP client

The final chapter of this book will look ahead to the new network tools and resources enabled by new forms of Internet connection such as broadband and wireless. Everything possible now — and covered to this point in the book — will be possible with broadband, but will happen much faster, and you'll notice the difference if you do a lot of uploading and downloading.

A Quick Look Back

This chapter introduces some of the useful and fun Internet software you can use with AOL to expand and enrich your Internet experience. The sample is very small; hundreds of program are available at sites like those profiled in "Where to Find Internet Software . . . on the Web." Here are the high points:

- ▶ The differences between freeware and shareware; one thing to note–there is usually no difference in quality
- ▶ Where to find Internet software on AOL (Keyword: FileSearch) and on the Web (TUCOWS, Stroud, ZDNET, CNET)
- ▶ How to download, decompress and install Internet software (it's getting more and more automatic)
- ▶ Ten Internet programs worth looking into

Chapter 18

What's Next on the Internet: Broadband and Beyond

A big-city Internet Service Provider on the eastern seaboard advertises its services on TV with a highly realistic video clip of a sporting event, while the audio track repeatedly plays the sound of a modem whooshing and gurgling as it connects to the Internet. The message: our modem-based Internet connection delivers cool multimedia.

What's wrong with this picture? First of all, there's something wrong with the *sound*: does anyone really actually enjoy listening to a modem's caterwauling? In Chapter 3, you can find out how to turn off that annoying sound. In this chapter you'll see how a new type of very fast, or *broadband*, Internet connection does away with the slow and noisy modem; with broadband, the Internet is always on.

Another thing about that TV ad: how realistic is the high-quality video it portrays? What about all those multimedia-choked pages that can take a couple of minutes to download? Pages with the most powerful effects — using Shockwave and Java — often take the longest to retrieve (see Figure 18-1). Take DisneyBlast, which delivers its games and stories in the form of Shockwave (for more about Shockwave, see Chapter 5). These games take so long to download that kids are given smaller Shockwave games to fiddle with while the main show is crawling through the network pipes — the current Net's version of movie previews? Even simple tasks like opening up a full mailbox can take too much time over a modem-based connection.

Definition

Bandwidth refers to the capacity of a digital network to carry a certain amount of data (measured in bits) in a certain amount of time (usually one second). Narrowband networks (such as telephone lines) can carry data at a maximum of about 56Kbps (56,000 bits per second). Broadband networks blow the lid off this limit. Coaxial networks (the kind used by the cable TV companies) can send up to 160MB (160 million bits) per second, and fiber (the stuff used in long-distance network and phone trunk lines) is expected to carry up to 100GB (100 billion bits) per second.

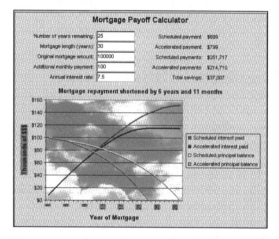

Figure 18-1. Life's too short to wait for indispensable information. You could pay off your mortgage while this Java calculator downloads.

Enter broadband — a set of technologies designed to dramatically increase *bandwidth,* thanks to data compression and technologies for delivering more data, faster over cable and even the phone companies' old-fashioned copper. This chapter focuses on two emerging, popular broadband choices, coming to your community soon if they're not already there: cable and ADSL (short for *asymmetric digital subscriber line*). Cable uses existing cable wiring, while ADSL squeezes every bit of capacity out of existing copper telephone lines. This chapter also looks into other options such as ISDN, satellite, wireless, and TV. AOL is actively exploring all these options for improving your future Internet connection.

AOL 5.0 can detect a live Internet connection (such as an ADSL or cable connection) and prompt you to sign on to AOL. It can also make AOL your primary Internet application when you read e-mail or browse the Web. Click a link offline and you'll go immediately to AOL's browser or e-mail program, online.

As this book was being completed, AOL started testing a new version of the AOL software, AOL Plus, customized to support ADSL connections. For more information, go to Keyword: **DSL**.

Sucking Jello Through a Straw

"Downloading Web pages with narrowband technology has been likened to sucking jello through a straw," say the authors of a *McKinsey Quarterly* article, "The Last Mile to the Internet." "Broadband technologies, on the other hand, promise to deliver crisp text, video and sound as quickly as if the user were watching television" (from the ADSL Forum's Web site, `www.adsl.com/adsl_forum.html`).

With broadband solutions like cable and ADSL, your connection to the Internet is always on. No more noisy dial-up modems or busy signals or conflicts with people who need to use the phone or fax. Just open AOL and sign on whenever you want!

The delays associated with the Web (sometimes called the World Wide Wait — or World Wide Cobweb) have made broadband a necessity for business and home users alike. Broadband removes limitations on doing things like downloading files, downloading e-mail messages with big files attached, viewing multimedia Web pages, and uploading your Web pages. Faster connections will not only speed up everyday tasks but will also make possible new network applications including video on demand, CD-quality audio broadcasting, authentic distance-learning, interactive shopping, telemedicine and telesurgery, and telecommuting with impressive tools, such as full access to fast workplace networks.

Making Data Networks Sing

In the broadband world, you'll hear references to data networks and voice networks. What's the difference and why does it matter? Put simply, a voice network supports telephone calls and some data traffic. The Internet, by contrast, provides the channel for a river of bits and bytes of data (numbers and letters, reduced to 0s and 1s) generated by the millions of people transferring files, browsing the Web, sending e-mail, and in general doing stuff on the Net.

When you make a phone call, you're attempting to create a *dedicated circuit* between you and another person. When your call connects, a circuit opens and stays open until one of you hangs up. Why *dedicated*? Because for voice to be comprehensible over a network it must be transmitted quickly, accurately, and in a continuous stream. You appreciate the phenomenon when its reverse is evident — using a cell phone and getting a less-than-dedicated circuit with a friend.

The sort of data you get on the Internet is different from voice. Ordinarily, it's enough for all the data to arrive at the other end and to be usable by the other person; in most cases the recipient doesn't have to use it right away. E-mail and newsgroup messages, for example, don't have to be received at once, and a reply often isn't even necessary. Data can even be dropped or lost along the way; it will be retransmitted. Data does not even need to be transmitted continuously in order to be comprehensible at the other end.

While phone networks rely on dedicated circuits, data networks like the Internet usually rely on something called *packet switching*. Before being sent over the Internet, your messages and search queries are divided into small packets of data. Packets from the same message can travel by different paths. Each is addressed so it knows where to go and is sequenced so it can be correctly put together at the other end. Likewise, the Web pages that you surf and the e-mail messages you receive come in little pieces but reassembled for your use. What distinguishes the Internet from other networks is reliance on a specific packet-switching technology called TCP/IP, which makes it possible for widely diverse computers and operating systems to share information over the same network. Invented in 1982 by Vint Cerf, TCP/IP has enabled the Net's spectacular growth.

Definition

TCP/IP (the Internet's Transmission Control Protocol/Internet Protocol) manages the segmenting of data into packets and the routing of packets across a wide variety of computer networks based on different operating systems and every kind of computer hardware. It makes the Internet possible.

18

What's Next on the Internet

What Can You Do with Broadband?

Broadband refers to the many new ways of connecting to AOL and from there to the Internet. The two most important, for now, are cable and ADSL. The two differ in how they work and in their costs, benefits, and availability, all of which will be discussed a little later. For now it's enough to recognize that they bring data to you 20-25 times faster than your standard 56K modem. Both ADSL and cable send data (when you upload a file or send an e-mail message) at a pokier speed. Hence the *asymmetric* in ADSL's name — it's faster *downstream* (from the Net to you) than *upstream* (from you to the Net). So, while the downstream multimedia quality of cable and ADSL are 20 times faster than your modem, the upstream quality is about the same. Unless you're operating your own Web radio station, you probably won't notice the slower upstream rate, however.

Some applications, such as distance learning, are not new, but are getting dramatically better in quality, thanks to broadband. Some will flourish because of competitive pressures. Video on demand and home-shopping services, for example, are favorites of the cable industry, so the telephone companies pioneering ADSL will emphasize their use. Keep your eye on *new* network uses, such as teleconferencing so realistic you'll forget the *tele* part. Conferencing will make possible collaborative projects between schools, and effective teamwork in business among workers at different locations and at home. Maybe those rare family reunions can, in the future, be supplemented by more frequent virtual reunions?

Video on Demand—and Internet TV

Just before the Internet became so popular in the mid-1990s, U.S. newspapers were filled with talk of 500 channels on demand. The "channels" in question referred to cable channels broadcasting TV shows to consumers. This dream fizzled. People seemed to want something more interactive than TV.

Broadband will enable broadcast TV over the Internet — at a level of quality approaching the real thing. A sign of the times: Hugh Downs, the long-time anchor of ABC's 20/20 show, recently resigned in order to take on the same role for a start-up company that's creating Internet TV broadcasts.

With broadband, individuals, businesses, and teachers won't just be consuming other people's programming; they'll be making and broadcasting their own video. The commercial applications of video on demand will allow you to see travel destinations and potential hotels before you leave home or book a room, or watch music videos as well as hear audio clips at your favorite online CD store or music site (see Figure 18-2), or watch TV-quality previews of upcoming movies (instead of the jerky Net trailers you get now).

Figure 18-2. Waiting for broadband: the faster your connection, the better the videos (*(c)Tunes.com*).

Virtual Learning Gets Real

School has become a life-long proposition in the information age, with the need for perpetual skill-tuning and knowledge-building. If you didn't get enough of school the first time around (who does?), distance learning will let you take the courses you need — Java programming or medieval philosophy — at your own pace and without the classroom format.

Current efforts to deliver courses as part of work toward college and advanced degrees suffer in many ways from bandwidth restrictions. PowerPoint demonstrations can take too long to download and provide too few interactive opportunities. Low-resolution streaming video clips can be distracting. Instructors too often rehash their yellowing lectures for the Web, typing miniature lectures, throw in a few links, and don't really go beyond the traditional lecture. Such online lectures do give students access to information at any time, removing the obligation to show up early for that early morning lecture, but they don't capitalize on the ability of the new medium to engage attention, illuminate and support concepts, facilitate student-to-student communication, and support collaborative work.

Whether it's a sixth grade biology class, college-level American history class, or post-graduate business training, distance training can support learning in many ways:

▶ Connect students with experts in their field, providing the tools to do interviews, solicit help with problem-solving, and encourage follow-up questions.

▶ Make it easier for students to take part in class activities.

▶ Give students the tools to brainstorm, do research, compare notes, write joint documents, and create joint presentations, which they may want to maintain after the project is over.

Videoconferencing in Education

Videoconferencing allows students to visit distant places, interview experts, and communicate with other classrooms in order to exchange information about locales and to learn from different cultures.

The idea is not new. For several years schoolrooms have been using a product called CUSeeMe (short for Can You See Me), to create a simple conferencing system. Though not fancy, the CUSeeMe software grabbed the imagination of thousands of classrooms. A directory of classrooms around the world that use CUSeeMe shows what classes are actually doing with the software (www.gsn.org/cu/_cfm/countrylist.cfm). See Figures 18-3 and 18-4.

CUSeeMe currently makes the most sense where it overcomes distances or provides experiences not possible in the current location. Broadband Internet connections should improve broadcast quality and thus also increase the opportunities for classroom-to-classroom communication using CUSeeMe and similar products.

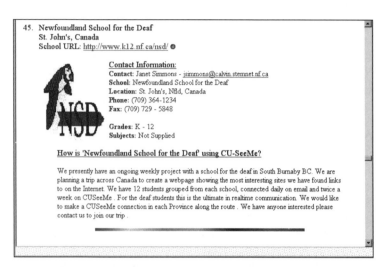

Figure 18-3. Videoconferencing makes a difference: The Newfoundland School for the Deaf

Figure 18-4. Prime Minister Blair and President Clinton's visit to a Maryland high school, broadcast over CUSeeMe. Imagine how it would look with broadband, with schools around the country actively participating.

You've Got a Phone Call!

Do you keep a telephone by your desktop PC? Why not use the computer as your telephone? Chapter 17 includes a section on cool software called Internet Phone, which lets you communicate with others by phone, video, audio, and shared white boards. If it's possible over a modem, imagine what will be possible over connections twenty times as fast.

Interactive Gaming

Role-playing games, science-fiction fantasy games, action games, and the like are standard fare on the Internet. Most interactive games have come to compensate for the restrictions of narrow bandwidth in several ways. MUDs and MOOs, for example, have been predominantly text based. Action takes place more in the imagination than on the screen. (See Chapter 16 on these virtual communities.) By the way, MUD means a multiuser dimension or dungeon — a text-based interactive game; a sort of highly structured chat, with rooms, roles, special commands, and so forth. A MOO is a MUD that's object-oriented (pretty much the same thing as a MUD).

"Bandwidth is the Holy Grail of online gaming," someone wrote on CNET recently; the person with the fastest connection literally wins. The problem with modems is something called *latency*. In an interactive game, for example, the video, audio, and other multimedia segments must be perfectly coordinated; user actions must be nearly instantaneously displayed across the Net, or the game breaks down. Response time must be rapid.

Awesome ADSL

ADSL is short for what sounds like a lot of gibberish: Asymmetric Digital Subscriber Line. Instead of all that, just think *fast*. ADSL began as the phone companies' answer to the limitations of both cable modems and an older, slower, more complex type of broadband called ISDN, both of which are discussed later in this chapter.

Approximately 750 million phone lines reach into the world's homes and businesses, creating a huge market for services that capitalize on copper — the stuff phone lines are made of. The phone companies have found it expensive and technically too tricky to rewire the world with fiber or to provide a wireless phone connection like a satellite. (Don't rule out a fiber future, but for now it's best to make the best of existing wired and wireless connections.)

ADSL is one member of a larger family of DSL technologies, which vary mostly in their data-transmission speed (especially how fast they move data from you to the Internet). DSL technologies have 20-50 times higher modem speeds from existing phone lines. Higher bandwidth doesn't affect copper's purpose: transmitting voice. Why? There's a huge band of frequencies that simply aren't required to transmit the human voice. ADSL uses every bit of those unused frequencies to transmit data.

Note

AOL has made an arrangement with several phone companies, including Bell Atlantic, to offer ADSL service to AOL members at an additional charge. AOL has committed itself to provide a range of broadband solutions.

18

What's Next on the Internet

What Is Required with ADSL?

Here's what you'll need to use ADSL:

- ▶ With ADSL you must purchase and probably get someone to install something called a network interface card. Soon, USB (Universal Serial Bus) plugs will be available, meaning you will be able to simply plug the ADSL phone connection into a newer-model PC's USB jack in the back of the computer. Some new PCs include ADSL modems and related equipment.
- ▶ You'll need the ADSL service, which will incur a setup charge and monthly fee.

ADSL's Advantages

ADSL has some clear advantages over other types of bandwidth.

- ▶ Unlike cable (and more cost effectively than ISDN), ADSL can deliver both data (AOL and the Net) and voice (phone calls) at the same time, over a single line. You can use the phone and the Internet at the same time, and experience the Net at lightning speeds. ISDN, an older technology, also combines voice and data, but it's expensive, complex to install, and does not achieve anything close to ADSL's speed (see "What about ISDN?").

ADSL is being tested on five continents, and more than 300 companies have joined the ADSL Forum to promote the standard. For a Web page with current information on the status of U.S. ADSL trials, see the ADSL Forum's ADSL Trials Worldwide chart (www.adsl.com/trial_matrix.html). The chart includes the upstream and downstream data rates of the new networks. The easiest way to find out about local service is to call your phone company — or any other phone-service providers in your area.

The xDSL FAQ, a readable set of frequently asked questions about the whole subject, grows out of the **comp.dcom.xdsl** newsgroup (the FAQ can be found at homepage.interaccess.com/~jkristof/xdsl-faq.txt). See Figure 18-5; there's a ton of information here.

▶ Also unlike cable, with ADSL, the line by which you connect to the Internet is *your* line, not a shared line, which is especially important if you'll be transmitting sensitive business data.

▶ Like cable, your Internet connection will always be *on*, so you don't have to dial-in and potentially get a busy signal. With ADSL, connecting to AOL becomes about as simple as turning on the light.

AOL Plus

New in AOL 5.0, AOL automatically detects whether you have a fast Internet connection, no matter what kind of connection it is (cable, ADSL, satellite, ISDN, or something else). If you do have a fast connection, AOL has additional software available that allows you to take full advantage of multimedia content such as streaming video, CD-quality music, animation, and much more.

AOL Plus allows members with a high-speed Internet connection to enjoy the newest audio, video, and download features from AOL's top content partners. With AOL Plus you use AOL as you always have. As you navigate, you'll notice a tower in the lower-right corner of your AOL display. This tower refreshes itself as you move through the service. Where there are high-speed features for you to enjoy, links to them appear in the tower. Just click on a link and AOL Plus automatically launches these features.

AOL Plus includes the latest video news and sports highlights, plus in-depth interviews and feature stories. You'll also find the newest movie trailers, top music videos, and AOL Plus Radio — continuous, CD-quality audio in a variety of musical styles. Dynamic, high-speed content is being added daily.

DSL on AOL

Usually, getting ADSL means finding a provider, having your phone wires checked, installing a modem, and signing up for the phone-based service, which is billed monthly. Working with providers around the country, AOL offers the entire package for a very competitive price (see Keyword: **AOL Plus** for the details). With your local DSL provider (often your regional telephone company), AOL coordinates the services, software, and hardware required for your new, fast connection. With AOL Plus DSL, you use your existing screen names and have full access to all your favorite areas.

▶ The service itself, when purchased through the AOL Plus program, adds a set amount to your monthly or hourly AOL fee.

▶ AOL can also provide a DSL modem, installation kit, the AOL Plus software, and simple manual.

▶ The phone company charges an additional activation fee.

▶ A CD containing a special version of the AOL software and DSL drivers (so you can use the DSL modem). The package also includes the phone filters you need to convert your existing phone jacks to DSL (including your PC's modem jack) to the new fast connection.

ADSL Resources on the Internet

Need ADSL information? Here's where to look:

▶ AOL's information center (Keyword: **AOL Plus**). Despite the name, this area focuses on ADSL, not the business-oriented xDSL services. This is the place to learn about AOL's field trials and the AOL Plus enhancements. Most valuable here, the message boards let you ask questions of and share experiences with other AOL members.

▶ The Internet newsgroup, **comp.dcom.xdsl**. Like other comp.dcom.* newsgroups, this one attracts knowledgeable professionals.

▶ ADSL Forum (www.adsl.com). A major consortium of the big players in the ADSL business; the public area contains information about worldwide trials and actual ADSL deployment (click ADSL deployment). Includes an ADSL tutorial (www.adsl.com/adsl_tutorial.html). See Figure 18-6.

▶ The Universal ADSL Working Group (www.uawg.org/). Made up of big companies such as Microsoft — trying to make ADSL more friendly, standardized, and affordable for consumers.

Note

Remember, with ADSL you can use your phone and PC at the same time; if you've got two lines already, you may be able to give up a line when you get ADSL — offsetting the cost of the DSL service.

18

What's Next on the Internet

Find It Online

To find out whether your cable provider offers Internet services, you can check out the availability chart at www.catv.org/helper/frame/state.html.

Note

If you have AOL's Bring Your Own Access billing plan, you can access AOL over your cable company's Internet connection, as explained at Keyword: **Cable**. Currently, AOL itself isn't directly available over cable.

▶ Telco Exchange (www.telcoexchange.com/). A searchable guide to the availability and pricing of DSL services sold by your area's phone companies and Internet Service Providers.

▶ What is ADSL? (www.gte.com/dsl/whatdsl.html). Good questions, and a pitch by GTE, which offers ADSL in some areas.

Cable, the Familiar Broadband Alternative

More than 65 million Americans have cable TV. Many cable companies also offer Internet services. So, if you have cable service and your cable company just happens to offer Internet service, you should be able to connect to the Internet over your cable TV network; once connected to the Net, you can then sign on to AOL and run circles around all your friends who are still using an old-fashioned modem.

The major requirement for cable modem Net access (other than that cable subscription, of course) is a cable modem, a piece of hardware that connects your PC to the high-speed cabling ordinarily used for cable TV transmission (see Figure 18-7). You'll need a network card inside your PC, just as with ASDL. The cable modem plugs into both the cable outlet on the wall and this card. Unlike your standard dial-up modem, you may not have a choice when you purchase a cable modem, just as you might not have a vast array of cable companies to choose from in the first place; your cable company can tell you which cable modems you must use.

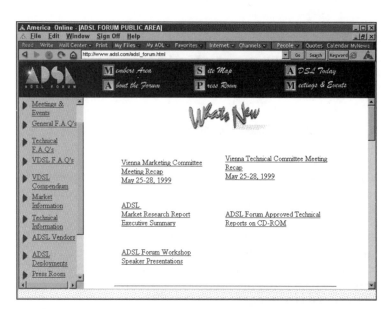

Figure 18-7. Using the same cabling that brings you cable TV, your PC can connect to the Internet at very high speeds (from CNET).

Why Cable?

Why would you want to access AOL using *cable*? Speed is the short answer: with a fast cable connection you can take advantage of some of the cool new applications discussed in the first half of this chapter.

Cable TV networks are based on a kind of thick wire cabling called coaxial, which can move data at a rate of anywhere from 10 to 30Mbps (a couple hundred times faster than a 56Kbps modem). It's been calculated that a 10MB file that takes 24 minutes to download over a 56Kbps modem would take just *20 seconds* over a 4Mbps cable modem and 8 seconds over a 10Mbps cable modem.

Like ADSL, cable modems' *potential* "upstream" data rate is lower, typically under 1Mbps; they download files a lot faster than they upload them. Cable companies have begun to upgrade their upstream connections to the Internet to increase their speed (using fiber as well as coax).

Once your system is attached to a cable network via network card and cable modem, you sign on to AOL as described in Chapter 2 in the "Signing on to AOL over a Network" section.

Note

Some experts consider the high-end numbers a bit deceptive, since your network card can't do much better than a more leisurely 4Mbps, or less. In addition, cable wires are often shared by hundreds of families, creating *local* traffic jams. Finally, data zooming to your cable operator's gateway to the Internet will begin to crawl along the Internet at a slower rate and then encounter congestion at popular Web sites. *In any network, the slowest link sets the pace for the rest of the network.*

18

What's Next on the Internet

From the Welcome screen, click Set Up. Create a new location for use with an ISP, LAN, DSL, or cable modem CSL. Add a custom (TCP/IP) connection, and when you're done simply sign on to AOL using this new location. Look for instructions at Keyword: **Cable**.

Cable's Flip Side: Congestion and Security Issues

Cable is often criticized for putting your connection onto a shared line with hundreds of other neighbors who connect at the same point of the larger cable network.

If everyone uses a cable connection, performance can slip. Also, your data probably passes through the local stretch of the network in an unencrypted form, meaning its contents can be detected and monitored (that is, *hacked*) by a network-savvy snoop.

A more serious concern for some is security. If you run a small business or do defense work, you might not want to entrust your mission-critical data to your cable company. Seek the opinion of a networking or business consultant if you have concerns here.

ADSL or Cable?

First, you are not likely to notice a speed difference between the two broadband options. Both can achieve downstream data rates (from the Net to you — for example, when you download a file) that far surpass what you are probably used to with a dial-up connection and modem. In fact, your cable or ADSL connection may be faster than you can achieve on the Internet itself, with its irregular traffic patterns and frequent congestion. Yet, the more people who use cable in your community, the greater your local congestion.

Second, the availability of cable and ADSL Net access varies from region to region; you may not even have a choice! Cable may be less prevalent in less-developed and rural areas than in cities, so if you don't have cable to begin with, you'll have to factor a monthly cable subscription into your calculations. If you don't have cable, you might want to look into satellite or wireless options, described in the next section.

Because conditions vary so widely, AOL is working to offer as many solutions as possible. It's working with the regional telephone companies to provide low-cost ADSL connections. And it's trying to persuade the cable companies to provide direct access to AOL (and the Internet) over cable. At the same time, AOL has launched several satellite and wireless initiatives with big companies such as Hughes Electronic.

The best solution — cable, ADSL, satellite, wireless — will depend on where you are, what you need, and what's available right now.

Other Broadband Options: ISDN, Wireless, Satellite, AOLTV

Because of their likely availability throughout the U.S. in the near future, cable and ADSL have a lot to recommend themselves. Other broadband options may make sense in specific circumstances. Some of these options, like wireless and satellite, may make more and more sense over time. Others, like ISDN, may well be a thing of the past.

▶ ISDN can help small businesses requiring a dedicated Internet connection where high speed, low cost, and easy maintenance are not issues.

▶ Wireless may make sense for business travelers, for people in larger metropolitan areas, and for anyone who needs timely communication *anywhere*.

▶ Satellite can make sense for rural consumers who already have satellite TV connections.

▶ AOL TV is for consumers who otherwise have no use for an expensive computer.

Tip

For an exhaustive introduction to ISDN, with lots of links, see Broadcast ISDN User Guide and Directory (www.britton2000.com/isdn/). The site includes large directories of ISDN manufacturers and service providers. IDG Books Worldwide publishes *ISDN For Dummies*, if you're feeling overwhelmed by the choices and the complexity.

What About ISDN?

Find It Online

These examples come from a series of articles on wireless computing, available at *Network Computing* (www.nwc.com/netdesign/wireless1.html). On AOL, start at Keyword: **Wireless**.

Since the mid-1980s, a type of service called Integrated Services Digital Network (ISDN) has been aiming to beat modem speeds using existing mostlycopper telephone wires. As a technology ISDN can send more data, more densely, in digital form, at higher speeds, but it has failed to make a dent in broadband demand. At the same time, plain old modems have gotten faster. ISDN combines voice (telephone) and data (computer information) on one line, while delivering the data speeds of only about 128K, approximately double today's standard 56K modems. ADSL can download from the Internet ten times that fast, while also combining voice and data.

Cost remains an issue with ISDN. Customers have to buy special equipment called a terminal adapter (similar to a modem), pay a setup fee, and then shell out a sometimes high monthly service fee to their telephone company because of the telco's special ISDN equipment. They must sometimes also pay an ISDN fee to their Internet service provider.

Even though a bit costly and less speedy than newer alternatives, ISDN can cut your AOL costs by speeding those time-consuming downloads, Automatic AOL sessions, and Web browsing. Such speed can cut the time you spend online and thus lower your phone bills. ISDN also makes sense for smaller businesses (under ten employees) that require a shared Internet connection that's always on. If it's speed you need, however, it may make sense to bet on cable or wait for ADSL.

Being Wired or Going Wireless?

Some people see a brilliant future in wireless. What's special about wireless? It untethers you from the desktop and its tangle of plugs and cords. You can work and play anywhere. Like ADSL and cable, some types of wireless promise high data-transmission rates (1.5Mbps and higher). Other types offer the great convenience of wireless at about the speed of your current modem, however, so you need to look into the transmission speeds of any wireless option you might consider.

Wireless works by sending data over radio waves. It uses different kinds of transmission techniques, such as satellite and base stations (towers). Wireless networks can be used to transmit and retrieve data to and from the Internet.

Right now, wireless access often depends on fixed links over local towers. Your location must have a clear "line of sight" to one of these *relay stations*, which send your data using ultra highfrequency infrared waves. You'll need to find out whether you have access in your area and then ask your wireless provider whether you meet this line-of-sight condition.

As with ADSL and cable, the flavor of wireless you choose can have a lot to do with where you live — and the longer you wait, the more the choices. The reason to wait: wireless connections to AOL and the Net are just starting to proliferate.

Going Wireless on AOL

AOL offers three wireless services now. Look for more in the not-so-distant future.

- ▶ On AOL you can initiate a page to someone with a wireless pager and (currently) either the Mobilecom or Metrocall services. Paging is a one-way thing. To respond to your page, the recipient can send you another page or an e-mail message, or use the phone. Keyword: **Paging** lets you send a page to a Mobilecom or Metrocall subscriber whose number you know.

  If you are a Metrocall subscriber and have a new word pager, which displays text messages, you can be automatically notified of your AOL e-mail. Just tell anyone sending you e-mail to send a CC of the message to you at yourpagernumber@page.metrocall.com. When someone sends you a pager message, the pager tells you who sent the message and what it's about, and displays up to 80 characters of the message itself.

- ▶ In some regions of the country, you can currently purchase a wireless modem and subscribe to certain Internet Service Providers in order to connect your laptop to the Internet without being anywhere near a phone jack or network cable. This type of wireless access requires a wireless modem. One such service, Metrocom's Ricochet, offers local service in several large U.S. cities. Ricochet sends data at less-than-blaz-

Tip

To find out about service in your area, as well as nationwide, do an AOL Search search for **wireless modem [type your area here].** Also, use a comprehensive list of Internet Service Provides such as The List (www.thelist.com) to find ISPs offering wireless.

Note

AOL Mail for Palm will not yet work with a TCP/IP connection (Bring Your Own Access billing plan) or the Palm VII wireless network.

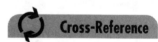

Cross-Reference

Chapter 9 has a section called "AOL Anywhere: New Ways To Do Mail" that includes a brief discussion of AOL Mail. The new program was still being tested as this book was being written. Keyword: **Anywhere** has the details about doing e-mail using a Palm Connected Organizer.

18

What's Next on the Internet

Note

Satellite dishes receive data at up to about 400Kbps, but they don't send it at that speed — or send it at all, at least for now. For that you'll need to dial up AOL using a regular modem. Two-way satellite connections are in development, but in the meantime satellite, like cable and ADSL, is lopsided: downloading is a lot faster than uploading. In the case of satellite, downstream and upstream travel over different paths: satellite (downstream) and over the phone lines (upstream).

Tip

AOL recently announced important agreements with Sprint PCS, Motorola, Nokia, Bell South, NeoPoint, and other leading makers of pagers, cell phones, smart phones, and other mobile wireless devices. In the near future you will be able to use AOL Mail and the AOL Instant Messenger service on a wide range of wireless devices.

ing speeds (under 56Kbps); a higher-speed network is in the works. Using a wireless ISP like Ricochet, and AT&T or Bell Atlantic, you can then connect to AOL over that connection, if you're using the Bring Your Own Access billing plan.

AOL Anywhere

AOL Mail provides access to your AOL e-mail through your Palm Connected Organizer and Windows CE organizers. The basic software and service are free; make sure to check the details for your billing plan at Keyword: **AOLMail**. (Choose Palm or CE, then click the Frequently Asked Questions tab.)

To use AOL Mail on a Palm Connected Organizer:

▶ **Requirements.** You'll need a Palm Connected Organizer III (or higher), with the Palm operation system (version 3.0 or higher), and at least 424K of RAM. You'll also need a snap-on Palm modem. Palm's built-in infrared connection, TCP connection, and cellular modems are not fully supported. AOL Mail for the Palm Connected Organizer is available for the Macintosh as well as the PC; instructions and up-to-date lists of supported devices are available at Keyword: **AOLMail**.

▶ **Installing and using AOL Mail.** The free AOL Mail software (contained in a small file called aolmail.prc) can be downloaded to your PC from Keyword: **AOLMail**. You'll then need to transfer it to your Palm and install it during a Palm HotSync session. (That's when you transfer information back and forth between your PC and your Palm.) Please see your Palm documentation for the specific instructions for HotSyncing, which requires a cradle in which to rest your Palm Connected Organizer. AOL Mail will then be available by tapping your Palm's Application icon. You can then dial into AOL using your Palm modem, and read, write, send, and delete e-mail messages.

To use AOL Mail on a Windows CE organizer:

▶ **Requirements.** You'll need to be running Windows CE version 2.11. Supported devices include the Casio E-15, E-100, and E-105; the Compaq Aero 1530, 2110, 2150, and 2160; the HP Jornado 420/30; and Phillips Nino 500. You'll need 200K of storage memory and 1.1MB of program memory. For any of these devices you'll also need a clip-on modem or built-in/PCMIA modem. Network (Ethernet) cards work as well, as long as they're PCMIA- or CompactFlash-compatible, depending on the standard your organizer supports.

▶ **Installing and using AOL Mail.** To use AOL Mail, you download the free software (AOLWinCE.exe) from Keyword: **AOLMail**, then run the software on your PC (with your organizer connected), following the on-screen directions to install AOL Mail on your organizer. Tap Start⊅AOL Mail to bring up a setup wizard to guide you through the process of setting up your modem and location. You'll be ready to read, write, send, and delete messages.

In the Stars: AOL's Satellite Access

So much is going on in space that it's easy to feel dizzy or get vertigo. If you don't have access to cable or ADSL, but do have satellite TV, read on. If you don't have satellite and live in the countryside, you can use a satellite dish and subscription to service like Hughes's DirecPC to get AOL on your PC at broadband speeds.

With Hughes Electronics Corp. (the huge GM-owned provider of satellite and digital TV services), AOL will make its online content available to subscribers of Hughes' **DirecTV** (satellite) service. This service will use the set-top box just described. The new service is to be called AOL TV, which delivers the AOL you know through the TV set, which you also know. AOL TV marks a step toward truly interactive TV as an alternative to cable TV's one-way transmission model, with its limited choice and absence of interactivity. Most AOL and Internet features will be available to the AOL TV user, including the ability to chat, shop, use Instant Messages, send and receive e-mail, and browse the Web.

Keyword: **PDAs** can help if you are just getting started with a Palm Connected Organizer or other gadget. The area offers tutorials, product reviews, links to vendors, and downloadable games.

AOL Mail for both Palm and Window CE organizers supports the core e-mail functions of writing, sending, reading, and deleting e-mail messages.

A Quick Look Back . . . and Ahead

Imagine what a super-fast AOL connection could make possible:

▶ Chatting by talking instead of typing

▶ Cool Web multimedia, Shockwave, and Java in a flash

▶ Getting immersed in a multimedia art gallery or 3D playground

▶ Browsing a fashion catalog, and discussing your needs, choices, and payment options with a person shown and heard onscreen

AOL is creating a range of broadband alternatives to make all this possible, including

▶ ADSL

▶ Cable

▶ Satellite

▶ Wireless

America Online is playing the whole field of new technologies and will make them as easy to use as possible. When you're ready for broadband, AOL is ready with the services you want.

Index

Notes

Notes

Notes

Notes

Notes

Notes

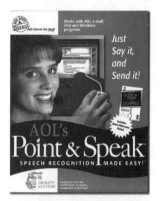

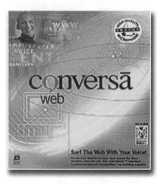

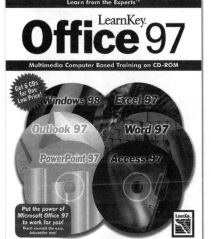

Created Exclusively for AOL Members

The Fast, Easy Way to Share Your Photos Online!

Order Today!
1-888-299-0329

AOL's PhotoCam

Everything you need in one great package to get you started with digital imaging. Just point, click, connect and send! Save money and time. There is no film or developing costs. It is easy to share your photos with family and friends through your email or view pictures on your TV/VCR with the video output connector. AOL's PhotoCam includes an easy to use manual, MGI's PhotoSuite SE, 2MB of built-in memory to shoot and store up to 32 pictures, beautiful black vinyl carrying case, 4AA batteries, and more.
$199.95 (s&h $7.90)   #0010373N 11712

Just Point, Click, Connect and Send!

AMERICA
Online.

*So easy to use,
no wonder it's #1*

AOL SHOP Direct

AOL Selects the Best

Protect Your PC From Internet Viruses!

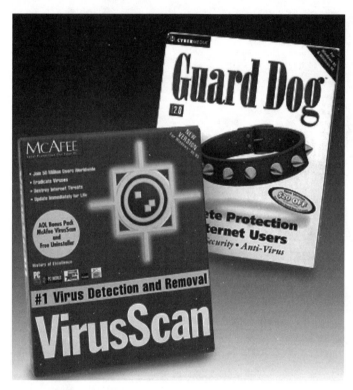

Order Today!
1-888-299-0329

VirusScan/Free Guard Dog 2.0

VirusScan detects viruses from floppy disks, Internet downloads, email attachments, Intranets, shared files, CD-ROMs and online services. In addition, we are including as a Bonus, Guard Dog 2.0. Guard Dog is reliable way to safeguard your personal files and keep your web browsing habits private. A must have duo of robust protection programs!
$29.95 (s&h $5.60)   #0010374N 11271

2 for 1 exclusive AOL offer!

AMERICA
Online.

So easy to use,
no wonder it's #1

AOL Selects the Best

Get the Most Out of Your Computing Experience!

AOL Shop Direct Upgrade Shop

In general, when accessing AOL and the Internet - and uploading or downloading pictures, files or information - the speed and performance of your computer are tied to three primary components:

--The central processing unit (CPU)
--The memory capacity (hard drive and RAM)
--The modem speed

AOL is dedicated to help you have the best online and computing experience. In AOL's Upgrade Shop we have devoted an entire area on "Quick Tips," handy information and popular computing terms to better aid and assist you in upgrading your computer. In addition, we have tested, selected, and priced the best products to turbo-charge your system.

*So easy to use
no wonder it's #1*

Go to AOL Keyword: Upgrade Shop

AOL Selects the Best

Send and receive email anywhere, anytime!

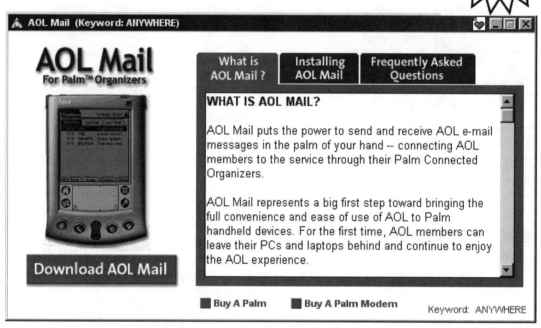

AOL Mail For Palm™ Organizers

AOL Mail represents a significant first step toward bringing the full convenience and ease of use of AOL to Palm™ handheld devices. For the first time, AOL members can leave their PCs and laptops behind and continue to enjoy the AOL experience. All you need to get going is a compatible Palm™ device*, a Palm™ snap-on modem, and an AOL account. AOL Mail connects members directly to AOL using their regular screen names and passwords. Leveraging AOL's global network of access numbers, AOL Mail allows members to connect with the service from just about anywhere. AOL Mail requires a Palm III, IIIe, IIIx, V, VII, or an earlier Palm that has been upgraded to Palm III compatibility, and 425K of free RAM.

Coming Soon... AOL Mail for Windows CE Palm-Size PCs

AMERICA Online.

*So easy to use,
no wonder it's #1*